OCA Oracle Database 12c: SQL Fundamentals I Exam Guide

(Exam 1Z0-061)

Roopesh Ramklass

New York   Chicago   San Francisco
Athens   London   Madrid   Mexico City
Milan   New Delhi   Singapore   Sydney   Toronto

Cataloging-in-Publication Data is on file with the Library of Congress

OCA Oracle Database 12c: SQL Fundamentals I Exam Guide (Exam 1Z0-061)

1234567890 DOC DOC 10987654

ISBN: Book p/n 978-0-07-182027-1 and CD p/n 978-0-07-182026-4
of set 978-0-07-182028-8

MHID: Book p/n 0-07-182027-2 and CD p/n 0-07-182026-4
of set 0-07-182028-0

Sponsoring Editor Stephanie Evans	**Technical Editor** Cecil Strydom	**Production Supervisor** James Kussow
Editorial Supervisor Jody McKenzie	**Copy Editor** Lunaea Weatherstone	**Composition** Cenveo Publisher Services
Project Manager Tania Andrabi, Cenveo® Publisher Services	**Proofreaders** Emily Rader, Claire Splan	**Illustration** Cenveo Publisher Services
Acquisitions Coordinator Mary Demery	**Indexer** Ted Laux	**Art Director, Cover** Jeff Weeks

With love to Ameetha for sharing your journey with me.

Acknowledgments

This book was written amidst emigrating from South Africa to Canada and completed during one of the most brutal winters in Canadian history. Concluding the task to a standard I am satisfied with during this tumultuous time would not have been possible without the love, support, encouragement, and friendship of my wife, Dr. Ameetha Garbharran.

- I am grateful too for the meticulous attention to detail and wisdom of the technical editor, my esteemed colleague and friend Cecil Strydom, who kept me focused on the quality of this endeavor.
- Finally, thank you to the team at McGraw-Hill Education, specifically Mary Demery and Stephanie Evans, who kept me on track with my deadlines and showed empathy and understanding during our intercontinental transition.

ABOUT THE AUTHOR

Roopesh Ramklass (Canada) is an Oracle Certified Master with expertise in infrastructure, middleware, and database architecture. He has worked for Oracle Global Support, Advanced Customer Services, and Oracle University. He has run an IT consultancy and is experienced with infrastructure systems provisioning, software development, and systems integration. He has spoken at numerous Oracle User Group conferences and is the author of several technology books.

About the Technical Editor

Cecil Strydom has been working exclusively as an Oracle DBA for the last 13 years, covering everything from performance tuning to disaster recovery. He has worked with Oracle database versions 8 through 11g and has experience with RAC, Data Guard, eBusiness, Portal, Apex, and various other Oracle applications. Cecil is an OCP-certified Oracle DBA and is currently a systems consultant for a multinational company based in Johannesburg, South Africa.

CONTENTS AT A GLANCE

CONTENTS

PREFACE

The objective of this study guide is to prepare you for the 1Z0-061 exam by familiarizing you with the knowledge tested in the exam. Because the primary focus of the book is to help you pass the test, we don't always cover every aspect of the related technology. Some aspects of the technology are only covered to the extent necessary to help you understand what you need to know to pass the exam, but we hope this book will serve you as a valuable professional resource after your exam.

In This Book

This book is organized in such a way as to serve as an in-depth review for the Oracle Database 12c: SQL Fundamentals exam for both novice and experienced Oracle professionals. Each chapter covers a major aspect of the exam, with an emphasis on the "why" as well as the "how to" of working with and supporting Oracle SQL.

On the CD-ROM

For more information on the CD-ROM, please see the "About the CD-ROM" appendix at the back of the book.

Exam Objective Map

At the end of the Introduction you will find an Exam Objective Map. This table has been constructed to allow you to cross-reference the official exam objectives with the objectives as they are presented and covered in this book. The objectives are listed as presented by the certifying body with a chapter and page reference.

In Every Chapter

We've created a set of chapter components that call your attention to important items, reinforce key points, and provide helpful exam-taking hints. Take a look at what you'll find in each chapter:

- Every chapter begins with **Certification Objectives**—what you need to know in order to pass the section in the exam dealing with the chapter topic. The Certification Objective headings identify the objectives within the chapter, so you'll always know an objective when you see it!

- **Exam Watch** notes call attention to information about, and potential pitfalls in, the exam. These helpful hints are written by authors who have taken the exam and received their certification—who better to tell you what to worry about? They know what you're about to go through!

- **Exercises** are interspersed throughout the chapters. These are designed to give you a feel for the real-world experience you need in order to pass the exam. They help you master skills that are likely to be an area of focus in the exam. Don't just read through the exercises; they are hands-on practice that you should be comfortable completing. Learning by doing is an effective way to increase your competency with a product.

- **On the Job** notes describe the issues that come up most often in real-world settings. They provide a valuable perspective on certification- and product-related topics. They point out common mistakes and address questions that have arisen from on-the-job discussions and experience.

- **Inside the Exam** sidebars highlight some of the most common and confusing problems that students encounter when taking a live exam. Designed to anticipate what the exam will emphasize, getting inside the exam will help ensure you know what you need to know to pass. You can get a leg up on how to respond to those difficult-to-understand questions by focusing extra attention on these sidebars.

■ **Scenario & Solution** sections lay out potential problems and solutions in a quick-to-read format.

SCENARIO & SOLUTION

When querying the JOBS table for every row containing just the JOB_ID and MAX_SALARY columns, is a projection, selection, or join being performed?	A projection is performed since the columns in the JOBS table have been restricted to the JOB_ID and MAX_SALARY columns.
An alias provides a mechanism to rename a column or an expression. Under what conditions should you enclose an alias in double quotes?	If an alias contains more than one word or if the case of an alias must be preserved, then it should be enclosed in double quotation marks. Failure to double quote a multi-worded alias will raise an Oracle error. Failure to double quote a single-word alias will result in the alias being returned in uppercase.
The SELECT list of a query contains a single column. Is it possible to sort the results retrieved by this query by another column?	Yes. Unless positional sorting is used, the ORDER BY clause is independent of the SELECT clause in a statement.

■ The **Certification Summary** is a succinct review of the chapter and a restatement of salient points regarding the exam.

✔ ■ The **Two-Minute Drill** at the end of every chapter is a checklist of the main points. It can be used for last-minute review.

Q&A ■ The **Self Test** offers questions similar to those in the exam. The answers to these questions, as well as explanations of the answers, can be found at the end of each chapter. By taking the Self Test after completing each chapter, you'll reinforce what you've learned from that chapter while becoming familiar with the structure of the exam questions.

■ The **Lab Question** at the end of the Self Test section offers a unique and challenging question format that requires you to understand multiple chapter concepts in order to answer correctly. These questions are more complex and more comprehensive than the other questions, as they test your ability to take all the knowledge you've gained from reading the chapter and apply it to complicated, real-world situations. These questions are aimed to be more difficult than what you will find in the exam. If you can answer these questions, you have proven that you know the subject!

Some Pointers

Once you've finished reading this book, set aside some time to do a thorough review. You might want to return to the book several times and make use of all the methods it offers for reviewing the material:

1. *Reread all the Two-Minute Drills,* or have someone quiz you. You also can use the drills as a way to do a quick cram before the exam. You may want to make flashcards out of 3 × 5 index cards with the Two-Minute Drill material.

2. *Reread all the Exam Watch notes and Inside the Exam elements.* Remember that these notes are written by authors who have taken the exam and passed. They know what you should expect—and what you should be on the lookout for.

3. *Review all the Scenario & Solution sections* for quick problem solving.

4. *Retake the Self Tests.* Taking the tests right after you've read the chapter is a good idea, because the questions help reinforce what you've just learned. However, it's an even better idea to go back later and answer all the questions in the book in a single sitting. Pretend that you're taking the live exam. When you go through the questions the first time, you should mark your answers on a separate piece of paper. That way, you can run through the questions as many times as you need to until you feel comfortable with the material.

5. *Complete the exercises.* Did you do the exercises when you read through each chapter? If not, do them! These exercises are designed to cover exam topics, and there's no better way to get to know this material than by practicing. Be sure you understand why you are performing each step in each exercise. If there is something you are not clear on, reread that section in the chapter.

INTRODUCTION

There is an ever-increasing demand for staff with IT industry certification. The benefits to employers are significant—they can be certain that staff have a certain level of competence—and the benefits to the individuals, in terms of demand for their services, are equally great. Many employers now require technical staff to have certifications. The Oracle certifications are among the most sought after. But apart from rewards in a business sense, knowing that you are among a relatively small pool of elite Oracle professionals and that you have proved your competence is a personal reward well worth attaining.

There are several Oracle certification *tracks*—this book is concerned with the Oracle Database Administration certification track, specifically for release 12c of the database. There are three levels of DBA certification: Certified Associate (OCA), Certified Professional (OCP), and Certified Master (OCM). The OCA qualification is based on two examinations, the first of which is covered in this book and may be taken online. The OCP qualification requires passing a third examination. These examinations can be taken at many Oracle Testing Centers or Pearson VUE Authorized Test Centers and consist of 60 to 70 questions to be completed in 90 minutes. The OCM qualification requires completing a further two-day evaluation at an Oracle testing center, involving simulations of complex environments and use of advanced techniques.

To prepare for the first OCA examination, you can attend an Oracle University instructor-led training course, you can study Oracle University online learning material, or you can read this book. In all cases, you should also refer to the Oracle Documentation Library for details on syntax. This book will be a valuable addition to other study methods, but it is also sufficient by itself. It has been designed with the examination objectives in mind, though it also includes a great deal of information that will be useful to you in the course of your work. For readers working in development, the subject matter of this book is also the starting point for studying Oracle Corporation's development tools: SQL, PL/SQL, and the APEX development environment.

SQL is an amazing language and the exam and this book are the first steps in a journey that is likely to last the length of your career. Study the material and experiment and as you work through the exercises and sample questions and become more familiar with the Oracle environment, you will realize that there is one golden rule:

When in doubt, try it out.

In a multitude of cases, you will find that a simple test that takes a couple of minutes can save hours of speculation and poring through manuals. If anything is ever unclear, construct an example and see what happens. This book was developed using Windows and Linux, but to carry out the exercises and your further investigations you can use any platform that is supported for Oracle.

Your initiation into the exciting world of Oracle database administration is about to begin.

Exam 1Z0-061

Official Objective	Ch No.	Pg No.
1.0 Retrieving Data Using the SQL SELECT Statement		
1.1 List the capabilities of SQL SELECT statements	2	56
1.2 Execute a basic SELECT statement	2	64
2.0 Restricting and Sorting Data		
2.1 Limit the rows that are retrieved by a query	3	110
2.2 Sort the rows that are retrieved by a query	3	143
2.3 Use ampersand substitution to restrict and sort output at runtime	3	150
3.0 Using Single-Row Functions to Customize Output		
3.1 Describe various types of functions available in SQL	4	176
3.2 Use character, number, and date functions in SELECT statements	4	183
4.0 Using Conversion Functions and Conditional Expressions		
4.1 Describe various types of conversion functions that are available in SQL	5	234
4.2 Use the TO_CHAR, TO_NUMBER, and TO_DATE conversion functions	5	237
4.3 Apply conditional expressions in a SELECT statement	5	250
5.0 Reporting Aggregated Data Using the Group Functions		
5.1 Identify the available group functions	6	283
5.2 Describe the use of group functions	6	278

1
Relational Database Design Using Oracle

CERTIFICATION OBJECTIVES

T he content of this chapter is not directly tested by the Oracle certification examination, but it is vital in understanding the purpose of SQL. This is considered prerequisite knowledge that every student should have, beginning with an appreciation of how the Oracle server technologies fit together and the positioning of each product.

The Oracle server technologies product set is more than a database. There are also the Oracle WebLogic Server and the Oracle Enterprise Manager. Taken together, these are the server technologies that make up the Oracle Cloud. Cloud computing is an emerging environment for managing the complete IT environment and providing services to users on demand.

Databases fundamentally provide the infrastructure for the organization, storage, and retrieval of data in an efficient manner. Oracle Database 12c has evolved from a Relational Database Management System (RDBMS) to an Object RDBMS supporting the organization of virtually any type of information with no practical limit on the volume of data that may be stored. The vast data volumes generated by Amazon.com, the Large Hadron Collider (LHC) at CERN in Europe, and many financial institutions and governments are organized and managed in Oracle databases. Although Oracle databases have features addressing demands for scalability, high availability, and superb performance, this guide will focus on the data organization problem. Structured Query Language (SQL, pronounced "sequel") is an international standard for managing data stored in relational databases. Oracle Database 12c offers an implementation of SQL that is generally compliant with the current standard, which is Core SQL:2011. Full details of the compliancy are in Appendix C of the SQL Language Reference, which is part of the Oracle Database Documentation Library. As a rule, compliancy can be assumed.

Throughout this book, two tools are used extensively for exercises: SQL*Plus and SQL Developer. These are tools that developers use every day in their work. The exercises and many of the examples are based on two demonstration sets of data, known as the HR and OE schemas. There are instructions on how to launch the tools and create the demonstration schemas, though you may need assistance from your local database administrator to get started.

This chapter consists of summarized descriptions of the Oracle server technologies, the SQL language, the client tools, and the demonstration schemas. Several real-world data organization scenarios are considered while discussing the concepts behind the relational paradigm and normalizing of data into relational structures.

CERTIFICATION OBJECTIVE 1.01

Position the Server Technologies

There is a family of products that makes up the Oracle server technologies:

- The Oracle database
- The Oracle WebLogic Server
- The Oracle Enterprise Manager
- Various application development tools and languages

These products each have a position in the Oracle product set. The database is the repository for data and the engine that manages access to it. The Oracle WebLogic Server runs software that generates the web user interfaces that submit calls for data retrieval and modification to the database for execution. The Oracle Enterprise Manager is a comprehensive administration tool for monitoring, managing, and tuning the Oracle processes and also (through plug-ins) third-party products. Lastly, there are tools and languages for developing applications; either applications that run on end users' machines in the client-server model or applications that run centrally on application servers.

The combination of the server technologies and the development tools make up a platform for application development and delivery that enables the cloud. The cloud is an approach to the delivery of IT services that maximizes the cost efficiency of the whole environment by delivering computing power from a pool of available resources to wherever it is needed, on demand.

The Oracle Server Architecture

An Oracle database is a set of files on disk. It exists until these files are deliberately deleted. There are no practical limits to the size and number of these files, and therefore no practical limits to the size of a database. Access to the database is through the Oracle instance. The instance is a set of processes and memory structures: it exists on the CPU(s) and in the memory of the server node, and this existence is temporary. An instance can be started and stopped. Users of the database establish sessions against the instance, and the instance then manages all access to the database. It is absolutely impossible in the Oracle environment for any user to have direct contact with the database. An Oracle instance with an Oracle database makes up an Oracle server.

The processing model implemented by the Oracle server is that of client-server processing, often referred to as *two-tier*. In the client-server model, the generation of the user interface and much of the application logic is separated from the management of the data. For an application developed using SQL (as all relational database applications will be), this means that the client tier generates the SQL commands, and the server tier executes them. This is the basic client-server split, with (as a general rule) a local area network between the two sides. The network communications protocol used between the user process and the server process is Oracle's proprietary protocol, Oracle Net.

The client tier consists of two components: the users and the user processes. The server tier has three components: the server processes that execute the SQL, the instance, and the database itself. Each user interacts with a user process. Each user process interacts with a server process, usually across a local area network. The server processes interact with the instance, and the instance with the database. Figure 1-1 shows this relationship diagrammatically. A *session* is a user process in communication with a server process. There will usually be one user process per user and one server process per user process. The user and server processes that make up sessions are launched on demand by users and terminated when no longer required; this is the log-on and log-off cycle. The instance processes and memory structures are launched by the database administrator and persist until the administrator deliberately terminates them; this is the database startup and shutdown cycle.

The user process can be any client-side software that is capable of connecting to an Oracle server process. Throughout this book, two user processes will be used extensively: SQL*Plus and SQL Developer. These are simple processes provided by Oracle for establishing sessions against an Oracle server and issuing ad hoc SQL. A widely used alternative is TOAD (the Tool for Application Developers) from Quest Software, though this is licensed software. End-user applications will need to be written with something more sophisticated than these tools, something capable of

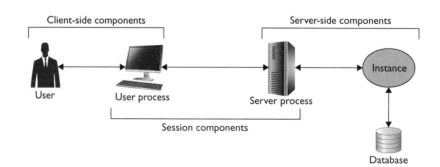

FIGURE 1-1

The indirect connection between a user and a database

managing windows, menus, proper onscreen dialogs, and so on. Such an application could be written with the Oracle Development Tools, with Microsoft Access linked to the Oracle ODBC drivers, with any third-generation language (such as C or Java) for which Oracle has provided a library of function calls that will let it interact with the server, or with any number of Oracle-compatible third-party tools. What the user process actually is does not matter to the Oracle server at all. When an end user fills in a form and clicks a Submit button, the user process will be generating an INSERT statement (detailed in Chapter 10) and sending it to a server process for execution against the instance and the database. As far as the server is concerned, the INSERT statement might just as well have been typed into SQL*Plus as what is known as ad hoc SQL.

Never forget that all communication with an Oracle server follows this client-server model. The separation of user code from server code dates back to the earliest releases of the database and is unavoidable. Even if the user process is running on the same machine as the server (as is the case if, for example, one is running a database on one's own laptop for development or training purposes), the client-server split is still enforced. Applications running in an application server environment (described in the next section) also follow the client-server model for their database access.

The simplest form of the database server is one instance connected to one database, but in a more complex environment one database can be opened by many instances concurrently. This is known as a RAC (Real Application Cluster). RAC can bring many potential benefits, which may include scalability, performance, and zero downtime. The ability to dynamically add further instances running on supplementary nodes to a database is a major part of the database's contribution to the cloud.

The Oracle WebLogic Server

With the emergence of the Web as the standard communications platform for delivering applications to end users has come the need for application servers. An application server replaces the client-side software traditionally installed on end-user terminals; it runs applications centrally, presenting them to users in windows displayed locally in web browsers. The applications make use of data stored in one or more database servers.

The Oracle WebLogic Server is a platform for developing, deploying, and managing *web applications*. A web application can be defined as any application with which users communicate with HTTP. Web applications usually run in at least three tiers: a database tier manages access to the data, the client tier (often implemented as a web browser) handles the local window management for communications with the users, and an application tier in the middle executes the program logic that generates the user interface and the SQL calls to the database.

Web applications can be developed with a number of technologies, among which Java is predominant. Applications written in Java should conform to the Java EE (Java Enterprise Edition) standard, which defines how such applications should be packaged and deployed. JEE and related standards are controlled by Oracle and accepted by virtually all software developers. Oracle WebLogic Server is a JEE-compliant application server. Oracle's implementation of the standards allows for automatic load balancing and fault tolerance across multiple application servers on multiple machines through JEE clustering. Clustering virtualizes the provision of the application service; users ask for an application that might be available from a number of locations, and the cluster works out from where any one session or request can best be serviced. If one location fails, others will take up the load, and more resources can be made available to an application as necessary. The ability to separate the request for a service from the location of its provision and to add or remove JEE servers from a cluster dynamically is a major part of the Oracle WebLogic Server's contribution to the cloud.

It is important to note that Oracle's commitment to international standards is very strong. Applications running in the Oracle WebLogic Server environment can connect to any database for which there are Java-compliant drivers; it is not necessary to use an Oracle database. Applications developed with the Oracle WebLogic Server toolkits can be deployed to any third-party JEE-compliant application server.

The simplest processing model of web applications is three-tier: a client tier that manages the user interface, a middle tier that generates the interface and issues SQL statements to the data tier, and a data tier that manages the data itself. In the Oracle environment, the client tier will be a browser (such as Mozilla Firefox or Windows Internet Explorer) that handles local window management, controls the keyboard, and tracks mouse movements. The middle tier will be an Oracle WebLogic Server running the software (probably written in Java) that generates the windows sent to the client tier for display and the SQL statements sent to the data tier for execution. The data tier will be an Oracle server: an instance and a database. In this three-tier environment, there are two types of sessions: end-user sessions from the client tier to the middle tier, and database sessions from the middle tier to the data tier. The end-user sessions will be established with HTTP. The database sessions are client-server sessions consisting of a user process and a server process, as described in the previous section.

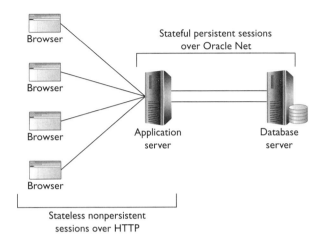

FIGURE 1-2

The connection
pooling model

It is possible for an application to use a one-for-one mapping of end-user session to database session: each user, from their browser, will establish a session against the application server, and the application server will then establish a session against the database server on the user's behalf. However, this model has been proven to be very inefficient when compared to the *connection pooling* model. With connection pooling, the application server establishes a relatively small number of persistent database sessions and makes them available on demand (queuing requests if necessary) to a relatively large number of end-user sessions against the application server. Figure 1-2 illustrates the three-tier architecture using connection pooling.

From the point of view of the database, it makes no difference whether a SQL statement comes from a client-side process such as SQL*Plus or Microsoft Access or from a pooled session to an application server. In the former case, the user process all happens on one machine; in the latter, the user process has been divided into two tiers: an application tier that generates the user interface and a client tier that displays it.

Oracle Enterprise Manager

The increasing size and complexity of IT installations makes management a challenging task. This is hardly surprising: no one ever said that managing a powerful environment should necessarily be simple. However, management tools can make the task easier and the administration staff more productive.

Oracle Enterprise Manager comes in three forms:

- Database Express
- Fusion Middleware Control
- Cloud Control

Oracle Enterprise Manager Database Express is a graphical tool for managing one database, which may be a RAC clustered database. It consists of a Java process running on the database server machine. Administrators connect to Database Express from a browser, and Database Express then connects to the database server. Database Express has facilities for real-time management, performance monitoring, and running scheduled jobs. Oracle Enterprise Manager Fusion Middleware Control is a graphical tool for managing a Fusion Middleware deployment. These deployments typically include Oracle WebLogic Server, an industry-leading application server which provides the container Java virtual machines (JVMs) that host Oracle or custom Java applications.

Oracle Enterprise Manager Cloud Control globalizes the management environment. A management repository (residing in an Oracle database) and one or more management servers manage the complete environment: all the databases and application servers, wherever they may be. Cloud Control can also manage the nodes, or machines, on which the servers run, as well as (through plug-ins) a wide range of third-party products. Each managed node runs an agent process, which is responsible for monitoring the managed target on the node: executing jobs against them and reporting status, activity levels, and alert conditions back to the management server(s).

Cloud Control provides a holistic view of the environment and, if well configured, makes administration staff far more productive than they are without it. It becomes possible for one administrator to effectively manage hundreds of targets.

Cloud Computing

Critical to the concept of cloud computing is *service virtualization*. This means that at all levels there is a layer of abstraction between what is requested and what is provided. End users ask for an application service and let the cloud work out which clustered JEE application server can best provide it. Application servers ask for a database service and let the cloud work out from which RAC node the data can best be served. Within the cloud there is a mapping of possible services to available service providers, and there are algorithms for assigning the workload and resources appropriately. The result is that end users have neither the need nor the capacity to know from where their computing resources are actually being provided. The analogy often drawn is with delivery of domestic electricity: it is supplied on demand, and the home owner has no way of telling which power station is currently supplying him.

The cloud is not exclusive to Oracle. At the physical level, some operating system and hardware vendors are providing cloud-like capabilities. These include the ability to partition servers into virtual machines and dynamically add or remove CPU(s) and RAM from the virtual machines according to demand. This is conceptually similar to Oracle's approach of dynamically assigning application server and database server resources to logical services. There is no reason why the two approaches cannot be combined. Both are working toward the same goal and can work together. The result should be an environment where adequate resources are always available on demand, without facing the issues of excess capacity at some times and under-performance at others. It should also be possible to design a cloud environment with no single point of failure, thus achieving the goal of 100 percent uptime that is being demanded by many users.

The SQL application developer need not know how the cloud has been implemented. The SQL will be invoked from an application server and executed by an instance against a database: the cloud will take care of making sure that at any moment pools of application servers and instances sized appropriately for the current workload are available.

EXERCISE 1-1

Investigate Your Database and Application Environment

This is a paper-based exercise, with no specific solution.

Attempt to identify the user processes, application servers, and database servers used in your environment. Try to work out where the SQL is being generated and where it is being executed. Bear in mind that usually the user processes used by end users will be graphical and will frequently go through application servers; the database administration and development staff will often prefer to use client-server tools that connect to the database server directly.

Development Tools and Languages

The Oracle server technologies include various facilities for developing applications, some existing within the database, others external to it.

Within the database, it is possible to use three languages. The one that is unavoidable, and the subject of this book, is SQL. SQL is used for data access, but it cannot be used for developing complete applications. It has no real facilities for developing user interfaces, and it also lacks the procedural structures needed for manipulating rows individually. The other two languages available within the database fill these gaps. They are PL/SQL and Java, although Java may also be used outside the database. PL/SQL is a third-generation language (3GL) proprietary to Oracle. It has the usual procedural constructs (such as if-then-else and looping) and facilities for user interface design. In the PL/SQL code, one can embed calls to SQL. Thus, a PL/SQL application might use SQL to retrieve one or more rows from the database, then perform various actions based on their content, and then issue more SQL to write rows back to the database. Java offers a similar capability to embed SQL calls within the Java code. This is industry standard technology: any Java programmer should be able write code that will work with an Oracle database (or indeed with any other Java-compliant database).

Other languages are available for developing client-server applications that run externally to the database. The most commonly used are C and Java, but it is possible to use most of the mainstream 3GLs. For all these languages, Oracle Corporation provides OCI (Oracle Call Interface) libraries that let code written in these languages establish sessions against an Oracle database and invoke SQL commands.

Many organizations will not want to use a 3GL to develop database applications. Oracle Corporation provides rapid application development tools such as Oracle Application Express, JDeveloper, ADF, and many other products. These can make programmers far more productive than if they were working with a 3GL. Like the languages, all these application development tools end up doing the same thing: constructing SQL statements that are sent to the database server for execution.

on the
job

All developers and administrators working in the Oracle environment must know PL/SQL. C and Java are not necessary, unless the project specifically uses them.

CERTIFICATION OBJECTIVE 1.02

Understand Relational Structures

Several real-world data organization scenarios are introduced to discuss the relational paradigm and introduce some practical modeling techniques. Critical to an understanding of SQL is an understanding of the relational paradigm and the ability to *normalize* data into relational structures. Normalization is the work of systems analysts, as they model business data into a form suitable for storing in relational tables. It is a science that can be studied for years, and there are many schools of thought that have developed their own methods and notations.

Real-World Scenarios

This guide uses several hypothetical scenarios, including the two canned scenarios called HR and OE provided by Oracle and frequently used as the context for exam questions to illustrate various SQL concepts. The following scenarios evolve further as new concepts are discussed.

Car Dealership

Sid runs a car dealership and needs a system to keep track of the cars that she buys and sells. She has noticed business taking a dive and wants to move into the twenty-first century and create a website that advertises available stock. She needs a system to keep records of the cars she has bought and sold and the details of these transactions.

Geological Cores

Core samples of the earth have been collected by your local geological survey agency. To ensure scientific rigor, the developers at GeoCore have determined that the system must track the exact geographical location, the elemental content of the core samples, and the dates of collection.

Order Entry

The Order Entry (OE) scenario provided as a sample by Oracle contains information for a fictitious commercial system that tracks products, customers, and the sales orders that have been placed.

Human Resources

The Human Resources (HR) scenario provided as a sample by Oracle records employees, departments, office locations, and job-related information for a typical HR department.

Although the hypothetical scenarios described above vary in complexity, they share several characteristics, including a potential data growth that may eventually overwhelm a paper-based or spreadsheet-based data organization solution, as well as a requirement for data to be manipulated (inserted, updated, and deleted) and retrieved in an efficient manner. The challenge of producing an efficient data organization design (also known as a data model) may be overcome with both an understanding of how the data being organized is likely to be utilized and a few basic data modeling techniques. The goal is to achieve an optimal balance between data storage and data access which will provide long-term downstream cost-saving benefits.

Data Modeling

Various formalized data modeling approaches are available, such as the Zachman framework and the Rational Unified Process, that ultimately seek to provide a systematic, standards-based approach to representing objects in an enterprise. There are a multitude of notations available to model entities and their relationships. A popular notation adopted by Oracle in its CASE tools (Computer Aided Software Engineering) and more recently in SQL Developer is the crow's foot notation, which will be discussed below. Other notations, such as Relational Schema notation and UML (Universal Markup Language), are also popular, but you must choose a notation that is comfortable and sensible for you.

Logical modeling is based on conceptualizing objects of interest as *entities* and their interactions with each other as *relationships*. There are many approaches to entity-relationship diagrams, each with their benefits and limitations. A brief discussion of entity-relationship diagrams and their notation follows.

Entities and Relations

Many Oracle professionals have adopted a framework that consists of three modeling stages for relational database modeling. A logical model is conceived when high-level constructs called *entities*, comprising various *attributes* and their *relationships*, are typically represented together in a diagram. Entities in logical models are usually depicted as rectangles with rounded corners, which comprise attributes or identifiers sometimes denoted by an "o" symbol. Attributes that uniquely identify an instance of an entity are designated as primary keys and are sometimes denoted by "#*". Data typing the attributes may be done at this stage, but it is generally not reflected in the design.

The logical model is then turned into a relational model by translating the entities into *relations*, commonly referred to as tables. The idea here is that sets of instances of the entities are collectively modeled as a table. The attributes are turned into table *columns*. Each instance of an entity is reflected as a *tuple* or *row* of data, each having values for its different attributes or columns. The number of "rows in the table" is the "cardinality of the tuples." Usually the attributes that are unique for each row are called *unique keys*, and typically a unique key is chosen to be the *primary key* (which is discussed later). The relationships between the entities are often modeled as *foreign keys*, which will also be explored below.

Relations in relational models are usually depicted as rectangles. At this stage there is typically more detail in terms of data typing for the attributes, and primary and foreign key attributes are also reflected with a "P" and an "F," respectively, in the relational model. Finally, the relational model is engineered into a physical model by implementing the design in a relational database.

Crow's foot notation is often used to depict relationships in logical and relational data models. The relationships between the entities can be one of the following and will be explored in the context of the Car Dealership scenario.

- **1:N**   One-to-many
- **N:1**   Many-to-one
- **1:1**   One-to-one
- **M:N**   Many-to-many

Consider the scenario of Sid's car dealership introduced earlier. You could model the likely data as an entity consisting of the following car-related attributes: Make, Model, Engine Capacity, and Color. Information regarding the buying and selling of cars is also required, so you could add Purchase Date, Sold Date, Sellers Name, Sellers SSN (Social Security number), Sellers Company, the same details for the buyer, and finally the Purchase Price and Selling Price, as in Figure 1-3.

FIGURE 1-3

A single car
dealership entity

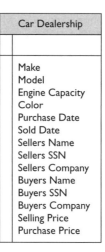

Car Dealership
Make
Model
Engine Capacity
Color
Purchase Date
Sold Date
Sellers Name
Sellers SSN
Sellers Company
Buyers Name
Buyers SSN
Buyers Company
Selling Price
Purchase Price

Sample transactional data stored in a table based on this entity may look like Figure 1-4, which shows three rows of data in a table comprising fourteen columns called CAR_DEALERSHIP. The commands to create tables and populate them with data will be discussed later in this book. For now, there are several more fundamental important things to notice. Tables store data in rows, also called records. Each data element is found at the intersection of a row and a column, also called a cell. It is fairly intuitive and much like a spreadsheet.

The first two records in the CAR_DEALERSHIP table include the following information:

- A silver Mercedes A160 with a 1600cc engine capacity that belonged to Coda, a private seller with SSN 12345, was bought by Sid with SSN 12346 from Sid's Cars, for $10,000 on 1 June 2013.

- A silver Mercedes A160 with a 1600cc engine capacity that belonged to Sid, with SSN 12346, from Sid's Cars, was bought by Wags, with SSN 12347, from Wags Auto, for $12,000 on 1 August 2013.

FIGURE 1-4

Sample data in the
CAR_
DEALERSHIP
table

Notice the repetition of data. Each record contains duplicate information for the cars being bought or sold and for the customer doing the buying or selling. Unnecessary duplication of data usually indicates poor design since it is wasteful and often requires needless maintenance. If this maintenance is not carefully done, this design allows errors (sometimes referred to as *insert update and deletion anomalies*) to creep in and reduces the overall integrity of the data.

Database normalization refers to modeling data using multiple entities with relationships between them, which may reduce or entirely eliminate data redundancy. There are many types of normal forms that have been defined theoretically, but relational database design primarily focuses on the following three:

- First normal form (1NF) deals with the issue of eliminating unnecessary repeating groups of data. An example of a repeating group in Figure 1-4 would be the first four columns on the first two rows where descriptive information about the car is repeated. You could define a new Cars entity that uniquely identifies a specific car using the Car ID primary key attribute as well as the Make, Model, Engine Capacity, and Color attributes. The Car ID identifier is then used in the related Transactions entity to avoid repeating groups of data.

- Second normal form removes attributes from the entity (1NF) that are not dependent on the primary key. In the proposed Cars entity described above, the Color attribute is not dependent on a specific car. You could define a new Colors entity that uniquely identifies a specific color using the Color ID primary key attribute. The Color ID can then be referenced by the Cars entity.

- Third normal form removes all interdependent attributes from a 2NF entity. The buyers and sellers of cars each have a uniquely identifying Social Security number (SSN). Their names, however, are interdependent on the SSN attribute. You could define a new Customers entity that uniquely identified a customer using the Customer ID primary key attribute, where interdependent information like the customer's name and company are stored.

on the **Job** *There are often several possible normalized models for an application. It is important to use the most appropriate—if the systems analyst gets this wrong, the implications can be serious for performance, storage needs, and development effort.*

Note: In the context of performance tuning, it is intentional and acceptable to duplicate data in entities. When data is normalized across multiple entities instantiated as multiple tables that must be joined together, the Oracle server processes need to physically fetch data from multiple tables and join them in memory buffers to produce the required results set. The extra IO required to query or manipulate normalized data sometimes justifies denormalizing data models to reduce disk IO operations and hence increase performance. This is common in Data Warehouse (DWH) and Decision Support Systems (DSS) but is an exception rather than the rule in Online Transaction Processing (OLTP) systems.

Consider the logical data model in Figure 1-5. The car-related data has been modeled as the Cars entity. The customer's (buyers and sellers) information is essentially the same, so they have been modeled as the Customers entity with the

FIGURE 1-5

The car dealership entity-relationship diagram

Customer Type attribute to differentiate between Purchasers and Sellers. The sales and purchases are recorded in the Transactions entity, while a *lookup* entity called Colors keeps track of different colors.

There are several advantages to conceptualizing this design as four interrelated entities. Firstly, the data has been normalized and there is no duplication of data. A practical benefit of multiple entities, each tracking a single construct like Cars, Customers, Colors, and even Transactions, is the ease of data maintenance. New colors can be added, each with a unique code, and as new cars are purchased, these colors, defined and maintained in one place, can be used to describe multiple cars with the same color. You could improve the sophistication of this model by defining entities for Tires, Security Systems, Tracking Devices, or Audio Visual add-ons. You could equally enhance the details collected for each car, such as VIN and engine numbers; or for each customer, such as address and bank details; but this hypothetical scenario serves to illustrate several concepts and obviously cannot be used in a production application scenario without further enhancements.

Primary Keys

Each entity in Figure 1-5 has a primary key attribute that uniquely identifies a tuple or row of data denoted by a #* adjacent to the attribute name. Each value of the Car ID primary key is unique in the entity. Multiple rows cannot share the same primary key value. Similarly, Color ID uniquely identifies each row in the Colors entity, as do Customer ID and Transaction ID in the Customers and Transactions entities, respectively.

Relationships

The lines in Figure 1-5 linking the various entities are known as *relations*. The crow's foot notation expresses the cardinality of the relationships between the entities—one-to-one, one-to-many, many-to-one, and many-to-many. The crow's foot notation explicitly illustrates the entity with the *many* side of the relationship with multiple "feet," while the entity on the *one* side has one foot. Attributes in a one-to-one relationship are identical, while many-to-many relationships indicate that multiple tuples in entity A have the same attribute values as many tuples in entity B. Both one-to-one and many-to-many relationships are not very common and sometimes point to flaws in the relational model. One-to-many and many-to-one relationships occur frequently when modeling relational entities. They relate attributes in two entities in a *master-detail* relationship. From the point of view of the relationship between the Cars and Colors entities (the order is significant), for example, *many* records in the Cars entity will be *one* Color. Many cars could have the same single Color ID attribute indicating they are the same color. The Colors entity is the *master* or *lookup* entity, while the Cars entity is the *detail* entity in this relationship. From the point of view of the relationship between Colors and Cars, *one* Color can be associated with *many* Cars. So it is just a matter of perspective whether a relationship is one-to-many or many-to-one; it all depends on which direction of the relationship you consider. The other relationships indicated by the crow's feet show that a single car can be bought and sold multiple times, hence the one-to-many relationship between the Cars and Transactions entities and lastly that one customer can perform many transactions (like buying and selling many cars).

Referential Integrity and Foreign Keys

These relationships introduce the concept of referential integrity, which ensures data consistency and integrity by guaranteeing that an attribute (say attribute A) belonging to the entity on the *one* side of the relationship must be unique, while the attribute (say attribute B) on the entity on the *many* side must have a value that is in the set of unique values described by attribute A. Attribute B is called a foreign key since it has a referential dependency on attribute A. Consider the Colors-Cars relationship based on the Color ID attribute. Referential integrity ensures that the Color ID attribute in each tuple in the Cars entity must have a value that is identical to exactly one instance of the Color ID attribute in the Colors entity. This guarantee is central to relational modeling since the *joining* of the Cars and Colors entities on the Color ID attribute allows the Colors.Color (this is *dot notation*) attribute to be matched with a related tuple in the Cars entity. The Color ID attribute in the Cars entity is the foreign key that is related to the unique key, which is the Color ID attribute in the Colors entity, where it also happens to be the primary key. It is very common that foreign keys in an entity are based on primary keys in a related entity, but this is not the rule.

Note: Foreign keys in an entity are based on unique keys in a related entity, but those unique keys do not have to be the primary key; they just have to be unique.

The logical model in Figure 1-5 would typically evolve into a relational model typically with more data-typing details and clearer primary and foreign keys, as in Figure 1-6.

The relational model could be engineered into a physical model where actual tables and other database constructs (discussed later in this chapter) are created.

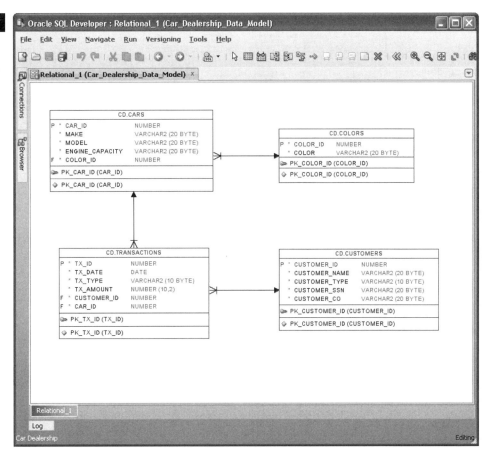

FIGURE 1-6

Relational
model of the car
dealership

The sample data in Figure 1-4 transferred into the physical model built from the
relational model above would produce four datasets, as in Figure 1-7.

The first two rows of data in the Transactions dataset can be interpreted as
follows:

- A transaction with TX ID 100 describes the purchase of a car with Car ID 1
  by Sid's dealership from a customer with Customer ID 2 for $10,000 on 1 June
  2013. You *lookup* Customer ID 2 and see it was a sale from Coda, a private
  seller with SSN 12345. You *lookup* Car ID 1 and determine that it was a 2001-
  A160 Mercedes with Color ID 1, which you further resolve to be Silver.

- A transaction with TX ID 101 describes the sale of Car ID 1 to Customer ID
  4, which you resolve to be a dealer called Wags from Wags Auto with SSN
  12347, for $12,000 on 1 August 2013.

Sample data using the car dealership relational model

Based on the earlier descriptions offered in a single-entity design, nothing has been lost by organizing the sample data across the four-entity design. However, much has been gained. There is no duplication of data. There is a clarity and elegance that will facilitate ease of maintenance of this data as new cars are bought and sold and as new customers transact with Sid's dealership.

EXERCISE 1-2

Design an Entity-Relationship Diagram for the Geological Cores Scenario

In this exercise, you will gain familiarity with basic relational modeling by completing an entity-relationship diagram for the Geological Core scenario introduced earlier. To recap: Core samples of the earth have been collected by your local geological agency. To ensure scientific rigor, the developers at GeoCore have determined that the system must track the exact geographical location, the elemental contents of the core samples, and the date of collection.

1. The GeoCore developers have proposed four entities with their respective attributes as per the following table. Draw a diagram with these entities reflecting the primary keys.

Entity	Attribute
Elements	Atomic Number (Primary Key)
	Element Description
	Symbol
	Atomic Mass
Contents	Content ID (Primary Key)
	Atomic Number
	Quantity
Depth	Depth ID (Primary Key)
	Start Depth
	End Depth
Cores	Core ID (Primary Key)
	Depth ID
	Collection Date
	Longitude
	Latitude
	Content ID

2. The Elements and Contents entities share a many-to-one relationship through the Atomic Number attribute. The Cores entity shares a many-to-one relationship with the Depth entity through the Depth ID attribute and a many-to-one relationship with the Contents entity through the Content ID attribute. Your task is to update the entity diagram to reflect these

relationships. Your completed Entity-Relationship diagram should closely resemble this illustration:

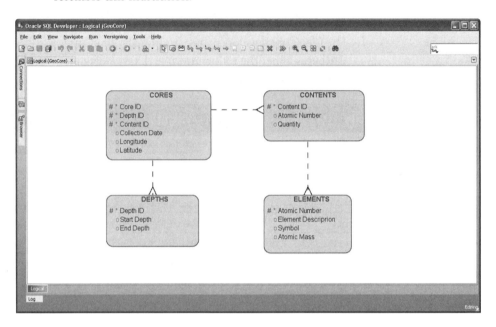

Rows and Tables

The relational paradigm models data as two-dimensional tables. A table consists of a number of rows, each consisting of a set of columns. Within a table, all the rows have the same column structure, though it is possible that in some rows some columns may have nothing in them. An example of a table would be a list of one's employees, each employee being represented by one row. The columns might be employee number, name, and a code for the department in which the employee works. Any employees not currently assigned to a department would have that column blank. Another table could represent the departments: one row per department, with columns for the department's code and the department's name.

Relational tables conform to certain rules that constrain and define the data. At the column level, each column must be of a certain data type, such as numeric, date-time, or character. The character data type is the most general, in that it can accept any type of data. At the row level, usually each row must have some uniquely identifying characteristic: this could be the value of one column, such as the employee number and department number in the preceding examples, which cannot be repeated in different rows. There may also be rules that define links between the tables, such as a rule that every employee must be assigned a department code that can be matched to a row in the departments table. Tables 1-1 through 1-4 are examples of the tabulated data definitions (a subset of data and structures from the sample schema known as SCOTT provided by Oracle):

TABLE 1-1

The DEPT Table

Column Name	Description	Data Type	Length
DEPTNO	Department number	Numeric	2
DNAME	Department name	Character	14

TABLE 1-2

The EMP Table

Column Name	Description	Data Type	Length
EMPNO	Employee number	Numeric	4
ENAME	Employee name	Character	10
DEPTNO	Department number	Numeric	2

TABLE 1-3

Row Data from the DEPT Table

DEPTNO	DNAME
10	ACCOUNTING
20	RESEARCH
30	SALES
40	OPERATIONS

EMPNO	ENAME	DEPTNO
7369	SMITH	20
7499	ALLEN	30
7521	WARD	30
7566	JONES	20
7654	MARTIN	30
7698	BLAKE	30
7782	CLARK	10
7788	SCOTT	20

Looking at the layout of the DEPT and EMP Tables 1-1 and 1-2, the two-dimensional structure is clear. Each row is of fixed length, each column is of fixed length (padded with spaces when necessary), and the rows are delimited with a new line. Table 1-3 shows the rows in the DEPT table stored in DEPTNO order, but this is a matter of chance, not design: relational tables do not impose any particular ordering on their rows. Table 1-4 shows that department number 10 has one employee, and department number 40 has none. Changes to data are usually very efficient with the relational model. New employees can be appended to the employees table, or they can be moved from one department to another simply by changing the DEPTNO value in their row.

Consider an alternative structure, where the data is stored according to the hierarchical paradigm. The hierarchical model was developed before the relational model, for technology reasons. In the early days of computing, storage devices lacked the capability for maintaining the many separate files that were needed for the many relational tables. Note that this problem is avoided in the Oracle database by abstracting the physical storage (files) from the logical storage (tables): there is no direct connection between tables and files and certainly not a one-to-one mapping. In effect, many tables can be stored in a very few files.

A hierarchical structure stores all related data in one unit. For example, the record for a department would include all that department's employees. The hierarchical paradigm can be very fast and very space efficient. One file access may be all that is needed to retrieve all the data needed to satisfy a query. The employees and departments listed previously could be stored hierarchically as follows:

10,ACCOUNTING,7782,CLARK
20,RESEARCH,7369,SMITH,7566,JONES,7788,SCOTT
30,SALES,7499,ALLEN,7521,WARD,7654,MARTIN,7698,BLAKE
40,OPERATIONS

In this example layout, the rows and columns are of variable length. Columns are delimited with a comma, rows with a new line. Data retrieval is typically very efficient if the query can navigate the hierarchy: if one knows an employee's department, the employee can be found quickly. If one doesn't, the retrieval may be slow. Changes to data can be a problem if the change necessitates movement. For example, to move employee 7566, JONES from RESEARCH to SALES would involve considerable effort on the part of the database because the move has to be implemented as a removal from one line and an insertion into another. Note that in this example, while it is possible to have a department with no employees (the OPERATIONS department), it is absolutely impossible to have an employee without a department: there is nowhere to put him or her. This is excellent if there is a business rule stating that all employees must be in a department but not so good if that is not the case.

The relational paradigm is highly efficient in many respects for many types of data, but it is not appropriate for all applications. As a general rule, a relational analysis should be the first approach taken when modeling a system. Only if it proves inappropriate should one resort to nonrelational structures. Applications where the relational model has proven highly effective include virtually all OLTP and DSS systems. The relational paradigm can be demanding in its hardware requirements and in the skill needed to develop applications around it, but if the data fits, it has proved to be the most versatile model. There can be, for example, problems caused by the need to maintain the indexes that maintain the links between tables and the space requirements of maintaining multiple copies of the indexed data in the indexes themselves and in the tables in which the columns reside. Nonetheless, relational design is in most circumstances the optimal model.

A number of software publishers have produced database management systems that conform (with varying degrees of accuracy) to the relational paradigm; Oracle is only one. IBM was perhaps the first company to commit major resources to it,

SCENARIO & SOLUTION	
Your organization is designing a new application. Who should be involved?	Everyone! The project team must involve business analysts (who model the business processes), systems analysts (who model the data), system designers (who decide how to implement the models), developers, database administrators, system administrators, and (most importantly) end users.
It is possible that relational structures may not be suitable for a particular application. How can this be determined, and what should be done next? Can Oracle help?	Attempt to normalize the data into two-dimensional tables, linked with one-to-many relationships. If this really cannot be done, consider other paradigms. Oracle may well be able to help. For instance, maps and other geographical data really don't work relationally. Neither does text data (such as word processing documents). But the Spatial and Text database options can be used for these purposes. There is also the possibility of using user-defined objects to store nontabular data.

but their product (which later developed into DB2) was not ported to non-IBM platforms for many years. Microsoft's SQL Server is another relational database that has been limited by the platforms on which it runs. Oracle databases, by contrast, have always been ported to every major platform from the first release. It may be this that gave Oracle the edge in the RDBMS market place.

A note on terminology: Confusion can arise when discussing relational databases with people used to working with Microsoft products. SQL is a language and SQL Server is a database, but in the Microsoft world, the term *SQL* is often used to refer to either.

CERTIFICATION OBJECTIVE 1.03

Summarize the SQL Language

SQL is defined, developed, and controlled by international bodies. Oracle Corporation does not have to conform to the SQL standard but chooses to do so. The language itself can be thought of as being very simple (there are only 16 commands), but in practice SQL coding can be phenomenally complicated. That is why a whole book is needed to cover the bare fundamentals.

SQL Standards

Structured Query Language (SQL) was first invented by an IBM research group in the '70s, but in fact Oracle Corporation (then trading as Relational Software, Inc.) claims to have beaten IBM to market by a few weeks with the first commercial implementation: Oracle 2, released in 1979. Since then the language has evolved enormously and is no longer driven by any one organization. SQL is now an international standard. It is managed by committees from ISO and ANSI. ISO is the Organisation Internationale de Normalisation, based in Geneva; ANSI is the American National Standards Institute, based in Washington, DC. The two bodies cooperate, and their SQL standards are identical.

Earlier releases of the Oracle database used an implementation of SQL that had some significant deviations from the standard. This was not because Oracle was being deliberately different: it was usually because Oracle implemented features that were ahead of the standard, and when the standard caught up, it used different syntax. An example is the outer join (detailed in Chapter 7), which Oracle implemented long before standard SQL; when standard SQL introduced an outer join, Oracle added support for the new join syntax while retaining support for its own proprietary syntax. Oracle Corporation ensures future compliance by inserting personnel onto the various ISO and ANSI committees and is now assisting with driving the SQL standard forward.

SQL Commands

These are the 16 primary SQL commands, separated into commonly used groups:
The Data Manipulation Language (DML) commands:

- SELECT
- INSERT
- UPDATE
- DELETE
- MERGE

The Data Definition Language (DDL) commands:

- CREATE
- ALTER
- DROP

- RENAME
- TRUNCATE
- COMMENT

The Data Control Language (DCL) commands:

- GRANT
- REVOKE

The Transaction Control Language (TCL) commands:

- COMMIT
- ROLLBACK
- SAVEPOINT

The first command, SELECT, is the main subject of Chapters 2 through 9. The remaining DML commands are covered in Chapter 10, along with the TCL commands. DDL is detailed in Chapter 11. DCL, which has to do with security, is only briefly mentioned: it falls more into the domain of the database administrator than the developer.

on the
ⓘ o b   *According to all the documentation, SELECT is a DML statement. In practice, no one includes it when they refer to DML—they talk about it as though it were a language in its own right (it almost is) and use DML to mean only the commands that change data.*

A Set-Oriented Language

Most 3GLs are procedural languages. Programmers working in procedural languages specify what to do with data, one row at a time. Programmers working in a set-oriented language say what they want to do to a group (a "set") of rows and let the database work out how to do it to all the rows in the set.

Procedural languages are usually less efficient than set-oriented languages at managing data, as regards both development and execution. A procedural routine for looping through a group of rows and updating them one by one will involve many lines of code, where SQL might do the whole operation with one command. The result: programmers' productivity increases. During program execution, procedural code gives the database no options; it must run the code as it has been written. With SQL, the programmer states what he or she wants to do but not how to do it; the database has the freedom to work out how best to carry out the operation. This will usually give better results.

Where SQL fails to provide a complete solution is that it is purely a data access language. Most applications will need procedural constructs, such as flow control: conditional branching and iteration. They will also usually need screen control, user interface facilities, and variables. SQL has none of these. SQL is a set-oriented language capable of nothing other than data access. For application development, one will therefore need a procedural language that can invoke SQL calls. It is therefore necessary for SQL to work with a procedural language.

Consider an application that prompts a user for a name, retrieves all the people with that name from a table, prompts the user to choose one of them, and then deletes the chosen person. The procedural language will draw a screen and generate a prompt for a name. The user will enter the name. The procedural language will construct a SQL SELECT statement using the name and submit the statement through a database session to the database server for execution. The server will return a set of rows (all the people with that name) to the procedural language, which will format the set for display to the user and prompt him to choose one (or more) of them. The identifier for the chosen person (or people) will then be used to construct a SQL DELETE statement for the server to execute. If the identifier is a unique identifier (the primary key), then the set of rows to be deleted will be a set of just one row; if the identifier is nonunique, then the set selected for deletion would be larger. The procedural code will know nothing about the likely size of the sets retrieved or deleted.

CERTIFICATION OBJECTIVE 1.04

Use the Client Tools

There are numerous tools that can be used to connect to an Oracle database. Two of the most basic are SQL*Plus and SQL Developer. These are provided by Oracle Corporation and are perfectly adequate for much of the work that a developer or a database administrator needs to do. The choice between them is partly a matter of personal preference, partly to do with the environment and partly to do with functionality. SQL Developer undoubtedly offers far more functionality that SQL*Plus, but it is more demanding in that it needs a graphical terminal, whereas SQL*Plus can be used on character mode devices.

The tool that has lasted longest is SQL*Plus, and even though Oracle Corporation is promoting SQL Developer very strongly as a replacement, all people working in the Oracle environment will be well advised to become familiar with it.

on the
Job

Many experienced developers and database administrators (perhaps including the author of this book) treat the newer tools with a certain degree of skepticism—though this may be nothing more than an indication that these people are somewhat old-fashioned. Throughout this book both tools will be used.

SQL*Plus

SQL*Plus is a client-server tool for connecting to a database and issuing ad hoc SQL commands. It can also be used for creating PL/SQL code and has facilities for formatting results. It is available on all platforms to which the database has been ported—the sections that follow give some detail on using SQL*Plus on Linux and Windows. There are no significant differences with using SQL*Plus on any other platform.

In terms of architecture, SQL*Plus is a user process written in C. It establishes a session against an instance and a database over the Oracle Net protocol. The platforms for the client and the server can be different. For example, there is no reason not to use SQL*Plus on a Windows PC to connect to a database running on a Unix server (or the other way round) provided that Oracle Net has been configured to make the connection.

SQL*Plus on Linux

The SQL*Plus executable file on a Linux installation is `sqlplus`. The location of this file will be installation specific but will typically be something like:

```
/u01/app/oracle/product/12.1.0/db_1/bin/sqlplus
```

Your Linux account should be set up appropriately to run SQL*Plus. There are some environment variables that will need to be set. These are

ORACLE_HOME

PATH

LD_LIBRARY_PATH

The ORACLE_HOME variable points to the Oracle Home. An Oracle Home is the Oracle software installation: the set of files and directories containing the executable code and some of the configuration files. The PATH must include the `bin` directory contained within the Oracle Home. The LD_LIBRARY_PATH should include the `lib` directory also contained within the Oracle Home, but in practice you may get away without setting this. Figure 1-8 shows a Linux terminal window and some tests to see if the environment is correct.

In Figure 1-8, first the `echo` command checks whether the three variables have been set up correctly: there is an ORACLE_HOME, and the `bin` and `lib` directories in it have been set as the last element of the PATH and the first element of the LD_LIBRARY_PATH variables, respectively. Then `which` confirms that the SQL*Plus executable file really is available, in the PATH. Finally, SQL*Plus is launched with a username, a password, and a connect identifier passed to it on the command line. If the tests do not return acceptable results and SQL*Plus fails to launch, this should be discussed with your system administrator and your database administrator. Some common errors with the logon itself are described in the section "Creating and Testing a Database Connection" later in this chapter.

The format of the logon string is the database username followed by a forward slash character as a delimiter, then a password followed by an @ symbol as a delimiter, and finally an Oracle Net connect identifier. In this example, the username is `system`, whose password is `admin123`, and the database is identified by `coda`.

FIGURE 1-8	

Checking the Linux session setup

```
[oracle@hades ~]$
[oracle@hades ~]$ echo $ORACLE_HOME
/u01/app/oracle/product/12.1.0/dbhome_1
[oracle@hades ~]$
[oracle@hades ~]$ echo $LD_LIBRARY_PATH
/u01/app/oracle/product/12.1.0/dbhome_1/lib
[oracle@hades ~]$
[oracle@hades ~]$ echo $PATH
/usr/lib64/qt-3.3/bin:/usr/local/bin:/bin:/usr/bin:/usr/local/sbin:/usr/sbin:/sbin:/home/oracle/bin:/u01/app/oracle/product/12.1.0/dbhome_1/bin
[oracle@hades ~]$
[oracle@hades ~]$ which sqlplus
/u01/app/oracle/product/12.1.0/dbhome_1/bin/sqlplus
[oracle@hades ~]$
[oracle@hades ~]$ sqlplus system/admin123@coda

SQL*Plus: Release 12.1.0.0.2 Beta on Sat Jun 8 22:38:13 2013

Copyright (c) 1982, 2012, Oracle.  All rights reserved.

Last Successful login time: Sat Jun 2013 22:31:51 +02:00

Connected to:
Oracle Database 12c Enterprise Edition Release 12.1.0.0.2 - 64bit Beta
With the Partitioning, OLAP, Data Mining and Real Application Testing options

SQL>
```

Following the logon, the next lines of text display the version of SQL*Plus being used, which is 12.1.0.0.2, the version of the database to which the connection has been made (which happens to be the same as the version of the SQL*Plus tool), and which options have been installed within the database. The last line is the prompt to the user, SQL> , at which point the user can enter any SQL*Plus or SQL command. If the logon does not succeed with whatever username (probably not system) you have been allocated, this should be discussed with your database administrator.

SQL*Plus on Windows

Historically, there were always two versions of SQL*Plus for Microsoft Windows: the character version and the graphical version. The character version is the executable file sqlplus.exe, and the graphical version was sqlplusw.exe. With the current release and 11g, the graphical version no longer exists, but many developers will prefer to use it, and the versions shipped with earlier releases are perfectly good tools for working with a 12c database. There are no problems with mixing versions: a 12c SQL*Plus client can connect to a 10g database, and a 10g SQL*Plus client can connect to a 12c database. Following a default installation of either the Oracle database or just the Oracle client on Windows, SQL*Plus will be available as a shortcut on the Windows Start menu. The location of the executable file launched by the shortcut will, typically, be something like the following:

```
D:\app\oracle\product\12.1.0\dbhome_1\BIN\sqlplus.exe
```

However, the exact path will be installation specific. Figure 1-9 shows a logon to a database with SQL*Plus, launched from the shortcut. The first line of text shows the version of SQL*Plus, which is the 12.1.0.0.2 release, and the time the program was launched. The third line of text is a logon prompt:

```
Enter user-name:
```

followed by the logon string entered manually, which was

```
system/admin123@coda
```

A change some people like to make to the shortcut that launches SQL*Plus is to prevent it from immediately presenting a logon prompt. To do this, add the NOLOG switch to the end of the command:

```
sqlplus /nolog
```

FIGURE I-9

A database logon with SQL*Plus for Windows

```
C:\Windows\system32\cmd.exe - D:\app\oracle\product\12.1.0\dbhome_1\BIN\sqlplus.exe

SQL*Plus: Release 12.1.0.0.2 Beta on Tue Sep 17 16:45:17 2013

Copyright (c) 1982, 2012, Oracle.  All rights reserved.

Enter user-name: system/admin123@coda
Last Successful login time: Tue Sep 17 2013 16:44:38 +02:00

Connected to:
Oracle Database 12c Enterprise Edition Release 12.1.0.0.2 - 64bit Beta
With the Partitioning, OLAP, Advanced Analytics and Real Application Testing options

SQL>
```

There is no reason not to launch SQL*Plus from an operating system prompt rather than from the Start menu shortcut: simply open a command window and run it. The program will immediately prompt for a logon, unless you invoke it with the NOLOG switch described above.

The tests of the environment and the need to set the variables if they are not correct, previously described for a Linux installation, are not usually necessary on a Windows installation. This is because the variables are set in the Windows Registry by the Oracle Universal Installer when the software is installed. If SQL*Plus does not launch successfully, check the Registry variables. Figure 1-10 shows the relevant section of the Registry, viewed with the Windows `regedit.exe` Registry Editor utility. Within the Registry Editor, navigate to the key:

HKEY_LOCAL_MACHINE

SOFTWARE

ORACLE

KEY_OraDb12c_home1

The final element of this navigation path will have a different name if there have been several 12c installations on the machine.

FIGURE 1-10

The Oracle
Registry variables

Note the values of the Registry variables ORACLE_HOME and ORACLE_HOME_NAME. These will relate to the location of the `sqlplus.exe` executable and the Start menu navigation path to reach the shortcut that will launch it.

Creating and Testing a Database Connection

SQL*Plus does not have any way of storing database connection details. Each time a user wishes to connect to a database, the user must tell SQL*Plus who they are and where the database is. There are variations depending on site-specific security facilities, but the most common means of identifying oneself to the database is by presenting a username and a case-sensitive password. There are two typically used forms of connect identifier for identifying the database: either by providing an alias that is resolved into the full connect details or by entering the full details.

From an operating system prompt, these commands will launch SQL*Plus and connect as database user SCOTT, whose password is tiger using each technique:

```
sqlplus scott/tiger@orcl
sqlplus scott/tiger@ocp12c.oracle.com:1521/orcl.oracle.com
```

The first example uses an alias, orcl, to identify the database. This must be *resolved* into the full connect details. This resolution can be done in a number of ways, but one way or another it must be accomplished. The usual techniques for this are to use a locally stored text file called the `tnsnames.ora` file (typically contained within the network/admin subdirectory of the ORACLE_HOME) or to contact an LDAP directory such as Microsoft's Active Directory or Oracle's Oracle Internet Directory (OID).

The second example provides all the connect details in line. The connect details needed are the hostname of the computer on which the database instance is running, the TCP port on which the Oracle Net database listener can be contacted, and the database service to which the user wishes the database listener to connect him. The first technique, where the user need only enter an alias, requires the database administrator to configure a name resolution mechanism; the second technique can only work if the user knows the details himself.

There are a number of circumstances that will cause a SQL*Plus connection attempt to fail. Figure 1-11 illustrates some of the more common problems.

First, the user launches SQL*Plus from a Windows operating system prompt, using the NOLOG switch to prevent the immediate logon prompt. No problem so far.

FIGURE 1-11

Some common logon problems

```
C:\Windows\system32\cmd.exe - sqlplus /nolog

C:\>sqlplus /nolog

SQL*Plus: Release 12.1.0.0.2 Beta on Thu Jul 4 22:51:04 2013

Copyright (c) 1982, 2012, Oracle.  All rights reserved.

SQL> connect hr/hr@wrongalias
ERROR:
ORA-12154: TNS:could not resolve the connect identifier specified


SQL> conn hr/hr@orcl
ERROR:
ORA-12541: TNS:no listener


SQL> conn hr/hr@orcl
ERROR:
ORA-12514: TNS:listener does not currently know of service requested in connect
descriptor


SQL> conn hr/wrongpassword@orcl
ERROR:
ORA-01017: invalid username/password; logon denied


SQL> conn hr/hr@orcl
Connected.
SQL>
```

Second, from the SQL> prompt, the user issues a connection request, which fails with a well-known error:

```
ORA-12154: TNS: could not resolve the connect identifier specified
```

This error is because the connect identifier given, wrongalias, cannot be resolved into database connection details by the TNS (Transparent Network Substrate—not an acronym particularly worth remembering) layer of Oracle Net. The name resolution method to be used and its configuration is a matter for the database administrator. In this case, the error is obvious: the user entered the wrong connect identifier.

The second connect attempt gives the correct identifier, orcl. This fails with

```
ORA-12541: TNS:no listener
```

This indicates that the connect identifier has resolved correctly into the address of a database listener, but that the listener is not actually running. Note that another possibility would be that the address resolution is faulty and is sending SQL*Plus to the wrong address. Following this error, the user should contact the database administrator and ask him or her to start the listener. Then try again.

The third connect request fails with

```
ORA-12514: TNS:listener does not currently know of service requested in connect descriptor
```

This error is generated by the database listener. SQL*Plus has found the listener with no problems, but the listener cannot make the onward connection to the database service. The most likely reason for this is that the database instance has not been started, so the user should ask the database administrator to start it and then try again.

The fourth connect request fails with

```
ORA-01017: invalid username/password; logon denied
```

To receive this message, the user must have contacted the database. The user has got through all the possible network problems, the database instance is running, and the database itself has been opened by the instance. The user just has the password or username wrong. Note that the message does not state whether it is the password or the username that is wrong; if it were to do so, it would be giving out information to the effect that the other one was right.

Finally, the fifth connect attempt succeeds.

on the
job
The preceding example demonstrates a problem-solving technique you will use frequently. If something fails, work through what it is doing step by step. Read every error message.

SQL Developer

SQL Developer is a tool for connecting to an Oracle database (or, in fact, some non-Oracle databases, too) and issuing ad hoc SQL commands. It can also manage PL/SQL objects. Unlike SQL*Plus, it is a graphical tool with wizards for commonly needed actions. SQL Developer is written in Java and requires a Java Runtime Environment (JRE) to run.

Being written in Java, SQL Developer is available on all platforms that support the appropriate version of the JRE. There are no significant differences between platforms.

Installing and Launching SQL Developer

SQL Developer is not installed with the Oracle Universal Installer, which is used to install all other Oracle products. It does not exist in an Oracle Home but is a completely self-contained product. The latest version can be downloaded from Oracle Corporation's website.

on the
ⓘ o b   *An installation of the 12c database will include a copy of SQL Developer, but it will not be the current version. Even if you happen to have an installation of the database, you will usually want to install the current version of SQL Developer as well.*

To install SQL Developer, unzip the ZIP file. That's all. It does require a JDK, the Java Runtime Environment, to be available; this comes from Oracle. But if an appropriate JDK is not already available on the machine being used, there are downloadable versions of SQL Developer for Windows that include it. For platforms other than Windows, the JDK must be preinstalled. Download it from Oracle's website and install according to the platform-specific directions. To check that the JDK is available with the correct version, from an operating system prompt run the following command:

```
java -version
```

This should return something like the following:

```
java version "1.7.0_21"
Java(TM) SE Runtime Environment (build 1.7.0_21-b11)
Java HotSpot(TM) 64-Bit Server VM (build 23.21-b01, mixed mode)
```

If it does not, using `which java` may help identify the problem: the search path could be locating an incorrect version.

Once SQL Developer has been unzipped, change your current directory to the directory in which SQL Developer was unzipped and launch it. On Windows, the executable file is `sqldeveloper.exe`. On Linux, it is the `sqldeveloper.sh` shell script. Remember to check that the DISPLAY environment variable has been set to a suitable value (such as 127.0.0.1:0.0, if SQL Developer is being run on the system console) before running the shell script.

Any problems with installing the JRE and launching SQL Developer should be referred to your system administrator.

The SQL Developer User Interface

Figure 1-12 shows the SQL Developer User Interface after connecting to a database.

The general layout of the SQL Developer window is a left pane for navigation around objects, and a right pane to display and enter information.

In the figure, the left pane shows that a connection has been made to a database. The connection is called orcl_sys. This name is just a label chosen when the connection was defined, but most developers will use some sort of naming convention—in this case, the name chosen is the database identifier, which is orcl, and the name of the user the connection was made as, which was sys. The

FIGURE 1-12

The SQL Developer User Interface

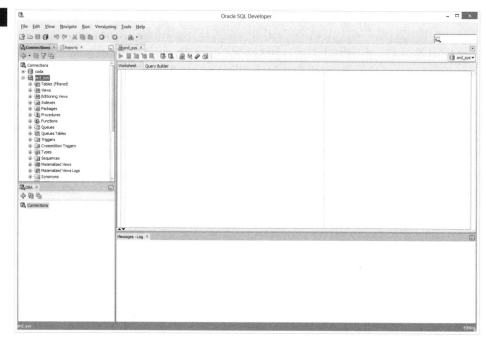

branches beneath list all the possible object types that can be managed. Expanding the branches would list the objects themselves. The right pane has an upper part prompting the user to enter a SQL statement and a lower part that will display the result of the statement. The layout of the panes and the tabs visible on them are highly customizable.

The menu buttons across the top menu bar give access to standard facilities:

- **File**   A normal Windows-like file menu, from which one can save work and exit from the tool.
- **Edit**   A normal Windows-like edit menu, from which one can undo, redo, copy, paste, find, and so on.
- **View**   The options for customizing the SQL Developer user interface.
- **Navigate**   Facilities for moving between panes and for moving around code that is being edited.
- **Run**   Enables execution and debugging of the SQL statements, SQL script, or PL/SQL block that is being worked on. Debugging facilitates stepping through code line by line rather than running the entire block of code.
- **Versioning**   Supports the creation of a code versioning repository to track different versions of your SQL programs.
- **Tools**   Links to external programs, including Data Modeler and SQL Worksheet
- **Help**   It's pretty good.

SQL Developer can be a very useful tool, as it is highly customizable. Experiment with it, read the Help, and set up the user interface the way that works best for you.

Creating a Database Connection

Database connections can be created and saved for reuse. Figure 1-13 shows the window where connections can be defined. To reach this window, click the "+" symbol visible on the Connections tab shown previously in Figure 1-12.

The name for the connection is arbitrary. In this example, the name chosen is the name of the database connect identifier (orcl) suffixed with the username (hr) that will be embedded in the connection.

The username and password must both be supplied, but only the username will be saved unless the Save Password check box is selected. Saving a password means that future connections can be made without any password prompt. This is convenient

How to define
a new database
connection

but highly dangerous if there is any possibility that the computer you are working on is not secure. In effect, you are delegating the authentication to your local operating system: if you can log on to that, you can log on to the database.

Assuming that you are using SQL Developer to connect to an Oracle database rather than to a third-party database, select the Oracle tab.

The Role drop-down box gives you the option to connect as *sysdba*. A sysdba connection is required before certain particularly serious operations (such as database startup and shutdown) can be carried out. It will never be needed for the exercises covered in this book.

The Connection Type radio buttons let you choose among five options:

- **Basic**   This prompts for the machine name of the database server, the port on which the database listener will accept connection requests, and the instance (the SID) or the service to which the connection will be made.

- **TNS**   If a name resolution method has been configured, then an alias for the database can be selected (from the local tnsnames.ora file) or entered, rather than the full details needed by the Basic option.

- **LDAP**   Database service definitions and their connection details that are stored in a LDAP directory service may be queried by specifying the LDAP Server details.

- **Advanced**   This allows entry of a full JDBC (Java Database Connectivity) connect string. This is completely Oracle independent and could be used to connect to any database that conforms to the JDBC standard.
- **Local/Bequeath**   If the database is running on the same machine as your SQL Developer client, this option allows you to connect directly to a server process bypassing the network listener.

Selecting Basic requires the user to know how to connect to the database; selecting TNS requires some configuration to have been done on the client machine by the database administrator, in order that the alias can be resolved into the full connection details.

After you enter the details, the Test button will force SQL Developer to attempt a logon. If this returns an error, then either the connection details are wrong, or there is a problem on the server side. Typical server-side problems are that the database listener is not running or that the database has not been started. Whatever the error is, it will be prefixed with an error number—some of the common errors were described in the preceding section, which described the use of SQL*Plus.

SCENARIO & SOLUTION

If a connection fails, what can you do? How should you try to fix the problem?	If a connection attempt fails, there should be some sort of error message. Read it! If it isn't immediately self-explanatory, look it up in the Oracle documentation and on My Oracle Support. Try to follow the flow of a connection—from the user process to the database listener to the instance to the database—and check each step.
If you can't fix the problem yourself, where can you go for help?	The documentation and My Oracle Support will get you a long way. Most support groups will refuse to talk to you unless you can show that you have tried to solve the problem yourself. Then talk to your network administrators, system administrators, and database administrators.

CERTIFICATION OBJECTIVE 1.05

Create the Demonstration Schemas

Throughout this book, there are hundreds of examples of running SQL code against tables of data. For the most part, the examples use tables in two demonstration schemas provided by Oracle: the HR schema, which is sample data that simulates a simple human resources application, and the OE schema, which simulates a more complicated order entry application.

These schemas can be created when the database is created; it is an option presented by the Database Configuration Assistant (DBCA). If they do not exist, they can be created later by running some scripts that will exist in the database Oracle Home.

on the
Ö o b
An earlier demonstration schema was SCOTT (password tiger). This schema is simpler than HR or OE. Many people with long experience of Oracle will prefer to use this. The creation script is still supplied; it is utlsampl.sql.

Users and Schemas

First, two definitions. In Oracle parlance, a database *user* is a person who can log on to the database. A database *schema* is all the objects in the database owned by one user. The two terms can often be used interchangeably, as there is a one-to-one relationship between users and schemas. Note that while there is in fact a CREATE SCHEMA command, this does not actually create a schema—it is only a quick way of creating objects in a schema. A schema is initially created empty, when a user is created with the CREATE USER command.

Schemas are used for storing objects. These may be data objects such as tables or programmatic objects such as PL/SQL stored procedures. User logons are used to connect to the database and access these objects. By default, users have access to the objects in their own schema and to no others, but most applications change this. Typically, one schema may be used for storing data that is accessed by other users who have been given permission to use the objects, even though they do not own them. In practice, very few users will ever have objects in their own schema, or permission to create them: they will have access rights (which will be strictly controlled) only to objects in another schema. These objects will be used by all users who run the application whose data that schema stores. Conversely, the users who own the data-storing schemas may never in fact log on: the only purpose of their schemas is to contain data used by others.

It is impossible for a data object to exist independently of a schema. Or in other words, all tables must have an owner. The owner is the user in whose schema the table resides. The unique identifier for a table (or any other schema object) is the username, followed by the object name. It follows that it is not possible for two tables with the same name to exist in the same schema, but that two tables with the same name (though possibly different structures or contents) can exist in different schemas. If an object does not exist in one's own schema, to access it one must qualify its name with the name of the schema in which it resides. For example, HR.EMPLOYEES is the table called EMPLOYEES in user HR's schema. Unless synonyms are available, only a user connected as HR could get to the table by referring to EMPLOYEES without a schema name qualifier. A synonym is a construct that makes an object accessible to other users without requiring its schema name as a prefix.

The HR and OE Schemas

The HR demonstration schema consists of seven tables, linked by primary key to foreign key relationships. Figure 1-14 illustrates the relationships between the tables, as an entity relationship diagram.

FIGURE 1-14

The HR entity relationship diagram

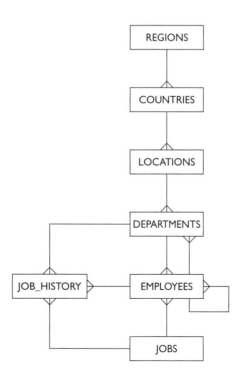

Two of the relationships shown in Figure 1-14 may not be immediately comprehensible. First, there is a many-to-one relationship from EMPLOYEES to EMPLOYEES. This is what is known as a *self-referencing foreign key*. This means that many employees can be connected to one employee, and it's based on the fact that many employees may have one manager, but the manager is also an employee. The relationship is implemented by the column manager_id being a foreign key to employee_id, which is the table's primary key.

The second relationship that may require explanation is between DEPARTMENTS and EMPLOYEES, which is bidirectional. The one-department-to-many-employees relationship simply states that there may be many staff members in each department, based on the EMPLOYEES dept_id column being a foreign key to the DEPARTMENTS primary key dept_id column. The one-employee-to-many-departments relationship shows that one employee could be the manager of several departments and is implemented by the manager_id column in DEPARTMENTS being a foreign key to the primary key employee_id column in EMPLOYEES.

Table 1-5 shows the columns of each table in the HR schema, using the notation described in the earlier section "Data Normalization" to indicate primary keys (#), foreign keys (\ ), and whether columns are optional (o) or mandatory (*).

The tables are:

- REGIONS has rows for major geographical areas.
- COUNTRIES has rows for each country, which are optionally assigned to a region.
- LOCATIONS includes individual addresses, which are optionally assigned to a country.
- DEPARTMENTS has a row for each department, optionally assigned to a location and optionally with a manager (who must exist as an employee).
- EMPLOYEES has a row for every employee, each of whom must be assigned to a job and optionally to a department and to a manager. The managers must themselves be employees.
- JOBS lists all possible jobs in the organization. It is possible for many employees to have the same job.
- JOB_HISTORY lists previous jobs held by employees, uniquely identified by employee_id and start_date; it is not possible for an employee to hold two jobs concurrently. Each job history record will refer to one employee, who will have had one job at that time and may have been a member of one department.

TABLE 1-5	Table	Columns	
	REGIONS	#*	region_id
The Tables and		o	region_name
Columns on the	COUNTRIES	#*	country_id
HR Schema		o	country_name
		\o	region_id
	LOCATIONS	#*	location_id
		o	street_address
		o	postal_code
		*	city
		o	state_province
		\o	country_id
	DEPARTMENTS	#*	department_id
		*	department_name
		\o	manager_id
		\o	location_id
	EMPLOYEES	#*	employee_id
		o	first_name
		*	last_name
		*	e-mail
		o	phone_number
		*	hire_date
		*	job_id
		o	salary
		o	commission_pct
		\o	manager_id
		\o	department_id
	JOBS	#*	job_id
		*	job_title
		o	min_salary
		o	max_salary
	JOB_HISTORY	#*	employee_id
		#*	start_date
		*	end_date
		*	job_id
		\o	department_id

This HR schema is used for most of the exercises and many of the examples embedded in the chapters of this book and does need to be available.

on the **Job**

There are rows in EMPLOYEES that do not have a matching parent row in DEPARTMENTS. This could be by design but might well be a design mistake that is possible because the DEPARTMENT_ID column in EMPLOYEES is not mandatory. There are similar possible errors in the REGIONS—COUNTRIES—LOCATIONS hierarchy, which really does not make a lot of sense.

The OE schema is considerably more complex than the HR schema. The table structures are much more complicated: they include columns defined as nested tables, user-defined data types, and XML data types. There are a number of optional exercises at the end of each chapter that are usually based on the OE schema. The objects referred to are described as they are used.

Demonstration Schema Creation

If the database you are using was created specifically for studying for the SQL examination, the demonstration schemas should have been created already. They are an option presented by the Database Configuration Assistant when it creates a database. After database creation, the schemas may have to be unlocked and their passwords set; by default the accounts are locked, which means you cannot log on to them. These commands, which could be issued from SQL*Plus or SQL Developer, will make it possible to log on as users HR and OE using the passwords hr and oe:

```
alter user hr account unlock identified by hr;
alter user oe account unlock identified by oe;
```

These `alter user` commands can only be issued when connected to the database as a user with DBA privileges, such as the user SYSTEM.

If the schemas were not created at database creation time, they can be created later by running scripts installed into the Oracle Home of the database. These scripts will need to be run from SQL*Plus or SQL Developer as a user with SYSDBA privileges. The script will prompt for certain values as it runs. For example, on Linux, first launch SQL*Plus from an operating system prompt:

```
sqlplus / as sysdba
```

There are various options for this connection, but the preceding syntax will usually work if the database is running on the same machine where you are running SQL*Plus. Then invoke the script from the SQL> prompt:

```
SQL> @?/demo/schema/human_resources/hr_main.sql
```

The "?" character is a variable that SQL*Plus will expand into the path to the Oracle Home directory. The script will prompt for HR's password, default tablespace, and temporary tablespace; the SYS password; and a destination for a logfile of the script's execution. Typical values for the default tablespace and temporary tablespace are USERS and TEMP, but these must already exist. After completion, you will be connected to the database as the new HR user. To verify this, run these statements.

```
SQL> show user;
```

You will see that you are currently connected as HR; then run:

```
SQL> select table_name from user_tables;
```

You will see a list of the seven tables in the HR schema.

To create the OE schema, follow the same process, nominating the script:

```
?/demo/schema/order_entry/oe_main.sql
```

The process for creating the schemas on Windows is identical, except for the path delimiters—where most operating systems use forward slashes, Windows uses back slashes. So the path to the Windows HR creation script becomes:

```
@?\demo\schema\human_resources\hr_main.sql
```

Note that running these schema creation scripts will *drop* the schemas first if they already exist. Dropping a schema means removing every item in it and then removing the user. This should not be a problem, unless the schema has been used for some development work that needs to be kept.

If the demonstration creation schema scripts do not exist as just described, this will be because the Oracle Home installation has not been completed. Installing a database Oracle Home can be done from one CD, but there is a second CD (called the *companion* or *example* CD) that includes a number of components that are, strictly speaking, optional. These include the demonstration schemas. The companion CD should normally be installed; if this has not been done, this must be discussed with the database administrator.

on the **job**

The demonstration schemas should not exist in production databases. It is not good, for security reasons, to have unnecessary schemas in a database that have well known usernames, capabilities, and (possibly) passwords.

CERTIFICATION SUMMARY

SQL is a language for managing access to normalized data stored in relational databases. It is not an application development language, but is invoked by such languages when they need to access data. The Oracle server technologies provide a platform for developing and deploying such applications. The combination of the Oracle server technologies and SQL result in an environment conforming to the relational database paradigm that is an enabling technology for Cloud computing.

Numerous client tools can be used to connect to an Oracle database. Two provided by Oracle Corporation are SQL*Plus and SQL Developer: SQL*Plus is installed as part of every Oracle client and Oracle database install, but SQL Developer can be installed as a separate product. Both tools can be used for preparing for the OCP examinations, and students should be familiar with both.

The demonstration schemas store example data that is used to illustrate the use of SQL, and also of more advanced Oracle development facilities.

TWO-MINUTE DRILL

Position the Server Technologies

❑ The Oracle database stores and manages access to user data.

❑ The Oracle WebLogic Server runs applications that connect users to the database.

❑ Oracle Enterprise Manager is a tool for managing databases, application servers, and, if desired, the entire computing environment.

❑ Languages built into the database for application development are SQL, PL/SQL, and Java.

Understand Relational Structures

❑ Data must be normalized into two-dimensional tables.

❑ Tables are linked through primary and foreign keys.

❑ Entity-relationship diagrams represent the tables graphically.

Summarize the SQL Language

❑ The DML commands are SELECT, INSERT, UPDATE, DELETE, and MERGE.

❑ The DDL commands are CREATE, ALTER, DROP, RENAME, TRUNCATE, and COMMENT.

❑ The DCL commands are GRANT and REVOKE.

❑ The TCL commands are COMMIT, ROLLBACK, and SAVEPOINT.

Use the Client Tools

❑ SQL*Plus is a command-line utility installed into the Oracle Home.

❑ SQL Developer is a graphical tool installed into its own directory.

❑ Both tools require a database connection, consisting of a username, a password, and a connect identifier.

Create the Demonstration Schemas

❑ The demonstration schemas are provided by Oracle to facilitate learning but must be created before they can be used.

SELF TEST

Position the Server Technologies

1. What components of the IT environment can Oracle Enterprise Manager Cloud Control manage? (Choose the best answer.)
   A. Oracle databases
   B. Oracle application servers
   C. Third-party products
   D. The server machines
   E. All of the above

2. What languages can run within the database? (Choose all that apply.)
   A. SQL
   B. C
   C. PL/SQL
   D. Java
   E. Any other language linked to the OCI libraries

Understand Relational Structures

3. Data that is modeled into a form suitable for processing in a relational database may be described as being (Choose the best answer.)
   A. First normal form
   B. Third normal form
   C. Abnormal form
   D. Paranormal form

4. An entity-relationship diagram shows data modeled into (Choose the best answer.)
   A. Two-dimensional tables
   B. Multidimensional tables
   C. Hierarchical structures
   D. Object-oriented structures

Summarize the SQL Language

5. SQL is a set-oriented language. Which of these features is a consequence of this? (Choose the best answer.)

   A.   Individual rows must have a unique identifier.

   B.   Sets of users can be managed in groups.

   C.   SQL statements can be placed within blocks of code in other languages, such as Java and PL/SQL.

   D.   One statement can affect multiple rows.

6. Which of these constructs is not part of the SQL language? (Choose all that apply.)

   A.   Iteration, based on WHILE..

   B.   Iteration, based on FOR..DO

   C.   Branching, based on IF..THEN..ELSE

   D.   Transaction control, based on COMMIT

   E.   Transaction control, based on ROLLBACK

Use the Client Tools

7. Which of these statements regarding SQL Developer are correct? (Choose two answers.)

   A.   SQL Developer cannot connect to databases earlier than release 10*g*.

   B.   SQL Developer can be installed outside an Oracle Home.

   C.   SQL Developer can store passwords.

   D.   SQL Developer relies on an LDAP directory for name resolution.

8. Which of the following are requirements for using SQL Developer? (Choose two correct answers.)

   A.   A Java Runtime Environment

   B.   The OCI libraries

   C.   A name resolution method such as LDAP or a TNSNAMES.ORA file

   D.   The SQL*Plus libraries

   E.   A graphical terminal

Create the Demonstration Schemas

9. Where may the demonstration schemas be created? (Choose the best answer.)

    A. The demonstration schemas must be created in a demonstration database.

    B. The demonstration schemas cannot be created in a production database.

    C. The demonstration schemas can be created in any database.

    D. The demonstration schemas can be created in any database if the demonstration user is created first.

10. How can you move a schema from one user to another? (Choose the best answer.)

    A. Use the ALTER SCHEMA MOVE… command.

    B. You cannot move a schema from one user to another.

    C. A schema can only be moved if it is empty (or if all objects within it have been dropped).

    D. Attach the new user to the schema, then detach the old user from the schema.

LAB QUESTION

The OE schema includes these tables:

- ❑ CUSTOMERS
- ❑ INVENTORIES
- ❑ ORDERS
- ❑ ORDER_ITEMS
- ❑ PRODUCT_DESCRIPTIONS
- ❑ PRODUCT_INFORMATION
- ❑ WAREHOUSES

A CUSTOMER can place many ORDERS, and an order can have many ORDER_ITEMS. Each item will be of one product, described by its PRODUCT_INFORMATION, and each product may have several PRODUCT_DESCRIPTIONS, in different languages. There are a number of WAREHOUSES, each of which can store many products; one product may be stored in many warehouses. An INVENTORIES entry relates products to warehouses, showing how much of each product is in each warehouse.

Sketch out this schema as an entity-relationship diagram, showing the many-to-one connections between the tables and ensuring that there are no many-to-many connections.

SELF TEST ANSWERS

Position the Server Technologies

1. ☑ **E.** Cloud Control can manage the complete environment (according to Oracle Corporation).
☒ **A, B, C,** and **D** are incorrect. All of these can be managed by Cloud Control.

2. ☑ **A, C,** and **D.** SQL, PL/SQL, and Java can all run in the database.
☒ **B** and **E** are incorrect. C cannot run inside the database, and OCI is used by external processes to connect to the database; it does not run within it.

Understand Relational Structures

3. ☑ **B.** Third normal form is the usual form aimed for by systems analysts when they normalize data into relational structures.
☒ **A, C,** and **D** are incorrect. A is incorrect because first normal form is only the first stage of data normalization. C and D would be more suitable to the X-Files than to a database.

4. ☑ **A.** The relational model uses two-dimensional tables.
☒ **B, C,** and **D** are incorrect. B is incorrect because two dimensions is the limit for relational structures. C and D are incorrect because they refer to nonrelational structures (though there are facilities within the Oracle database for simulating them).

Summarize the SQL Language

5. ☑ **D.** In a set-oriented language, one command can affect many rows (a set), whereas a procedural language processes rows one by one.
☒ **A, B,** and **C** are incorrect. A is incorrect because while rows should have a unique identifier in a well designed application, this is not actually a requirement. B is incorrect because users cannot be grouped in the Oracle environment. C is incorrect because (even though the statement is correct) it is not relevant to the question.

6. ☑ **A, B,** and **C.** These are all procedural constructions, which are not part of a set-oriented language. They are all used in PL/SQL.
☒ **D** and **E** are incorrect. These are SQL's transaction control statements.

Use the Client Tools

7. ☑ **B** and **C.** B is correct because SQL Developer can be installed in its own directory. C is correct because passwords can be saved as part of a connection definition (though this may not be a good idea).
☒ **A** and **D** are incorrect. A is incorrect because the Oracle Net protocol lets SQL Developer connect to a number of versions of the database. D is incorrect because LDAP is only one of several techniques for name resolution.

8. ☑ **A** and **E.** A is correct because SQL Developer is written in Java and therefore requires a Java Runtime Environment. E is correct because SQL Developer needs a graphics terminal to display windows.
☒ **B, C,** and **D** are incorrect. B is incorrect because SQL Developer uses JDBC to connect to databases, not OCI. C is incorrect because, while SQL Developer can use LDAP or a TNSNAMES.ORA file, it can also use and store the basic connection details. D is incorrect because SQL Developer is a completely independent product.

Create the Demonstration Schemas

9. ☑ **C.** The demonstration schemas can be created in any database, either at database creation time or by running scripts later.
☒ **A, B,** and **D** are incorrect. A and B are incorrect because, while they may be good practice, they are not a technical requirement. D is incorrect because it fails to understand that a schema can only be (and always is) created with a user.

10. ☑ **B.** A schema and a user are inseparable.
☒ **A, C,** and **D** are incorrect. A is incorrect because there is no such command. C and D are incorrect because they assume the impossible: that you can separate a user from his or her schema.

LAB ANSWER

Figure 1-15 shows a solution.

FIGURE 1-15

An entity-relationship diagram describing the OE schema

2

Data Retrieval Using the SQL SELECT Statement

CERTIFICATION OBJECTIVES

T his chapter explores the concepts of extracting or retrieving data stored in relational tables using the SELECT statement. The statement is introduced in its basic form and is progressively built on to extend its core functionality. As you learn the rules governing this statement, an important point to remember is that the SELECT statement never alters information stored in the database. Instead, it provides a read-only method of extracting information. When you ask a question using SQL SELECT, you are guaranteed to extract results, even from the difficult questions.

CERTIFICATION OBJECTIVE 2.01

List the Capabilities of SQL SELECT Statements

Knowing how to retrieve data in a set format using a query language is the first step toward understanding the capabilities of SELECT statements. Describing the relations involved provides a tangible link between the theory of how data is stored in tables and the practical visualization of the structure of these tables. These topics form an important precursor to the discussion of the capabilities of the SELECT statement. The three primary areas explored are as follows:

- Introducing the SQL SELECT statement
- The DESCRIBE table command
- Capabilities of the SELECT statement

Introducing the SQL SELECT Statement

The SELECT statement from Structured Query Language (SQL) has to be the single most powerful nonspoken language construct. The SELECT statement is an elegant, flexible, and highly extensible mechanism created to retrieve information from a database table. A database would serve little purpose if it could not be queried to answer all sorts of interesting questions. For example, you may have a database that contains personal financial records like your bank statements, your utility bills, and your salary statements. You could easily ask the database for a date-ordered list of your electrical utility bills for the last six months or query your bank statement for a list of payments made to a certain account over the same period. The beauty of the SELECT statement is encapsulated in its simple English-like format that allows questions to be asked of the database in a natural manner.

Tables, also known as relations, consist of *rows* of information divided by *columns*. Consider two of the sample tables introduced in the previous chapter: the EMPLOYEES table and the DEPARTMENTS table. This sample dataset is based on the Human Resources (HR) information for some fictitious organization. In Oracle terminology, each table belongs to a schema (owner), in this case the HR schema. The EMPLOYEES table stores rows or records of information. These contain several attributes (columns) that describe each employee in this organization. The DEPARTMENTS table contains descriptive information about each department within this organization, stored as rows of data divided into columns.

Assuming a connection to a database containing the sample HR schema is available, then using either SQL*Plus or SQL Developer you can establish a user session. Once connected to the database, you are ready to begin your tour of SQL.

on the
Job

SQL*Plus has an extensive runtime command environment which can be explored using the online documentation or the HELP INDEX command. This lists available SQL*Plus commands such as the SHOW command, which shows the value of a SQL*Plus variable. For example, SHOW USER shows the name of the currently connected user.

The DESCRIBE Table Command

To get the answers one seeks, one must ask the correct questions. An understanding of the terms of reference, which in this case are relational tables, is essential for the formulation of the correct questions. A structural description of a table is useful to establish what questions can be asked of it. The Oracle server stores information about all tables in a special set of relational tables called the *data dictionary*, in order to manage them. The data dictionary is quite similar to a regular language dictionary. It stores definitions of database objects in a centralized, ordered, and structured format.

A clear distinction must be drawn between storing the definition and the contents of a table. The definition of a table includes information such as table name, table owner, details about the columns that comprise it, and its physical storage size on disk. This information is also referred to as *metadata*. The contents of a table are stored in rows and are referred to as *data*.

The structural metadata of a table may be obtained by querying the database for the list of columns that comprise it using the DESCRIBE command. The general form of the syntax for this command is intuitive:

DESC[RIBE] <SCHEMA>.*tablename*

This command will be systematically unpacked. The DESCRIBE keyword can be shortened to DESC. All tables belong to a schema or owner. If you are describing a table that belongs to the schema to which you are connected, the "<SCHEMA>." portion of the command may be omitted. Figure 2-1 illustrates the use of the SHOW user command to verify that the current connected user is HR. While connected to the database as the HR user, the EMPLOYEES table is described from SQL*Plus with the DESCRIBE employees command and the DEPARTMENTS table is described using the shorthand notation DESC hr.departments. The HR. notational prefix could be omitted since the DEPARTMENTS table belongs to the HR schema. The HR schema (and every other schema) has access to a special table called *DUAL*, which belongs to the SYS schema. This table can be structurally described with the command DESCRIBE sys.dual.

Describing tables yields interesting and useful results. You know which columns of a table can be selected since their names are exposed. You also know the nature of the data contained in these columns since the column data type is exposed. Column

---

FIGURE 2-1

Describing the EMPLOYEES, DEPARTMENTS, and DUAL tables

```
                                     SQL Plus                          _  □  ×

SQL> SHOW user
USER is "HR"
SQL> DESCRIBE employees;
 Name                                      Null?    Type
 ---------------------------------------- -------- -----------------------------

 EMPLOYEE_ID                              NOT NULL NUMBER(6)
 FIRST_NAME                                        VARCHAR2(20)
 LAST_NAME                                NOT NULL VARCHAR2(25)
 EMAIL                                    NOT NULL VARCHAR2(25)
 PHONE_NUMBER                                      VARCHAR2(20)
 HIRE_DATE                                NOT NULL DATE
 JOB_ID                                   NOT NULL VARCHAR2(10)
 SALARY                                            NUMBER(8,2)
 COMMISSION_PCT                                    NUMBER(2,2)
 MANAGER_ID                                        NUMBER(6)
 DEPARTMENT_ID                                     NUMBER(4)

SQL> desc hr.departments;
 Name                                      Null?    Type
 ---------------------------------------- -------- -----------------------------

 DEPARTMENT_ID                            NOT NULL NUMBER(4)
 DEPARTMENT_NAME                          NOT NULL VARCHAR2(30)
 MANAGER_ID                                        NUMBER(6)
 LOCATION_ID                                       NUMBER(4)

SQL> desc sys.dual;
 Name                                      Null?    Type
 ---------------------------------------- -------- -----------------------------

 DUMMY                                             VARCHAR2(1)
```

data types are discussed in detail in Chapter 11. For the current discussion, the following explanation of the different column data types is sufficient.

Numeric columns are often specified as NUMBER(*p,s*), where the first parameter is *precision* and the second is *scale*. In Figure 2-1, the SALARY column of the EMPLOYEES table has a data type of NUMBER(8,2). This means that the values stored in this column can have at most 8 digits. Of these 8 digits, 2 may be to the right of the decimal point and up to 6 may be to the left. If more than two digits are to the right of the decimal point, the number will be rounded to 2 decimal places as long as there are at most 8 digits. A SALARY value of 999999.99 is acceptable, but a SALARY value of 9999999.9 is not, even though both these numbers contain 8 digits.

VARCHAR2(*length*) data type columns store variable length alphanumeric character data, where *length* determines the maximum number of characters a column can contain. The FIRST_NAME column of the EMPLOYEES table has data type VARCHAR2(20), which means it can store employees' names of up to 20 characters. Note that if this column contains no data or its content is less than 20 characters, it will not necessarily use the same space as it would use to store a name that is 20 characters long. The CHAR(*size*) column data type specifies fixed-length columns, where row space is preallocated to contain a fixed number of characters regardless of its contents. CHAR is much less commonly used than VARCHAR2. Unless the length of the data is predictable and constant, the CHAR data type utilizes storage inefficiently, padding any unused components with spaces.

DATE and TIMESTAMP column data types store date and time information. DATE stores a moment in time with precision, including day, month, year, hours, minutes, and seconds. TIMESTAMP(f) stores the same information as DATE but is also capable of storing fractional seconds.

on the
job

A variety of data types is available for use as column data types. Many have a specialized purpose like Binary Large Objects (BLOBs), used for storing binary data like music or video data. The vast majority of tables, however, use the primitive column data types of NUMBER, VARCHAR2, and DATE. The TIMESTAMP data type has become widely used since its introduction in Oracle 9i. Becoming familiar and interacting with these generic primitive data types prepares you for dealing with a significant range of database-related queries.

Mandatory columns, which are forced to store data for each row, are exposed by the *"Null?"* column output from the DESCRIBE command having the value *NOT NULL*. You are guaranteed that any column of data that is restricted by the NOT

NULL constraint when the table is created must contain some data. It is important to note that NULL has special meaning for the Oracle server. NULL refers to an absence of data. Blank spaces do not count as NULL since they are present in the row and have some length even though they are not visible.

EXERCISE 2-1

Describing the Human Resources Schema

The HR schema contains seven tables representing a data model of a fictitious Human Resources department. The EMPLOYEES table, which stores details of the staff, and the DEPARTMENTS table, which contains the details of the departments in the organization, have been described. In this step-by-step exercise, a connection is made using SQL Developer as the HR user and the remaining five sample tables are described. They are the JOBS table, which keeps track of the different job types available in the organization, and the JOB_HISTORY table, which keeps track of the job details of employees who changed jobs but remained in the organization. To understand the data model further, the LOCATIONS, COUNTRIES, and REGIONS tables, which keep track of the geographical information pertaining to departments in the organization, will be described.

1. Launch SQL Developer and choose New from the File menu. Choose Database Connection. If this is the first time you are connecting to the database from SQL Developer, you are required to create a connection. Provide a descriptive connection name and input HR as the username. The remaining connection details should be obtained from your database administrator. Once the connection is saved, click the Connect button.

2. Navigate to the SQL Worksheet, which is the tab titled Worksheet.

3. Type in the command DESCRIBE jobs. Terminating this command with a semicolon is optional.

4. Execute the DESCRIBE command, either by pressing the F5 key or by clicking the solid green triangular arrow icon located on the toolbar above the SQL Editor.

5. The JOBS table description appears in the Results frame as shown in the following illustration.

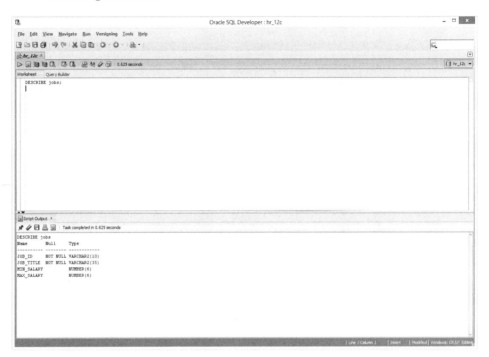

6. Steps 3 to 5 can be repeated to describe the remaining JOB_HISTORY, LOCATIONS, COUNTRIES, and REGIONS tables.

   SQL Developer provides an alternative to the DESCRIBE command when it comes to obtaining the structural information of tables.

7. Navigate to the LOCATIONS table using the Tree navigator located on the left frame underneath the connection name.

8. SQL Developer describes the table automatically on the right side of the tool as shown in the following illustration.

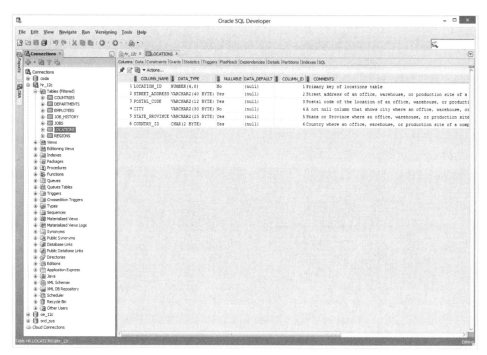

Capabilities of the **SELECT** Statement

Relational database tables are built on a strong mathematical foundation called *relational theory*. In this theory, relations, or tables, are operated on by a formal language called *relational algebra*. SQL is a commercial interpretation of the relational algebraic constructs. Three concepts from relational theory encompass the capability of the SELECT statement: projection, selection, and joining.

Projection refers to the restriction of attributes (columns) selected from a relation or table. When requesting information from a table, you can ask to view all the columns. For example, in the HR.DEPARTMENTS table, you can retrieve all rows and all columns with a simple SELECT statement. This query will return DEPARTMENT_ID, DEPARTMENT_NAME, MANAGER_ID, and LOCATION_ID information for every department record stored in the table. What if you wanted a list containing only the DEPARTMENT_NAME and MANAGER_ID columns? Well, you would request just those two columns from the table. This restriction of columns is called projection.

Selection refers to the restriction of the tuples or rows selected from a relation (table). It is often not desirable to retrieve every row from a table. Tables may contain many rows and, instead of asking for all of them, selection provides a means to restrict the rows returned. Perhaps you have been asked to identify only the employees who belong to department 30. With selection it is possible to limit the results set to those rows of data which have a DEPARTMENT_ID value of 30.

Joining, as a relational concept, refers to the interaction of tables with each other in a query. Third normal form, as discussed in Chapter 1, presented the notion of separating different types of data into autonomous tables to avoid duplication and maintenance anomalies and to associate related data using primary and foreign key relationships. These relationships provide the mechanism to join tables with each other. Joining is discussed extensively in Chapter 7.

Assume there is a need to retrieve the e-mail addresses for all employees who work in the Sales department. The EMAIL column belongs to the EMPLOYEES table, while the DEPARTMENT_NAME column belongs to the DEPARTMENTS table. Projection and selection from the DEPARTMENTS table may be used to obtain the DEPARTMENT_ID value that corresponds to the Sales department. The matching rows in the EMPLOYEES table may be joined to the DEPARTMENTS table based on this common DEPARTMENT_ID value. The EMAIL column may then be projected from this set of results.

The SQL SELECT statement is mathematically governed by these three tenets. An unlimited combination of projections, selections, and joins provides the language to extract the relational data required.

CERTIFICATION OBJECTIVE 2.02

Execute a Basic SELECT Statement

The practical capabilities of the SELECT statement are realized in its execution. The key to executing any query language statement is a thorough understanding of its syntax and the rules governing its usage. This topic is discussed first. It is followed by a discussion of the execution of a basic query before expressions and operators, which exponentially increase the utility of data stored in relational tables, are introduced. Next, the concept of a null value is demystified, as its pitfalls are exposed. These topics will be covered in the following four sections:

- The primitive SELECT statement
- Syntax rules
- SQL expressions and operators
- The NULL concept

The Primitive SELECT Statement

In its most primitive form, the SELECT statement supports the projection of columns and the creation of arithmetic, character, and date expressions. It also facilitates the elimination of duplicate values from the results set. The basic SELECT statement syntax is as follows:

SELECT * | {[DISTINCT] *column* | *expression* [*alias*],…}

FROM *table*;

The special keywords or reserved words of the SELECT statement syntax appear in uppercase. When using the commands, however, the case of the reserved words in your query statement does not matter. The reserved words cannot be used as column names or other database object names. SELECT, DISTINCT, and FROM are three keyword elements. A SELECT statement always comprises two or more clauses. The two mandatory clauses are the SELECT clause and the FROM clause. The pipe symbol | is used to denote OR. So you can read the first form of the above SELECT statement as:

SELECT *

FROM *table*;

In this format, the asterisk symbol (*) is used to denote all columns. SELECT *
is a succinct way of asking the Oracle server to return all possible columns. It is
used as a shorthand, time-saving symbol instead of typing in SELECT *column1*,
column2,…,*columnX*, to select all the columns. The FROM clause specifies which
table to query to fetch (project) the columns requested in the SELECT clause.

You can issue the following SQL command to retrieve all the columns and all the
rows from the REGIONS table in the HR schema:

```
SELECT * FROM regions;
```

As shown in Figure 2-2, when this command is executed in SQL*Plus, it returns
all the rows of data and all the columns that belong to this table. Use of the asterisk
in a SELECT statement is sometimes referred to as a "blind" query because the exact
columns to be fetched are not specified.

The second form of the basic SELECT statement has the same FROM clause as
the first form, but the SELECT clause is different:

SELECT {[DISTINCT] *column* | *expression* [*alias*],…}

FROM *table*;

This SELECT clause can be simplified into two formats:

SELECT *column1* (*possibly other columns or expressions*) [alias optional]

OR

SELECT DISTINCT *column1* (*possibly other columns or expressions*) [alias optional]

FIGURE 2-2	
Projecting all columns from the REGIONS table	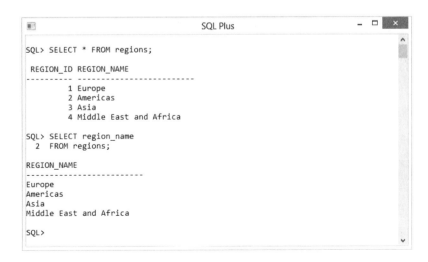

An *alias* is an alternative name for referencing a column or expression. Aliases are typically used for displaying output in a user-friendly manner. They also serve as shorthand when referring to columns or expressions to reduce typing. Aliases will be discussed in detail later in this chapter. By explicitly listing only the relevant columns in the SELECT clause, you, in effect, *project* the exact subset of the results you wish to retrieve. The following statement will return just the REGION_NAME column subset of the REGIONS table, as shown in Figure 2-2:

```
SELECT region_name
FROM regions;
```

You may be asked to obtain all the job roles in the organization that employees have historically fulfilled. For this you can issue the command SELECT * FROM JOB_HISTORY. However, in addition, the SELECT * construct returns the EMPLOYEE_ID, START_DATE, and END_DATE columns. The uncluttered results set containing only JOB_ID and DEPARTMENT_ID columns can be obtained with the statement shown in Figure 2-3, executed in SQL*Plus.

Using the DISTINCT keyword allows duplicate rows to be eliminated from the results set. In numerous situations a unique set of rows is required. It is important to note that the criterion employed by the Oracle server in determining whether a row is unique or distinct depends entirely on what is specified after the DISTINCT keyword in the SELECT clause. Selecting distinct JOB_ID values from the JOB_HISTORY table will return the eight distinct job types, as shown in Figure 2-4.

FIGURE 2-3

Projecting specific columns from the JOB_HISTORY table

```
SQL> SELECT job_id, department_id
  2  FROM job_history;

JOB_ID      DEPARTMENT_ID
----------  -------------
IT_PROG                60
AC_ACCOUNT            110
AC_MGR               110
MK_REP                20
ST_CLERK              50
ST_CLERK              50
AD_ASST               90
SA_REP                80
SA_MAN                80
AC_ACCOUNT            90

10 rows selected.

SQL>
```

FIGURE 2-4

Selecting unique JOB_IDs from the JOB_HISTORY table

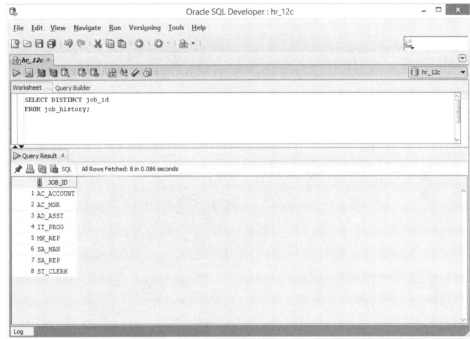

Compare this output to Figure 2-3, where ten rows are returned. Can you see that there are two occurrences of the AC_ACCOUNT and ST_CLERK JOB_ID values? These are the two duplicate rows that have been eliminated by looking for distinct JOB_ID values. Selecting the distinct DEPARTMENT_ID column from the JOB_HISTORY table returns only six rows, as Figure 2-5 demonstrates. DEPARTMENT_ID values 50, 80, 90, and 110 each occur twice in the JOB_HISTORY table, and thus four rows have been eliminated by searching for distinct DEPARTMENT_ID values.

An important feature of the DISTINCT keyword is the elimination of duplicate values from *combinations* of columns. There are ten rows in the JOB_HISTORY table. Eight rows contain distinct JOB_ID values. Six rows contain distinct DEPARTMENT_ID values. Can you guess how many rows contain distinct combinations of JOB_ID and DEPARTMENT_ID values? As Figure 2-6 reveals, there are nine rows returned in the results set that contain distinct JOB_ID and DEPARTMENT_ID combinations, with one row from Figure 2-3 having been eliminated. This is, of course, the row that contains a JOB_ID value of ST_CLERK and a DEPARTMENT_ID value of 50.

FIGURE 2-5

Selecting unique
DEPARTMENT_
IDs from the
JOB_HISTORY
table

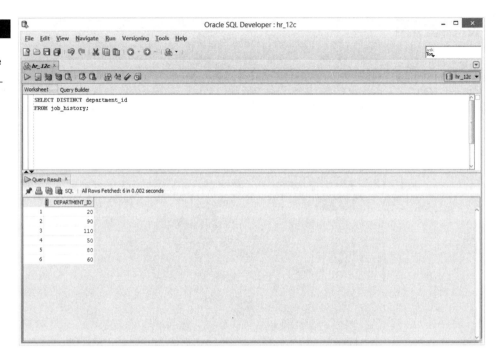

FIGURE 2-6

Unique JOB_ID,
DEPARTMENT_
ID combinations
from JOB_
HISTORY

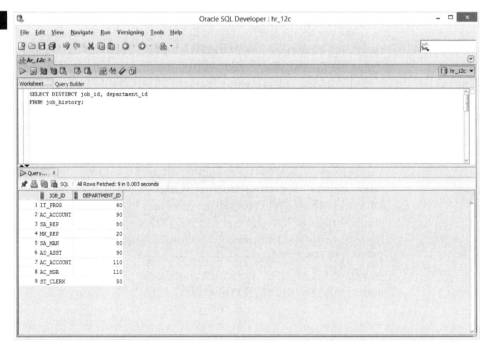

The ability to project specific columns from a table is very useful. Coupled with the ability to remove duplicate values or combinations of values this empowers you to assist with basic user reporting requirements. In many application databases, tables can sometimes store duplicate data. End user reporting frequently requires this data to be presented as a manageable set of unique records. This is something you now have the ability to do. Be careful, though, when using blind queries to select data from large tables. Executing a `SELECT * FROM huge_table;` *statement may cause performance issues if the table contains millions of rows of data.*

Syntax Rules

SQL is a fairly strict language in terms of syntax rules, but it remains simple and flexible enough to support a variety of programming styles. This section discusses some of the basic rules governing SQL statements.

Uppercase or Lowercase

It is a matter of personal taste about the case in which SQL statements are submitted to the database. The examples used thus far have been written in mixed case, uppercase for reserved words and lowercase for the remainder of the statement for illustrative purposes. Many developers, including the author of this book, prefer to write their SQL statements in lowercase. There is also a common misconception that SQL reserved words need to be specified in uppercase. Again, this is up to you. Adhering to a consistent and standardized format is advised.

The following three statements are syntactically equivalent:

```
SELECT * FROM LOCATIONS;
SELECT * FROM locations;
select * from locations;
```

There is one caveat regarding case sensitivity. When interacting with literal values, case does matter. Consider the JOB_ID column from the JOB_HISTORY table. This column contains rows of data which happen to be stored in the database in uppercase, for example, SA_REP and ST_CLERK. When requesting that the results set be restricted by a literal column, the case is critical. The Oracle server treats the request for all the rows in the JOB_HISTORY table that contain a value of St_Clerk in the JOB_ID column differently from the request for all rows which have a value of ST_CLERK in the JOB_ID column.

exam

ⓦatch   *SQL statements may be submitted to the database in lowercase, uppercase, or mixed case. You must pay careful attention to case when interacting with character literal data and aliases. Asking for a column called JOB_ID or*   *job_id returns the same column, but asking for rows where the JOB_ID value is PRESIDENT is different from asking for rows where the JOB_ID value is President. Character literal data should always be treated in a case-sensitive manner.*

Metadata about different database objects is stored by default in uppercase in the data dictionary. If you query a database dictionary table to return a list of tables owned by the HR schema, it is likely that the table names returned are stored in uppercase. This does not mean that a table cannot be created with a lowercase name; it can be. It is just more common and is the default behavior of the Oracle server to create and store tables, columns, and other database object metadata in uppercase in the database dictionary.

Statement Terminators

Semicolons are generally used as SQL statement terminators. SQL*Plus always requires a statement terminator, and usually a semicolon is used. A single SQL statement or even groups of associated statements are often saved as script files for future use. Individual statements in SQL scripts are commonly terminated by a line break (or carriage return) and a forward slash on the next line, instead of a semicolon. You can create a SELECT statement, terminate it with a line break, include a forward slash to execute the statement, and save it in a script file. The script file can then be called from within SQL*Plus. Note that SQL Developer does not require a statement terminator if only a single statement is present, but it will not object if one is used. It is good practice to always terminate your SQL statements with a semicolon. Several examples of SQL*Plus statements follow:

```
SELECT country_name, country_id, region_id FROM countries;
SELECT city, location_id,
       state_province, country_id
FROM locations
/
```

The first example of code demonstrates two important rules. First, the statement is terminated by a semicolon. Second, the entire statement is written on one line. It is entirely acceptable for a SQL statement to either be written on one line or to span multiple lines as long as no words in the statement span multiple lines. The second sample of code demonstrates a statement that spans three lines that is terminated by a new line and executed with a forward slash.

Indentation, Readability, and Good Practice

Consider the following query:

```
SELECT city, location_id,
       state_province, country_id
FROM locations
/
```

This example highlights the benefits of indenting your SQL statement to enhance the readability of your code. The Oracle server does not object if the entire statement is written on one line without indentation. It is good practice to separate different clauses of the SELECT statement onto different lines. When an expression in a clause is particularly complex, it is often better to separate that term of the statement onto a new line. When developing SQL to meet your reporting needs, the process is often iterative. The SQL interpreter is far more useful during the development process if complex expressions are isolated on separate lines, since errors are usually thrown in the format of: "ERROR at line X:". This makes the debugging process much simpler.

exam

watch *A common technique employed by some exam question designers measures attention to detail. A single missing punctuation mark like a semicolon may make the difference between a correct answer and an incorrect one. Incorrect spelling of object names further tests attention to detail. You may be asked to choose the correct statement that queries the REGIONS table. One of the options may appear correct but references the REGION table. This misspelling can lead to an incorrect statement being chosen.*

SCENARIO & SOLUTION

You want to construct and execute queries against tables stored in an Oracle database. Are you confined to using SQL*Plus or SQL Developer?	No. Oracle provides SQL*Plus and SQL Developer as free tools to create and execute queries. There are numerous tools available from Oracle (for example, Discoverer, APEX, and JDeveloper) and other third-party vendors that provide an interface to the tables stored in an Oracle database.
To explore your database environment further, you would like a list of tables, owned by your current schema, available for you to query. How do you interrogate the database dictionary to provide this metadata?	The data dictionary is a set of tables and views of other tables that can be queried via SQL. The statement SELECT table_name FROM user_tables; queries the database dictionary for a list of table names that belong to the current user.
When querying the JOBS table for every row containing just the JOB_ID and MAX_SALARY columns, is a projection, selection, or join being performed?	A projection is performed since the columns in the JOBS table have been restricted to the JOB_ID and MAX_SALARY columns.

EXERCISE 2-2

Answering Our First Questions with SQL

In this step-by-step exercise, a connection is made using SQL*Plus as the HR user to answer two questions using the SELECT statement.

Question 1: How many unique departments have employees currently working in them?

1. Start SQL*Plus and connect to the HR schema.

2. You may initially be tempted to find the answer in the DEPARTMENTS table. A careful examination reveals that the question asks for information about employees. This information is contained in the EMPLOYEES table.

3. The word "unique" should guide you to use the DISTINCT keyword.

4. Combining steps 2 and 3, you can construct the following SQL statement:

```
SELECT distinct department_id
FROM employees;
```

5. As shown in the following illustration, this query returns 12 rows. Notice that the third row is empty. This is a null value in the DEPARTMENT_ID column.

6. The answer to the first question is therefore: Eleven unique departments have employees working in them, but at least one employee has not been assigned to a department.

Question 2: How many countries are there in the Europe region?

1. This question comprises two parts. Consider the REGIONS table, which contains four regions each uniquely identified by a REGION_ID value, and the COUNTRIES table, which has a REGION_ID column indicating which region a country belongs to.

2. The first query needs to identify the REGION_ID of the Europe region. This is accomplished by the SQL statement:

```
SELECT * FROM regions;
```

3. The following illustration shows that the Europe region has a REGION_ID value of 1:

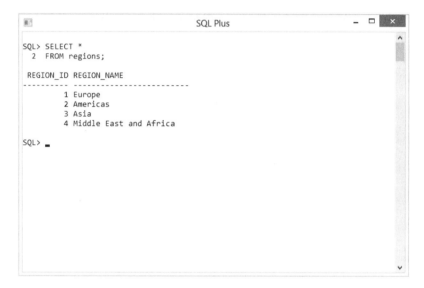

4. To identify which countries have 1 as their REGION_ID, you need to execute the following SQL query:

```
SELECT region_id, country_name FROM countries;
```

5. Manually counting the country rows with a REGION_ID of 1 in the following illustration helps answer the second question:

```
SQL> SELECT region_id, country_name
  2  FROM countries;

 REGION_ID COUNTRY_NAME
---------- ------------------------------------
         2 Argentina
         3 Australia
         1 Belgium
         2 Brazil
         2 Canada
         1 Switzerland
         3 China
         1 Germany
         1 Denmark
         4 Egypt
         1 France
         4 Israel
         3 India
         1 Italy
         3 Japan
         4 Kuwait
         3 Malaysia
         2 Mexico
         4 Nigeria
         1 Netherlands
         3 Singapore
         1 United Kingdom
         2 United States of America
         4 Zambia
         4 Zimbabwe

25 rows selected.

SQL>
```

6. The answer to the second question is therefore: There are eight countries in the Europe region as far as the HR data model is concerned.

SQL Expressions and Operators

The general form of the SELECT statement introduced the notion that columns and expressions are selectable. An expression is usually made up of an operation being performed on one or more column values. The operators that can act upon column values to form an expression depend on the data type of the column. They are the four cardinal arithmetic operators (addition, subtraction, multiplication, and division) for numeric columns; the concatenation operator for character or

	Precedence Level	Operator Symbol	Operation
TABLE 2-1	Highest	( )	Brackets or parentheses
	Medium	/	Division
Precedence	Medium	*	Multiplication
of Arithmetic	Lowest	−	Subtraction
Operators	Lowest	+	Addition

string columns; and the addition and subtraction operators for date and timestamp columns. As in regular arithmetic, there is a predefined order of evaluation (operator precedence) when more than one operator occurs in an expression. Round brackets have the highest precedence. Division and multiplication operations are next in the hierarchy and are evaluated before addition and subtraction, which have lowest precedence. These precedence levels are shown in Table 2-1.

Operators with the same level of precedence are evaluated from left to right. Round brackets may therefore be used to enforce nondefault operator precedence. Using brackets generously when constructing complex expressions is good practice and is encouraged. It leads to readable code that is less prone to error. Expressions expose a large number of useful data manipulation possibilities.

Arithmetic Operators

Consider the example of the JOB_HISTORY table, which stores the start date and end date of an employee's term in a previous job role. It may be useful for tax or pension purposes, for example, to calculate how long an employee worked in that role. This information can be obtained using an arithmetic expression. There are a few interesting elements of both the SQL statement and the results returned from Figure 2-7 that warrant further discussion.

Seven terms have been specified in the SELECT clause. The first four are regular columns of the JOB_HISTORY table, namely: EMPLOYEE_ID, JOB_ID, START_DATE, and END_DATE. The latter two terms provide the source information required to calculate the number of days and hours that an employee filled a particular position. Consider employee number 176 on the ninth row of output. This employee started as a Sales Manager on January 1, 2007, and ended employment on December 31, 2007. Therefore, this employee worked for exactly one year, which, in 2007, consisted of 365 days or 2,920 hours.

FIGURE 2-7

Arithmetic expression to calculate number of hours worked

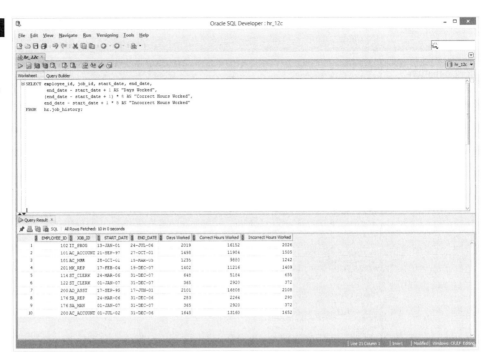

The number of days for which an employee was employed can be calculated by using the fifth term in the SELECT clause, which is an expression. This expression demonstrates that arithmetic performed on columns containing date information returns numeric values that represent a certain number of days. The sixth term closely resembles the fifth but calculates the number of hours worked by additionally multiplying by 8 (assuming an 8-hour workday).

To enforce operator precedence of the subtraction and addition operations in the sixth term, the subexpression *end_date-start_date+1* is enclosed in round brackets and then multiplied by 8 to obtain the correct number of hours worked. The seventh term is evaluated by first multiplying 1 by 8, which is added to *end_date-start_date*, which returns the incorrect results.

A hypothetical formula for predicting the probability of a meteor shower in a particular geographic region has been devised. The two expressions listed in Figure 2-8 are identical except for the Meteor Shower Probability % expression. However, as the results in the following table demonstrate, a different calculation is being made by each expression. Notice that the two expressions differ very slightly. Expression 2 has a pair of parentheses at the very end, enclosing (10 - 5). Consider

FIGURE 2-8

Use of the concatenation and arithmetic operators

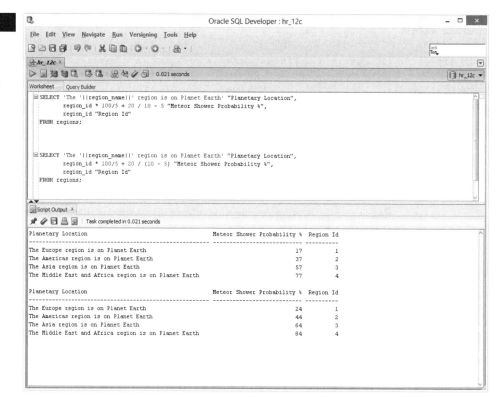

```
SELECT 'The '||region_name||' region is on Planet Earth' "Planetary Location",
       region_id * 100/5 + 20 / 10 - 5 "Meteor Shower Probability %",
       region_id "Region Id"
FROM regions;


SELECT 'The '||region_name||' region is on Planet Earth' "Planetary Location",
       region_id * 100/5 + 20 / (10 - 5) "Meteor Shower Probability %",
       region_id "Region Id"
FROM regions;
```

```
Planetary Location                               Meteor Shower Probability %  Region Id
-----------------------------------------------  ---------------------------  ---------
The Europe region is on Planet Earth                                      17          1
The Americas region is on Planet Earth                                    37          2
The Asia region is on Planet Earth                                        57          3
The Middle East and Africa region is on Planet Earth                     77          4

Planetary Location                               Meteor Shower Probability %  Region Id
-----------------------------------------------  ---------------------------  ---------
The Europe region is on Planet Earth                                      24          1
The Americas region is on Planet Earth                                    44          2
The Asia region is on Planet Earth                                        64          3
The Middle East and Africa region is on Planet Earth                     84          4
```

how the expressions are evaluated for the Asia region where REGION_ID is 3 as shown in the following table:

Step	Expression 1	Expression 2
1.	region_id * 100/5 + 20 / 10 − 5	region_id * 100/5 + 20 / (10 − 5)
2.	Substitute region_id with value: 3 * 100 /5 + 20 / 10 − 5	Substitute region_id with value: 3 * 100 / 5 + 20 / (10 − 5)
3.	The operators with the highest precedence are the two division and one multiplication operators. These must be evaluated first. If more than one operator with the same level of precedence is present in an expression, then these will be evaluated from left to right. Therefore, the first subexpression to be evaluated is: 3*100: **300** / 5 + 20 / 10 − 5	The operator with the highest precedence is the pair of parentheses and these must be evaluated first. Therefore, the first subexpression to be evaluated is: (10 − 5): 3*100/5 + 20/5

Step	Expression 1	Expression 2
4.	The next subexpression to be evaluated is: 300/5:	The next operators in the expression with the highest precedence are the two division and one multiplication operators. If more than one operator with the same level of precedence is present in an expression, then these will be evaluated from left to right. Therefore, the next subexpression to be evaluated is: 3*100:
	60 + 20/10 - 5	**300**/5 + 20/5
5.	The next subexpression to be evaluated is: 20/10:	The next subexpression to be evaluated is: 300/5:
	60 + 2 – 5	*60 + 20/5*
6.	The remaining operators are one addition and one subtraction operator which share the same level of precedence. These will therefore be evaluated from left to right. The next subexpression to be evaluated is: 60+2:	The next subexpression to be evaluated is: 20/5:
	62 – 5=57	*60 + 4 = 64*

on the **job**

Expressions offer endless possibilities and are one of the fundamental constructs in SELECT statements. As you practice SQL on your test database environment, you may encounter two infamous Oracle errors: "ORA-00923: FROM keyword not found where expected" and "ORA-00942: table or view does not exist". These are generally indicative of spelling or punctuation errors, such as missing enclosing quotes around character literals. Do not be perturbed by these messages. Remember, you cannot cause damage to the database if all you are doing is selecting data. It is a read-only operation, and the worst you can do is execute a nonperformant query.

Expression and Column Aliasing

Figure 2-7 introduced a new concept called column aliasing. Notice how the expression column has a meaningful heading named Days Worked. This heading is an alias. An *alias* is an alternate name for a column or an expression. If this expression did not make use of an alias, the column heading would be (END_DATE-START_DATE)+1, which is unattractive and not very descriptive. Aliases are especially useful with expressions or calculations and may be implemented in several ways. There are a few rules governing the use of column aliases in SELECT statements. In Figure 2-7, the alias given for the calculated expression called "Days Worked" was specified by leaving a space and entering the alias in double quotation marks. These quotation marks are necessary for two reasons. First, this alias is made up of more than one word. Second, case preservation of an alias is only possible if the alias is double quoted. As Figure 2-9 shows, an "ORA-00923: FROM keyword not found where expected" error is returned when a multi-worded alias is not double quoted.

The ORA-00923 error is not randomly generated by the server. The Oracle interpreter tries to process the statement and finds a problem with it. As it processes this particular statement, it finds a problem with line 2, column 43 at the point of the problem: the word Worked. Line 2 was processed and the expression was aliased with the word Days. The space after Days indicates to the Oracle interpreter that, since there is no additional comma to indicate another term belonging to the SELECT clause, it is complete. Therefore, it expects to find the FROM clause next. Instead it finds the word Worked and yields this error. Error messages from the Oracle server are informative, and you should read them carefully to resolve problems. This error is avoided by enclosing an alias that contains a space or other special characters, such as # and $, in double quotation marks, as shown around the alias "Days Worked" in Figure 2-7.

The second example in Figure 2-9 illustrates another interesting characteristic of column aliasing. Double quotation marks have once again been dispensed with, and an underscore character is substituted for the space between the words to avoid an error being returned. The Oracle interpreter processes the statement, finds no problem, and executes it. Notice that, although the alias was specified as Days_Worked, with only the title letters of the alias being capitalized, the expression heading was returned as DAYS_WORKED: all letters were automatically converted to uppercase. Thus, to preserve the case of the alias, it must be enclosed in double quotation marks.

The aliases encountered so far have been specified by leaving a space after a column or expression and inserting the alias. SQL offers a more formal way of inserting aliases. The AS keyword is inserted between the column or expression and the alias. Figure 2-10 illustrates the mixed use of the different types of column aliasing. Both the EMPLOYEE_ID and JOB_ID columns are aliased using the AS keyword, while the "Days Worked" expression is aliased using a space. The AS keyword is optional since it is also possible to use a space before specifying an alias, as discussed earlier. Use of the AS keyword does, however, improve the readability of SQL statements, and the author believes it is a good SQL coding habit to form.

FIGURE 2-10

Use of the AS keyword to specify column aliases

```
SQL Plus                                                        -  □  ×

SQL> SELECT employee_id AS "Employee Id",
  2         job_id AS "Occupation",
  3         start_date, end_date,
  4         (end_date-start_date)+1 "Days Worked"
  5  FROM job_history;

Employee Id Occupation START_DAT END_DATE  Days Worked
----------- ---------- --------- --------- -----------
        102 IT_PROG    13-JAN-01 24-JUL-06        2019
        101 AC_ACCOUNT 21-SEP-97 27-OCT-01        1498
        101 AC_MGR     28-OCT-01 15-MAR-05        1235
        201 MK_REP     17-FEB-04 19-DEC-07        1402
        114 ST_CLERK   24-MAR-06 31-DEC-07         648
        122 ST_CLERK   01-JAN-07 31-DEC-07         365
        200 AD_ASST    17-SEP-95 17-JUN-01        2101
        176 SA_REP     24-MAR-06 31-DEC-06         283
        176 SA_MAN     01-JAN-07 31-DEC-07         365
        200 AC_ACCOUNT 01-JUL-02 31-DEC-06        1645

10 rows selected.

SQL> ▪
```

Character and String Concatenation Operator

The double pipe symbols | | represent the character *concatenation* operator. This operator is used to join character expressions or columns together to create a larger character expression. Columns of a table may be linked to each other or to strings of literal characters to create one resultant character expression.

Figure 2-8 shows that the concatenation operator is flexible enough to be used multiple times and almost anywhere in a character expression. Here, the character literal "The" is concatenated to the data contents of the REGION_NAME column. This new string of characters is further concatenated to the character literal "region is on Planet Earth", and the whole expression is aliased with the friendly column heading "Planetary Location". Notice how each row in the results set is constructed by the systematic application of the expression to every row value from the table.

Consider the first data row from the "Planetary Location" expression column. It returns "The Europe region is on Planet Earth". A legible sentence for the rows of data has been created by concatenating literal strings of characters and spaces to either side of each row's REGION_NAME column value. The REGION_ID column has been aliased to show that regular columns as well as expressions may be aliased. Further, column headings are by default displayed in uppercase but can be overridden using an alias like "Region Id". The data types of the columns being queried determine how SQL*Plus and SQL Developer present their default data outputs. If the data type is numeric, then the column data is formatted to be right aligned. If the data type is character or date, then the column data is formatted to be left aligned.

Literals and the DUAL Table

Literal values in expressions are a common occurrence. These values refer to numeric, character, or date and time values found in SELECT clauses that do not originate from any database object. Concatenating character literals to existing column data can be useful, as introduced in Figure 2-8. What about processing literals that have nothing to do with existing column data? To ensure relational consistency, Oracle offers a clever solution to the problem of using the database to evaluate expressions that have nothing to do with any tables or columns. To get the database to evaluate an expression, a syntactically legal SELECT statement must be submitted. What if you wanted to know the sum of two numbers or two numeric literals? These questions can only be answered by interacting with the database in a relational manner. Oracle solves the problem of relational interaction with the database operating on literal expressions by offering a special table called DUAL. Recall the DUAL table described in Figure 2-1. It contains one column called DUMMY of character data type. You can execute the query SELECT * FROM dual, and the data value "X" is returned as the contents of the DUMMY column. The DUAL table allows literal expressions to be selected from it for processing and returns the expression results in its single row. It is exceptionally useful since it enables a variety of different processing requests to be made from the database. You may want to know how many seconds there are in a year. Figure 2-11 demonstrates an arithmetic expression executed against the DUAL table. Testing complex expressions during development, by querying the DUAL table, is an effective method to evaluate whether these expressions are working correctly. Literal expressions can be queried from any table, but remember that the expression will be processed for every row in the table.

```
SELECT 'literal '||'processing using the REGIONS table'
FROM regions;
```

FIGURE 2-11

Using the DUAL table

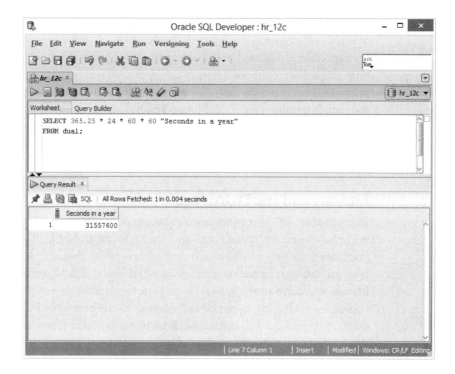

The preceding statement will return four lines in the results set, since there are four rows of data in the REGIONS table.

Two Single Quotes or the Alternative Quote Operator

The literal character strings concatenated so far have been singular words prepended and appended to column expressions. These character literals are specified using single quotation marks. For example:

```
SELECT 'I am a character literal string' FROM dual;
```

What about character literals that contain single quotation marks? For example, plural possessives pose a particular problem for character literal processing (the possessive case of most English plural nouns are formed by adding an apostrophe to the end if it ends with an "s"; an apostrophe and an "s" are added to singular nouns). Consider the following statement:

```
SELECT 'Plural's have one quote too many' FROM dual;
```

FIGURE 2-12

Error while
dealing with
literals with
implicit quotes

```
SQL> SELECT 'Plural's have one quote too many'
  2   FROM dual;
ERROR:
ORA-01756: quoted string not properly terminated


SQL>
```

As the example in Figure 2-12 shows, executing this statement causes an ORA-01756 Oracle error to be generated. It might seem like an odd error, but upon closer examination, the Oracle interpreter successfully processes the SELECT statement until position 16, at which point it expects a FROM clause. Position 1 to position 16 is:

```
select 'Plural's
```

The Oracle server processes this segment to mean that the character literal `'Plural'` is aliased as column "s". At this point, the interpreter expects a FROM clause, but instead finds the word "have". It then generates an error.

So, how are words that contain single quotation marks dealt with? There are essentially two mechanisms available. The most popular of these is to add an additional single quotation mark next to each naturally occurring single quotation mark in the character string. Figure 2-13 demonstrates how the previous error is avoided by replacing the character literal `'Plural's` with the literal `'Plural''s`.

The second example in Figure 2-13 shows that using two single quotes to handle each naturally occurring single quote in a character literal can become messy and error prone as the number of affected literals increases. Oracle offers a neat way to deal with this type of character literal in the form of the alternative quote (q) operator. Notice that the problem is that Oracle chose the single quote characters as the special pair of symbols that enclose or wrap any other character literal. These character-enclosing symbols could have been anything other than single quotation marks.

Bearing this in mind, consider the alternative quote (q) operator. The q operator enables you to choose from a set of possible pairs of wrapping symbols for character literals as alternatives to the single quote symbols. The options are any single-byte or multibyte character or the four brackets: (round brackets), {curly braces}, [square

FIGURE 2-13

Use of two
single quotes
with literals with
implicit quotes

brackets], or <angle brackets>. Using the q operator, the character delimiter can effectively be changed from a single quotation mark to any other character, as shown in Figure 2-14.

The syntax of the alternative quote operator is as follows:

q'*delimiter*character literal which may include the single quotes *delimiter*'

where *delimiter* can be any character or bracket. The first and second examples in Figure 2-14 show the use of angle and square brackets as character delimiters, while the third example demonstrates how an uppercase "X" has been used as the special character delimiter symbol through the alternative quote operator.

FIGURE 2-14

The alternate quote (q) operator

The NULL Concept

The concept of a null value was introduced in the earlier discussion of the DESCRIBE command. Both the number zero and a blank space are different from null since they occupy space. *Null* refers to an absence of data. A row that contains a null value lacks data for that column. Null is formally defined as a value that is unavailable, unassigned, unknown, or inapplicable. In other words, the rules of engaging with null values need careful examination. Failure to heed the special treatment that null values require will almost certainly lead to an error, or worse, an inaccurate answer.

Null values may be a tricky concept to come to grips with. The problem stems from the absence of null on a number line. It is not a real, tangible value that can be related to the physical world. Null is a placeholder in a nonmandatory column until some real data is stored in its place. Until then, beware of conducting arithmetic with null columns.

This section focuses on interacting with null column data with the SELECT statement and its impact on expressions.

Not Null and Nullable Columns

Tables store rows of data that are divided into one or more columns. These columns have names and data types associated with them. Some of them are constrained by database rules to be mandatory columns. It is compulsory for some data to be stored in the NOT NULL columns in each row. When columns of a table, however, are not compelled by the database constraints to hold data for a row, these columns run the risk of being empty.

In Figure 2-15, the EMPLOYEES table is described, and a few columns are selected from it. There are five NOT NULL columns and six NULLABLE columns. *Nullable* is a term sometimes used to describe a column that is allowed to contain null values. One of the nullable columns is the COMMISSION_PCT column. Figure 2-15 shows the first five rows of data from the EMPLOYEES table. This is sufficient to illustrate that all these employee records have null values in their COMMISSION_PCT columns.

SQL Developer makes it simple to observe null values in columns, as displayed in Figure 2-16. Here, the word (null) is displayed in the Query Result tab when a null value is encountered, as with the COMMISSION_PCT column. SQL Developer supports customizing this default description of null column data.

FIGURE 2-16

Null arithmetic always returns a null value.

The column aliased as "Null Arithmetic" is an expression made up of COMMISSION_PCT + SALARY + 10. Instead of returning a numeric value, this column returns null. There is an important reason for this:

Any arithmetic calculation with a NULL value always returns NULL.

Oracle offers a mechanism for interacting arithmetically with NULL values using the general functions discussed in Chapter 5. As the column expression aliased as "Division by Null" illustrates, even division by a null value results in null, unlike division by zero, which results in an error. Finally, notice the impact of the null keyword when used with the character concatenation operator. Null is concatenated between the FIRST_NAME and LAST_NAME columns, yet it has no impact. The character concatenation operators ignore null, while the arithmetic operations involving null values always result in null.

Foreign Keys and Nullable Columns

Data model design sometimes leads to problematic situations when tables are related to each other via a primary and foreign key relationship, but the column that the foreign key is based on is nullable.

The DEPARTMENTS table has as its primary key the DEPARTMENT_ID column. The EMPLOYEES table has a DEPARTMENT_ID column that is constrained by its foreign key relationship to the DEPARTMENT_ID column in the DEPARTMENTS table. This means that no record in the EMPLOYEES table is allowed to have in its DEPARTMENT_ID column a value that is not in the DEPARTMENTS table. This referential integrity forms the basis for third normal form and is critical to overall data integrity.

But what about NULL values? Can the DEPARTMENT_ID column in the DEPARTMENTS table contain nulls? The answer is *no*. Oracle insists that any column that is a primary key is implicitly constrained to be mandatory. But what about implicit constraints on foreign key columns? This is a quandary for Oracle, since in order to remain flexible and cater to the widest audience, it cannot insist that columns related through referential integrity constraints must be mandatory. Further, not all situations demand this functionality.

SCENARIO & SOLUTION

You are constructing an arithmetic expression that calculates taxable income based on an employee's SALARY and COMMISSION_PCT columns, both of which are nullable. Is it possible to convert the null values in either column to zero to always return a numeric taxable income?	Yes, but not with the information you have covered so far. Null values require special handling. In Chapter 5, we discuss the NVL function, which provides a mechanism to convert null values into more arithmetic-friendly data values.
An alias provides a mechanism to rename a column or an expression. Under what conditions should you enclose an alias in double quotes?	If an alias contains more than one word or if the case of an alias must be preserved, then it should be enclosed in double quotation marks. Failure to double quote a multi-worded alias will raise an Oracle error. Failure to double quote a single-word alias will result in the alias being returned in uppercase.
When working with character literal values that include single quotation marks, how should you specify these literals in the SELECT clause without raising an error?	There are two mechanisms available. The more common approach is to replace each naturally occurring single quote with two single quotes. The other approach is to make use of the alternate quote operator to specify an alternate pair of characters with which to enclose character literals.

The DEPARTMENT_ID column in the EMPLOYEES table is actually nullable. Therefore, the risk exists that there are records with null DEPARTMENT_ID values present in this table. In fact, there are such records in the EMPLOYEES table. The HR data model allows employees, correctly or not, to belong to no department. When performing relational joins between tables, it is entirely possible to miss or exclude certain records that contain nulls in the join column. Chapter 7 explores ways to deal with this challenge by making use of outer joins.

EXERCISE 2-3

Experimenting with Expressions and the DUAL Table

In this step-by-step exercise, a connection is made using SQL Developer as the HR user. Use expressions and operators to answer three questions related to the SELECT statement:

Question 1: It was demonstrated earlier how the number of days in which staff worked in a job could be calculated. For how many years did staff work while fulfilling these job roles and what were their EMPLOYEE_ID, JOB_ID, START_DATE, and END_DATE values? Alias the expression column in your query with the alias Years Worked. Assume that a year consists of 365.25 days.

1. Start SQL Developer and connect to the HR schema.
2. The projection of columns required includes EMPLOYEE_ID, JOB_ID, START_DATE, END_DATE, and an expression called Years Worked from the JOB_HISTORY table.
3. The expression can be calculated by dividing 1 plus the difference between END_DATE and START_DATE by 365.25 days, as shown next:

```
SELECT employee_id, job_id, start_date, end_date,
((end_date-start_date) + 1)/365.25 "Years Worked"
FROM job_history;
```

4. Executing the preceding SELECT statement yields the results displayed in the following illustration:

Question 2: Query the JOBS table and return a single expression of the form: The Job Id for the <job_title's> job is: <job_id>.

Take note that the job_title should have an apostrophe and an "s" appended to it to read more naturally. A sample of this output for the organization president is: "The Job Id for the President's job is: AD_PRES." Alias this column expression as "Job Description" using the AS keyword.

1. There are multiple solutions to this problem. The approach chosen here is to handle the naturally occurring single quotation marks with an additional single quote.

2. A single expression aliased as Job Description is required and may be constructed by dissecting the requirement into the literal `"The Job Id for the"` being concatenated to the JOB_TITLE column. This string is then concatenated to the literal `"'s job is: "` which is further concatenated to the JOB_ID column. An additional single quotation mark is added to yield the SELECT statement that follows:

```
SELECT 'The Job Id for the '||job_title||'''s job is: '||job_id
AS "Job Description"
FROM jobs;
```

3. The results of this SQL query are shown in the following illustration:

```
SQL> SELECT 'The Job Id for the '||job_title||'''s job is: '||job_id
  2  AS "Job Description"
  3  FROM jobs;

Job Description
-----------------------------------------------------------------------
The Job Id for the President's job is: AD_PRES
The Job Id for the Administration Vice President's job is: AD_VP
The Job Id for the Administration Assistant's job is: AD_ASST
The Job Id for the Finance Manager's job is: FI_MGR
The Job Id for the Accountant's job is: FI_ACCOUNT
The Job Id for the Accounting Manager's job is: AC_MGR
The Job Id for the Public Accountant's job is: AC_ACCOUNT
The Job Id for the Sales Manager's job is: SA_MAN
The Job Id for the Sales Representative's job is: SA_REP
The Job Id for the Purchasing Manager's job is: PU_MAN
The Job Id for the Purchasing Clerk's job is: PU_CLERK
The Job Id for the Stock Manager's job is: ST_MAN
The Job Id for the Stock Clerk's job is: ST_CLERK
The Job Id for the Shipping Clerk's job is: SH_CLERK
The Job Id for the Programmer's job is: IT_PROG
The Job Id for the Marketing Manager's job is: MK_MAN
The Job Id for the Marketing Representative's job is: MK_REP
The Job Id for the Human Resources Representative's job is: HR_REP
The Job Id for the Public Relations Representative's job is: PR_REP

19 rows selected.

SQL>
```

Question 3: Using the DUAL table, calculate the area of a circle with radius 6,000 units, with pi being approximately 22/7. Use the formula: Area = pi × radius × radius. Alias the result as "Area".

1. Working with the DUAL table may initially seem curious. You get used to it as its functionality becomes more apparent. This question involves selecting

a literal arithmetic expression from the DUAL table to yield a single row calculated answer that is not based on the column values in any table.

2. The expression may be calculated using the following SQL statement; note the use of brackets for precedence.

```
SELECT (22/7) * (6000 * 6000) Area
FROM dual;
```

3. The results returned show the approximate area of the circle as 113,142,857 square units.

CERTIFICATION SUMMARY

The SELECT statement construct forms the basis for the majority of interactions that occur with an Oracle database. These interactions may take the form of queries issued from SQL Developer, SQL*Plus, or any number of Oracle or other third-party client tools. At their core, these tools translate requests for information into SELECT statements, which are then executed by the database.

The structure of a table has been described. Rows of data have been retrieved and the set-oriented format of the results was revealed. The results were refined by projection. In other words, your queries can include only the columns you are interested in retrieving and exclude the remaining columns in a table.

SELECT syntax rules are basic and flexible, and language errors should be rare due to its English-like grammar. Statement termination using semicolons, regard for character literal case-sensitivity, and awareness of null values should assist with avoiding errors.

Expressions expose a vista of data manipulation possibilities through the interaction of arithmetic and character operators with column or literal data, or a combination of the two.

The general form of the SELECT statement was explored, and the foundation for the expansion of this statement was constructed.

The Self Test exercises are made up of two components. The first component is comprised of questions that give you an idea about what you may be asked during the exam. The second component enables you to practice the language skills discussed in this chapter in a lab format. The solutions to both categories of questions are discussed in detail in the solutions section.

TWO-MINUTE DRILL

List the Capabilities of SQL SELECT Statements

❑ The three fundamental operations that SELECT statements are capable of are projection, selection, and joining.

❑ Projection refers to the restriction of columns selected from a table. Using projection, you retrieve only the columns of interest and not every possible column.

❑ Selection refers to the extraction of rows from a table. Selection includes the further restriction of the extracted rows based on various criteria or conditions. This allows you to retrieve only the rows that are of interest and not every row in the table.

❑ Joining involves linking two or more tables based on common attributes. Joining allows data to be stored in third normal form in discrete tables, instead of in one large table.

❑ An unlimited combination of projections, selections, and joins provides the language to extract the relational data required.

❑ A structural definition of a table can be obtained using the DESCRIBE command.

❑ Columns in tables store different types of data using various data types, the most common of which are NUMBER, VARCHAR2, DATE, and TIMESTAMP.

❑ The data type NUMBER(x,y) implies that numeric information stored in this column can have at most x digits, but the whole number portion can have at most (x-y) digits.

❑ The DESCRIBE command lists the names, data types, and nullable status of all columns in a table.

❑ Mandatory columns are also referred to as NOT NULL columns.

Execute a Basic SELECT Statement

❑ The syntax of the primitive SELECT clause is as follows:
SELECT * | {[DISTINCT] column | expression [alias],…}

❑ The SELECT statement is also referred to as a SELECT query and comprises at least two clauses, namely the SELECT clause and the FROM clause.

❑ The SELECT clause determines the *projection* of columns. In other words, the SELECT clause specifies which columns are included in the results returned.

❑ The asterisk (*) operator is used as a wildcard symbol to indicate all columns. So, the statement SELECT * FROM accounts returns all the columns available in the ACCOUNTS table.

❑ The FROM clause specifies the source table or tables from which items are selected.

❑ The DISTINCT keyword preceding items in the SELECT clause causes duplicate combinations of these items to be excluded from the returned results set.

❑ SQL statements should be terminated with a semicolon. As an alternative, a new line can be added after a statement and a forward slash can be used to execute the statement.

❑ SQL statements can be written and executed in lowercase, uppercase, or mixed case. Be careful when interacting with character literals since these are case-sensitive.

❑ Arithmetic operators and the string concatenation operator acting on column and literal data form the basis of SQL expressions.

❑ Expressions and regular columns may be aliased using the AS keyword or by leaving a space between the column or expression and the alias.

❑ If an alias contains multiple words or the case of the alias is important, it must be enclosed in double quotation marks.

❑ Naturally occurring single quotes in a character literal can be selected by making use of either an additional single quote per naturally occurring quote or the alternative quote operator.

❑ The DUAL table is a single column and single row table that is often used to evaluate expressions that do not refer to specific columns or tables.

❑ Columns which are not governed by a NOT NULL constraint have the potential to store null values and are sometimes referred to as nullable columns.

❑ NULL values are not the same as a blank space or zero. NULL values refer to an absence of data. Null is defined as a value that is unavailable, unassigned, unknown, or inapplicable.

❑ Caution must be exercised when working with null values since arithmetic with a null value always yields a null result.

SELF TEST

The following questions will help you measure your understanding of the material presented in this chapter. Read all the choices carefully because there might be more than one correct answer. Choose all the correct answers for each question.

The following test is typical of the questions and format of the OCA 12c examination for the topic "Retrieving Data Using the SQL SELECT Statement." These questions often make use of the Human Resources schema.

List the Capabilities of SQL SELECT Statements

1. Which query creates a projection of the DEPARTMENT_NAME and LOCATION_ID columns from the DEPARTMENTS table? (Choose the best answer.)
   A. SELECT DISTINCT DEPARTMENT_NAME, LOCATION_ID
      FROM DEPARTMENTS;
   B. SELECT DEPARTMENT_NAME, LOCATION_ID
      FROM DEPARTMENTS;
   C. SELECT DEPT_NAME, LOC_ID
      FROM DEPT;
   D. SELECT DEPARTMENT_NAME AS "LOCATION_ID"
      FROM DEPARTMENTS;

2. After describing the EMPLOYEES table, you discover that the SALARY column has a data type of NUMBER(8,2). Which SALARY value(s) will not be permitted in this column? (Choose all that apply.)
   A. SALARY=12345678
   B. SALARY=123456.78
   C. SALARY=12345.678
   D. SALARY=123456
   E. SALARY=12.34

3. After describing the JOB_HISTORY table, you discover that the START_DATE and END_DATE columns have a data type of DATE. Consider the expression END_DATE-START_DATE. (Choose two correct statements.)
   A. A value of DATE data type is returned.
   B. A value of type NUMBER is returned.
   C. A value of type VARCHAR2 is returned.
   D. The expression is invalid since arithmetic cannot be performed on columns with DATE data types.
   E. The expression represents the days between the END_DATE and START_DATE less one day.

4. The DEPARTMENTS table contains a DEPARTMENT_NAME column with data type VARCHAR2(30). (Choose two true statements about this column.)
    A. This column can store character data up to a maximum of 30 characters.
    B. This column must store character data that is at least 30 characters long.
    C. The VARCHAR2 data type is replaced by the CHAR data type.
    D. This column can store data in a column with data type VARCHAR2(50) provided that the contents are at most 30 characters long.

Execute a Basic SELECT Statement

5. Which statement reports on unique JOB_ID values from the EMPLOYEES table? (Choose all that apply.)
    A. SELECT JOB_ID FROM EMPLOYEES;
    B. SELECT UNIQUE JOB_ID FROM EMPLOYEES;
    C. SELECT DISTINCT JOB_ID, EMPLOYEE_ID FROM EMPLOYEES;
    D. SELECT DISTINCT JOB_ID FROM EMPLOYEES;

6. Choose the two illegal statements. The two correct statements produce identical results. The two illegal statements will cause an error to be raised:
    A. SELECT DEPARTMENT_ID||' represents the '||
        DEPARTMENT_NAME||' Department' as "Department Info"
        FROM DEPARTMENTS;
    B. SELECT DEPARTMENT_ID||' represents the ||
        DEPARTMENT_NAME||' Department' as "Department Info"
        FROM DEPARTMENTS;
    C. select department_id||' represents the '||department_name||
        ' Department' "Department Info"
        from departments;
    D. SELECT DEPARTMENT_ID represents the DEPARTMENT_NAME Department as
        "Department Info"
        FROM DEPARTMENTS;

7. Which expressions do not return NULL values? (Choose all that apply.)
    A. select ((10 + 20) * 50) + null from dual;
    B. select 'this is a '||null||'test with nulls' from dual;
    C. select null/0 from dual;
    D. select null||'test'||null as "Test" from dual;

8. Choose the correct syntax to return all columns and rows of data from the EMPLOYEES table.

   A. select all from employees;

   B. select employee_id, first_name, last_name, first_name, department_id
   from employees;

   C. select % from employees;

   D. select * from employees;

   E. select *.* from employees;

9. The following character literal expression is selected from the DUAL table:
SELECT 'Coda''s favorite fetch toy is his orange ring' FROM DUAL;
(Choose the result that is returned.)

   A. An error would be returned due to the presence of two adjacent quotes

   B. Coda's favorite fetch toy is his orange ring

   C. Coda''s favorite fetch toy is his orange ring

   D. Coda''s favorite fetch toy is his orange ring'

10. There are four rows of data in the REGIONS table. Consider the following SQL statement:
SELECT '6 * 6' "Area" FROM REGIONS;
How many rows of results are returned and what value is returned by the Area column?
(Choose the best answer.)

   A. 1 row returned, Area column contains value 36

   B. 4 rows returned, Area column contains value 36 for all 4 rows

   C. 1 row returned, Area column contains value 6 * 6

   D. 4 rows returned, Area column contains value 6 * 6 for all 4 rows

   E. A syntax error is returned.

LAB QUESTION

In this chapter you worked through examples in the Human Resources schema. Oracle provides a number of example schemas for you to experiment with and to learn different concepts from. For the practical exercises, you will be using the Order Entry, or OE, schema. The solutions for these exercises will be provided later using SQL Developer. Using SQL Developer or SQL*Plus, connect to the OE schema and complete the following tasks.

   1. Obtain structural information for the PRODUCT_INFORMATION and ORDERS tables.

   2. Select the unique SALES_REP_ID values from the ORDERS table. How many different sales representatives have been assigned to orders in the ORDERS table?

3. Create a results set based on the ORDERS table that includes the ORDER_ID, ORDER_DATE, and ORDER_TOTAL columns. Notice how the ORDER_DATE output is formatted differently from the START_DATE and END_DATE columns in the HR.JOB_HISTORY table.

4. The PRODUCT_INFORMATION table stores data regarding the products available for sale in a fictitious IT hardware store. Produce a set of results that will be useful for a salesperson. Extract product information in the format <PRODUCT_NAME> with code: <PRODUCT_ID> has status of: <PRODUCT_STATUS>. Alias the expression as "Product." The results should provide the LIST_PRICE, the MIN_PRICE, the difference between LIST_PRICE, and MIN_PRICE aliased as "Max Actual Savings", along with an additional expression that takes the difference between LIST_PRICE and MIN_PRICE and divides it by the LIST_PRICE and then multiplies the total by 100. This last expression should be aliased as "Max Discount %".

5. Calculate the surface area of the earth using the DUAL table. Alias this expression as "Earth's Area". The formula for calculating the area of a sphere is: $4\pi r^2$. Assume, for this example, that the earth is a simple sphere with a radius of 3,958.759 miles and that π is 22/7.

SELF TEST ANSWERS

List the Capabilities of SQL SELECT Statements

1. ☑ **B.** A projection is an intentional restriction of the columns returned from a table.
☒ **A, C,** and **D** are incorrect. **A** is eliminated since the question has nothing to do with duplicates, distinctiveness, or uniqueness of data. **C** incorrectly selects nonexistent columns called DEPT_NAME and LOC_ID from a nonexistent table called DEPT. **D** returns just one of the requested columns: DEPARTMENT_NAME. Instead of additionally projecting the LOCATION_ID column from the DEPARTMENTS table, it attempts to alias the DEPARTMENT_NAME column as LOCATION_ID.

2. ☑ **A.** Columns with NUMBER(8,2) data type can store, at most, eight digits, of which, at most, six digits are to the left of the decimal point. Although **A** is the correct answer, note that since the question is phrased in the negative, these values are NOT allowed to be stored in such a column. **A** is not allowed because it contains eight whole number digits, but the data type is constrained to store six whole number digits and two fractional digits.
☒ **B, C, D,** and **E** are incorrect, as they can legitimately be stored in this data type. **C** is allowed since the fractional portion is rounded to two decimal places. **D** shows that numbers with no fractional part are legitimate values for this column, as long as the number of digits in the whole number portion does not exceed six digits.

3. ☑ **B and E.** The result of arithmetic between two date values represents a certain number of days.
☒ **A, C,** and **D** are incorrect. It is a common mistake to expect the result of arithmetic between two date values to be a date as well, so **A** may seem plausible, but it is false.

4. ☑ **A and D.** The scale of the VARCHAR2 data type, specified in brackets, determines its maximum capacity for storing character data as mentioned by **A**. If a data value that is at most 30 characters long is stored in any data type, it can also be stored in this column as stated by **D**.
☒ **B and C** are incorrect. **B** is incorrect because it is possible to store character data of any length up to 30 characters in this column. **C** is false, since the CHAR data type exists in parallel with the VARCHAR2 data type.

Execute a Basic SELECT Statement

5. ☑ **D.** Unique JOB_ID values are projected from the EMPLOYEES table by applying the DISTINCT keyword to just the JOB_ID column.
☒ **A, B,** and **C** are incorrect, since **A** returns an unrestricted list of JOB_ID values including duplicates, **B** makes use of the UNIQUE keyword in the incorrect context, and **C** selects the distinct combination of JOB_ID and EMPLOYEE_ID values. This has the effect of returning

all the rows from the EMPLOYEES table since the EMPLOYEE_ID column contains unique values for each employee record. Additionally, **C** returns two columns, which is not what was originally requested.

6. ☑ **B and D. B** and **D** represent the two illegal statements that will return syntax errors if they are executed. This is a tricky question because it asks for the illegal statements and not the legal statements. **B** is illegal because it is missing a single quote enclosing the character literal `"represents the"`. **D** is illegal because it does not make use of single quotes to enclose its character literals.

   ☒ **A and C** are incorrect, as they are the legal statements. **A** and **C** appear to be different since the case of the SQL statements are different and **A** uses the alias keyword AS, whereas **C** just leaves a space between the expression and the alias. Yet both **A** and **C** produce identical results.

7. ☑ **B and D. B** and **D** do not return null values since character expressions are not affected in the same way by null values as arithmetic expressions. **B** and **D** ignore the presence of null values in their expressions and return the remaining character literals.

   ☒ **A and C** are incorrect. They return null values because any arithmetic expression that involves a null will return a null.

8. ☑ **D.** An asterisk is the SQL operator that implies that all columns must be selected from a table.

   ☒ **A, B, C,** and **E** are incorrect. **A** uses the ALL reserved word but is missing any column specification and will, therefore, generate an error. **B** selects some columns but not all columns and, therefore, does not answer the question. **C** and **E** make use of illegal selection operators.

9. ☑ **B.** The key to identifying the correct result lies in understanding the role of the single quotation marks. The entire literal is enclosed by a pair of quotes to avoid the generation of an error. The two adjacent quotes are necessary to delimit the single quote that appears in literal **B**.

   ☒ **A, C,** and **D** are incorrect. **A** is eliminated since no error is returned. **C** inaccurately returns two adjacent quotes in the literal expression and **D** returns a literal with all the quotes still present. The Oracle server removes the quotes used as character delimiters after processing the literal.

10. ☑ **D.** The literal expression `'6 * 6'` is selected once for each row of data in the REGIONS table.

    ☒ **A, B, C,** and **E** are incorrect. **A** returns one row instead of four and calculates the product 6 * 6. The enclosing quote operators render 6 * 6 a character literal and not a numeric literal that can be calculated. **B** correctly returns four rows but incorrectly evaluates the character literal as a numeric literal. **C** incorrectly returns one row instead of four and **E** is incorrect, because the given SQL statement can be executed.

LAB ANSWER

The assumption is made that an Oracle database is available for you to practice on. The database administrator (DBA) in your organization may assist you with installing and setting this up. In order for any client tool such as SQL*Plus or SQL Developer to connect to the database, a listener process should be running and the database must be opened. Additionally, you may have to request that the HR and OE schema accounts be unlocked and that the passwords be reset. If these sample schemas are not present, it is a simple matter to get the DBA to run the scripts, which are installed when the database is installed, to create them. Connect to the OE schema using either SQL*Plus or SQL Developer.

1. The DESCRIBE command gives us the structural description of a table. The following illustration shows these two tables being described:

2. The request for unique values usually involves using the DISTINCT keyword as part of your SELECT statement. The two components of the statement involve the SELECT clause and the FROM clause. You were asked for unique SALES_REP_ID values FROM the ORDERS table. It is simple to translate this request into the following SELECT statement:

```
SELECT DISTINCT sales_rep_id
FROM orders;
```

From the results in the illustration, you can answer the original question: There are nine different sales representatives responsible for orders listed in the ORDERS table, but there is at least one order that contains null values in their SALES_REP_ID fields.

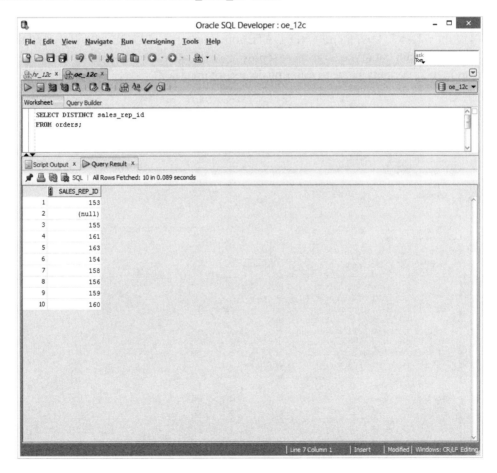

3. When asked to create a results set, it translates to SELECT one or more columns from a table. In this case, your SELECT clause is constructed from the three columns requested. There is no request for unique values, so there is no need to consider the DISTINCT keyword. The FROM clause need only include the ORDERS table to build the following SELECT statement:

```
SELECT order_id, order_date, order_total
FROM orders;
```

Consider the output in the following illustration, specifically the ORDER_DATE column. This column contains the day, month, year, hours, minutes, seconds, and fractional seconds up to six decimal places or accurate up to a millionth of a second. The description of the ORDERS table exposes ORDER_DATE as a TIMESTAMP(6) with LOCAL TIMEZONE column. This means that the data in this column can be stored with fractional precision up to six decimal places and that the data is time zone-aware. Basically, data may be worked on by people in different time zones. So Oracle provides a data type that normalizes the local time to the database time zone to avoid confusion. Compared to the START_DATE and END_DATE columns in the HR.JOB_HISTORY table, the ORDER_DATE column data type is far more sophisticated. Essentially, though, both these data types store date and time information but to differing degrees of precision.

4. The SELECT clause to answer this question should contain an expression aliased as "Product" made up of concatenations of character literals with the PRODUCT_NAME, PRODUCT_ID, and PRODUCT_STATUS columns. Additionally, the SELECT clause must contain the LIST_PRICE and MIN_PRICE columns and two further arithmetic expressions aliased as "Max Actual Savings" and "Max Discount %". The FROM clause need only include the PRODUCT_INFORMATION table. Proceed by constructing each of the three expressions in turn and put them all together. The "Product" expression could be derived with the following SELECT statement:

```
SELECT product_name||' with code: '||product_id||' has status
of:'||product_status AS "Product"
```

The "Max Actual Savings" expression could be derived with the following SELECT statement:

```
SELECT list_price - min_price AS "Max Actual Savings"
```

The "Max Discount %" expression takes the calculation for "Max Actual Savings", divides this amount by the LIST_PRICE, and multiplies it by 100. It could be derived with the following SELECT statement:

```
SELECT ((list_price-min_price)/list_price) * 100 AS "Max Discount %"
```

These three expressions, along with the two regular columns, form the SELECT clause executed against the PRODUCT_INFORMATION table as shown next:

5. The versatile DUAL table clearly forms the FROM clause. The SELECT clause is more interesting, since no actual columns are being selected, just an arithmetic expression. A possible SELECT statement to derive this calculation could be:

```
SELECT (4 * (22/7) * (3958.759 * 3958.759)) AS "Earth's Area"
FROM dual;
```

This calculation approximates that planet Earth's surface area is 197,016,573 square miles.

3
Restricting and Sorting Data

L imiting the columns retrieved by a SELECT statement is known as *projection* and was introduced in Chapter 2. Restricting the rows returned is known as *selection*. This chapter discusses the *WHERE* clause, which is an enhancement to the selection functionality of the SELECT statement. The WHERE clause specifies one or more conditions that the Oracle server evaluates to restrict the rows returned by the statement. A further language enhancement is introduced with the ORDER BY clause, which provides data sorting capabilities. Ampersand substitution provides a way to reuse the same statement to execute different queries by substituting query elements at runtime. This chapter concludes with an exploration of this technique of runtime binding in SQL statements.

CERTIFICATION OBJECTIVE 3.01

Limit the Rows Retrieved by a Query

One of the cornerstone principles in relational theory is selection. Selection is actualized using the WHERE clause of the SELECT statement. Conditions that restrict the dataset returned take many forms and operate on columns as well as expressions. Only those rows in a table that conform to these conditions are returned. Conditions restrict rows using comparison operators in conjunction with columns and literal values. Boolean operators provide a mechanism to specify multiple conditions to restrict the rows returned. Boolean, conditional, concatenation, and arithmetic operators are discussed to establish their order of precedence when they are encountered in a SELECT statement. The following four areas are investigated:

- The WHERE clause
- Comparison operators
- Boolean operators
- Precedence rules

The WHERE clause

The WHERE clause extends the SELECT statement by providing the language to restrict rows returned based on one or more conditions. Querying a table with just the SELECT and FROM clauses results in every row of data stored in the table being returned. Using the DISTINCT keyword, duplicate values are excluded, and the resultant rows are restricted to some degree. What if very specific information is required from a table, for example, only the data where a column contains a specific value? How would you retrieve the countries that belong to the Europe region from the COUNTRIES table? What about retrieving just those employees who work as sales representatives? These questions are answered using the WHERE clause to specify exactly which rows must be returned. The format of the SQL SELECT statement that includes the WHERE clause is:

SELECT * | {[DISTINCT] *column* | *expression* [*alias*],…}
FROM *table*
[WHERE *condition(s)*];

The SELECT and FROM clauses were examined in Chapter 2. The WHERE clause always follows the FROM clause. The square brackets indicate that the WHERE clause is optional. One or more conditions may be simultaneously applied to restrict the result set. A condition is specified by comparing two terms using a conditional operator. These terms may be column values, literals, or expressions. The *equality* operator is most commonly used to restrict result sets. Two examples of WHERE clauses are shown next:

```
SELECT country_name
FROM countries
WHERE region_id=3;

SELECT last_name, first_name
FROM employees
WHERE job_id='SA_REP';
```

The first example projects the COUNTRY_NAME column from the COUNTRIES table. Instead of selecting every row, the WHERE clause restricts the rows returned to only those that contain a 3 in the REGION_ID column. The second example projects two columns, LAST_NAME and FIRST_NAME from the EMPLOYEES table. The rows returned are restricted to those that contain the value SA_REP in their JOB_ID columns.

Numeric-Based Conditions

Conditions must be formulated appropriately for different column data types. The conditions restricting rows based on numeric columns can be specified in several different ways. Consider the SALARY column in the EMPLOYEES table. This column has a data type of NUMBER(8,2). Figure 3-1 shows two different ways in which the SALARY column has been restricted. The first and second examples retrieve the LAST_NAME and SALARY values of the employees who earn $10,000. Notice the difference in the WHERE clauses of the following queries. The first query specifies the number 10000, while the second encloses the number within single quotes like a character literal. Both formats are acceptable to Oracle since an implicit data type conversion is performed when necessary.

```
SELECT last_name, salary
FROM employees
WHERE salary = 10000;

SELECT last_name, salary
FROM employees
WHERE salary = '10000';
```

A numeric column can be compared to another numeric column in the same row to construct a WHERE clause condition, as the following query demonstrates:

```
SELECT last_name, salary, department_id
FROM employees
WHERE salary = department_id;
```

FIGURE 3-1

Two ways to select numeric values in a WHERE clause

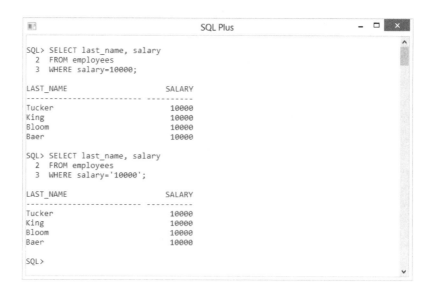

The first example in Figure 3-2 shows how the WHERE clause is too restrictive and results in no rows being selected. This is because the range of SALARY values is 2100 to 24000, and the range of DEPARTMENT_ID values is 10 to 270. Since there is no overlap in the range of DEPARTMENT_ID and SALARY values, there are no rows that satisfy this condition and therefore nothing is returned. The example also illustrates how a WHERE clause condition compares one numeric column to another.

The second example in Figure 3-2 demonstrates extending the WHERE clause condition to compare a numeric column, SALARY, to the numeric expression: DEPARTMENT_ID*100. For each row, the value in the SALARY column is compared to the product of the DEPARTMENT_ID value and 100. The WHERE clause also permits expressions on either side of the comparison operator. You could issue the following statement to yield identical results:

```
SELECT last_name, salary
FROM employees
WHERE salary/10 = department_id*10;
```

As in regular algebra, the expression (SALARY = DEPARTMENT_ID * 100) is equivalent to (SALARY/10 = DEPARTMENT_ID * 10). The notable feature about this example is that the terms on either side of the comparison operator are expressions.

FIGURE 3-2	
Using the WHERE clause with numeric expressions	

```
SQL> SELECT last_name, salary, department_id
  2  FROM employees
  3  WHERE salary = department_id;

no rows selected

SQL> SELECT last_name, salary, department_id
  2  FROM employees
  3  WHERE salary = department_id * 100;

LAST_NAME                      SALARY DEPARTMENT_ID
------------------------- ---------- -------------
Ernst                            6000            60
Olsen                            8000            80
Smith                            8000            80

SQL>
```

Character-Based Conditions

Conditions determining which rows are selected based on character data are specified by enclosing character literals in the conditional clause within single quotes. The JOB_ID column in the EMPLOYEES table has a data type of VARCHAR2(10). Suppose you wanted a report consisting of the LAST_NAME values of those employees currently employed as sales representatives. The JOB_ID value for a sales representative is SA_REP. The following statement produces such a report:

```
SELECT last_name
FROM employees
WHERE job_id='SA_REP';
```

If you tried specifying the character literal without the quotes, an Oracle error would be raised. Remember that character literal data is case sensitive, so the following WHERE clauses are not equivalent.

```
Clause 1: WHERE job_id=SA_REP

Clause 2: WHERE job_id='Sa_Rep'

Clause 3: WHERE job_id='sa_rep'
```

Clause 1 generates an "ORA-00904: "SA_REP": invalid identifier" error since the literal SA_REP is not wrapped in single quotes. Clause 2 and Clause 3 are syntactically correct but not equivalent. Further, neither of these clauses yields any data since there are no rows in the EMPLOYEES table that have JOB_ID column values that are either Sa_Rep or sa_rep, as shown in Figure 3-3.

FIGURE 3-3	
Using the WHERE clause with character data	

```
SQL Plus                                          _ □ ✕

SQL> SELECT last_name
  2  FROM employees
  3  WHERE job_id=SA_REP;
WHERE job_id=SA_REP
             *
ERROR at line 3:
ORA-00904: "SA_REP": invalid identifier


SQL> SELECT last_name
  2  FROM employees
  3  WHERE job_id='Sa_Rep';

no rows selected

SQL> SELECT last_name
  2  FROM employees
  3  WHERE job_id='sa_rep';

no rows selected

SQL>
```

Character-based conditions are not limited to comparing column values with literals. They may also be specified using other character columns and expressions. The LAST_NAME and FIRST_NAME columns are both specified as VARCHAR2(25) data typed columns. Consider the query:

```
SELECT employee_id, job_id, last_name, first_name
FROM employees
WHERE last_name=first_name;
```

Both the LAST_NAME and FIRST_NAME columns appear on either side of the equality operator in the WHERE clause. No literal values are present; therefore no single quote characters are necessary to delimit them. This condition stipulates that only rows that contain the same data value (an exact case-sensitive match) in the LAST_NAME and FIRST_NAME columns will be returned. This condition is too restrictive and, as Figure 3-4 shows, no rows are returned.

Character-based expressions form either one or both parts of a condition separated by a conditional operator. These expressions can be formed by concatenating literal

FIGURE 3-4

Character column-based WHERE clause

values with one or more character columns. The following four clauses demonstrate some of the options for character-based conditions:

```
Clause 1: WHERE 'A '||last_name||first_name = 'A King'

Clause 2: WHERE first_name||' '||last_name = last_name||' '||first_name

Clause 3: WHERE 'SA_REP'||'King' = job_id||last_name

Clause 4: WHERE job_id||last_name ='SA_REP'||'King'
```

Clause 1 concatenates the string literal "A" to the LAST_NAME and FIRST_NAME columns. This expression is compared to the literal "A King" and any row that fulfils this condition is returned. Clause 2 demonstrates that character expressions may be placed on both sides of the conditional operator. Clause 3 illustrates that literal expressions may also be placed on the left of the conditional operator. It is logically equivalent to Clause 4, which has swapped the operands in Clause 3 around. Both Clauses 3 and 4 result in the same row of data being returned, as shown in Figure 3-5.

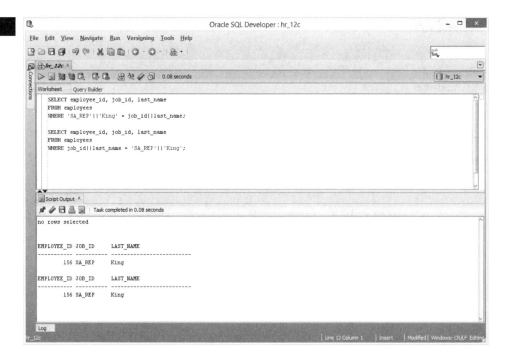

FIGURE 3-5

Equivalence
of conditional
expressions

Date-Based Conditions

DATE columns are useful when storing date and time information. Date literals must be enclosed in single quotation marks just like character data; otherwise an error is raised. When used in conditional WHERE clauses, DATE columns are compared to other DATE columns or to_date literals. The literals are automatically converted into DATE values based on the default date format, which is DD-MON-RR. If a literal occurs in an expression involving a DATE column, it is automatically converted into a date value using the default format mask. DD represents days, MON represents the first three letters of a month, and RR represents a Year 2000–compliant year (that is, if RR is between 50 and 99, then the Oracle server returns the previous century, else it returns the current century). The full four-digit year, YYYY, can also be specified. Consider the following four SQL statements:

```
Statement 1:
SELECT employee_id
FROM job_history
WHERE start_date = end_date;

Statement 2:
SELECT employee_id
FROM job_history
WHERE start_date = '01-JAN-2001';

Statement 3:
SELECT employee_id
FROM job_history
WHERE start_date = '01-JAN-01';

Statement 4:
SELECT employee_id
FROM job_history
WHERE start_date = '01-JAN-99';
```

The first statement tests equality between two DATE columns. Rows that contain the same values in their START_DATE and END_DATE columns will be returned. Note, however, that DATE values are only equal to each other if there is an exact match between all their components including day, month, year, hours, minutes, and seconds. Chapter 4 discusses the details of storing DATE values. Until then, don't worry about the hours, minutes, and seconds components.

In the WHERE clause of the second statement, the START_DATE column is compared to the character literal '01-JAN-2001'. The entire four-digit year component (YYYY) has been specified. This is acceptable to the Oracle server, and all rows in the JOB_HISTORY table with START_DATE column values equal to the first of January 2001 will be returned.

The third statement is equivalent to the second since the literal `'01-JAN-01'` is converted to the date value 01-JAN-2001. This is due to the RR component being less than 50, so the current (twenty-first) century, 20, is prefixed to the year RR component to provide a century value. All rows in the JOB_HISTORY table with START_DATE column values = 01-JAN-2001 will be returned.

The century component for the literal `'01-JAN-99'` becomes the previous (twentieth) century, 19, and yields a date value of 01-JAN-1999 for the fourth statement, since the RR component, 99, is greater than 50. Rows in the JOB_HISTORY table with START_DATE column values = 01-JAN-1999 will be returned.

Arithmetic using the addition and subtraction operators is supported in expressions involving DATE values. An expression like END_DATE – START_DATE returns a numeric value representing the number of days between START_DATE and END_DATE. An expression like START_DATE + 1 returns a DATE value that is 1 day later than START_DATE. So the following expression is legitimate, as shown in Figure 3-6:

```
SELECT start_date, employee_id
FROM job_history
WHERE start_date + 1 = '25-MAR-06';
```

FIGURE 3-6

Using the WHERE clause with numeric expressions

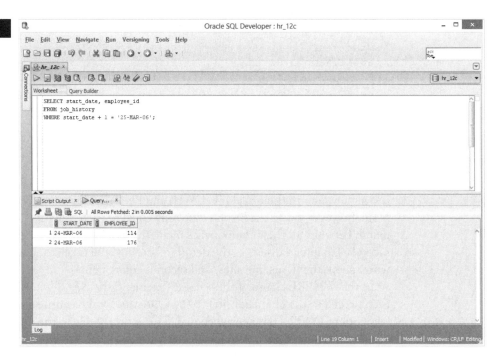

This query returns rows from the JOB_HISTORY table containing a START_DATE value equal to 1 day before 25-MAR-2006. Therefore, only rows with a value of 24-MAR-2006 in the START_DATE column will be retrieved.

e x a m

ⓦatch   *Conditional clauses compare two terms using comparison operators. It is important to understand the data types of the terms involved so they can be enclosed in single quotes, if necessary. A common mistake is to assume that a WHERE clause is syntactically correct when, in fact, it is missing quotation*   *marks that delimit character or date literals. Another common oversight is not being aware that the terms to the left and right of the comparison operator in a conditional clause may be expressions, columns, or literal values. Both these concepts may be tested in the exam.*

Comparison Operators

The *equality* operator is used extensively to illustrate the concept of restricting rows using a WHERE clause. There are several alternative operators that may also be used. The *inequality* operators like "less than" or "greater than or equal to" may be used to return rows conforming to inequality conditions. The *BETWEEN* operator facilitates range-based comparison to test whether a column value lies between two values. The *IN* operator tests set membership, so a row is returned if the column value tested in the condition is a member of a set of literals. The pattern matching comparison operator *LIKE* is extremely powerful, allowing components of character column data to be matched to literals conforming to a specific pattern. The last comparison operator discussed in this section is the *IS NULL* operator, which returns rows where the column value contains a null value. These operators may be used in any combination in the WHERE clause and will be discussed next.

Equality and Inequality

Limiting the rows returned by a query involves specifying a suitable WHERE clause. If the clause is too restrictive, then few or no rows are returned. If the conditional clause is too broadly specified, then more rows than are required are returned.

Exploring the different available operators should equip you with the language to request exactly those rows you are interested in. Testing for *equality* in a condition is both natural and intuitive. Such a condition is formed using the "is equal to" (=) operator. A row is returned if the equality condition is true for that row. Consider the following query:

```
SELECT last_name, salary
FROM employees
WHERE job_id='SA_REP';
```

The JOB_ID column of every row in the EMPLOYEES table is tested for equality with the character literal SA_REP. For character information to be equal, there must be an exact case-sensitive match. When such a match is encountered, the values for the projected columns, LAST_NAME and SALARY, are returned for that row, as shown in Figure 3-7. Note that although the conditional clause is based on the JOB_ID column, it is not necessary for this column to be projected by the query.

Inequality-based conditions enhance the WHERE clause specification. Range and pattern matching comparisons are possible using inequality and equality operators,

FIGURE 3-7

Conditions based on the equality operator

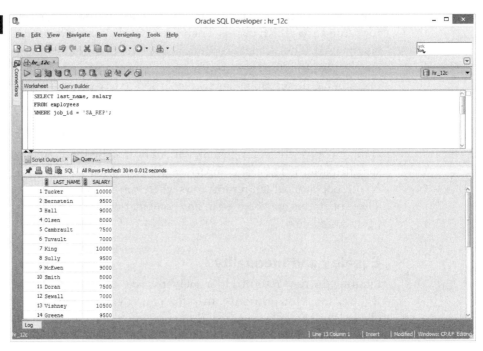

but it is often preferable to use the BETWEEN and LIKE operators for these comparisons. The inequality operators are described in Table 3-1.

Inequality operators allow range-based queries to be fulfilled. You may be required to provide a set of results where a column value is *greater than* another value. For example, the following query may be issued to obtain a list of LAST_NAME and SALARY values for employees who earn more than $5,000:

```
SELECT last_name, salary
FROM employees
WHERE salary > 5000;
```

Similarly, to obtain a list of employees who earn less than $3,000, the following query may be submitted:

```
SELECT last_name, salary
FROM employees
WHERE salary < 3000;
```

The *composite inequality operators* (made up of more than one symbol) are utilized in the following four clauses:

```
Clause 1: WHERE salary <= 3000;

Clause 2: WHERE salary >= 5000;

Clause 3: WHERE salary <> department_id;

Clause 4: WHERE salary != 4000+department_id;
```

Clause 1 returns those rows that contain a SALARY value that is less than or equal to 3000. Clause 2 obtains data where the SALARY value is greater than or equal to 5000, while Clauses 3 and 4 demonstrate the two forms of the

	Operator	Description
TABLE 3-1		
	<	Less than
Inequality	>	Greater than
Operators	<=	Less than or equal to
	>=	Greater than or equal to
	<>	Not equal to
	!=	Not equal to

"not equal to" operators. Clause 3 returns the rows that have SALARY column values that are not equal to the DEPARTMENT_ID values. The alternate "not equal to" operator in Clause 4 illustrates that columns, literals, and expressions may all be compared using inequality operators. Clause 4 returns those rows that contain a SALARY value that is not equal to the sum of the DEPARTMENT_ID for that row and 4000.

Numeric inequality is naturally intuitive. The comparison of character and date terms, however, is more complex. Testing character inequality is interesting since the strings being compared on either side of the inequality operator are compared in lexicographical order. Based on the database character set and NLS (National Language Support) settings, each character string is either evaluated using a binary or linguistic comparison method. In English type character sets, the comparison semantics operate as discussed in this chapter. With the default binary comparison method, characters are assigned a numeric value with blanks having a lesser value than other characters. These numeric values form the basis for the evaluation of the inequality comparison. Consider the following statement:

```
SELECT last_name
FROM employees
WHERE last_name < 'King';
```

The character literal 'King' is converted to a numeric representation. Assuming a US7ASCII database character set with AMERICAN NLS settings, the literal 'King' is converted into its ordinal character values: K (75), i (105), n (110), and g (103). For each row in the EMPLOYEES table, the LAST_NAME column data is similarly converted into numeric values for each character which are then compared in turn with the numeric values of the characters in the literal 'King'. For example, the row with LAST_NAME='Kaufling' is compared as follows: The first character in both strings is 'K' with an equal ordinal value of 75. So the second character (i=105) is compared with (a=97). Since (97 < 105) or (a < i), 'Kaufling' < 'King' and the row is selected. The same process for comparing numeric data using the inequality operators applies to character data. The only difference is that character data is converted implicitly by the Oracle server to a numeric value based on certain database settings.

Inequality comparisons operating on date values follow a similar process to character data. The Oracle server stores dates in an internal numeric format, and these values are compared within the conditions. The second of June always occurs earlier than the third of June of the same year. Therefore, the numeric value of the date 02-JUN-2008 is less than the numeric value of the date 03-JUN-2008. Consider the following query:

```
SELECT last_name, hire_date
FROM employees
WHERE hire_date < '01-JAN-2003';
```

This query retrieves the last name and hire date of each employee record containing a HIRE_DATE value that is earlier than '01-JAN-2003'. Rows with employee HIRE_DATE on or before 31-DEC-2002 will be returned, while rows with employee HIRE_DATE values later than the first of January 2003 will not be returned, as shown in Figure 3-8.

on the **Job**

The WHERE clause is a fundamental extension to the SELECT statement and forms part of most queries. Although many comparison operators exist, the majority of conditions are based on comparing two terms using both the equality and the inequality operators.

FIGURE 3-8

Conditions based on the inequality operators

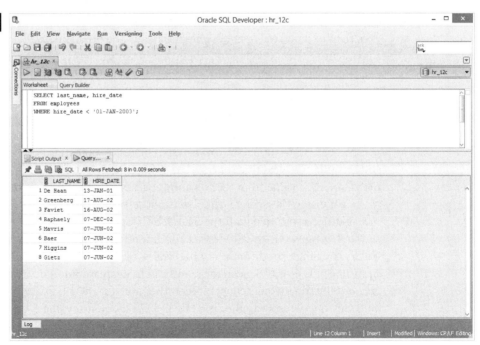

Range Comparison with the BETWEEN Operator

The BETWEEN operator tests whether a column or expression value falls within a range of two boundary values. The item must be at least the same as the lower boundary value, or at most the same as the higher boundary value, or fall within the range, for the condition to be true.

Suppose you want the last names and salaries of employees who earn a salary in the range of $3,400 and $4,000. A possible solution using the BETWEEN operator is as follows:

```
SELECT last_name, salary
FROM employees
WHERE salary BETWEEN 3400 AND 4000;
```

This operator allows the WHERE condition to read in a natural English manner. The last names of all the employees earning from $3,400 to $4,000 will be returned. *Boolean* operators like AND, OR, and NOT are discussed later in this chapter, but they are introduced here to enhance the description of the BETWEEN operator. The AND operator is used to specify multiple WHERE conditions, all of which must be satisfied for a row to be returned. Using the AND operator, the BETWEEN operator is equivalent to two conditions using the "greater than or equal to" and "less than or equal to" operators, respectively. The preceding SQL statement is equivalent to the following statement, as shown in Figure 3-9.

```
SELECT last_name
FROM employees
WHERE salary >= 3400
AND salary <= 4000;
```

The SALARY value for a row is tested first if it is greater than or equal to 3400 and second if it is less than or equal to 4000. If both conditions are satisfied, the LAST_NAME value from the row forms part of the results set. If only one or neither of the conditions is satisfied, the row is not selected.

Conditions specified with the BETWEEN operator can therefore be equivalently denoted using two inequality-based conditions, but it is shorter and simpler to specify the range condition using the BETWEEN operator. The implication of this equivalence is that the mechanism utilized to evaluate numeric, character, and date operands by the inequality operators is the same for the BETWEEN operator. The following query tests whether the HIRE_DATE column value is on or after 24-JUL-1994 but on or before 07-JUN-1996:

```
SELECT first_name, hire_date
FROM employees
WHERE hire_date BETWEEN '24-JUL-1994' AND '07-JUN-1996';
```

FIGURE 3-9

The BETWEEN
operator

You are not restricted to specifying literal values as the operands to the BETWEEN
operator, since these may be column values and expressions such as the following:

```
SELECT first_name, hire_date
FROM employees
WHERE '24-JUL-1994' BETWEEN hire_date+30 AND '07-JUN-1996';
```

For a row to be returned by this query, the date literal 24-JUL-1994 must fall
between the row's HIRE_DATE column value plus 30 days and the date literal
07-JUN-1996.

Set Comparison with the IN Operator

The *IN* operator tests whether an item is a member of a set of literal values. The set
is specified by a comma separating the literals and enclosing them in round brackets.
If the literals are character or date values, then these must be delimited using

single quotes. You may include as many literals in the set as you wish. Consider the following example:

```
SELECT last_name, salary
FROM employees
WHERE salary IN (3000,4000,6000);
```

The SALARY value in each row is compared for equality to the literals specified in the set. If the SALARY value equals 3000, 4000, or 6000, the LAST_NAME and SALARY values for that row are returned. The Boolean OR operator, discussed later in this chapter, is used to specify multiple WHERE conditions, at least one of which must be satisfied for a row to be returned. The IN operator is therefore equivalent to a series of OR conditions. The preceding SQL statement may be written using multiple OR condition clauses, for example:

```
SELECT last_name, salary
FROM employees
WHERE salary = 3000
OR salary = 4000
OR salary = 6000;
```

This statement will return an employee's LAST_NAME and SALARY if at least one of the WHERE clause conditions is true; it has the same meaning as the previous statement that uses the IN operator, as shown in Figure 3-10.

FIGURE 3-10

The IN operator

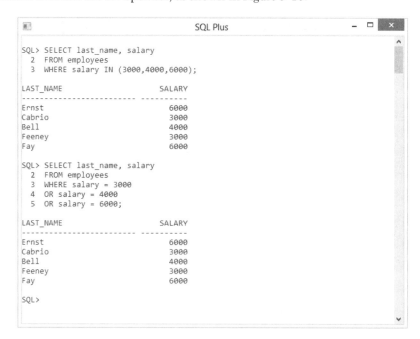

Testing set membership using the IN operator is more succinct than using multiple OR conditions, especially as the number of members in the set increases. The following two statements demonstrate use of the IN operator with DATE and CHARACTER data.

```
SELECT last_name
FROM employees
WHERE last_name IN ('King','Garbharran','Ramklass');

SELECT last_name
FROM employees
WHERE hire_date IN ('01-JAN-1998','01-DEC-1999');
```

Pattern Comparison with the LIKE Operator

To review, the BETWEEN operator provides a concise way to specify range-based conditions, and the IN operator provides an optimal method to test set membership. Now we introduce the *LIKE* operator, which is designed exclusively for character data and provides a powerful mechanism for searching for letters or words. Numeric values compared using the LIKE operator are automatically typecast as character data.

LIKE is accompanied by two wildcard characters: the percentage symbol (%) and the underscore character (_). The percentage symbol is used to specify zero or more characters, while the underscore character specifies one wildcard character. A wildcard may represent any character.

You may be requested to provide a list of employees whose first names begin with the letter "A". The following query can be used to provide this set of results:

```
SELECT first_name
FROM employees
WHERE first_name LIKE 'A%';
```

The character literal that the FIRST_NAME column is compared to is enclosed in single quotes like a regular character literal. In addition, it has a percentage symbol, which has a special meaning in the context of the LIKE operator. The percentage symbol substitutes zero or more characters appended to the letter "A". Employee records with FIRST_NAME values beginning with the letter "A" are returned.

The wildcard characters can appear at the beginning, middle, or end of the character literal. They can even appear alone, as in:

```
WHERE first_name LIKE '%';
```

In this case, every row containing a FIRST_NAME value that is not null will be returned. Wildcard symbols are not mandatory when using the LIKE operator.

In such cases, LIKE behaves as an equality operator testing for exact character matches; so the following two WHERE clauses are equivalent:

```
WHERE last_name LIKE 'King';

WHERE last_name = 'King';
```

The underscore wildcard symbol substitutes exactly one other character in a literal. Consider searching for employees whose last names are four letters long, begin with a "K", have an unknown second letter, and end with "ng". You may issue the following statement:

```
WHERE last_name LIKE 'K_ng';
```

Depending on the dataset, you may retrieve employees named King, Kong, and Kung. An alternate way to perform pattern matching is to use an interminable series of OR conditions, but to achieve the preceding results without using the LIKE operator is prohibitively complex. For example, it may be achieved with the following series of OR conditions:

```
WHERE last_name = 'Kang'
OR last_name ='Kbng'
OR last_name ='Kcng'
...
OR last_name ='Kzng'
```

This example is incomplete, since it is not feasible to list every possible character that could be substituted. This example demonstrates the sheer effort required to substitute a single character without using the LIKE operator and the underscore wildcard symbol. For an unknown number (zero or more) of character substitutions, the possibilities are exponentially larger than for single-character substitution. It is not practically possible to perform character pattern matching without the use of the LIKE operator and the wildcard symbols.

As Figure 3-11 shows, the two wildcard symbols can be used independently, together, or even multiple times in a single WHERE condition. The first query retrieves those records where COUNTRY_NAME begins with the letter "I" followed by zero or more characters, followed by a lowercase "a" which in turn is followed by zero or more characters.

The second query retrieves those countries whose names contain the letter "i" as its fifth character. The length of the COUNTRY_NAME values and the letter they begin with are unimportant. The four underscore wildcard symbols preceding the lowercase "i" in the WHERE clause represent exactly four characters (which

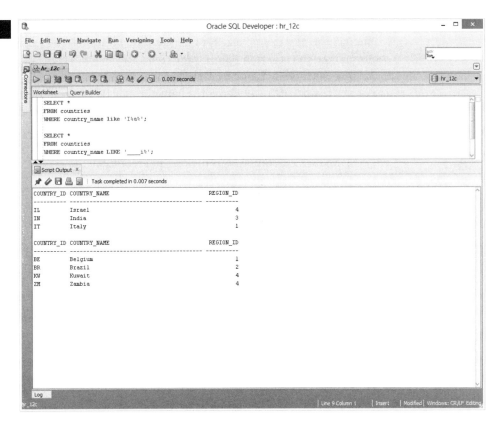

FIGURE 3-11

The wildcard
symbols of the
LIKE operator

could be any characters). The fifth letter must be an "i", and the percentage symbol
specifies that the COUNTRY_NAME can have zero or more characters from the
sixth character onward.

What about the scenario when you are searching for a literal that contains a
percentage or underscore character? Oracle provides a way to temporarily disable
their special meaning and regard them as regular characters using the *ESCAPE*
identifier. The JOBS table contains JOB_ID values that are literally specified with
an underscore character, such as SA_MAN, AD_VP, MK_REP, and SA_REP.
Assume there is, in addition, a row in the JOBS table with a JOB_ID of SA%MAN.
Notice there is no underscore character in this JOB_ID. How can values be retrieved
from the JOBS table if you are looking for JOB_ID values beginning with the
characters SA_? Consider the following SQL statement:

```
SELECT *
FROM jobs
WHERE job_id LIKE 'SA_%';
```

This query will return the rows SA_REP, SA_MAN, and SA%MAN. The requirement in this example is not met since an additional row, SA%MAN, not conforming to the criterion that it begins with the characters SA_, is also returned, as the first example in Figure 3-12 shows.

A naturally occurring underscore character may be escaped (or treated as a regular nonspecial symbol) using the ESCAPE identifier in conjunction with an ESCAPE character. The second example in Figure 3-12 shows the SQL statement that retrieves the JOBS table records with JOB_ID values equal to SA_MAN and SA_REP and which conforms to the original requirement:

```
SELECT *
FROM jobs
WHERE job_id LIKE 'SA\_%' ESCAPE '\';
```

The ESCAPE identifier instructs the Oracle server to treat any character found after the backslash character as a regular nonspecial symbol with no wildcard meaning. In the preceding WHERE clause, any JOB_ID values that begin with the three characters "SA_" will be returned. Traditionally, the ESCAPE character is the backslash symbol, but it does not have to be. The following statement is equivalent to the previous one but uses a dollar symbol as the ESCAPE character instead.

```
SELECT job_id
FROM jobs
WHERE job_id LIKE 'SA$_%' ESCAPE '$';
```

FIGURE 3-12

The ESCAPE identifier and the LIKE operator

```
                                        SQL Plus                              _ □ ✕

SQL> SELECT *
  2  FROM jobs
  3  WHERE job_id LIKE 'SA_%';

JOB_ID     JOB_TITLE                            MIN_SALARY MAX_SALARY
---------- ------------------------------------ ---------- ----------
SA%MAN     Contrived Sales Manager
SA_MAN     Sales Manager                             10000      20080
SA_REP     Sales Representative                       6000      12008

SQL>
SQL> SELECT *
  2  FROM jobs
  3  WHERE job_id LIKE 'SA\_%' ESCAPE '\';

JOB_ID     JOB_TITLE                            MIN_SALARY MAX_SALARY
---------- ------------------------------------ ---------- ----------
SA_MAN     Sales Manager                             10000      20080
SA_REP     Sales Representative                       6000      12008

SQL>
```

The percentage symbol may be similarly escaped when it occurs naturally as character data. Suppose there is a requirement to retrieve the row with the hypothetical JOB_ID: SA%MAN introduced earlier. Querying the JOBS table for JOB_ID values such as SA%MAN using the following code results in the records SA_MAN and SA%MAN being returned.

```
SELECT job_id
FROM jobs
WHERE job_id LIKE 'SA%MAN';
```

The Oracle server interprets the percentage symbol in the WHERE clause as a wildcard symbol when used with the LIKE operator. To obtain the row with JOB_ID: SA%MAN using the LIKE operator, the percentage symbol may be escaped using the following statement:

```
SELECT job_id
FROM jobs
WHERE job_id LIKE 'SA\%MAN' ESCAPE '\';
```

The backslash is defined as the ESCAPE character that instructs the Oracle server to ignore the wildcard properties of the symbol occurring immediately after the backslash. In this way, both wildcard symbols can be used as either specialized or regular characters in different segments of the same character string.

EXERCISE 3-1

Using the LIKE Operator

Retrieve a list of DEPARTMENT_NAME values that end with the three letters "ing" from the DEPARTMENTS table.

1. Start SQL*Plus and connect to the HR schema.
2. The SELECT clause is

   ```
   SELECT DEPARTMENT_NAME
   ```

3. The FROM clause is

   ```
   FROM DEPARTMENTS
   ```

4. The WHERE clause must perform a comparison between the DEPARTMENT_NAME column values and a pattern of characters beginning with zero or more characters but ending with three specific characters, "ing".

5. The operator enabling character pattern matching is the LIKE operator. The pattern the DEPARTMENT_NAME column must conform to is `'%ing'`. The percentage wildcard symbol indicates that zero or more characters may precede the "ing" string of characters.

6. Thus, the WHERE clause is

```
WHERE DEPARTMENT_NAME LIKE '%ing'
```

7. Executing this statement returns the set of results matching this pattern as shown in the following illustration:

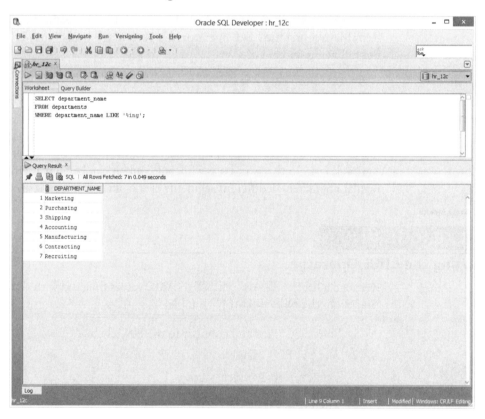

Null Comparison with the IS NULL Operator

NULL values inevitably find their way into database tables. It is often required that only those records that contain a NULL value in a specific column are sought. The *IS NULL* operator selects only the rows where a specific column value is NULL.

Testing column values for equality to NULL is performed using the IS NULL operator instead of the "is equal to" operator (=).

Consider the following query that fetches the LAST_NAME and COMMISSION_PCT columns from the EMPLOYEES table for those rows that have NULL values stored in the COMMISSION_PCT column:

```
SELECT last_name, commission_pct
FROM employees
WHERE commission_pct IS NULL;
```

This WHERE clause reads naturally and retrieves only the records that contain NULL COMMISSION_PCT values. As Figure 3-13 shows, the query using the "is equal to" operator does not return any rows, while the query using the IS NULL operator does.

Boolean Operators

Data is restricted using a WHERE clause with a single condition. *Boolean* or *logical* operators enable multiple conditions to be specified in the WHERE clause of the SELECT statement. This facilitates a more refined data extraction capability.

FIGURE 3-13

Using the IS
NULL operator

```
SQL> SELECT last_name, commission_pct
  2  FROM employees
  3  WHERE commission_pct = NULL;

no rows selected

SQL>
SQL> SELECT last_name, commission_pct
  2  FROM employees
  3  WHERE commission_pct IS NULL;

LAST_NAME                 COMMISSION_PCT
------------------------- --------------
King
Kochhar
De Haan
Hunold
Ernst
Austin
Pataballa
Lorentz
Greenberg
Faviet
Chen
Sciarra
Urman
Popp
Raphaely
Khoo
Baida
Tobias
```

Consider isolating those employee records with FIRST_NAME values that begin with the letter "J" and who earn a COMMISSION_PCT greater than 10 percent. First, the data in the EMPLOYEES table must be restricted to FIRST_NAME values like "J%", and second, the COMMISSION_PCT values for the records must be tested to ascertain if they are larger than 10 percent. These two separate conditions may be associated using the Boolean *AND* operator and are applied consecutively in a WHERE clause. A result set conforming to any or all conditions or to the negation of one or more conditions may be specified using Boolean operators.

The AND Operator

The *AND* operator merges conditions into one larger condition to which a row must conform to be included in the results set. Boolean operators are defined using *truth tables*. Table 3-2, the AND operator truth table, summarizes its functionality.

If two conditions specified in a WHERE clause are joined with an AND operator, then a row is tested consecutively for conformance to both conditions before being retrieved. If it conforms to neither or only one of the conditions, the row is excluded since the result is FALSE. If the row contains a NULL value that causes one of the conditions to evaluate to NULL, then that row is excluded. A row will only be returned if every condition joined with an AND operator evaluates to TRUE. In a scenario with more than two conditions joined with the AND operator, only data conforming to every condition will be returned.

TABLE 3-2	Condition X	Condition Y	Result
	FALSE	FALSE	FALSE
AND Operator	TRUE	FALSE	FALSE
Truth Table	FALSE	TRUE	FALSE
	TRUE	TRUE	TRUE
	TRUE	NULL	NULL
	NULL	TRUE	NULL
	FALSE	NULL	FALSE
	NULL	FALSE	FALSE
	NULL	NULL	NULL

Employee records with FIRST_NAME values beginning with the letter "J" and COMMISSION_PCT greater than 10 percent can be retrieved using the following query:

```
SELECT first_name, last_name, commission_pct, hire_date
FROM employees
WHERE first_name LIKE 'J%'
AND commission_pct > 0.1;
```

Notice that the WHERE clause now has two conditions but only one WHERE keyword. The AND operator separates the two conditions. To specify further mandatory conditions, simply add them and ensure that they are separated by additional AND operators. You can specify as many conditions as you wish. Remember, though, the more AND conditions specified, the more restrictive the query becomes. Figure 3-14 shows the preceding query followed by two additional restrictions. The HIRE_DATE value must be larger than 01-JUN-1996, and the LAST_NAME must contain the letter "o".

FIGURE 3-14

Using the AND operator

The first query returns four rows. Notice that the additional AND conditions in the second query are satisfied by only two rows.

The OR Operator

The *OR* operator separates multiple conditions, at least one of which must be satisfied by the row selected to warrant inclusion in the results set. Table 3-3, the OR operator truth table, summarizes its functionality.

If two conditions specified in a WHERE clause are joined with an OR operator, then a row is tested consecutively for conformance to either or both conditions before being retrieved. Conforming to just one of the OR conditions is sufficient for the record to be returned. If it conforms to none of the conditions, the row is excluded since the result is FALSE. A row will only be returned if at least one of the conditions associated with an OR operator evaluates to TRUE.

Retrieving employee records having FIRST_NAME values beginning with the letter "B" or those with a COMMISSION_PCT greater than 35 percent can be written as:

```
SELECT first_name, last_name, commission_pct, hire_date
FROM employees
WHERE first_name LIKE 'B%'
OR commission_pct > 0.35;
```

Notice that the two conditions are separated by the OR keyword. All employee records with FIRST_NAME values beginning with an uppercase "B" will be returned regardless of their COMMISSION_PCT values, even if they are NULL. All those records having COMMISSION_PCT values greater that 35 percent, regardless of what letter their FIRST_NAME begins with are also returned.

TABLE 3-3	Condition X	Condition Y	Result
OR Operator Truth Table	FALSE	FALSE	FALSE
	TRUE	FALSE	TRUE
	FALSE	TRUE	TRUE
	TRUE	TRUE	TRUE
	TRUE	NULL	TRUE
	NULL	TRUE	TRUE
	FALSE	NULL	NULL
	NULL	FALSE	NULL
	NULL	NULL	NULL

FIGURE 3-15

Using the OR operator

Further OR conditions may be specified by separating them with an OR operator. The more OR conditions you specify, the less restrictive your query becomes. Figure 3-15 shows the preceding query with two additional OR conditions. The HIRE_DATE value must be larger than 01-MAR-2008 or the LAST_NAME must begin with the letter "B". The first query returns fewer rows than the second query since more rows meet the less restrictive conditions in the second query than in the first.

The NOT Operator

The *NOT* operator negates conditional operators. A selected row must conform to the logical opposite of the condition in order to be included in the results set. Table 3-4, the NOT operator truth table, summarizes its functionality.

Conditional operators may be negated by the NOT operator as shown by the WHERE clauses listed in Table 3-5.

TABLE 3-4	Condition **X**	NOT Condition **X**
	FALSE	TRUE
The NOT Operator Truth Table	TRUE	FALSE
	NULL	NULL

TABLE 3-5	Positive	Negative
	WHERE last_name='King'	WHERE NOT (last_name='King')
Conditions Negated by the NOT Operator	WHERE first_name LIKE 'R%'	WHERE first_name NOT LIKE 'R%'
	WHERE department_id IN (10,20,30)	WHERE department_id NOT IN (10,20,30)
	WHERE salary BETWEEN 1 and 3000	WHERE salary NOT BETWEEN 1 AND 3000
	WHERE commission_pct IS NULL	WHERE commission_pct IS NOT NULL

As the examples in Table 3-5 suggest, the NOT operator can be very useful. It is important to understand that the NOT operator negates the comparison operator in a condition, whether it's an equality, inequality, range based, pattern matching, set membership, or null testing operator.

SCENARIO & SOLUTION

You have a complex query with multiple conditions. Is there a restriction on the number of conditions you can specify in the WHERE clause? Is there a limit to the number of comparison operators you can use in a single query?	No. You may specify any number of conditions in the WHERE clause separated by the Boolean operators. There is no limit when using the comparison operators, and they may be specified multiple times if necessary in a single query.
You have been tasked to locate rows in the EMPLOYEES table where the SALARY values contain the numbers 8 and 0 adjacent to each other. The SALARY column has a NUMBER data type. Is it possible to use the LIKE comparison operator with numeric data?	Yes. Oracle automatically casts the data into the required data type, if possible. In this case, the numeric SALARY values are momentarily "changed" into character data allowing the use of the LIKE operator to locate matching patterns. The following query locates the required rows: `SELECT * FROM employees` `WHERE salary LIKE '%80%';"`
By restricting the rows returned from the JOBS table to those that contain the value SA_REP in the JOB ID column, is a projection, selection or join performed?	A selection is performed since rows are restricted.

Retrieving employee records with FIRST_NAME values that do NOT begin with the letter "B" or those that do NOT comply with a COMMISSION_PCT greater than 35 percent can be written as:

```
SELECT first_name, last_name, commission_pct, hire_date
FROM employees
WHERE first_name NOT LIKE 'B%'
OR NOT (commission_pct > 0.35);
```

Notice that the two conditions are still separated by the OR operator and the NOT operator has just been added to them.

on the

Job *AND and OR are Boolean operators that enable multiple WHERE clause conditions to be specified in a single query. All conditions separated by an AND operator must evaluate to true after testing a row's values to prevent it from being excluded from the final results set. However, only one of the conditions separated by an OR operator must evaluate to true to avoid its exclusion from the final results set. If five conditions, A, B, C, D, and E, occur in a WHERE clause as WHERE A and B or C or D and E, then a row will be returned if both conditions A and B are fulfilled, or only condition C is met, or both conditions D and E are true.*

Precedence Rules

Arithmetic, character comparison, and Boolean expressions were examined in the context of the WHERE clause. But how do these operators interact with each other? Arithmetic operators subscribe to a precedence hierarchy. Bracketed expressions are evaluated before multiplication and division operators, which are evaluated before subtraction and addition operators. Similarly, there is a precedence hierarchy for the previously mentioned operators, as shown in Table 3-6.

Operators at the same level of precedence are evaluated from left to right if they are encountered together in an expression. When the NOT operator modifies the LIKE, IS NULL, and IN comparison operators, their precedence level remains the same as the positive form of these operators.

Consider the following SELECT statement that demonstrates the interaction of various different operators:

```
SELECT last_name,salary,department_id,job_id,commission_pct
FROM employees
WHERE last_name LIKE '%a%' AND salary > department_id * 200
OR
job_id IN ('MK_REP','MK_MAN') AND commission_pct IS NOT NULL;
```

TABLE 3-6

Operator
Precedence
Hierarchy

Precedence Level	Operator Symbol	Operation
1	()	Parentheses or brackets
2	/,*	Division and multiplication
3	+,−	Addition and subtraction
4	||	Concatenation
5	=,<,>,<=,>=	Equality and inequality comparison
6	[NOT] LIKE, IS [NOT] NULL, [NOT] IN	Pattern, null, and set comparison
7	[NOT] BETWEEN	Range comparison
8	!=,<>	Not equal to
9	NOT	NOT logical condition
10	AND	AND logical condition
11	OR	OR logical condition

The LAST_NAME, SALARY, DEPARTMENT_ID, JOB_ID, and COMMISSION_PCT columns are projected from the EMPLOYEES table based on two discrete conditions. The first condition retrieves the records containing the character "a" in the LAST_NAME field AND with a SALARY value greater than 200 times the DEPARTMENT_ID value. The product of DEPARTMENT_ID and 200 is processed before the inequality operator since the precedence of multiplication is higher than inequality comparison.

The second condition fetches those rows with JOB_ID values of either MK_MAN or MK_REP in which COMMISSION_PCT values are not null. For a row to be returned by this query, either the first OR second conditions need to be fulfilled. Figure 3-16 illustrates three queries. Query 1 returns four rows. Query 2 is based on the first condition just discussed and returns four rows. Query 3 is based on the second condition and returns zero rows.

Changing the order of the conditions in the WHERE clause changes its meaning due to the different precedence of the operators. Consider the following code sample:

```
SELECT last_name,salary,department_id,job_id,commission_pct
FROM employees
WHERE last_name LIKE '%a%'
AND salary > department_id * 100
AND commission_pct IS NOT NULL
OR
job_id = 'MK_MAN';
```

FIGURE 3-16

Operator
precedence in the
WHERE clause

There are two composite conditions in this query. The first condition retrieves
the records with the character "a" in the LAST_NAME field AND a SALARY
value greater than 100 times the DEPARTMENT_ID value AND where the
COMMISSION_PCT value is not null. The second condition fetches those rows
with JOB_ID values of MK_MAN. A row is returned by this query if it conforms to
either condition one OR condition two but not necessarily to both.

As Figure 3-17 illustrates, this query returns six rows. It further shows the division
of the query into two queries based on its two composite conditions. The first condition
results in five rows being returned while the second results in the retrieval of just one
row with a JOB_ID value of MK_MAN.

Boolean operators OR and AND allow multiple WHERE clause conditions to be specified. The Boolean NOT operator negates a conditional operator and may be used several times within the same condition. The equality, inequality, BETWEEN, IN, and LIKE comparison operators test two terms within a single condition. Only one comparison operator is used per conditional clause. The distinction between Boolean and comparison operators is important and forms the basis for many questions related to this chapter in the exam.

FIGURE 3-17

Effect of condition clause ordering due to precedence rules

CERTIFICATION OBJECTIVE 3.02

Sort the Rows Retrieved by a Query

Regular language dictionaries sort words in alphabetical order. Pages printed in a book are sorted numerically in ascending order from beginning to end. The practical implementations of selection and projection have been covered thus far. The usability of the retrieved datasets may be significantly enhanced with a mechanism to order or sort the information. Information may be sorted alphabetically, numerically, from earliest to latest, or in ascending or descending order. Further, the data may be sorted by one or more columns, including columns that are not listed in the SELECT clause. Sorting is performed once the results of a SELECT statement have been fetched. The sorting parameters do not influence the records returned by a query, just the presentation of the results. Exactly the same rows are returned by a statement including a sort clause as are returned by a statement excluding a sort clause. Only the ordering of the output may differ. Sorting the results of a query is accomplished using the ORDER BY clause.

The ORDER BY Clause

When tables are created, they are initially empty and contain no rows. As rows are inserted, updated, and deleted by one or more users or application systems, the original ordering of the stored rows is lost. The Oracle server cannot and does not guarantee that rows are stored sequentially. This is not a problem since a mechanism to sort the retrieved dataset is available in the form of the *ORDER BY* clause.

This clause is responsible for transforming the output of a query into more practical, user-friendly sorted data. The ORDER BY clause is always the last clause in a SELECT statement. As the full syntax of the SELECT statement is progressively exposed, you will observe new clauses added but none of them will be positioned after the ORDER BY clause. The format of the ORDER BY clause in the context of the SQL SELECT statement is as follows:

SELECT * | {[DISTINCT] *column* | *expression* [*alias*],...}
FROM *table*
[WHERE *condition(s)*]
[ORDER BY {*col(s)* | *expr* | *numeric_pos*} [ASC | DESC] [NULLS FIRST | LAST]];

Ascending and Descending Sorting

Ascending sort order is natural for most types of data and is therefore the default sort order used whenever the ORDER BY clause is specified. An ascending sort order for numbers is lowest to highest, while it is earliest to latest for dates and alphabetically for characters. The first form of the ORDER BY clause shows that results of a query may be sorted by one or more columns or expressions:

ORDER BY *col(s)* | *expr*;

Suppose that a report is requested that must contain an employee's LAST_NAME, SALARY, and COMMISSION_PCT information, sorted alphabetically by the LAST_NAME column for all sales representatives and marketing managers. This report could be extracted with the following SELECT statement:

```
SELECT last_name, salary, commission_pct
FROM employees
WHERE job_id IN ('SA_MAN','MK_MAN')
ORDER BY last_name;
```

The data selected may be ordered by any of the columns from the tables in the FROM clause, including those that do not appear in the SELECT list. The results from the preceding query may be sorted by the COMMISSION_PCT column, as shown in Figure 3-18.

The second example in Figure 3-18 shows that by appending the keyword *DESC* to the ORDER BY clause, the rows are returned sorted in descending order based on the COMMISSION_PCT column. The third example demonstrates the optional *NULLS LAST* keywords, which specify that if the sort column contains null values, then these rows are to be listed last after sorting the remaining rows based on their NOT NULL values. To specify that rows with null values in the sort column should be displayed first, append the *NULLS FIRST* keywords to the ORDER BY clause.

The following example sorts a dataset based on an expression. This expression calculates an employee's value to a company based on their HIRE_DATE and SALARY values. This formula takes the HIRE_DATE value and subtracts a specified number of days to return an earlier date. The number of days subtracted is calculated by dividing the SALARY value by 10. The expression is aliased as EMP_VALUE, as follows:

```
SELECT last_name, salary, hire_date, hire_date-(salary/10) emp_value
FROM employees
WHERE job_id IN ('SA_REP','MK_MAN')
ORDER BY emp_value;
```

FIGURE 3-18

Sorting data using the ORDER BY clause

```
SQL Plus                                            _ □  ✕
SQL> SELECT last_name, salary, commission_pct
  2  FROM employees
  3  WHERE job_id IN ('SA_MAN','MK_MAN')
  4  ORDER BY commission_pct;

LAST_NAME                    SALARY COMMISSION_PCT
------------------------- ---------- --------------
Zlotkey                       10500             .2
Partners                      13500             .3
Cambrault                     11000             .3
Errazuriz                     12000             .3
Russell                       14000             .4
Hartstein                     13000

6 rows selected.

SQL>
SQL> SELECT last_name, salary, commission_pct
  2  FROM employees
  3  WHERE job_id IN ('SA_MAN','MK_MAN')
  4  ORDER BY commission_pct DESC;

LAST_NAME                    SALARY COMMISSION_PCT
------------------------- ---------- --------------
Hartstein                     13000
Russell                       14000             .4
Partners                      13500             .3
Errazuriz                     12000             .3
Cambrault                     11000             .3
Zlotkey                       10500             .2

6 rows selected.

SQL>
SQL> SELECT last_name, salary, commission_pct
  2  FROM employees
  3  WHERE job_id IN ('SA_MAN','MK_MAN')
  4  ORDER BY commission_pct DESC NULLS LAST;

LAST_NAME                    SALARY COMMISSION_PCT
------------------------- ---------- --------------
Russell                       14000             .4
Partners                      13500             .3
Cambrault                     11000             .3
Errazuriz                     12000             .3
Zlotkey                       10500             .2
Hartstein                     13000

6 rows selected.

SQL> _
```

The EMP_VALUE expression is initialized with the HIRE_DATE value and is offset further into the past based on the SALARY field. The earliest EMP_VALUE date appears first in the result set output since the ORDER BY clause specifies that the results will be sorted by the expression alias. Note that the results could be sorted by the explicit expression, and the alias could be omitted, as in ORDER BY HIRE_DATE-(SALARY/10), but using aliases renders the query easier to read.

Several implicit default options are selected when you use the ORDER BY clause. The most important of these is that unless DESC is specified, the sort order is assumed to be ascending. If null values occur in the sort column, the default sort order is assumed to be NULLS LAST for ascending sorts and NULLS FIRST for descending sorts. If no ORDER BY clause is specified, the same query executed at different times may return the same set of results in different row order, so no assumptions should be made regarding the default row order.

Positional Sorting

Oracle offers an alternate and shorter way to specify the sort column or expression. Instead of specifying the column name, the position of the column as it occurs in the SELECT list is appended to the ORDER BY clause. Consider the following example:

```
SELECT last_name, hire_date, salary
FROM employees
WHERE job_id IN ('SA_REP','MK_MAN')
ORDER BY 2;
```

The ORDER BY clause specifies the numeric literal 2. This is equivalent to specifying ORDER BY HIRE_DATE, since the HIRE_DATE column is the second column selected in the SELECT clause.

Positional sorting applies only to columns in the SELECT list that have a numeric position associated with them. Modifying the preceding query to sort the results by the JOB_ID column is not possible using positional sorting since this column does not occur in the SELECT list.

Composite Sorting

Results of a query may be sorted by more than one column using *composite sorting*. Two or more columns may be specified (either literally or positionally) as the composite sort key by commas separating them in the ORDER BY clause. Consider the requirement to fetch the JOB_ID, LAST_NAME, SALARY, and HIRE_DATE values from the EMPLOYEES table. The further requirements are that the results must be sorted in reverse alphabetical order by JOB_ID first, then in ascending alphabetical order by LAST_NAME, and finally in numerically descending order based on the SALARY column. The following SELECT statement fulfills these requirements:

```
SELECT job_id, last_name, salary, hire_date
FROM employees
WHERE job_id IN ('SA_REP','MK_MAN')
ORDER BY job_id DESC, last_name, 3 DESC;
```

Each column involved in the sort is listed left to right in order of importance separated by commas in the ORDER BY clause, including the modifier DESC, which occurs twice in this clause. This example also demonstrates mixing literal and positional column specifications. As Figure 3-19 shows, there are several rows with the same JOB_ID value, for example, SA_REP. For these rows, the data is sorted alphabetically by the secondary sort key, which is the LAST_NAME column.

For the rows with the same JOB_ID and same LAST_NAME column values such as SA_REP and Smith, these rows are sorted in numeric descending order by the third sort column, SALARY.

FIGURE 3-19

Composite sorting using the ORDER BY clause

```
                              SQL Plus                    _ □ ×

SQL> SELECT job_id, last_name, salary, hire_date
  2  FROM employees
  3  WHERE job_id IN ('SA_REP','MK_MAN')
  4  ORDER BY job_id DESC, last_name, 3 DESC;

JOB_ID     LAST_NAME                  SALARY HIRE_DATE
---------- ------------------------- ---------- ---------
SA_REP     Abel                       11000 11-MAY-04
SA_REP     Ande                        6400 24-MAR-08
SA_REP     Banda                       6200 21-APR-08
SA_REP     Bates                       7300 24-MAR-07
SA_REP     Bernstein                   9500 24-MAR-05
SA_REP     Bloom                      10000 23-MAR-06
SA_REP     Cambrault                   7500 09-DEC-06
SA_REP     Doran                       7500 15-DEC-05
SA_REP     Fox                         9600 24-JAN-06
SA_REP     Grant                       7000 24-MAY-07
SA_REP     Greene                      9500 19-MAR-07
SA_REP     Hall                        9000 20-AUG-05
SA_REP     Hutton                      8800 19-MAR-05
SA_REP     Johnson                     6200 04-JAN-08
SA_REP     King                       10000 30-JAN-04
SA_REP     Kumar                       6100 21-APR-08
SA_REP     Lee                         6800 23-FEB-08
SA_REP     Livingston                  8400 23-APR-06
SA_REP     Marvins                     7200 24-JAN-08
SA_REP     McEwen                      9000 01-AUG-04
SA_REP     Olsen                       8000 30-MAR-06
SA_REP     Ozer                       11500 11-MAR-05
SA_REP     Sewall                      7000 03-NOV-06
SA_REP     Smith                       8000 10-MAR-05
SA_REP     Smith                       7400 23-FEB-07
SA_REP     Sully                       9500 04-MAR-04
SA_REP     Taylor                      8600 24-MAR-06
SA_REP     Tucker                     10000 30-JAN-05
SA_REP     Tuvault                     7000 23-NOV-07
SA_REP     Vishney                    10500 11-NOV-05
MK_MAN     Hartstein                  13000 17-FEB-04

31 rows selected.

SQL> _
```

e x a m

Ⓦatch   *The concept of sorting data is usually thoroughly tested. The syntax of the ORDER BY clause is straightforward, but multiple sort terms like expressions, columns, and positional specifiers, coupled with descending sort orders for some terms and ascending sort orders for others, provide a powerful data sorting mechanism that comes with a corresponding increase in complexity. This complexity is often tested, so ensure that you have a solid understanding of the ORDER BY clause.*

EXERCISE 3-2

Sorting Data Using the ORDER BY Clause

The JOBS table contains descriptions of different types of jobs an employee in the organization may occupy. It contains the JOB_ID, JOB_TITLE, MIN_SALARY, and MAX_SALARY columns. You are required to write a query that extracts the JOB_TITLE, MIN_SALARY, and MAX_SALARY columns, as well as an expression called VARIANCE, which is the difference between the MAX_SALARY and MIN_SALARY values, for each row. The results must include only JOB_TITLE values that contain either the word "President" or "Manager". Sort the list in descending order based on the VARIANCE expression. If more than one row has the same VARIANCE value, then, in addition, sort these rows by JOB_TITLE in reverse alphabetic order.

1. Start SQL Developer and connect to the HR schema.
2. The SELECT clause is

```
SELECT JOB_TITLE, MIN_SALARY, MAX_SALARY, (MAX_SALARY -
MIN_SALARY) VARIANCE
```

3. The FROM clause is

```
FROM JOBS
```

4. The WHERE conditions must allow only those rows whose JOB_TITLE column contains either the string "President" OR the string "Manager".
5. The WHERE clause is

```
WHERE JOB_TITLE LIKE '%President%' OR JOB_TITLE LIKE '
%Manager%'
```

6. Sorting is accomplished with the ORDER BY clause. Composite sorting is required using both the VARIANCE expression and the JOB_TITLE column in descending order.

7. The ORDER BY clause is

```
ORDER BY VARIANCE DESC, JOB_TITLE DESC
```

You may alternately specify the explicit expression in the ORDER BY clause instead of the expression alias.

8. Executing the statement returns a set of results matching this pattern as shown in the following illustration.

CERTIFICATION OBJECTIVE 3.03

Ampersand Substitution

As queries are developed and perfected, they may be saved for future use. Sometimes, queries differ very slightly, and it is desirable to have a more generic form of the query that has a variable or placeholder defined that can be substituted at runtime. Oracle offers this functionality in the form of *ampersand substitution*. Every element of the SELECT statement may be substituted, and the reduction of queries to their core elements to facilitate reuse can save you hours of tedious and repetitive work. The following areas are examined in this section:

- Substitution variables
- The DEFINE and VERIFY commands

Substitution Variables

The key to understanding substitution variables is to regard them as placeholders. A SQL query is composed of two or more clauses. Each clause can be divided into subclauses, which are in turn made up of character text. Any text, subclause or clause element, or even the entire SQL query, is a candidate for substitution. Consider the SELECT statement in its general form:

SELECT * | {[DISTINCT] *column* | *expression* [*alias*],...}
FROM *table*
[WHERE *condition(s)*]
[ORDER BY {*col(s)* | *expr* | *numeric_pos*} [ASC | DESC] [NULLS FIRST | LAST]];

Using substitution, you insert values into the italicized elements, choosing which optional keywords to use in your queries. When the LAST_NAME column in the EMPLOYEES table is required, the query is constructed using the general form of the SELECT statement and substituting the column name: LAST_NAME in place of the word *column* in the SELECT clause and the table name; EMPLOYEES in place of the word *table* in the FROM clause.

Single Ampersand Substitution

The most basic and popular form of substitution of elements in a SQL statement is *single ampersand substitution*. The ampersand character (&) is the symbol chosen to designate a substitution variable in a statement and precedes the variable name with no spaces between them. When the statement is executed, the Oracle server processes the statement, notices a substitution variable, and attempts to resolve this variable's value in one of two ways. First, it checks whether the variable is *defined* in the user session. (The *DEFINE* command is discussed later in this chapter.) If the variable is not defined, the user process prompts for a value that will be substituted in place of the variable. Once a value is submitted, the statement is complete and is executed by the Oracle server. The *ampersand substitution* variable is resolved at execution time and is sometimes known as *runtime binding* or *runtime substitution*.

A common requirement in the sample HR department may be to retrieve the same information for different employees at different times. Perhaps you are required to look up contact information like PHONE_NUMBER data given either LAST_NAME or EMPLOYEE_ID values. This generic request can be written as follows:

```
SELECT employee_id, last_name, phone_number
FROM employees
WHERE last_name = &LASTNAME
OR employee_id = &EMPNO;
```

As Figure 3-20 shows, when running this query, Oracle server prompts you to input a value for the variable called LASTNAME. You enter an employee's last name, if you know it, for example, `'King'`. If you don't know the last name but know the employee ID number, you can type in any value and press the ENTER key to submit the value. Oracle then prompts you to enter a value for the EMPNO variable.

FIGURE 3-20

Single ampersand substitution

```
SQL> SELECT employee_id, last_name, phone_number
  2  FROM employees
  3  WHERE last_name = &LASTNAME
  4  OR employee_id = &EMPNO;
Enter value for lastname: 'King'
old   3: WHERE last_name = &LASTNAME
new   3: WHERE last_name = 'King'
Enter value for empno: 0
old   4: OR employee_id = &EMPNO
new   4: OR employee_id = 0

EMPLOYEE_ID LAST_NAME                        PHONE_NUMBER
----------- -------------------------------- --------------------
        100 King                             515.123.4567
        156 King                             011.44.1345.429268

SQL>
```

After typing in a value, for example, 0, and hitting ENTER, there are no remaining substitution variables for Oracle to resolve, and the following statement is executed:

```
SELECT employee_id, last_name, phone_number
FROM employees
WHERE last_name = 'King'
OR employee_id = 0;
```

Variables can be assigned any alphanumeric name that is a valid identifier name. The literal you substitute when prompted for a variable must be an appropriate data type for that context; otherwise, an ORA-00904: invalid identifier error is returned. If the variable is meant to substitute a character or date value, the literal needs to be enclosed in single quotes. A useful technique is to enclose the *ampersand substitution* variable in single quotes when dealing with character and date values. In this way, the user is required to submit a literal value without worrying about enclosing it in quotes. The following statement rewrites the previous one but encloses the LASTNAME variable in quotes:

```
SELECT employee_id, last_name, phone_number, email
FROM employees
WHERE last_name = '&LASTNAME'
OR employee_id = &EMPNO;
```

When prompted for a value to substitute for the LASTNAME variable, you may, for example, submit the value King without any single quotes, as these are already present; and when the *runtime substitution* is performed, the first WHERE clause condition will resolve to WHERE LAST_NAME = 'King'.

Double Ampersand Substitution

There are occasions when a substitution variable is referenced multiple times in the same query. In such situations, the Oracle server will prompt you to enter a value for every occurrence of the single ampersand substitution variable. For complex scripts this can be very inefficient and tedious. The following statement appears to retrieve the FIRST_NAME and LAST_NAME columns from the EMPLOYEES table for those rows that contain the same set of characters in both fields:

```
SELECT first_name, last_name
FROM employees
WHERE last_name LIKE '%&SEARCH%'
AND first_name LIKE '%&SEARCH%';
```

The two conditions are identical but apply to different columns. When this statement is executed, you are first prompted to enter a substitution value for the SEARCH variable used in the comparison with the LAST_NAME column. Thereafter, you are prompted to enter a substitution value for the SEARCH variable used in the comparison with the FIRST_NAME column. This poses two problems. First, it is inefficient to enter the same value twice, but second and more importantly, typographical errors may confound the query since Oracle does not verify that the same literal value is entered each time substitution variables with the same name are used. In this example, the logical assumption is that the contents of the variables substituted should be the same, but the fact that the variables have the same name has no meaning to the Oracle server and it makes no such assumption. The first example in Figure 3-21 shows the results of running the preceding query and submitting two distinct values for the SEARCH substitution variable. In this particular example, the results are incorrect since the requirement was to retrieve FIRST_NAME and LAST_NAME pairs that contained the identical string of characters.

In situations when a substitution variable is referenced multiple times in the same query and your intention is that the variable must have the same value at each occurrence in the statement, it is preferable to make use of *double ampersand*

FIGURE 3-21	

Double ampersand substitution

```
                                    SQL Plus                        –  □  ×

SQL> SELECT first_name, last_name
  2  FROM employees
  3  WHERE last_name LIKE '%&SEARCH%'
  4  AND first_name LIKE '%&SEARCH%';
Enter value for search: K
old   3: WHERE last_name LIKE '%&SEARCH%'
new   3: WHERE last_name LIKE '%K%'
Enter value for search: S
old   4: AND first_name LIKE '%&SEARCH%'
new   4: AND first_name LIKE '%S%'

FIRST_NAME           LAST_NAME
-------------------- -------------------------
Steven               King
Sundita              Kumar

SQL> SELECT first_name, last_name
  2  FROM employees
  3  WHERE last_name LIKE '%&&SEARCH%'
  4  AND first_name LIKE '%&SEARCH%';
Enter value for search: G
old   3: WHERE last_name LIKE '%&&SEARCH%'
new   3: WHERE last_name LIKE '%G%'
old   4: AND first_name LIKE '%&SEARCH%'
new   4: AND first_name LIKE '%G%'

FIRST_NAME           LAST_NAME
-------------------- -------------------------
Girard               Geoni

SQL>
```

substitution. This involves prefixing the first occurrence of the substitution variable that occurs multiple times in a query, with two ampersand symbols instead of one. When the Oracle server encounters a *double ampersand substitution* variable, a session value is defined for that variable and you are not prompted to enter a value to be substituted for this variable in subsequent references.

The second example in Figure 3-21 demonstrates how the SEARCH variable is preceded by two ampersands in the condition with the FIRST_NAME column and thereafter is prefixed by one ampersand in the condition with the LAST_NAME column. When executed, you are prompted to enter a value to be substituted for the SEARCH variable only once for the condition with the FIRST_NAME column. This value is then automatically resolved from the session value of the variable in subsequent references to it, as in the condition with the LAST_NAME column. To undefine the SEARCH variable, you need to use the *UNDEFINE* command described later in this chapter.

on the
job

Whether you work as a developer, database administrator, or business end user, all SQL queries you encounter may be broadly classified as either ad hoc or repeated queries. Ad hoc queries are usually one-off statements written during some data investigation exercise that are unlikely to be reused. The repeated queries are those that are run frequently or periodically, which are usually saved as script files and run with little to no modification whenever required. Reuse prevents costly redevelopment time and allows these consistent queries to potentially benefit from Oracle's native automatic tuning features geared toward improving query performance.

Substituting Column Names

Literal elements of the WHERE clause have been the focus of the discussion on substitution thus far, but virtually any element of a SQL statement is a candidate for substitution. In the following statement, the FIRST_NAME and JOB_ID columns are static and will always be retrieved, but the third column selected is variable and specified as a substitution variable named COL. The result set is further sorted by this variable column in the ORDER BY clause:

```
SELECT first_name, job_id, &&col
FROM employees
WHERE job_id IN ('MK_MAN','SA_MAN')
ORDER BY &col;
```

As Figure 3-22 demonstrates, at runtime, you are prompted to provide a value for the double ampersand variable called COL. You could, for example, enter the

FIGURE 3-22

Substituting
column names

column named SALARY and submit your input. The statement that executes performs the substitution and retrieves the FIRST_NAME, JOB_ID, and SALARY columns from the EMPLOYEES table sorted by SALARY.

Unlike character and date literals, column name references do not require single quotes both when explicitly specified and when substituted via ampersand substitution.

Substituting Expressions and Text

Almost any element of a SQL statement may be substituted at runtime. The constraint is that Oracle requires at least the first word to be static. In the case of the SELECT statement, at the very minimum, the SELECT keyword is required and the remainder of the statement may be substituted as follows:

```
SELECT &rest_of_statement;
```

When executed, you are prompted to submit a value for the variable called REST_OF_STATEMENT, which could be any legitimate query, such as DEPARTMENT_NAME from DEPARMENTS. If you submit this text as input for the variable, the query that is run will be resolved to the following statement:

```
SELECT department_name FROM departments;
```

Consider the general form of the SQL statement rewritten using ampersand substitution, as shown next:

```
SELECT &SELECT_CLAUSE
FROM &FROM_CLAUSE
WHERE &WHERE_CLAUSE
ORDER BY &ORDER_BY_CLAUSE;
```

The usefulness of this statement is arguable, but it does illustrate the concept of substitution effectively. As Figure 3-23 shows, the preceding statement allows any query discussed so far to be submitted at runtime. The first execution queries

FIGURE 3-23

Substituting expressions and text

```
                                    SQL Plus                          _  □  ×
SQL> SELECT &SELECT_CLAUSE
  2    FROM &FROM_CLAUSE
  3    WHERE &WHERE_CLAUSE
  4    ORDER BY &ORDER_BY_CLAUSE;
Enter value for select_clause: *
old   1: SELECT &SELECT_CLAUSE
new   1: SELECT *
Enter value for from_clause: regions
old   2: FROM &FROM_CLAUSE
new   2: FROM regions
Enter value for where_clause: region_id=2
old   3: WHERE &WHERE_CLAUSE
new   3: WHERE region_id=2
Enter value for order_by_clause: region_name
old   4: ORDER BY &ORDER_BY_CLAUSE
new   4: ORDER BY region_name

 REGION_ID REGION_NAME
---------- ------------------------
         2 Americas

SQL> SELECT &SELECT_CLAUSE
  2    FROM &FROM_CLAUSE
  3    WHERE &WHERE_CLAUSE
  4    ORDER BY &ORDER_BY_CLAUSE;
Enter value for select_clause: *
old   1: SELECT &SELECT_CLAUSE
new   1: SELECT *
Enter value for from_clause: countries
old   2: FROM &FROM_CLAUSE
new   2: FROM countries
Enter value for where_clause: region_id=2
old   3: WHERE &WHERE_CLAUSE
new   3: WHERE region_id=2
Enter value for order_by_clause: country_name
old   4: ORDER BY &ORDER_BY_CLAUSE
new   4: ORDER BY country_name

CO COUNTRY_NAME                               REGION_ID
-- ---------------------------------------- ----------
AR Argentina                                        2
BR Brazil                                           2
CA Canada                                           2
MX Mexico                                           2
US United States of America                         2

SQL>
```

the REGIONS table, while the second execution queries the COUNTRIES table. Useful candidates for ampersand substitution are statements that are run multiple times and differ slightly from each other.

Define and Verify

Double ampersand substitution is used to avoid repetitive input when the same variable occurs multiple times in a statement. When a double ampersand substitution occurs, the variable is stored as a session variable. As the statement executes, all further occurrences of the variable are automatically resolved using the stored session variable. Any subsequent executions of the statement within the same session automatically resolve the substitution variables from stored session values. This is not always desirable and indeed limits the usefulness of substitution variables. Oracle does, however, provide a mechanism to *UNDEFINE* these session variables.

INSIDE THE EXAM

There are three certification objectives in this chapter. Limiting the rows retrieved by a query introduced the WHERE clause, which practically demonstrates the concept of selection. The conditions that limit the rows returned are based on comparisons using the BETWEEN, IN, LIKE, Equality, and Inequality operators. Your thorough understanding of these comparison operators and their behavior with character, numeric, and date data types will be examined, along with how they are different from the Boolean NOT, AND, and OR operators.

Using the ORDER BY clause to sort results retrieved is optional and extremely useful. Exam questions that test the concepts of traditional, positional, and composite sorting, along with how NULL values can be handled, are common. When multiple sort

terms are present in the ORDER BY clause, it is acceptable to specify ascending sort orders for some and descending sort orders for others. It is a common mistake to forget that Oracle provides this mixed sorting feature as well for the specification of the NULLS FIRST | LAST modifier.

Your understanding of substitution using single and double ampersands as well as the DEFINE and UNDEFINE commands will be tested. You may be given a statement that includes a double ampersand substitution variable that is subsequently referenced multiple times in the statement, along with a single ampersand substitution variable; you will be expected to understand the differences in their behavior. Your understanding of column name, expression, and text substitution will also be measured.

The *VERIFY* command is specific to SQL*Plus and controls whether or not substituted elements are echoed on the user's screen prior to executing a SQL statement that uses substitution variables. These commands are discussed in the next sections.

The DEFINE and UNDEFINE Commands

Session level variables are implicitly created when they are initially referenced in SQL statements using double ampersand substitution. They persist or remain available for the duration of the session or until they are explicitly undefined. A session ends when the user exits their client tool like SQL*Plus or when the user process is terminated abnormally.

The problem with persistent session variables is they tend to detract from the generic nature of statements that use ampersand substitution variables. Fortunately, these session variables can be removed with the UNDEFINE command. Within a script or at the command line of SQL*Plus or SQL Developer, the syntax for undefining session variables is as follows:

UNDEFINE *variable*;

Consider a simple generic example that selects a static and variable column from the EMPLOYEES table and sorts the output based on the variable column. The static column could be the LAST_NAME column.

```
SELECT last_name, &&COLNAME
FROM employees
WHERE department_id=30
ORDER BY &COLNAME;
```

The first time this statement executes, you are prompted to input a value for the variable called COLNAME, and SALARY is input. This value is substituted and the statement executes. A subsequent execution of this statement within the same session does not prompt for any COLNAME value since it is already defined as SALARY in the context of this session and can only be undefined with the UNDEFINE COLNAME command, as shown in Figure 3-24. Once the variable has been undefined, the next execution of the statement prompts the user for a value for the COLNAME variable and FIRST_NAME is substituted, changing the query.

The DEFINE command serves two purposes. It can be used to retrieve a list of all the variables currently defined in your SQL session; it can also be used to explicitly define a value for a variable referenced as a substitution variable by one or more

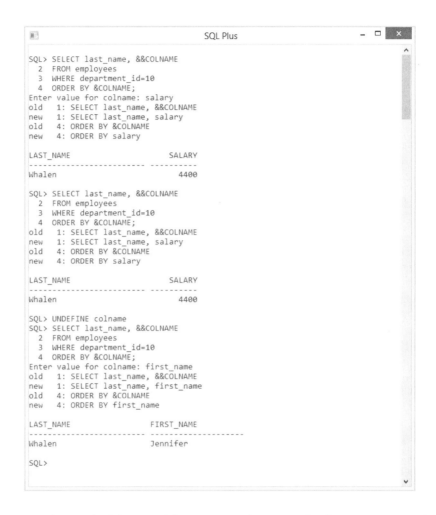

FIGURE 3-24

The UNDEFINE command

statements during the lifetime of that session. The syntax for the two variants of the DEFINE command are as follows:

DEFINE;
DEFINE *variable=value*;

As Figure 3-25 demonstrates, a variable called EMPNAME is defined explicitly to have the value 'King'. The stand-alone DEFINE command in SQL*Plus then returns a number of session variables prefixed with an underscore character as well as other familiar variables, including EMPNAME and double ampersand substitution variables implicitly defined earlier. Two different but simplistic query examples are

FIGURE 3-25

The DEFINE
command

```
                                  SQL Plus                           –  □  ×

SQL> DEFINE EMPNAME=King
SQL> DEFINE
DEFINE _DATE            = "04-AUG-13" (CHAR)
DEFINE _CONNECT_IDENTIFIER = "coda" (CHAR)
DEFINE _USER            = "HR" (CHAR)
DEFINE _PRIVILEGE       = "" (CHAR)
DEFINE _SQLPLUS_RELEASE = "1201000002" (CHAR)
DEFINE _EDITOR          = "Notepad" (CHAR)
DEFINE _O_VERSION       = "Oracle Database 12c Enterprise Edition Release 12.1.0.
0.2 - 64bit Beta
With the Partitioning, OLAP, Advanced Analytics and Real Application Testing opt
ions" (CHAR)
DEFINE _O_RELEASE       = "1201000002" (CHAR)
DEFINE _RC              = "0" (CHAR)
DEFINE SEARCH           = "G" (CHAR)
DEFINE COL              = "salary" (CHAR)
DEFINE COLNAME          = "first_name" (CHAR)
DEFINE EMPNAME          = "King" (CHAR)
SQL> SELECT last_name, salary
  2  FROM employees
  3  WHERE last_name='&EMPNAME';
old   3: WHERE last_name='&EMPNAME'
new   3: WHERE last_name='King'

LAST_NAME                    SALARY
------------------------ ----------
King                          10000
King                          24000

SQL> SELECT 'The EMPNAME variable is defined as:'||'&EMPNAME'
  2  FROM dual;
old   1: SELECT 'The EMPNAME variable is defined as:'||'&EMPNAME'
new   1: SELECT 'The EMPNAME variable is defined as:'||'King'

'THEEMPNAMEVARIABLEISDEFINEDAS:'||'KING
---------------------------------------
The EMPNAME variable is defined as:King

SQL> undefine EMPNAME
SQL>
```

executed, and the explicitly defined substitution variable EMPNAME is referenced
by both queries. Finally, the variable is UNDEFINED.

The capacity of the SQL client tool to support session-persistent variables may
be switched off and on as required using the *SET* command. The SET command is
not a SQL language command, but rather a SQL environment control command. By
specifying SET DEFINE OFF, the client tool (for example, SQL*Plus) does not save
session variables or attach special meaning to the ampersand symbol. This allows

the ampersand symbol to be used as an ordinary literal character if necessary. The SET DEFINE ON | OFF command therefore determines whether or not ampersand substitution is available in your session.

The following example uses the ampersand symbol as a literal value. When executed, you are prompted to submit a value for bind variable SID.

```
SELECT 'Coda & Sid' FROM dual;
```

By turning off the ampersand substitution functionality as follows, this query may be executed without prompts:

```
SET DEFINE OFF
SELECT 'Coda & Sid' FROM dual;
SET DEFINE ON
```

Once the statement executes, the SET DEFINE ON command may be used to switch the substitution functionality back on. If DEFINE is SET OFF and the context that an ampersand is used in a statement cannot be resolved literally, Oracle returns an error.

SCENARIO & SOLUTION

The SELECT list of a query contains a single column. Is it possible to sort the results retrieved by this query by another column?	Yes. Unless positional sorting is used, the ORDER BY clause is independent of the SELECT clause in a statement.
Ampersand substitution variables support reusability of repetitively executed SQL statements. If a substituted value is to be used multiple times at different parts of the same statement, is it possible to be prompted to submit a substitution value just once and for that value to automatically be substituted during subsequent references to the same variable?	Yes. The two methods that may be used are double ampersand substitution or the DEFINE command. Both methods result in the user providing input for a specific substitution variable once. This value remains bound to the variable for the duration of the session unless it is explicitly UNDEFINED.

You have been tasked to retrieve the LAST_NAME and DEPARTMENT_ID values for all rows in the EMPLOYEES table. The output must be sorted by the nullable DEPARTMENT_ID column, and all rows with NULL DEPARTMENT_ID values must be listed last. Is it possible to provide the results as requested?	Yes. The ORDER BY clause provides for sorting by columns that potentially contain NULL values by permitting the modifiers NULLS FIRST or NULLS LAST to be specified. The following query locates the required rows:
	`SELECT last_name, department_id FROM employees`
	`ORDER BY department_id NULLS LAST;`

The VERIFY Command

As discussed earlier, two categories of commands are available when dealing with the Oracle server: SQL language commands and the SQL client control commands. The SELECT statement is an example of a language command, while the SET command controls the SQL client environment. There are many different language and control commands available, but the control commands pertinent to substitution are DEFINE and *VERIFY*.

The VERIFY command controls whether the substitution variable submitted is displayed onscreen so you can *verify* that the correct substitution has occurred. A message is displayed showing the *old* clause followed by the *new* clause containing the substituted value. The VERIFY command is switched ON and OFF with the command SET VERIFY ON | OFF. As Figure 3-26 shows, VERIFY is first switched OFF, a query that uses ampersand substitution is executed, and you are prompted to input a value. The value is then substituted, the statement runs, and its results are displayed.

VERIFY is then switched ON, the same query is executed, and you are prompted to input a value. Once the value is input and before the statement commences execution, Oracle displays the clause containing the reference to the substitution variable as the *old* clause with its line number and, immediately below this, the *new* clause displays the statement containing the substituted value.

FIGURE 3-26

The VERIFY command

```
SQL> SET VERIFY OFF
SQL> SELECT last_name, salary
  2  FROM employees
  3  WHERE last_name='&EMPNAME';
Enter value for empname: King

LAST_NAME                      SALARY
------------------------- ----------
King                            10000
King                            24000

SQL> SET VERIFY ON
SQL> SELECT last_name, salary
  2  FROM employees
  3  WHERE last_name='&EMPNAME';
Enter value for empname: King
old   3: WHERE last_name='&EMPNAME'
new   3: WHERE last_name='King'

LAST_NAME                      SALARY
------------------------- ----------
King                            10000
King                            24000

SQL>
```

Using Ampersand Substitution

A common calculation performed by the Human Resources department relates to the calculation of taxes levied upon an employee. Although this is done for all employees, there are always a few staff members who dispute the tax deducted from their income. The tax deducted per employee is calculated by obtaining the annual salary for the employee and multiplying this by the current tax rate, which may vary from year to year. You are required to write a reusable query using the current tax rate and the EMPLOYEE_ID number as inputs and return the EMPLOYEE_ID, FIRST_NAME, SALARY, ANNUAL SALARY (SALARY * 12), TAX_RATE, and TAX (TAX_RATE * ANNUAL SALARY) information.

1. Start SQL*Plus and connect to the HR schema.

2. The SELECT list must include the four specified columns as well as two expressions. The first expression aliased as ANNUAL SALARY is a simple calculation, while the second expression aliased as TAX depends on the TAX_RATE. Since the TAX RATE may vary, this value must be substituted at runtime.

3. The SELECT clause is

```
SELECT &&EMPLOYEE_ID EMPLOYEE_ID, FIRST_NAME, SALARY, SALARY
* 12 AS "ANNUAL SALARY", &&TAX_RATE "TAX RATE", (&TAX_RATE *
(SALARY * 12)) AS TAX
```

4. The double ampersand preceding EMPLOYEE_ID and TAX_RATE in the SELECT clause stipulates to Oracle that when the statement is executed the user must be prompted to submit a value for each substitution variable that will be used wherever they are subsequently referenced as &EMPLOYEE_ID and &TAX_RATE, respectively.

5. The FROM clause is

```
FROM EMPLOYEES
```

6. The WHERE clause must allow only the row whose EMPLOYEE_ID value is specified at runtime.

7. The WHERE clause is

```
WHERE EMPLOYEE_ID = &EMPLOYEE_ID
```

8. Executing this statement returns the set of results shown in the following illustration.

```
                                   SQL Plus                          _  □  ×
SQL> SELECT &&EMPLOYEE_ID employee_id, first_name, salary,
  2          salary * 12 as "ANNUAL SALARY",
  3          &&TAX_RATE "TAX RATE", (&TAX_RATE * (salary * 12)) as TAX
  4   FROM employees
  5   WHERE employee_id = &EMPLOYEE_ID;
Enter value for employee_id: 101
old    1: SELECT &&EMPLOYEE_ID employee_id, first_name, salary,
new    1: SELECT 101 employee_id, first_name, salary,
Enter value for tax_rate: 0.1
old    3:          &&TAX_RATE "TAX RATE", (&TAX_RATE * (salary * 12)) as TAX
new    3:          0.1 "TAX RATE", (0.1 * (salary * 12)) as TAX
old    5: WHERE employee_id = &EMPLOYEE_ID
new    5: WHERE employee_id = 101

EMPLOYEE_ID FIRST_NAME               SALARY ANNUAL SALARY   TAX RATE        TAX
----------- -------------------- ---------- ------------- ---------- ----------
        101 Neena                     17000        204000         .1      20400

SQL>
```

CERTIFICATION SUMMARY

The *WHERE* clause provides the language that enables *selection* in SELECT statements. The criteria for including or excluding rows take the form of conditions. Using comparison operators, two terms are compared with each other and the condition is evaluated as being true or false for each row. These terms may be column values, literals, or expressions. If the Boolean sum of the results of each condition evaluates to true for a particular row, then that row is retrieved. Conditional operators allow terms to be compared to each other in a variety of ways, including equality, inequality, range based, set membership, and character pattern matching comparison.

Once a set of data is isolated by your query, the *ORDER BY* clause facilitates sorting the retrieved rows based on numeric, date, or character columns or expressions. Results may be sorted using combinations of columns or expressions, or both. Data is sorted in ascending order by default.

Generic, reusable statements may be constructed using ampersand substitution variables which prompt for runtime values during execution. Session-persistent substitution variables may be defined and are extremely convenient in situations where many substitutions of the same variable occur in a statement or script.

The simple SELECT statement has been expanded to include a WHERE and ORDER BY clause. These basic building blocks offer a practical and useful language that can be applied while you build your knowledge of SQL.

TWO-MINUTE DRILL

Limit the Rows Retrieved by a Query

❑ The WHERE clause extends the SELECT statement by providing the language that enables selection.

❑ One or more conditions constitute a WHERE clause. These conditions specify rules to which the data in a row must conform to be eligible for selection.

❑ For each row tested in a condition, there are terms on the left and right of a comparison operator. Terms in a condition can be column values, literals, or expressions.

❑ Comparison operators may test two terms in many ways. Equality or inequality tests are very common, but range, set, and pattern comparisons are also available.

❑ Range comparison is performed using the BETWEEN operator, which tests whether a term falls between (and including) given start and end boundary values.

❑ Set membership is tested using the IN operator. A condition based on a set comparison evaluates to true if the left-side term is listed in the parenthesized (single-quoted if nonnumeric), comma-delimited (if more than one value) set on the right side.

❑ The LIKE operator enables literal character patterns to be matched with other literals, column values, or evaluated expressions. The percentage symbol (%) behaves as a wildcard that matches zero or more characters. The underscore symbol (_) behaves as a single character wildcard that matches exactly one other character.

❑ Boolean operators include the AND, OR, and NOT operators. The AND and OR operators enable multiple conditional clauses to be specified. These are sometimes referred to as multiple WHERE clauses.

❑ The NOT operator negates the comparison operator involved in a condition.

Sort the Rows Retrieved by a Query

❑ Results are sorted using the ORDER BY clause. Rows retrieved may be ordered according to one or more columns by specifying either the column names or their numeric position in the SELECT clause.

❑ The sorted output may be arranged in descending or ascending order using the DESC or ASC modifiers after the sort terms in the ORDER BY clause.

Ampersand Substitution

❑ Ampersand substitution facilitates SQL statement reuse by providing a means to substitute elements of a statement at runtime. The same SQL statement may therefore be run multiple times with different input parameters.

❑ Single ampersand substitution requires user input for every occurrence of the substitution variable in the statement. Double ampersand substitution requires user input only once per occurrence of a substitution variable, since it defines a session-persistent variable with the given input value.

❑ Session-persistent variables may be set explicitly using the DEFINE command. The UNDEFINE command may be used to unset both implicitly (double ampersand substitution) and explicitly defined session variables.

❑ The VERIFY environmental setting controls whether SQL*Plus displays the old and new versions of statement lines that contain substitution variables.

SELF TEST

The following questions will help you measure your understanding of the material presented in this chapter. Read all the choices carefully because there may be more than one correct answer. Choose all the correct answers for each question.

Limit the Rows Retrieved by a Query

1. Which two clauses of the SELECT statement facilitate selection and projection?
   A. SELECT, FROM
   B. ORDER BY, WHERE
   C. SELECT, WHERE
   D. SELECT, ORDER BY

2. Choose the query that extracts the LAST_NAME, JOB_ID, and SALARY values from the EMPLOYEES table for records having JOB_ID values of either SA_REP or MK_MAN and having SALARY values in the range of $1,000 to $4,000. The SELECT and FROM clauses are SELECT LAST_NAME, JOB_ID, SALARY FROM EMPLOYEES:
   A. WHERE JOB_ID IN ('SA_REP','MK_MAN')
      AND SALARY > 1000 AND SALARY < 4000;
   B. WHERE JOB_ID IN ('SA_REP','MK_MAN')
      AND SALARY BETWEEN 1000 AND 4000;
   C. WHERE JOB_ID LIKE 'SA_REP%' AND 'MK_MAN%'
      AND SALARY > 1000 AND SALARY < 4000;
   D. WHERE JOB_ID = 'SA_REP'
      AND SALARY BETWEEN 1000 AND 4000
      OR JOB_ID='MK_MAN';

3. Which of the following WHERE clauses contains an error? The SELECT and FROM clauses are SELECT * FROM EMPLOYEES:
   A. WHERE HIRE_DATE IN ('02-JUN-2004');
   B. WHERE SALARY IN ('1000','4000','2000');
   C. WHERE JOB_ID IN (SA_REP,MK_MAN);
   D. WHERE COMMISSION_PCT BETWEEN 0.1 AND 0.5;

4. Choose the WHERE clause that extracts the DEPARTMENT_NAME values containing the character literal "er" from the DEPARTMENTS table. The SELECT and FROM clauses are SELECT DEPARTMENT_NAME FROM DEPARTMENTS:
   A. WHERE DEPARTMENT_NAME IN ('%e%r');
   B. WHERE DEPARTMENT_NAME LIKE '%er%';

   C. WHERE DEPARTMENT_NAME BETWEEN 'e' AND 'r';

   D. WHERE DEPARTMENT_NAME CONTAINS 'e%r';

5. Which two of the following conditions are equivalent to each other?

   A. WHERE COMMISSION_PCT IS NULL

   B. WHERE COMMISSION_PCT = NULL

   C. WHERE COMMISSION_PCT IN (NULL)

   D. WHERE NOT(COMMISSION_PCT IS NOT NULL)

6. Which two of the following conditions are equivalent to each other?

   A. WHERE SALARY <=5000 AND SALARY >=2000

   B. WHERE SALARY IN (2000,3000,4000,5000)

   C. WHERE SALARY BETWEEN 2000 AND 5000

   D. WHERE SALARY > 2000 AND SALARY < 5000

   E. WHERE SALARY >=2000 AND <=5000

Sort the Rows Retrieved by a Query

7. Choose one false statement about the ORDER BY clause.

   A. When using the ORDER BY clause, it always appears as the last clause in a SELECT statement.

   B. The ORDER BY clause may appear in a SELECT statement that does not contain a WHERE clause.

   C. The ORDER BY clause specifies one or more terms by which the retrieved rows are sorted. These terms can only be column names.

   D. Positional sorting is accomplished by specifying the numeric position of a column as it appears in the SELECT list, in the ORDER BY clause.

8. The following query retrieves the LAST_NAME, SALARY, and COMMISSION_PCT values for employees whose LAST_NAME begins with the letter "R". Based on the following query, choose the ORDER BY clause that first sorts the results by the COMMISSION_PCT column, listing highest commission earners first, and then sorts the results in ascending order by the SALARY column. Any records with NULL COMMISSION_PCT must appear last:

SELECT LAST_NAME, SALARY, COMMISSION_PCT

FROM EMPLOYEES

WHERE LAST_NAME LIKE 'R%'

   A. ORDER BY COMMISSION_PCT DESC, 2;

   B. ORDER BY 3 DESC, 2 ASC NULLS LAST;

   C. ORDER BY 3 DESC NULLS LAST, 2 ASC;

   D. ORDER BY COMMISSION_PCT DESC, SALARY ASC;

Ampersand Substitution

9. The DEFINE command explicitly declares a session-persistent substitution variable with a specific value. How is this variable referenced in an SQL statement? Consider an expression that calculates tax on an employee's SALARY based on the current tax rate. For the following session-persistent substitution variable, which statement correctly references the TAX_RATE variable?

   DEFINE TAX_RATE=0.14

   A. SELECT SALARY * :TAX_RATE TAX FROM EMPLOYEES;
   B. SELECT SALARY * &TAX_RATE TAX FROM EMPLOYEES;
   C. SELECT SALARY * :&&TAX TAX FROM EMPLOYEES;
   D. SELECT SALARY * TAX_RATE TAX FROM EMPLOYEES;

10. When using ampersand substitution variables in the following query, how many times will you be prompted to input a value for the variable called JOB the first time this query is executed?

    SELECT FIRST_NAME, '&JOB'
    FROM EMPLOYEES
    WHERE JOB_ID LIKE '%'||&JOB||'%'
    AND '&&JOB' BETWEEN 'A' AND 'Z';

    A. 0
    B. 1
    C. 2
    D. 3

LAB QUESTION

Using SQL Developer or SQL*Plus, connect to the OE schema and complete the following tasks.

A customer requires a hard disk drive and a graphics card for her personal computer. She is willing to spend between $500 and $800 on the disk drive but is unsure about the cost of a graphics card. Her only requirement is that the resolution supported by the graphics card should be either 1024×768 or 1280×1024. As the sales representative, you have been tasked to write one query that searches the PRODUCT_INFORMATION table where the PRODUCT_NAME value begins with HD (hard disk) or GP (graphics processor) and their list prices. Remember the hard disk list prices must be between $500 and $800 and the graphics processors need to support either 1024×768 or 1280×1024. Sort the results in descending LIST_PRICE order.

SELF TEST ANSWERS

Limit the Rows Retrieved by a Query

1. ☑ **C.** The SELECT clause facilitates projection by specifying the list of columns to be projected from a table, while the WHERE clause facilitates selection by limiting the rows retrieved based on its conditions.

☒ **A, B,** and **D** are incorrect. The FROM clause specifies the source of the rows being projected and the ORDER BY clause is used for sorting the selected rows.

2. ☑ **B.** The IN operator efficiently tests whether the JOB_ID for a particular row is either SA_REP or MK_MAN, while the BETWEEN operator efficiently measures whether an employee's SALARY value falls within the required range.

☒ **A, C,** and **D** are incorrect. **A** and **C** exclude employees who earn a salary of $1,000 or $4,000, since these SALARY values are excluded by the inequality operators. **C** also selects JOB_ID values like SA_REP% and MK_MAN%, potentially selecting incorrect JOB_ID values. **D** is half right. The first half returns the rows with JOB_ID equal to SA_REP having SALARY values between $1,000 and $4,000. However, the second part (the OR clause), correctly tests for JOB_ID equal to MK_MAN but ignores the SALARY condition.

3. ☑ **C.** The character literals being compared to the JOB_ID column by the IN operator must be enclosed by single quotation marks.

☒ **A, B,** and **D** are syntactically correct. Notice that **B** does not require quotes around the numeric literals. Having them, however, does not cause an error.

4. ☑ **B.** The LIKE operator tests the DEPARTMENT_NAME column of each row for values that contain the characters `"er"`. The percentage symbols before and after the character literal indicate that any characters enclosing the `"er"` literal are permissible.

☒ **A** and **C** are syntactically correct. **A** uses the IN operator, which is used to test set membership. **C** tests whether the alphabetic value of the DEPARTMENT_NAME column is between the letter `"e"` and the letter `"r"`. Finally, **D** uses the word `"contains"`, which cannot be used in this context.

5. ☑ **A** and **D.** The IS NULL operator correctly evaluates the COMMISSION_PCT column for NULL values. **D** uses the NOT operator to negate the already negative version of the IS NULL operator, IS NOT NULL. Two negatives return a positive, and therefore **A** and **D** are equivalent.

☒ **B** and **C** are incorrect. NULL values cannot be tested by the equality operator or the IN operator.

6. ☑ **A** and **C.** Each of these conditions tests for SALARY values in the range of $2,000 to $5,000.

   ☒ **B, D,** and **E** are incorrect. **B** excludes values like $2,500 from its set, **D** excludes the boundary values of $2,000 and $5,000, and **E** is illegal since it is missing the SALARY column name reference after the AND operator.

Sort the Rows Retrieved by a Query

7. ☑ **C.** The terms specified in an ORDER BY clause can include column names, positional sorting, numeric values, and expressions.

   ☒ **A, B,** and **D** are true.

8. ☑ **C.** Positional sorting is performed, and the third term in the SELECT list, COMMISSION_ PCT, is sorted first in descending order, and any NULL COMMISSION_PCT values are listed last. The second term in the SELECT list, SALARY, is sorted next in ascending order.

   ☒ **A, B,** and **D** are incorrect. **A** does not specify what to do with NULL COMMISSION_PCT values, and the default behavior during a descending sort is to list NULLS FIRST. **B** applies the NULLS LAST modifier to the SALARY column instead of the COMMISSION_PCT column, and **D** ignores NULLS completely.

Ampersand Substitution

9. ☑ **B.** A session-persistent substitution variable may be referenced using an ampersand symbol from within any SQL statement executed in that session.

   ☒ **A, C,** and **D** are incorrect. **A** and **D** attempt to reference the substitution variable using a colon prefix to its name and the variable name on its own. These are invalid references to substitution variables in SQL. **C** references a variable called TAX and not the variable TAX_RATE.

10. ☑ **D.** The first time this statement is executed, two single ampersand substitution variables are encountered before the third double ampersand substitution variable. If the first reference on line one of the query contained a double ampersand substitution, you would only be prompted to input a value once.

   ☒ **A, B,** and **C** are incorrect since you are prompted thrice to input a value for the JOB substitution variable. In subsequent executions of this statement in the same session, you will not be prompted to input a value for this variable.

LAB ANSWER

Using SQL Developer or SQL*Plus, connect to the OE schema and complete the following tasks.

You are required to query the PRODUCT_INFORMATION table in the OE schema for the PRODUCT_NAME and LIST_PRICE columns. The rows selected must conform to either of two conditions. The first condition is that the PRODUCT_NAME must begin with the characters 'HD' and their LIST_PRICE must fall in the range between $500 and $800. Alternately, the row can conform to the second condition that the PRODUCT_NAME must begin with the characters 'GP' and contain the characters '1024x768' or '1280x1024'. Finally, the results must be sorted in descending LIST_PRICE order.

1. Start SQL Developer and connect to the OE schema.

2. The SELECT clause is
   ```
   SELECT PRODUCT_NAME, LIST_PRICE
   ```

3. The FROM clause is
   ```
   FROM PRODUCT_INFORMATION
   ```

4. The first condition is
   ```
   PRODUCT_NAME LIKE 'HD%' AND LIST_PRICE BETWEEN 500 AND 800
   ```

5. The second conditions are:
   ```
   PRODUCT_NAME LIKE 'GP%1024x768%' or
   PRODUCT_NAME LIKE 'GP%1280x1024%'
   ```

6. Since either the first or second condition must be fulfilled by a row in order to be retrieved, these two conditions must be separated with the Boolean OR operator.

7. The WHERE clause is
   ```
   WHERE (PRODUCT_NAME LIKE 'HD%' AND LIST_PRICE BETWEEN 500 AND 800) OR
   (PRODUCT_NAME LIKE 'GP%1024x768%') OR (PRODUCT_NAME LIKE 'GP%1280x1024%')
   ```

8. The ORDER BY clause is
   ```
   ORDER BY LIST_PRICE DESC
   ```

9. Executing this statement returns the set of results matching this pattern as shown in the illustration:

4
Single-Row Functions

F unctions are a wonderful extension to SQL and provide a first glimpse of the procedural capabilities Oracle supports. Procedural languages allow a rich degree of programming that yields an almost unlimited range of data manipulation possibilities. Oracle server implements a proprietary procedural language called PL/SQL, or procedural SQL. A range of named programmatic objects may be constructed using PL/SQL. These include procedures, functions, and packages. Although writing PL/SQL is relatively straightforward, a thorough understanding of SQL is a prerequisite and the focus of this guide. The functions discussed in this chapter are confined to PL/SQL programs packaged and supplied by Oracle as built-in features.

CERTIFICATION OBJECTIVE 4.01

Describe Various Types of Functions Available in SQL

SQL functions are broadly divided into those that calculate and return a value for every row in a data set and those that return a single aggregated value for all rows. The following two areas are explored:

- Defining a function
- Types of functions

Defining a Function

A *function* is a program written to optionally accept input parameters, perform an operation, and return a single value. A function returns only one value per execution.

Three important components form the basis of defining a function. The first is the input parameter list. It specifies zero or more arguments that may be passed to a function as input for processing. These arguments or parameters may be of differing data types, and some may be mandatory while others may be optional. The second component is the data type of its resultant value. Upon execution, only one value of a predefined data type is returned by the function. The third encapsulates the details of the processing performed by the function and contains the program code that optionally manipulates the input parameters, performs calculations and operations, and generates a return value.

A function is often described as a *black box* that takes an input, performs a calculation, and returns a value as illustrated by the following equation. Instead of focusing on their implementation details, you are encouraged to concentrate on the features that built-in functions provide.

$F(x, y, z, …)$ = result;

Functions may be *nested* within other functions, such as $F1(x, y, F2(a, b), z)$, where F2, which takes two input parameters, a and b, and forms the third of four parameters submitted to F1. Functions can operate on any available data types, the most popular being character, date, and numeric data. These operands may be columns or expressions.

As an example, consider a function that calculates a person's age. The AGE function takes one date input parameter, which is the person's birthday. The result returned by the AGE function is a number representing a person's age. The black box calculation involves obtaining the difference in years between the current date and the birthday input parameter.

Operating on Character Data

Character data or strings are versatile since they facilitate the storage of almost any type of data. Functions that operate on character data are broadly classified as *case conversion* and *character manipulation* functions. The following string built-in functions are examined in detail later in this chapter, but a brief description is provided here.

LOWER, UPPER, and INITCAP are the case conversion functions that convert a given character column, literal, or expression into lowercase, uppercase, or initial case, respectively:

```
lower('SQL') = sql
upper('sql') = SQL
initcap('sql') = Sql
```

The character manipulation functions are exceptionally powerful and include the LENGTH, CONCAT, SUBSTR, INSTR, LPAD, RPAD, TRIM, and REPLACE functions.

The LENGTH(*string*) function uses a character string as an input parameter and returns a numeric value representing the number of characters present in that string:

```
length('A short string') = 14
```

The CONCAT(*string 1*, *string 2*) function takes two strings and concatenates or joins them in the same way that the concatenation operator || does:

```
concat('SQL is',' easy to learn.') = SQL is easy to learn.
```

The SUBSTR(*string*, *start position*, *number of characters*) function accepts three parameters and returns a string consisting of the number of characters extracted from the source string, beginning at the specified start position:

```
substr('http://www.domain.com',12,6) = domain
```

The INSTR(*source string*, *search item*, [*start position*],[*nth occurrence of search item*]) function returns a number that represents the position in the source string, beginning from the given start position, where the *nth* occurrence of the search item begins:

```
instr('http://www.domain.com','.',1,2) = 18
```

The LPAD(*string*, *length after padding*, *padding string*) and RPAD(*string*, *length after padding*, *padding string*) functions add a padding string of characters to the left or right of a string until it reaches the specified length after padding.

```
rpad('#PASSWORD#',11,'#') = #PASSWORD##
lpad('#PASSWORD#',11,'#') = ##PASSWORD#
```

The TRIM function literally trims off leading or trailing (or both) character strings from a given source string:

```
trim('#' from '#PASSWORD#') = PASSWORD
```

The REPLACE(*string*, *search item*, *replacement item*) function locates the search item in a given string and replaces it with the replacement item, returning a string with replaced values:

```
replace('#PASSWORD#','WORD','PORT') = #PASSPORT#
```

Operating on Numeric Data

Many numeric built-in functions are available. Some calculate square roots, perform exponentiation, and convert numbers into hexadecimal format. There are too many to mention, and many popular mathematical, statistical, and financial calculations have been exposed as built-in functions by Oracle.

Three common numeric functions, examined later in this chapter, are ROUND, TRUNC, and MOD. ROUND(*number, decimal precision*) facilitates rounding off a number to the lowest or highest value given a decimal precision format:

```
round(42.39,1) = 42.4
```

The TRUNC(*number, decimal precision*) function drops off or truncates the number given a decimal precision value:

```
trunc(42.39,1) = 42.3
```

The MOD(*dividend, divisor*) returns the remainder of a division operation:

```
mod(42,10) = 2
```

Operating on Date Information

Working with date values may be challenging. Performing date arithmetic that accommodates leap years and variable month lengths can be frustrating and error prone. Oracle addresses this challenge by providing native support for date arithmetic and several built-in date functions such as MONTHS_BETWEEN, ADD_MONTHS, LAST_DAY, NEXT_DAY, SYSDATE, ROUND, and TRUNC.

The MONTHS_BETWEEN(*date1, date2*) function returns the number of months between two dates, while the ADD_MONTHS(*date, number of months*) returns the date resulting from adding a specified number of months to a date:

```
months_between('01-FEB-2008','01-JAN-2008') = 1
add_months('01-JAN-2008',1) = 01-FEB-2008
```

The LAST_DAY(*date*) function returns the last day of the month that the specified date falls into, while the NEXT_DAY(*date, day of the week*) returns the date on which the next specified day of the week falls after the given date:

```
last_day('01-FEB-2008') = 29-FEB-2008
next_day('01-FEB-2008','Friday') = 08-FEB-2008
```

The SYSDATE function takes no parameters and returns a date value that represents the current server date and time. ROUND(*date, date precision format*) and TRUNC(*date, date precision format*) round and truncate a given date value to the nearest date precision format like day, month, or year:

```
sysdate = 17-DEC-2007
round(sysdate,'month') = 01-JAN-2008
trunc(sysdate,'month') = 01-DEC-2007
```

Single-row functions are used in almost every query issued by analysts, developers, and administrators. When searching for character data, the TRIM function is frequently used to eliminate extra spaces that occur in character fields. The case conversion functions are used to standardize the column data. This facilitates more accurate and efficient searching since the case in which character data is captured is often inconsistent.

Types of Functions

Two broad types of functions operating on single and multiple rows, respectively, are discussed next. This distinction is vital to understanding the larger context in which functions are used. Oracle continuously strives to ensure that its commercial interpretation of SQL conforms to international standards. This facilitates ease of systems and skills migration across vendors and suppliers of RDBMS software. Oracle's implementation of SQL is compliant with Core SQL:2011, a standard endorsed by both ISO (International Organization for Standardization) and ANSI (American National Standards Institute). SQL functions have been standardized, and Oracle has documented those that are fully or partially compliant to the SQL:2011 standard.

Single-Row Functions

There are several categories of *single-row* functions, including character, numeric, date, conversion, and general. The focus of this chapter is on the character, numeric, and date single-row functions. These are functions that operate on one row of a dataset at a time. If a query selects 10 rows, the function is executed 10 times, once per row, usually with the values from that row as input to the function.

As Figure 4-1 shows, two columns of the REGIONS table have been selected along with an expression using the LENGTH function with the REGION_NAME column.

The length of the REGION_NAME column is calculated for each row, proving that the function has executed four separate times, returning one result per row.

Single-row functions manipulate the data items in a row to extract and format them for display purposes. The input values to a single-row function can be user-specified constants or literals, column data, variables, or expressions optionally supplied by other nested single-row functions. The nesting of single-row functions is a commonly used technique. Functions can return a value with a different data type from its input parameters. As Figure 4-1 demonstrates, the LENGTH function accepts one character input parameter and returns a numeric output.

FIGURE 4-1

A single-row
function

Conversion functions like TO_CHAR, TO_NUMBER, and TO_DATE are discussed in Chapter 5. They change the data type of column data or expressions allowing other functions to operate on them. The *general* functions are also discussed in Chapter 5. They simplify working with NULL values and facilitate conditional logic within a SELECT statement. These include the NVL, NVL2, NULLIF, COALESCE, CASE, and DECODE functions.

Apart from their inclusion in the SELECT list of a SQL query, single-row functions may be used in the WHERE and ORDER BY clauses. Assume there is a requirement to list rows from the REGIONS table where the length of the REGION_NAME column data is at least five characters long. There is a further need for this list to be sorted in alphabetic order based on the value of the last character in the REGION_NAME column. The WHERE clause is shown here:

```
WHERE length(region_name) > 4
```

To obtain the last character in a string, the SUBSTR function is used with the REGION_NAME column as the source string. The length of the REGION_NAME is used as the start position (to obtain the position of the last character) producing the following ORDER BY clause:

```
ORDER BY substr(region_name, length(region_name),1)
```

FIGURE 4-2

Functions in
SELECT, WHERE,
and ORDER BY
clauses

As Figure 4-2 shows, only three of the four regions are returned, and the list
is sorted in alphabetic order based on the last character in the REGION_NAME
column for each row.

Multiple-Row Functions

As the name suggests, this category of functions operates on more than one row at a
time. Typical uses of *multiple-row* functions include calculating the sum or average of
the numeric column values or counting the total number of records in sets. These are
sometimes known as *aggregation* or *group* functions and are explored in Chapter 6.

exam

ⓦatch   *Single-row functions are
executed for each row in the selected
data set. This concept is implicitly tested
via practical examples in the exam.
Functions always return only one value of a
predetermined data type. They may accept
zero or more parameters of differing data
types. The single-row character functions*

*like LENGTH, SUBSTR, and INSTR are
frequently used together, and a thorough
understanding of these is required.
Remember that input parameters that can
be implicitly converted to the data types
required by functions are acceptable to
Oracle.*

CERTIFICATION OBJECTIVE 4.02

Use Character, Number, and Date Functions in SELECT Statements

This section conducts a detailed investigation of the single-row functions introduced earlier. A structured approach will be taken that includes function descriptions, syntax rules, parameter descriptions, and usage examples. The character case conversion functions are examined, followed by the character manipulation functions. Next, the numeric functions are examined, and the section concludes with a discussion of the date functions.

Using Character Case Conversion Functions

Character data may be saved in tables from numerous sources, including application interfaces and batch programs. It is not safe to assume that character data has been committed in a consistent manner. The character *case conversion* functions serve two important purposes. They may be used first, to modify the appearance of a character data item for display purposes and second, to render them consistent for comparison operations. It is simpler to search for a string using a consistent case format instead of testing every permutation of uppercase and lowercase characters that could match the string. It is important to remember that these functions do not alter the data stored in tables. They still form part of the read-only SQL query.

The character functions discussed next expect string parameters. These may be any string literal, character column value, or expression resulting in a character value. If it is a numeric or a date value, it is implicitly converted into a string.

The LOWER Function

The LOWER function converts a string of characters into their lowercase equivalents. It does not add extra characters or shorten the length of the initial string. Uppercase characters are converted into their lowercase equivalents. Numeric, punctuation, or special characters are ignored. The LOWER function can take only one parameter. Its syntax is:

LOWER(*s*),

The following queries illustrate the usage of this function:

```
Query 1: SELECT lower(100) FROM dual;
Query 2: SELECT lower(100+100) FROM dual;
Query 3: SELECT lower('The SUM '||'100 + 100'||' = 200') FROM dual;
```

Queries 1 and 2 return the strings "100" and "200", respectively. The parameter to the LOWER function in query 3 is a character expression and the string returned by the function is "the sum 100 + 100 = 200".

```
Query 4: SELECT lower(SYSDATE) FROM dual;
Query 5: SELECT lower(SYSDATE+2) FROM dual;
```

Assume that the current system date is: 17-DEC-2007. Queries 4 and 5 return the strings "17-dec-2007" and "19-dec-2007", respectively. The date expressions are evaluated and implicitly converted into character data before the LOWER function is executed.

As Figure 4-3 shows, the LOWER function is used in the WHERE clause to locate the records with the lowercase letters "u" and "r" adjacent to each other in the LAST_NAME field.

FIGURE 4-3	

The LOWER function

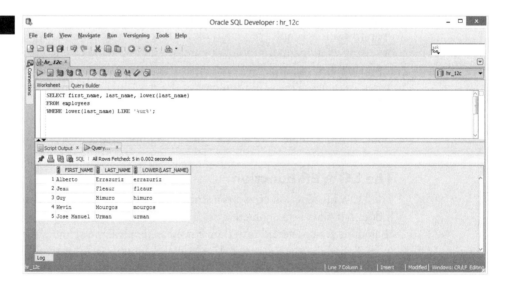

Consider writing an alternative query to return the same results without using the LOWER function in the WHERE clause. It could be done as follows:

```
SELECT first_name, last_name, lower(last_name)
FROM employees
WHERE last_name LIKE '%ur%'
OR last_name LIKE '%UR%'
OR last_name LIKE '%uR%'
OR last_name LIKE '%Ur%';
```

This query works but is cumbersome, and the number of OR clauses required increases exponentially as the length of the search string increases.

The UPPER Function

The UPPER function is the logical opposite of the LOWER function and converts a string of characters into their uppercase equivalents. It does not add extra characters or shorten the length of the initial string. All lowercase characters are converted into their uppercase equivalents. Numeric, punctuation, or special characters are ignored. The UPPER function takes only one parameter. Its syntax is:

UPPER(s),

The following queries illustrate the usage of this function:

```
Query 1: SELECT upper(1+2.14) FROM dual;
Query 2: SELECT upper(SYSDATE) FROM dual;
```

Query 1 returns the string "3.14". The parameter to the UPPER function in query 2 is SYSDATE, which returns the current system date. Since this value is returned in uppercase by default, no case conversion is performed.

The UPPER function is used in Figure 4-4 to extract the rows from the COUNTRIES table where the COUNTRY_NAME values contain the letters "U", "S", and "A" in that order. The letters "U," "S," and "A" do not have to be adjacent to each other.

Writing an alternative query to return the same results without using the UPPER or LOWER functions could be done using a query with eight conditions:

```
SELECT * FROM COUNTRIES
WHERE country_name LIKE '%u%s%a%' OR country_name LIKE '%u%s%A%'
OR country_name LIKE '%u%S%a%' OR country_name LIKE '%u%S%A%'
OR country_name LIKE '%U%s%a%' OR country_name LIKE '%U%s%A%'
OR country_name LIKE '%U%S%a%' OR country_name LIKE '%U%S%A%';
```

FIGURE 4-4

The UPPER function

The UPPER function

This query works but is cumbersome. The number of OR clauses required increases exponentially as the length of the search string increases.

The INITCAP Function

The INITCAP function converts a string of characters into capitalized case. It is often used for data presentation purposes. The first letters of each word in the string are converted to their uppercase equivalents, while the remaining letters of each word are converted to their lowercase equivalents. A word is usually a string of adjacent characters separated by a space or underscore, but other characters such as the percentage symbol, exclamation mark, or dollar sign are valid word separators. Punctuation or special characters are regarded as valid word separators. The INITCAP function can take only one parameter. Its syntax is:

INITCAP(s),

The following queries illustrate the usage of this function:

```
Query 1: SELECT initcap(21/7) FROM dual;
Query 2: SELECT initcap(SYSDATE) FROM dual;
Query 3: SELECT initcap('init cap or init_cap or init%cap') FROM dual;
```

Query 1 returns the quotient 3 as a string. Query 2 returns the character string value of the current system date, with the month portion changed from uppercase to initial case. Assuming that the current system date is 17-DEC-2007, query 2 therefore returns "17-Dec-2007". Query 3 returns "Init Cap Or Init_Cap Or Init%Cap".

The queries in Figure 4-5 select the LAST_NAME and JOB_ID values from the EMPLOYEES table for those employees with LAST_NAME values starting with the letter "H". The first query applies the INITCAP function to the entire SELECT clause. The second query shows how the INITCAP function is applied separately to each character component. Both queries yield identical results.

FIGURE 4-5

The INITCAP function

EXERCISE 4-1

Using the Case Conversion Functions

Retrieve a list of all FIRST_NAME and LAST_NAME values from the EMPLOYEES table where FIRST_NAME contains the character string "li".

1. Start SQL Developer and connect to the HR schema.

2. The SELECT clause is

```
SELECT FIRST_NAME, LAST_NAME
```

3. The FROM clause is

```
FROM EMPLOYEES
```

4. The WHERE clause must compare the FIRST_NAME column values with a pattern of characters containing all possible case combinations of the string "li". Therefore, if the FIRST_NAME contains the character strings "LI", "Li", "lI", or "li", that row must be retrieved.

5. The LIKE operator is used for character matching, and four combinations can be extracted with four WHERE clauses separated by the OR keyword. However, the case conversion functions can simplify the condition. If the LOWER function is used on the FIRST_NAME column, the comparison can be done with one WHERE clause condition. The UPPER or INITCAP functions could also be used.

6. The WHERE clause is

```
WHERE LOWER(FIRST_NAME) LIKE '%li%'
```

7. Executing this statement returns employees' names containing the characters "li" as shown in this illustration:

Using Character Manipulation Functions

Some of the most powerful features to emerge from Oracle are the *character manipulation* functions. Their usefulness in data manipulation is almost without peer, and many seasoned technical professionals whip together a quick script to massage data items with SQL *character manipulation* functions. Nesting these functions is common. The concatenation operator (||) is generally used instead of the CONCAT function. The LENGTH, INSTR, SUBSTR, and REPLACE functions often find themselves in each other's company as do RPAD, LPAD, and TRIM.

The CONCAT Function

The CONCAT function joins two character literals, columns, or expressions to yield one larger character expression. Numeric and date literals are implicitly cast as characters when they occur as parameters to the CONCAT function. Numeric or date expressions are evaluated before being converted to strings ready to be concatenated. The CONCAT function takes two parameters. Its syntax is:

CONCAT(*s1, s2*)

where *s1* and *s2* represent string literals, character column values, or expressions resulting in character values. The following queries illustrate the usage of this function:

```
Query 1: SELECT concat(1+2.14,' approximates pi') FROM dual;
Query 2: SELECT concat('Today is: ',SYSDATE) FROM dual;
```

Query 1 returns the string "3.14 approximates pi". The numeric expression is evaluated to return the number 3.14. This number is automatically changed into the character string "3.14", which is concatenated to the character literal in the second parameter. The second parameter to the CONCAT function in query 2 is SYSDATE, which returns the current system date. This value is implicitly converted to a string to which the literal in the first parameter is concatenated. If the system date is 17-DEC-2007, query 2 returns the string "Today is: 17-DEC-2007".

Consider using the CONCAT function to join three terms to return one character string. Since CONCAT takes only two parameters, it is only possible to join two terms with one instance of this function. The solution is to nest the CONCAT function within another CONCAT function, as shown here:

```
SELECT concat('Outer1 ', concat('Inner1',' Inner2'))
FROM dual;
```

The first CONCAT function has two parameters: the first is the literal "Outer1" while the second is a nested CONCAT function. The second CONCAT function takes two parameters: the first is the literal "Inner1" while the second is the literal "Inner2". This query results in the following string: "Outer1 Inner1 Inner2". Nested functions are described in detail in Chapter 5.

The CONCAT function was used in Figure 4-6 to extract the rows from the EMPLOYEES table where the DEPARTMENT_ID=100. The objective was to produce a single string literal output from the CONCAT function of the format FIRST_NAME LAST_NAME earns SALARY.

FIGURE 4-6

The CONCAT function

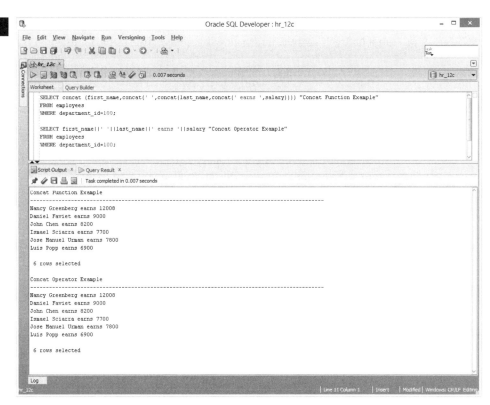

This simple task was transformed into a complex four-level-deep nested set of function calls. As the second example in Figure 4-6 demonstrates, the concatenation operator performs the equivalent task in a simpler manner.

The LENGTH Function

The LENGTH function returns the number of characters that constitute a character string. This includes character literals, columns, or expressions. Numeric and date literals are automatically cast as characters when they occur as parameters to the LENGTH function. Numeric or date expressions are evaluated before being converted to strings ready to be measured. Blank spaces, tabs, and special characters are all counted by the LENGTH function. The LENGTH function takes only one parameter. Its syntax is:

LENGTH(*s*),

where *s* represents any string literal, character column value, or expression resulting in a character value. The following queries illustrate the usage of this function:

```
Query 1: SELECT length(1+2.14||' approximates pi') FROM dual;
Query 2: SELECT length(SYSDATE) FROM dual;
```

Query 1 returns the number 20. The numeric expression is evaluated to return the number 3.14. This number is automatically cast as the character string "3.14" which is then concatenated to the character literal " approximates pi". The resultant character string contains 20 characters. Query 2 first evaluates the SYSDATE function, which returns the current system date. This value is automatically converted to a character string whose length is then determined. Assuming that the system date returned is "17-DEC-07", query 2 returns value 9.

The LENGTH function is used in Figure 4-7 to extract the COUNTRY_NAME value with length greater than 10 characters and the remaining columns from the COUNTRIES table.

The LPAD and RPAD Functions

The LPAD and RPAD functions, also known as left pad and right pad functions, return a string padded with a specified number of characters to the left or right of the source string, respectively. The character strings used for padding include character literals, column values, or expressions. Numeric and date literals are implicitly cast as characters

FIGURE 4-7

The LENGTH function

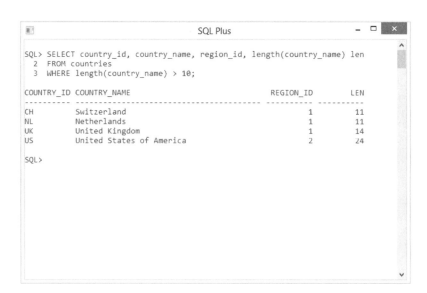

when they occur as parameters to the LPAD or RPAD functions. Numeric or date expressions are evaluated before being converted to strings destined for padding. Blank spaces, tabs, and special characters may be used as padding characters.

The LPAD and RPAD functions take three parameters. Their syntaxes are:

LPAD(*string, length,* [*padstring*]) and
RPAD(*string, length,* [*padstring*]),

where *string* represents the source string, *length* is an integer value that represents the final length of the string returned, and *padstring* specifies the character string to be used as padding. If LPAD (or RPAD) is used, the *padstring* is added to the left (or right) of the source *string* until it reaches the target *length*. Note that if the *length* parameter is smaller than or equal to the length of the source *string*, then no padding occurs and a substring of the source *string* having *length* number of characters is returned. If *padstring* is omitted, the character string used for padding defaults to a single blank space.

The following queries illustrate the usage of this function:

```
Query 1: SELECT lpad(1000+200.55,14,'*') FROM dual;
Query 2: SELECT rpad(1000+200.55,14,'*') FROM dual;
Query 3: SELECT lpad(SYSDATE,14,'$#') FROM dual;
Query 4: SELECT rpad(SYSDATE,4,'$#') FROM dual;
```

Query 1 returns a 14-character string: "*******1200.55". The numeric expression is evaluated to return the number 1200.55. This number is cast as the string "1200.55" of length seven (including the decimal point). To achieve the final length of 14 characters, 7 asterisks are left padded to the string. Query 2 returns the string "1200.55*******".

The LPAD function in query 3 has a target string length of 14 characters. Assume that SYSDATE returns a nine-character date value: "17-DEC-07". This date is converted into a string, and the padding string is systematically applied to reach the target length. It returns: "$#$#$17-DEC-07". Note that although the padding string consists of two characters ($#), the string was not applied evenly since there are three dollar symbols and two hash symbols. This is because LPAD and RPAD will pad the source string as much as possible with the padding string until the target length is reached. The RPAD function in query 4 has a target length of 4 characters, but the SYSDATE function alone returns a nine-character value. Therefore no padding occurs and, assuming the current system date is "17-DEC-07", the first four characters of the converted date are returned: "17-D".

FIGURE 4-8

The LPAD and
RPAD functions

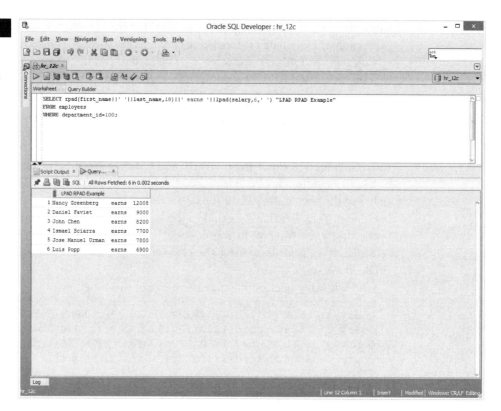

The LPAD and RPAD functions are used in Figure 4-8 to format the results in a neater and more presentable manner. The results returned by this query are identical to those in Figure 4-6 but have been rendered more readable using the LPAD and RPAD functions.

The TRIM Function

The TRIM function removes characters from the beginning or end of character literals, columns or expressions to yield one potentially shorter character item. Numeric and date literals are automatically cast as characters when they occur as parameters to the TRIM function. Numeric or date expressions are evaluated first before being converted to strings ready to be trimmed.

The TRIM function takes a parameter made up of an optional and a mandatory component. Its syntax is:

TRIM([*trailing* | *leading* | *both*] *trimstring* from *s*),

The string to be trimmed (*s*) is mandatory. The following points list the rules governing the use of this function:

- TRIM(*s*) removes spaces from both sides of the input string. When no direction of trimming is specified, then spaces are trimmed from *both* sides of the string.
- TRIM(*trailing trimstring* from *s*) removes all occurrences of *trimstring* from the end of the string *s* if it is present.
- TRIM(*leading trimstring* from *s*) removes all occurrences of *trimstring* from the beginning of the string *s* if it is present.
- TRIM(*both trimstring* from *s*) removes all occurrences of *trimstring* from the beginning and end of the string *s* if it is present.

The following queries illustrate the usage of this function:

```
Query 1: SELECT trim(TRAILING 'e' FROM 1+2.14||' is pie') FROM dual;
Query 2: SELECT trim(BOTH '*' FROM '*******Hidden*******') FROM dual;
Query 3: SELECT trim(1 from sysdate) FROM dual;
```

Query 1 evaluates the numeric expression to return the number 3.14. This number is then cast as the character string "3.14" which is then concatenated to the character literal to construct the string "3.14 is pie". The TRIM function then removes any occurrences of the character "e" from the end of the string to return "3.14 is pi". Query 2 peels away all occurrences of the asterisk trim character from the beginning and end of the character literal and returns the string "Hidden". Note that although one trim character is specified, multiple occurrences will be trimmed if they are consecutively present. Query 3 has two interesting aspects. The trim character is not enclosed in quotes and is implicitly converted to a character. The SYSDATE function returns the current system date, which is assumed to be 17-DEC-07. Since no keyword is specified for trailing, leading, or both trim directions, the default of both applies. Therefore, all occurrences of character 1 at the beginning or ending of the date string are trimmed, resulting in "7-DEC-07" being returned.

The TRIM function used in Figure 4-9 does not appear to do anything, but closer examination reveals a common practical use for it. As discussed earlier, data is frequently entered into application database tables through a variety of sources. It may happen that spaces are accidentally entered and saved in character fields unintentionally. The contrived trim string in the WHERE clause simulates the LAST_NAME field padded with spaces. This could hinder searching for employees with LAST_NAME values of Smith. Trimming the space padded LAST_NAME

FIGURE 4-9

The TRIM
function

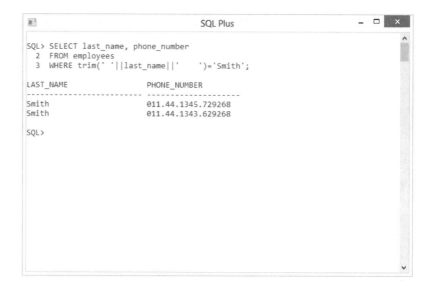

```
SQL Plus                                    _ □ ×

SQL> SELECT last_name, phone_number
  2  FROM employees
  3  WHERE trim(' '||last_name||'    ')='Smith';

LAST_NAME                   PHONE_NUMBER
-----------------------     --------------------
Smith                       011.44.1345.729268
Smith                       011.44.1343.629268

SQL>
```

field enables accurate searching and eliminates the risk of unintended spaces that
may be present in character data. Remember that when no parameters other than
the string *s* are specified to the TRIM function, then its default behavior is to
trim(both ' ' from *s*).

The INSTR Function (In-String)

The INSTR function locates the position of a search string within a given string. It
returns the numeric position at which the *n*th occurrence of the search string begins,
relative to a specified start position. If the search string is not present, the INSTR
function returns zero.

Numeric and date literals are implicitly cast as characters when they occur as
parameters to the INSTR function. Numeric or date expressions are first evaluated
before being converted to strings ready to be searched.

The INSTR function takes four parameters made up of two optional and two
mandatory arguments. The syntax is:

INSTR(*source string*, *search string*, [*search start position*], [*nth occurrence*]),

The default value for the *search start position* is 1 or the beginning of the *source
string*. The default value for the *n*th occurrence is 1 or the first occurrence. The
following queries illustrate the INSTR function with numeric and date expressions:

```
Query 1: SELECT instr(3+0.14,'.') FROM dual;
Query 2: SELECT instr(sysdate, 'DEC') FROM dual;
```

Query 1 evaluates the numeric expression to return the number 3.14. This number is implicitly cast as the string "3.14". The period character is searched for and the first occurrence of it is at position 2. Query 2 evaluates the SYSDATE function and converts the returned date into a string. Assume that the current system date is 17-DEC-07. The first occurrence of the characters DEC begins at position 4. Consider the following queries with character data illustrating the default values and the third and fourth parameters of the INSTR function:

```
Query 3: SELECT instr('1#3#5#7#9#','#') FROM dual;
Query 4: SELECT instr('1#3#5#7#9#','#',5) FROM dual;
Query 5: SELECT instr('1#3#5#7#9#','#',3,4) FROM dual;
```

Query 3 searches for the first occurrence of the hash symbol in the source string beginning at position 1 and returns position 2. Query 4 has the number 5 as its third parameter, indicating that the search for the hash symbol must begin at position 5 in the source string. The subsequent occurrence of the hash symbol is at position 6, which is returned by the query. Query 5 has the numbers 3 and 4 as its third and fourth parameters. This indicates that the search for the hash symbol must begin at position 3 in the source string. Query 5 then returns the number 10, which is the position of the fourth occurrence of the hash symbol when the search begins at position 3.

The INSTR function used in Figure 4-10 returns records from the DEPARTMENTS table where the string "on" is found beginning at the second position of the DEPARTMENT_NAME column.

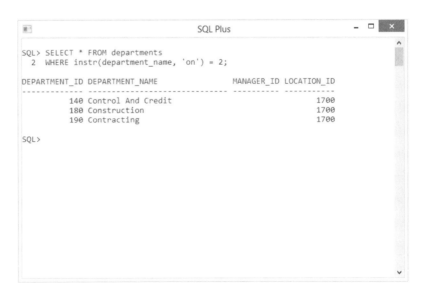

FIGURE 4-10

The INSTR function

```
SQL> SELECT * FROM departments
  2  WHERE instr(department_name, 'on') = 2;

DEPARTMENT_ID DEPARTMENT_NAME                 MANAGER_ID LOCATION_ID
------------- ------------------------------- ---------- -----------
          140 Control And Credit                               1700
          180 Construction                                     1700
          190 Contracting                                      1700

SQL>
```

The INSTR function is often used in combination with the SUBSTR function in utility programs designed to extract encoded data from electronic data streams.

The SUBSTR Function (Substring)

The SUBSTR function extracts and returns a segment from a given source string. It extracts a substring of a specified length from the source string beginning at a given position. If the start position is larger than the length of the source string, null is returned. If the number of characters to extract from a given start position is greater than the length of the source string, the segment returned is the substring from the start position to the end of the string.

Numeric and date literals are automatically cast as characters when they occur as parameters to the SUBSTR function. Numeric and date expressions are evaluated before being converted to strings ready to be searched.

The SUBSTR function takes three parameters, with the first two being mandatory. Its syntax is:

SUBSTR(*source string, start position,* [*number of characters to extract*]),

The default number of characters to extract is equal to the number of characters from the *start position* to the end of the *source string*. The following queries illustrate the SUBSTR function with numeric and date expressions:

```
Query 1: SELECT substr(10000-3,3,2) FROM dual;
Query 2: SELECT substr(sysdate,4,3) FROM dual;
```

Query 1 evaluates the numeric expression to return the number 9997. This number is automatically cast into the character string "9997". The search for the substring begins at position 3 and the two characters from that position onward are extracted, yielding the substring "97". Query 2 evaluates the SYSDATE function and converts the date returned into a character string. Assume that the current system date is 17-DEC-07. The search for the substring begins at position 4 and the three characters from that position onward are extracted, yielding the substring "DEC". Consider the following queries with character data illustrating the default behavior of the optional parameter of the SUBSTR function:

```
Query 3: SELECT substr('1#3#5#7#9#',5) FROM dual;
Query 4: SELECT substr('1#3#5#7#9#',5,6) FROM dual;
Query 5: SELECT substr('1#3#5#7#9#',-3,2) FROM dual;
```

Query 3 extracts the substring beginning at position 5. Since the third parameter is not specified, the default extraction length is equal to the number of characters from and including the *start position* (position 5 in this case) to the end of the *source string*, which is six characters long. Therefore query 3 is equivalent to query 4 and the substring returned by both queries is "5#7#9#". Query five has the number –3 as its start position. The negative start position parameter instructs Oracle to commence searching three characters from the end of the string. Therefore, the start position is three characters from the end of the string, which is position 8. The third parameter is 2, which results in the substring "#9" being returned.

The SUBSTR function used in Figure 4-11 returns records from the EMPLOYEES table, where the first two characters in the JOB_ID values are AD. This function has been further used in the SELECT list to extract the initial character from the FIRST_NAME field of each employee in the result set.

The REPLACE Function

The REPLACE function replaces all occurrences of a search item in a source string with a replacement term and returns the modified source string. If the length of the replacement term is different from that of the search item, then the lengths of the returned and source strings will be different. If the search string is not found, the source string is returned unchanged. Numeric and date literals and expressions are evaluated before being implicitly cast as characters when they occur as parameters to the REPLACE function.

FIGURE 4-11

The SUBSTR function

```
SQL Plus                                                    _ □ ×

SQL> SELECT 'Advertising Team Member: '||
  2          substr(first_name, 1,1)||'. '||
  3          last_name "Initial and Last Name"
  4  FROM employees
  5  WHERE substr(job_id,1,2) ='AD';

Initial and Last Name
--------------------------------------------------------
Advertising Team Member: J. Whalen
Advertising Team Member: S. King
Advertising Team Member: N. Kochhar
Advertising Team Member: L. De Haan

SQL>
```

SCENARIO & SOLUTION

You would like to search for a character string stored in the database. The case in which it is stored is unknown and there are potentially leading and trailing spaces surrounding the string. Can such a search be performed?	Yes. The simplest solution is to first TRIM the leading and trailing spaces from the column and then convert the column data using a case conversion function like LOWER, UPPER, or INITCAP to simplify the number of comparisons required in the WHERE clause condition.

You have been asked to extract the last three characters from the LAST_NAME column in the EMPLOYEES table. Can such a query be performed without using the LENGTH function?	Yes. The SUBSTR(*source string, start position, number of characters*) function takes three parameters. If the start position is set to –3, and the number of characters parameter is set to 3 or is omitted, the last three characters of the LAST_NAME column data is retrieved. The following query may be used:
	
	`SELECT SUBSTR(LAST_NAME,-3) FROM`
	`EMPLOYEES;`

You would like to extract a consistent ten-character string based on the SALARY column in the EMPLOYEES table. If the SALARY value is less than ten characters long, zeros must be added to the left of the value to yield a ten-character string. Is this possible?	Yes. The LPAD function may be used as follows:
	
	`SELECT LPAD(SALARY,10,0)`
	`FROM EMPLOYEES;`

The REPLACE function takes three parameters, with the first two being mandatory. Its syntax is:

REPLACE(*source string, search item,* [*replacement term*]),

If the *replacement term* parameter is omitted, each occurrence of the *search item* is removed from the *source string*. In other words, the *search item* is replaced by an empty string. The following queries illustrate the REPLACE function with numeric and date expressions:

```
Query 1: SELECT replace(10000-3,'9','85') FROM dual;
Query 2: SELECT replace(sysdate, 'DEC','NOV') FROM dual;
```

Query 1 evaluates the numeric expression to return the number 9997, which is cast as the character string "9997". The search string is the character "9" which occurs three times in the source. Each search character is substituted with the replacement string "85" yielding the string "8585857". Query 2 evaluates the SYSDATE function and converts the date returned into a character string. Assume that the current system date is 17-DEC-07. The search string "DEC" occurs once in the source string and is replaced with the characters "NOV" yielding the result "17-NOV-07". Note that this is a character string and not a date value. Consider the following queries with character data, which illustrate the default behavior of the optional parameter of the REPLACE function:

```
Query 3: SELECT replace('1#3#5#7#9#','#','->') FROM dual;
Query 4: SELECT replace('1#3#5#7#9#','#') FROM dual;
```

The hash symbol in query 3 is specified as the search character and the replacement string is specified as "->". The hash symbol occurs five times in the source, and the resultant string is: "1->3->5->7->9->". Query 4 does not specify a replacement string. The default behavior is therefore to replace the search string with an empty string which, in effect, removes the search character completely from the source, resulting in the string "13579" being returned.

The REPLACE function used in Figure 4-12 returns records from the EMPLOYEES table where the JOB_ID values are SA_MAN, but it modifies the SALARY column by replacing each 0 with 000 and aliasing the new expression as "Dream Salary".

FIGURE 4-12	

The REPLACE function

EXERCISE 4-2

Using the Character Manipulation Functions

Envelope printing restricts the addressee field to 16 characters. Ideally, the addressee field contains employees' FIRST_NAME and LAST_NAME values separated by a single space. When the combined length of an employee's FIRST_NAME and LAST_NAME exceeds 15 characters, the addressee field should contain their formal name. An employee's formal name is made up of the first letter of their FIRST_NAME and the first 14 characters of their LAST_NAME.

You are required to retrieve a list of FIRST_NAME and LAST_NAME values and formal names for employees where the combined length of FIRST_NAME and LAST_NAME exceeds 15 characters.

1. Start SQL*Plus and connect to the HR schema.

2. The formal name is constructed by concatenating the first character in the FIRST_NAME field with a space and the first 14 characters of the LAST_NAME field to return a string that is 16 characters long. The SUBSTR function is used to extract the initial and surname portions.

3. The SELECT clause is

```
SELECT FIRST_NAME, LAST_NAME, SUBSTR(FIRST_NAME,1,1)||'
'||SUBSTR(LAST_NAME,1,14)  FORMAL_NAME
```

4. The FROM clause is

```
FROM EMPLOYEES
```

5. The WHERE clause must limit the records returned to only those where the combined lengths of their FIRST_NAME and LAST_NAME exceeds 15 characters.

6. The WHERE clause is

```
WHERE LENGTH(FIRST_NAME) + LENGTH(LAST_NAME) > 15
```

7. Executing this statement returns the following set of results:

Using Numeric Functions

There is a range of built-in *numeric functions* provided by Oracle that rivals the mathematical toolboxes of popular spreadsheet software packages. A significant differentiator between numeric and other functions is that they accept and return only numeric data. Oracle provides numeric functions for solving trigonometric, exponentiation, and logarithmic problems, among others. This guide focuses on three *numeric single-row functions*, ROUND, TRUNC, and MOD, discussed next.

The Numeric ROUND Function

The ROUND function performs a rounding operation on a numeric value based on the decimal precision specified. The value returned is either rounded up or down based on the numeric value of the significant digit at the specified decimal precision position. If the specified decimal precision is *n*, the digit significant to the rounding is found (*n* + 1) places to the RIGHT of the decimal point. If it is negative, the digit significant to the rounding is found *n* places to the LEFT of the decimal point. If the numeric value of the significant digit is greater than or equal to 5, a "round up" occurs, else a "round down" occurs. The ROUND function takes two parameters. Its syntax is:

ROUND(*source number*, [*decimal precision*]),

The *source number* parameter represents any numeric literal, column, or expression. The *decimal precision* parameter specifies the degree of rounding and is optional. If the *decimal precision* parameter is absent, the default degree of rounding is zero, which means the source is rounded to the nearest whole number.

Consider the decimal degrees listed in Table 4-1 for the number 1234.5678. The negative decimal precision values are located to the left of the decimal point while the positive values are found to the right.

If the decimal precision parameter is zero, then the source number is rounded to the nearest whole number. If it is 1, then the source number is rounded to the nearest tenth. If it is 2, then the source is rounded to the nearest hundredth, and so on. The following queries illustrate the usage of this function:

```
Query 1: SELECT round(1601.916718,1) FROM dual;
Query 2: SELECT round(1601.916718,2) FROM dual;
Query 3: SELECT round(1601.916718,-3) FROM dual;
Query 4: SELECT round(1601.916718) FROM dual;
```

Query 1 has a decimal precision parameter (*n*) of 1, which implies that the source number is rounded to the nearest tenth. Since the hundredths (*n* + 1) digit is 1 (less than 5), no rounding occurs and the number returned is 1601.9. The decimal precision parameter in query 2 is 2, so the source number is rounded to the nearest hundredth. Since the thousandths unit is 6 (greater than 5), rounding up occurs and the number returned is 1601.92. The decimal precision parameter of the query 3 is −3. Since it is negative, the digit significant for rounding (6) is found three places

TABLE 4-1	Decimal Precision	Significant Rounding Digit	Decimal Position
	−3	1	Thousands (*n* ×1000)
Decimal Precision Descriptions	−2	2	Hundreds (*n* ×100)
	−1	3	Tens (*n* ×10)
	0	4	Units (*n* ×1)
	1	5	Tenths (*n* ÷10)
	2	6	Hundredths (*n* ÷100)
	3	7	Thousandths (*n* ÷1000)

to the left of the decimal point and the source number is rounded up to the nearest thousand to yield 2000. Query 4 has dispensed with the decimal precision parameter. This implies that rounding is done to the nearest whole number. Since the tenth unit is 9, the number is rounded up and 1602 is returned.

The example shown in Figure 4-13 selects employees working as sales managers and computes a loyalty bonus based on the number of days employed rounded to the nearest whole number. The ROUND function is used to round the fractional part of the difference between the current system date and the HIRE_DATE for each sales manager.

The Numeric TRUNC Function (Truncate)

The TRUNC function performs a truncation operation on a numeric value based on the decimal precision specified. A numeric truncation is different from rounding because the resulting value drops the numbers at the decimal precision specified and does not attempt to round up or down if the decimal precision is positive. However, if the decimal precision specified (n) is negative, the input value is zeroed down from the nth decimal position. The TRUNC function takes two parameters. Its syntax is:

TRUNC (*source number*, [*decimal precision*]),

FIGURE 4-13

The numeric
ROUND function

Source number represents any numeric literal, column, or expression. *Decimal precision* specifies the degree of truncation and is optional. If the *decimal precision* parameter is absent, the default degree of truncation is zero, which means the *source number* is truncated to the nearest whole number.

If the *decimal precision* parameter is 1, then the *source number* is truncated at its tenths unit. If it is 2, it is truncated at its hundredths unit, and so on. The following queries illustrate the usage of this function:

```
Query 1: SELECT trunc(1601.916718,1) FROM dual;
Query 2: SELECT trunc(1601.916718,2) FROM dual;
Query 3: SELECT trunc(1601.916718,-3) FROM dual;
Query 4: SELECT trunc(1601.916718) FROM dual;
```

Query 1 has a *decimal precision* parameter of 1, which implies that the *source number* is truncated at its tenths unit and the number returned is 1601.9. The *decimal precision* parameter (*n*) in query 2 is 2, so the *source number* is truncated at its hundredths unit and the number returned is 1601.91. Note that this result would be different if a round(1601.916718,2) was performed since the digit in position (*n* + 1 = 3) after the decimal point is 6 (greater than 5) and 1601.92 would have been returned. Query 3 specifies a negative number (−3) as its decimal precision. Three places to the left of the decimal point implies that the truncation happens to the nearest thousand, as shown earlier in Table 4-1. Therefore, the *source number* is truncated at its thousands position and the number returned is 1000. Finally, query 4 does not have a *decimal precision* parameter implying that truncation is done at the whole number degree of precision. The number returned is 1601.

The finance department has qualified for a top departmental award for which the company decided to reward its finance staff by adjusting their salaries. Since the fractional salary adjustment results in numbers with up to three decimal places, the TRUNC function is used to truncate the proposed salary increase to a whole number, as shown in Figure 4-14.

The MOD Function (Modulus)

The MOD function returns the numeric remainder of a division operation. Two numbers, the dividend (number being divided) and the divisor (number to divide by) are provided, and a division operation is performed. If the divisor is a factor of the dividend, MOD returns zero since there is no remainder. If the divisor is zero, no division by zero error is returned and the MOD function returns the dividend instead. If the divisor is larger than the dividend, then the MOD function returns the dividend as its result. This is because it divides zero times into the dividend, leaving

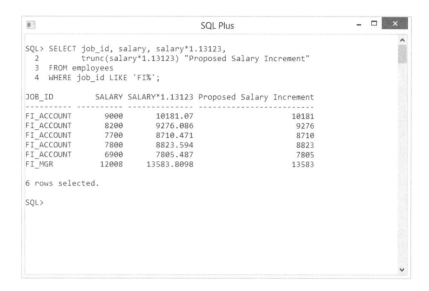

FIGURE 4-14

The numeric
TRUNC function

the remainder equal to the dividend. The MOD function takes two parameters. Its syntax is:

MOD(*dividend*, *divisor*),

The *dividend* and *divisor* parameters represent a numeric literal, column, or expression, which may be negative or positive. The following queries illustrate the usage of this function:

```
Query 1: SELECT mod(6,2) FROM dual;
Query 2: SELECT mod(5,3) FROM dual;
Query 3: SELECT mod(7,35) FROM dual;
Query 4: SELECT mod(5.2,3) FROM dual;
```

Query 1 divides 6 by 2 perfectly, yielding 0 as the remainder. Query 2 divides 5 by 3, yielding 2 as the remainder. Query 3 attempts to divide 7 by 35. Since the *divisor* is larger than the *dividend*, the number 7 is returned as the modulus value. Query 4 has an improper fraction as the *dividend*. Dividing 5.2 by 3 yields 2.2 as the remainder.

on the
job

Any even number divided by 2 naturally has no remainder, but odd numbers divided by 2 always have a remainder of 1. Therefore, the MOD function is often used to distinguish between even and odd numbers.

FIGURE 4-15

The MOD
function

```
                                   SQL Plus                          —  ☐  ✕
SQL> SELECT first_name, last_name, employee_id, mod(employee_id,4) team#
  2    FROM employees
  3    WHERE employee_id BETWEEN 100 AND 111
  4    ORDER BY employee_id;

FIRST_NAME           LAST_NAME            EMPLOYEE_ID      TEAM#
-------------------- -------------------- ----------- ----------
Steven               King                         100          0
Neena                Kochhar                      101          1
Lex                  De Haan                      102          2
Alexander            Hunold                       103          3
Bruce                Ernst                        104          0
David                Austin                       105          1
Valli                Pataballa                    106          2
Diana                Lorentz                      107          3
Nancy                Greenberg                    108          0
Daniel               Faviet                       109          1
John                 Chen                         110          2
Ismael               Sciarra                      111          3

12 rows selected.

SQL> _
```

The EMPLOYEE_ID column in the EMPLOYEES table stores a unique sequential number for each record beginning with employee number 100. The first 12 employees must be allocated to one of four teams in a round-robin manner for a particular task. Figure 4-15 shows how this is accomplished using the MOD function.

The 12 employees' records are isolated with a BETWEEN operator in the WHERE clause. The MOD function is applied to the division of the EMPLOYEE_ID column values by 4. As Figure 4-15 shows, the MOD function allocates the numbers 0 to 3 to each row in a round-robin manner.

exam

ⓦatch *The default values assumed by the optional parameters of functions are not always intuitive but are often tested. For example, calling the SUBSTR function with just the first two parameters results in the function extracting a substring from a start position to the end of the given source string. The optional parameter for both the numeric and date TRUNC and ROUND functions is the degree of precision. For example, calling the numeric TRUNC function without specifying degree of truncation results in the number being truncated to the nearest whole number. It is useful to be familiar with the default values assumed by optional parameters for these functions.*

Working with Dates

The *date* built-in functions provide a convenient way to solve date-related problems without needing to keep track of leap years or the number of days in particular months. We'll discuss storage of dates by Oracle and the default date format masks before we examine the SYSDATE function. We'll follow by discussing date arithmetic and the *date manipulation functions*: ADD_MONTHS, MONTHS_BETWEEN, LAST_DAY, NEXT_DAY, ROUND, and TRUNC.

Date Storage in the Database

Dates are stored internally in a numeric format that supports the storage of century, year, month, and day details, as well as time information such as hours, minutes, and seconds. These date attributes are available for every literal, column value, or expression that is of date data type.

When date information is accessed from a table, the default format of the results comprises two digits that represent the day, a three-letter abbreviation of the month, and two digits representing the year component. By default, these components are separated with hyphens in SQL*Plus and SQL Developer. Note that previous versions of SQL Developer used forward slashes as the default date separator when displaying dates. Figure 4-16 shows the contents of the START_DATE column after querying the JOB_HISTORY table using SQL*Plus.

FIGURE 4-16

Default date separators in SQL*Plus

```
SQL> SELECT employee_id, start_date
  2  FROM job_history;

EMPLOYEE_ID START_DAT
----------- ---------
        101 21-SEP-97
        101 28-OCT-01
        102 13-JAN-01
        114 24-MAR-06
        122 01-JAN-07
        176 24-MAR-06
        176 01-JAN-07
        200 17-SEP-95
        200 01-JUL-02
        201 17-FEB-04

10 rows selected.

SQL>
```

Although the century component is not displayed by default, it is stored in the database when the date value is inserted or updated and is available for retrieval. The format in which a date is displayed is referred to as its format mask. There are several formatting codes or date format masks available, as shown in Table 4-2.

The language to format date items using the full range of date format masks is discussed in Chapter 5. The DD-MON-RR format mask is the default for display and input. The RR date format mask differs from the YY format mask since it is used to specify different centuries based on the current and specified years. The century component assigned to a date value when it is inserted or updated when a two-digit year value is submitted depends on the NLS_DATE_FORMAT setting in that session. If the NLS_DATE_FORMAT is set to the default DD-MON-RR format, the century component is automatically assigned based on the following rules:

- If the last two digits of the current year and specified year lie between 0 and 49, the current century is returned. Suppose the current year is 2014. The date assigned for 24-JUL-04 is 24-JUL-2004.

- If the last two digits of the current year lie between 0 and 49 and the specified year falls between 50 and 99, the previous century is returned. Suppose the current year is 2014. The date assigned for 24-JUL-94 is 24-JUL-1994.

- If the last two digits of the current and specified years lie between 50 and 99, the current century is returned by default. If the current year is 2055, the date assigned for 24-JUL-94 is 24-JUL-2094.

TABLE 4-2		

Date Format
Masks

Format Mask	Format Description
DD	Day of the month
MON	Month of the year
YY	Two-digit year
YYYY	Four-digit year, including century
RR	Two-digit year (Year 2000–compliant)
CC	Two-digit century
HH	Hours with AM and PM
HH24	Twenty-four-hour time
MI	Minutes
SS	Seconds

■ If the last two digits of the current year lie between 50 and 99 and the specified year falls between 0 and 49, the next century is returned. If the current year is 1975, the date assigned for 24-JUL-17 is 24-JUL-2017.

The SYSDATE Function

The SYSDATE function takes no parameters and returns the current system date and time according to the database server. By default, the SYSDATE function returns the DD-MON-RR components of the current system date. It is important to remember that SYSDATE does not return the date and time as specified by your local system clock. If the database server is located in a different time zone from a client querying the database, the date and time returned will differ from the local operating system clock on the client machine. The query to retrieve the database server date is as follows:

```
SELECT sysdate FROM dual;
```

Date Arithmetic

Arithmetic with date columns and expressions were briefly discussed in Chapter 2. The following equations illustrate an important principle regarding *date arithmetic:*

```
Date1 - Date2 = Num1
Date1 - Num1 = Date2
Date1 = Date2 + Num1
Date1 = Date2 - Num1
```

A date can be subtracted from another date. The difference between two date items represents the number of days between them. Any number, including fractions, may be added to or subtracted from a date item. In this context the number represents a number of days. The sum or difference between a number and a date item always returns a date item.

To illustrate the time component of the SYSDATE function as it pertains to date arithmetic, the SQL Developer environment has been temporarily modified to display time information as well as date information.

on the
①ob
To modify the SQL Developer environment to display time information for date columns, by default, navigate to Tools | Preferences | Database | NLS | Date Format. Change the default display mask (DD-MON-RR) to (DD-MON-RR HH24:MI:SS).

A conversion function, which will be discussed in detail in Chapter 5, is introduced here to aid this example. Figure 4-17 demonstrates how the TO_DATE conversion function is used to convert the date literal 02-JUN-2008 with time component 12.10pm into a date data type.

The first query in the figure is dissected as follows: two days prior to the second of June, 12.10pm is the thirty-first of May, 12.10pm, which is the date and time returned by expression 1. Adding 0.5 days or 12 hours to 02-JUN-08 12:10pm, as expression 2 demonstrates, results in the date 03-JUN-08 and the time 00.10 being returned. Expression 3 adds 6/24 or six hours, resulting in the date 02-JUN-08, 18.10 being returned.

The HIREDATE column for employees with DEPARTMENT_ID values of 30 is subtracted from the date item 02-JUN-2006 12:10pm in the figure's second query. The number of days between these two dates is returned for each row. Notice that when the HIREDATE column value occurs later than 02-JUN-2006, a negative number is returned.

FIGURE 4-17

The SYSDATE function and date arithmetic

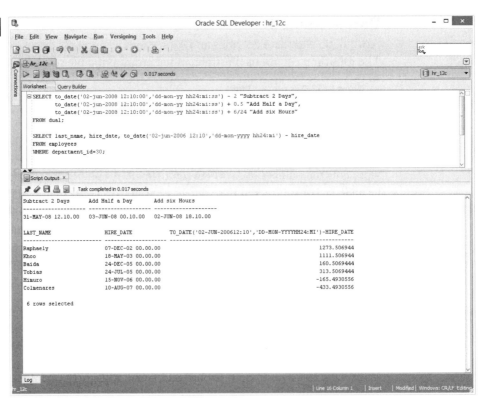

Using Date Functions

The *date manipulation* functions provide a reliable and accurate means of working with date items. These functions provide such ease and flexibility for date manipulation that many integration specialists, database administrators, and other developers make frequent use of them.

The MONTHS_BETWEEN Function

The MONTHS_BETWEEN function returns a numeric value representing the number of months between two date values. Date literals in the format DD-MON-RR or DD-MON-YYYY are automatically cast as date items when they occur as parameters to the MONTHS_BETWEEN function. The MONTHS_BETWEEN function takes two mandatory parameters. Its syntax is:

MONTHS_BETWEEN(*date1*, *date2*),

The function computes the difference in months between *date1* and *date2*. If the *date1* occurs before the *date2*, a negative number is returned. The difference between the two date parameters may consist of a whole number and a fractional component. The whole number represents the number of months between the two dates. The fractional component represents the days and time remaining after the integer difference between years and months is calculated and is based on a 31-day month. A whole number with no fractional part is returned if the day components of the dates being compared are either the same or the last day of their respective months.

The following queries illustrate the MONTHS_BETWEEN function:

```
Query 1: SELECT months_between(SYSDATE+31, SYSDATE),
                months_between(SYSDATE+61, SYSDATE),
                months_between(SYSDATE+92, SYSDATE)
         FROM dual;
Query 2: SELECT months_between('29-mar-2008','28-feb-2008')
         FROM dual;
Query 3: SELECT months_between('29-mar-2008','28-feb-2008') * 31
         FROM dual;
Assume that the current date is 29-DEC-2007.
```

The first expression in Query 1 returns the number 1, as the month between 29-DEC-2007 is 29-JAN-2008 (31 days later). The second expression similarly returns 2 months between 29-DEC-2007 and 29-FEB-2008 (62 days later). Since February 2008 has 29 days, 91 days must be added to 29-DEC-2007 to get 29-MAR-2008, and the MONTHS_BETWEEN (29-MAR-2008, 29-DEC-2007) function returns exactly three months.

Query 2 implicitly converts the date literals into date items of the format DD-MON-YYYY. Since no time information is provided, Oracle assumes the time to be midnight on both days, or 00:00:00. The MONTHS_BETWEEN function returns approximately 1.03225806. The whole number component indicates that there is one month between these two dates. Closer examination of the fractional component interestingly reveals that there is exactly one month between 28-MAR-2008 and 28-FEB-2008. The fractional component must therefore represent the one-day difference. It would include differences in hours, minutes, and seconds as well, but for this example, the time components are identical. Multiplying 0.03225806 by 31 returns 1, since the fractional component returned by MONTHS_BETWEEN is based on a 31-day month.

Query 3 is identical to Query 2 except it multiplies the result of Query 2 by 31. Expectedly it returns 1.03225806 × 31 = (1 x 31) + (0.03225806 × 31) = 31 + 1 = 32.

The MONTHS_BETWEEN function used in Figure 4-18 returns records from the JOB_HISTORY table. The months between the dates an employee started in a particular job and ended that job are computed, and the results are sorted in descending order.

FIGURE 4-18

The MONTHS_
BETWEEN
function

```
SQL> SELECT employee_id, end_date, start_date,
  2         months_between(end_date, start_date) duration
  3  FROM job_history
  4  ORDER BY duration DESC;

EMPLOYEE_ID END_DATE  START_DAT   DURATION
----------- --------- --------- ----------
        200 17-JUN-01 17-SEP-95         69
        102 24-JUL-06 13-JAN-01 66.3548387
        200 31-DEC-06 01-JUL-02 53.9677419
        101 27-OCT-01 21-SEP-97 49.1935484
        201 19-DEC-07 17-FEB-04 46.0645161
        101 15-MAR-05 28-OCT-01 40.5806452
        114 31-DEC-07 24-MAR-06 21.2258065
        176 31-DEC-07 01-JAN-07 11.9677419
        122 31-DEC-07 01-JAN-07 11.9677419
        176 31-DEC-06 24-MAR-06 9.22580645

10 rows selected.

SQL>
```

exam

ⓦatch

A common mistake is to assume that the return data type of single-row functions are the same as the category the function belongs to. This is only true of the numeric functions. Character and date functions can return values of other data types. For example, *the INSTR character function and the MONTHS_BETWEEN date function both return a numeric value. It is important to be familiar with the principles of date arithmetic, as it is common to erroneously assume that the difference between two dates is a date, when in fact it is a number.*

The ADD_MONTHS Function

The ADD_MONTHS function returns a date item calculated by adding a specified number of months to a given date value. Date literals in the format DD-MON-RR or DD-MON-YYYY are automatically cast as date items when they occur as parameters to the ADD_MONTHS function. The ADD_MONTHS function takes two mandatory parameters. Its syntax is:

ADD_MONTHS (*start date*, *number of months*),

The function computes the target date after adding the specified number of months to the *start date*. The number of months may be negative, resulting in a target date earlier than the start date being returned. The *number of months* may be fractional, but the fractional component is ignored and the integer component is used.

The three queries in Figure 4-19 illustrate the behavior of the ADD_MONTHS function.

The first query in the figure returns 07-MAY-2009 since the day component remains the same if possible and the month is incremented by one. The second query has two interesting dimensions. The parameter specifying the number of months to add contains a fractional component, which is ignored. Therefore, it is equivalent to ADD_MONTHS ('31-dec-2008',2). Adding two months to the date 31-DEC-2008 should return the date 31-FEB-2009, but there is no such date, so the last day of the month, 28-FEB-2009, is returned. Since the number of months added in the third query is –12, the date 07-APR-2008 is returned, which is 12 months prior to the start date.

FIGURE 4-19

The ADD_
MONTHS
function

EXERCISE 4-3

Using the Date Functions

You are required to obtain a list of EMPLOYEE_ID, LAST_NAME, and HIRE_
DATE values for the employees who have worked more than 100 months between
the date they were hired and 01-JAN-2012.

1. Start SQL Developer and connect to the HR schema.

2. The SELECT clause is

   ```
   SELECT EMPLOYEE_ID, LAST_NAME, HIRE_DATE
   ```

3. The FROM clause is

   ```
   FROM EMPLOYEES
   ```

4. The WHERE clause must compare the months between the given date literal and the HIRE_DATE value with the numeric literal 100.

5. The MONTHS_BETWEEN function may be used in the WHERE clause.

6. The WHERE clause is

```
WHERE MONTHS_BETWEEN('01-JAN-2012', HIRE_DATE) > 100
```

7. Executing this statement returns the set of results shown in the following illustration:

The NEXT_DAY Function

The NEXT_DAY function returns the date when the next occurrence of a specified day of the week occurs. Literals that may be implicitly cast as date items are acceptable when they occur as parameters to the NEXT_DAY function. The NEXT_DAY function takes two mandatory parameters. Its syntax is:

NEXT_DAY (*start date*, *day of the week*),

The function computes the date on which the *day of the week* parameter next occurs after the *start date*. The *day of the week* parameter may be either a character value or an integer value. The acceptable values are determined by the NLS_DATE_LANGUAGE database parameter, but the default values are at least the first three characters of the day name or integer values, where 1 represents Sunday, 2 represents Monday, and so on. The character values representing the days of the week may be specified in any case. The *day of the week* parameter may be longer than three characters, but any characters following a valid abbreviation are ignored; for example, Sunday may be referenced as "sun", "sun dance", "sun hat", or "Sunday".

The three queries in Figure 4-20 illustrate the behavior of the NEXT_DAY function.

01-JAN-2009 is a Thursday. Therefore, the next time a Tuesday occurs will be five days later, on 06-JAN-2009, which is what the first query in the figure retrieves. The second query specifies the character literal WEDNE, which is interpreted as Wednesday. The next Wednesday after 01-JAN-2009 is 07-JAN-2009. The third query uses the integer form to specify the fifth day of the week. Assuming the default values where Sunday is represented by the number 1, the fifth day is Thursday. The next time another Thursday occurs after 01-JAN-2009 is 08-JAN-2009.

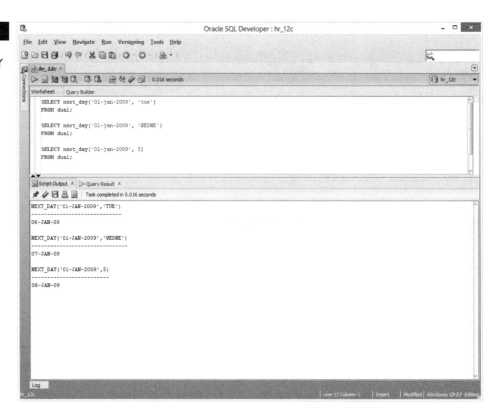

FIGURE 4-20

The NEXT_DAY function

SCENARIO & SOLUTION

You wish to retrieve the duration of employment in days for each employee. Is it possible to perform such a calculation?	Yes. The SYSDATE function may be used to obtain the current system date. The following query computes the duration by subtracting the HIRE_DATE column from the value returned by the SYSDATE function:
	
	`SELECT SYSDATE-HIRE_DATE`
	`FROM EMPLOYEES;`

You are tasked with identifying the date the end-of-year staff bonus will be paid. Bonuses are usually paid on the last Friday in December. Can the bonus date be computed using the NEXT_DAY function?	Yes. If the NEXT_DAY function is called with the start date parameter set to the last day in December and the search day set to Friday, then the first Friday in January is returned. Subtracting seven days from this date yields the date of the last Friday in December. Consider the following query for the year 2009:
	
	`SELECT NEXT_DAY('31-DEC-2009', 'Friday') -7`
	`FROM DUAL;`

Employees working in the IT department have moved to new offices and, although the last four digits of their phone numbers are the same, the set of the three digits 423 is changed to 623. A typical phone number of an IT staff member is 590.423.4567. You are required to provide a list of employees' names with their old and new phone numbers. Can this list be provided?	Yes. The REPLACE function is used. To replace every 4 with a 6 will change digits that should not be changed as well, so the string to be replaced must be uniquely specified. The following query provides the list:
	
	`SELECT FIRST_NAME, LAST_NAME, REPLACE( PHONE_`
	`NUMBER, '.423.','.623.') FROM EMPLOYEES WHERE`
	`DEPARTMENT_ID=60`

The LAST_DAY Function

The LAST_DAY function returns the date of the last day in the month a specified day belongs to. Literals that may be implicitly cast as date items are acceptable when they occur as parameters to the LAST_DAY function. The LAST_DAY function takes one mandatory parameter. Its syntax is:

LAST_DAY(*start date*),

The function extracts the month that the *start date* parameter belongs to and calculates the date of the last day of that month. The two queries in Figure 4-21 illustrate the behavior of the LAST_DAY function.

FIGURE 4-21

The LAST_DAY function

The last day in the month of January 2009 is 31-JAN-2009, which is returned by the `LAST_DAY('01-JAN-2009')` function call in the first query in the figure. The second query extracts the employees with JOB_ID values of IT_PROG. The number of days worked by these employees in their first month of employment is calculated by subtracting the HIRE_DATE values from the LAST_DAY of that month.

The Date ROUND Function

The date ROUND function performs a rounding operation on a value based on a specified date precision format. The value returned is either rounded up or down to the nearest date precision format.

The date ROUND function takes one mandatory and one optional parameter. Its syntax is:

ROUND(*source date*, [*date precision format*]),

The *source date* parameter represents any value that can be implicitly converted into a date item. The *date precision format* parameter specifies the degree of rounding and is optional. If it is absent, the default degree of rounding is *day*. This means the *source date* is rounded to the nearest day. The *date precision formats* include *century* (CC), *year* (YYYY), *quarter* (Q), *month* (MM), *week* (W), *day* (DD), *hour* (HH), and *minute* (MI). Many of these formats are discussed in Chapter 5.

Rounding up to *century* is equivalent to adding 1 to the current century. Rounding up to the next month occurs if the *day* component is greater than 16, else rounding down to the beginning of the current month occurs. If the month falls between 1 and 6, then rounding to *year* returns the date at the beginning of the current year, else it returns the date at the beginning of the following year. Figure 4-22 shows four items in the SELECT list, each rounding a date literal to a different degree of precision.

The first item rounds the date to the nearest day. Since the time is 13:00, which is after 12:00, the date is rounded to midnight on the following day, or 03-JUN-2009 00:00. The second item rounds the date to the same day of the week as the first day of the month and returns 01-JUN-2009. The third item rounds the date to the beginning of the following month, since the day component is 16 and returns 01-JUL-2009. The fourth item is rounded up to the date at the beginning of the following year since the month component is 7, and 01-JAN-2010 is returned.

FIGURE 4-22

The date
ROUND function

```
                              SQL Plus                    – □ ×

SQL> SELECT round(to_date('02-JUN-2009 13:00','DD-MON-YYYY HH24:MI')) DAY,
  2          round(to_date('02-JUN-2009','DD-MON-YYYY'),'w') week,
  3          round(to_date('16-JUN-2009','DD-MON-YYYY'),'month') MONTH,
  4          round(to_date('12-JUL-2009','DD-MON-YYYY'),'year') YEAR
  5  FROM dual;

DAY       WEEK      MONTH     YEAR
--------- --------- --------- ---------
03-JUN-09 01-JUN-09 01-JUL-09 01-JAN-10

SQL> _
```

INSIDE THE EXAM

There are two certification objectives in this chapter. Various types of SQL functions are described and the concept of a function is defined. A distinction is made between single-row functions, which execute once for each row in a dataset, and multiple-row functions, which execute once for all the rows in a dataset. Single-row functions may be used in the SELECT, WHERE, and ORDER BY clauses of the SELECT statement.

The second objective relates to the use of character, numeric, and date functions in queries. The exam tests your understanding of these functions by providing practical examples of their usage. You may be asked to predict the results returned or to identify errors inherent in the syntax of these examples.

Functions can take zero or more input parameters, some of which may be mandatory while others are optional. Mandatory parameters are listed first, and optional parameters are always last. Common errors relate to confusion about the meaning of positions of parameters in functions. A character function like INSTR takes four parameters, with the first two being mandatory. The first is the source string; the second is the search string, while the third and fourth are not always intuitive and may be easily forgotten or mixed up. Be sure to remember the meaning of parameters in different positions. Another frequent mistake relates to confusion about the default values used by Oracle when optional parameters are not specified. You may be expected to predict the results returned from function calls that do not have all their optional parameters specified.

The Date TRUNC Function

The date TRUNC function performs a truncation operation on a date value based on a specified date precision format. The date TRUNC function takes one mandatory and one optional parameter. Its syntax is:

TRUNC(*source date*, [*date precision format*]),

The *source date* parameter represents any value that can be implicitly converted into a date item. The *date precision format* parameter specifies the degree of truncation and is optional. If it is absent, the default degree of truncation is *day*. This means that any time component of the *source date* is set to midnight or 00:00:00 (00 hours, 00 minutes, and 00 seconds). Truncating at the month level sets the date of the *source*

FIGURE 4-23

The date TRUNC function

```
SQL Plus                                    _ □ ×

SQL> SELECT trunc(to_date('02-jun-2009 13:00','dd-mon-yyyy hh24:mi')) DAY,
  2         trunc(to_date('02-jun-2009','dd-mon-yyyy'),'w') week,
  3         trunc(to_date('16-jun-2009','dd-mon-yyyy'),'month') MONTH,
  4         trunc(to_date('12-jul-2009','dd-mon-yyyy'),'year') YEAR
  5  FROM dual;

DAY       WEEK      MONTH     YEAR
--------- --------- --------- ---------
02-JUN-09 01-JUN-09 01-JUN-09 01-JAN-09

SQL> _
```

date to the first day of the month. Truncating at the year level returns the date at the beginning of the current year. Figure 4-23 shows four items in the SELECT list, each truncating a date literal to a different degree of precision.

The first item sets the time component of 13:00 to 00:00 and returns the current day. The second item truncates the date to the same day of the week as the first day of the month and returns 01-JUN-2009. The third item truncates the date to the beginning of the current month and returns 01-JUN-2009. The fourth item is truncated to the date at the beginning of the current year and returns 01-JAN-2009.

CERTIFICATION SUMMARY

Single-row functions exponentially enhance the data manipulation possibilities offered by SQL statements. These functions execute once for each row of data selected. They may be used in SELECT, WHERE, and ORDER BY clauses in a SELECT statement.

The black box nature of the built-in PL/SQL functions was discussed, and a distinction between multiple and single-row functions was made. A high-level overview describing how character, numeric, and date information may be manipulated by single-row functions was provided before systematically exploring several key functions in detail.

Character-case conversion functions were described before introducing the character manipulation functions. The numeric functions ROUND, TRUNC, and MOD were discussed, but these represent the tip of the iceberg since Oracle provides a vast toolbox of mathematical and numeric functions. Date arithmetic and storage was briefly explored before taking a detailed look at the date functions.

There are numerous single-row functions available, and you are not required to memorize their every detail. Understanding the broad categories of single-row functions and being introduced to the common character, numeric, and date functions provide a starting point for your discovery of their usefulness.

TWO-MINUTE DRILL

Describe Various Types of Functions Available in SQL

❑ Functions accept zero or more input parameters but always return one result of a predetermined data type.

❑ Single-row functions execute once for each row selected, while multiple-row functions execute once for the entire set of rows queried.

❑ Character functions are either case-conversion or character-manipulation functions.

Use Character, Number, and Date Functions in SELECT Statements

❑ The INITCAP function accepts a string of characters and returns each word in title case.

❑ The function that computes the number of characters in a string including spaces and special characters is the LENGTH function.

❑ The INSTR function returns the positional location of the nth occurrence of a specified string of characters in a source string.

❑ The SUBSTR function extracts and returns a segment from a given source string.

❑ The REPLACE function substitutes each occurrence of a search item in the source string with a replacement term and returns the modified source string.

❑ A modulus operation returns the remainder of a division operation and is available via the MOD function.

❑ The numeric ROUND function rounds numbers either up or down to the specified degree of precision.

❑ The SYSDATE function is traditionally executed against the DUAL table and returns the current date and time of the database server.

❑ Date types store century, year, month, day, hour, minutes, and seconds information.

❑ The difference between two date items is always a number that represents the number of days between these two items.

❑ Any number, including fractions, may be added to or subtracted from a date item, and in this context the number represents a specified number of days.

❑ The MONTHS_BETWEEN function computes the number of months between two given date parameters. Any fractional component returned is based on a 31-day month.

❑ The LAST_DAY function is used to obtain the last day in a month given any valid date item.

SELF TEST

The following questions will help you measure your understanding of the material presented in this chapter. Read all the choices carefully because there might be more than one correct answer. Choose all the correct answers for each question.

Describe Various Types of Functions Available in SQL

I. Which statements regarding single-row functions are true? (Choose all that apply.)
   A. They may return more than one result.
   B. They execute once for each record processed.
   C. They may have zero or more input parameters.
   D. They must have at least one mandatory parameter.

2. Which of these are single-row character-case conversion functions? (Choose all that apply.)
   A. LOWER
   B. SMALLER
   C. INITCASE
   D. INITCAP

Use Character, Number, and Date Functions in SELECT Statements

3. What value is returned after executing the following statement? (Choose the best answer.)
   `SELECT LENGTH('How_long_is_a_piece_of_string?') FROM DUAL;`
   A. 29
   B. 30
   C. 24
   D. None of the above

4. What value is returned after executing the following statement? (Choose the best answer.)
   `SELECT SUBSTR('How_long_is_a_piece_of_string?', 5,4) FROM DUAL;`
   A. long
   B. _long
   C. ring?
   D. None of the above

5. What value is returned after executing the following statement? (Choose the best answer.)
```
SELECT INSTR('How_long_is_a_piece_of_string?','_',5,3) FROM DUAL;
```
   A. 4

   B. 14

   C. 12

   D. None of the above

6. What value is returned after executing the following statement? (Choose the best answer.)
```
SELECT REPLACE('How_long_is_a_piece_of_string?','_','') FROM DUAL;
```
   A. How long is a piece of string?

   B. How_long_is_a_piece_of_string?

   C. Howlongisapieceofstring?

   D. None of the above

7. What value is returned after executing the following statement? (Choose the best answer.)
```
SELECT MOD(14,3) FROM DUAL;
```
   A. 3

   B. 42

   C. 2

   D. None of the above

8. Assuming SYSDATE=07-JUN-1996 12:05pm, what value is returned after executing the following statement? (Choose the best answer.)
```
SELECT ADD_MONTHS(SYSDATE,-1) FROM DUAL;
```
   A. 07-MAY-1996 12:05pm

   B. 06-JUN-1996 12:05pm

   C. 07-JUL-1996 12:05pm

   D. None of the above

9. What value is returned after executing the following statement? Take note that 01-JAN-2009 occurs on a Thursday. (Choose the best answer.)
```
SELECT NEXT_DAY('01-JAN-2009','wed') FROM DUAL;
```
   A. 07-JAN-2009

   B. 31-JAN-2009

   C. Wednesday

   D. None of the above

10. Assuming SYSDATE=30-DEC-2007, what value is returned after executing the following statement? (Choose the best answer.)
```
SELECT TRUNC(SYSDATE,'YEAR') FROM DUAL;
```
   A. 31-DEC-2007

   B. 01-JAN-2008

   C. 01-JAN-2007

   D. None of the above

LAB QUESTION

Using SQL Developer or SQL*Plus, connect to the OE schema and complete the following tasks.

Several quotations were requested for prices on color printers. The supplier information is not available from the usual source, but you know that the supplier identification number is embedded in the CATALOG_URL column from the PRODUCT_INFORMATION table. You are required to retrieve the PRODUCT_NAME and CATALOG_URL values and to extract the supplier number from the CATALOG_URL column for all products that have both the words COLOR and PRINTER in the PRODUCT_DESCRIPTION column stored in any case.

SELF TEST ANSWERS

Describe Various Types of Functions Available in SQL

1. ☑ **B and C.** Single-row functions execute once for every record selected in a dataset and may either take no input parameters, like SYSDATE, or many input parameters.
   ☒ **A and D** are incorrect. A function by definition returns only one result and there are many functions with no parameters.

2. ☑ **A and D.** The LOWER function converts the case of the input string parameter to its lowercase equivalent, while INITCAP converts the given input parameter to title case.
   ☒ **B and C** are incorrect. They are not valid function names.

Use Character, Number, and Date Functions in SELECT Statements

3. ☑ **B.** The LENGTH function computes the number of characters in a given input string including spaces, tabs, punctuation marks, and other nonprintable special characters.
   ☒ **A, C,** and **D** are incorrect. The string literal has 30 characters including underscore characters and the question mark.

4. ☑ **A.** The SUBSTR function extracts a four-character substring from the given input string starting with and including the fifth character. The characters at positions 1 to 4 are How_. Starting with the character at position 5, the next four characters form the word "long".
   ☒ **B, C,** and **D** are incorrect. **B** is a five-character substring beginning at position 4, while ring?, which is also five characters long, starts five characters from the end of the given string.

5. ☑ **B.** The INSTR function returns the position that the nth occurrence of the search string may be found after starting the search from a given start position. The search string is the underscore character, and the third occurrence of this character starting from position 5 in the source string occurs at position 14.
   ☒ **A, C,** and **D** are incorrect. Position 4 is the first occurrence of the search string and position 12 is the third occurrence if the search began at position 1.

6. ☑ **C.** All occurrences of the underscore character are replaced by an empty string, which removes them from the string.
   ☒ **A, B,** and **D** are incorrect. **A** is incorrect because the underscore characters are not replaced by spaces, and **B** does not change the source string.

7. ☑ **C.** When 14 is divided by 3, the answer is 4 with remainder 2.
   ☒ **A, B,** and **D** are incorrect.

8. ☑ **A.** The –1 parameter indicates to the ADD_MONTHS function that the date to be returned must be one month prior to the given date.

☒ **B, C,** and **D** are incorrect. **B** is one day and not one month prior to the given date. **C** is one month after the given date.

9. ☑ **A.** Since the first of January 2009 falls on a Thursday, the date of the following Wednesday is six days later.

☒ **B, C,** and **D** are incorrect. **B** returns the last day of the month in which the given date falls, and **C** returns a character string instead of a date.

10. ☑ **C.** The date TRUNC function does not perform rounding and since the degree of truncation is YEAR, the day and month components of the given date are ignored and the first day of the year it belongs to is returned.

☒ **A, B,** and **D** are incorrect. **A** returns the last day in the month in which the given date occurs, and **B** returns a result achieved by rounding instead of truncation.

LAB ANSWER

Using SQL Developer or SQL*Plus, connect to the OE schema and complete the following tasks.

1. Start SQL Developer and connect to the OE schema.

2. A typical CATALOG_URL entry looks as follows: www.supp-102094.com/cat/hw/p1797.html. The supplier identification number is consistently six characters long and starts from the seventeenth character of the CATALOG_URL value. The SUBSTR function is used to extract this value.

3. The SELECT clause is therefore

```
SELECT PRODUCT_NAME, CATALOG_URL, SUBSTR(CATALOG_URL, 17, 6) SUPPLIER
```

4. The FROM clause is

```
FROM PRODUCT_INFORMATION
```

5. The records retrieved must be limited to those containing both the words COLOR and PRINTER. These words may occur in any order and may be present in uppercase, lowercase, or mixed case. Any of the case conversion functions may be used to deal with case issues, but because the two words can occur in any order, two conditions are necessary. The UPPER function will be used for case conversion for comparison.

6. The first condition is

```
UPPER(PRODUCT_DESCRIPTION) LIKE '%COLOR%'
```

7. The second condition is

```
UPPER(PRODUCT_DESCRIPTION) LIKE '%PRINTER%'
```

8. The WHERE clause is

```
WHERE UPPER(PRODUCT_DESCRIPTION) LIKE '%COLOR%' AND UPPER(PRODUCT_
DESCRIPTION) LIKE '%PRINTER%'
```

9. Executing the statement returns the set of results matching this pattern as shown in the following illustration:

5
Using Conversion Functions and Conditional Expressions

Functions that operate on numeric, date, and character information were discussed in Chapter 4, and familiarity with that content is assumed in this chapter. Sometimes data is not available in the exact format a function is defined to accept, resulting in a data type mismatch. To avoid mismatch errors, Oracle implicitly converts compatible data types. Implicit conversion is discussed before introducing explicit conversion functions, which are used for reliable data type conversions.

The concept of nesting functions is defined and a category of general functions aimed at simplifying interactions with NULL values is introduced. These include the NVL, NVL2, NULLIF, and COALESCE functions.

Conditional logic, or the ability to display different results depending on data values, is exposed by the conditional functions CASE and DECODE. These functions provide *if-then-else* logic in the context of a SQL query.

CERTIFICATION OBJECTIVE 5.01

Describe Various Types of Conversion Functions Available in SQL

SQL conversion *functions* are single row functions designed to alter the nature of the data type of a column value, expression, or literal. *TO_CHAR*, *TO_NUMBER*, and *TO_DATE* are the three most widely used conversion functions and are discussed in detail. The TO_CHAR function converts numeric and date information into characters, while TO_NUMBER and TO_DATE convert character data into numbers and dates, respectively. The concepts of implicit and explicit data type conversion are discussed in the next section.

Conversion Functions

Oracle allows columns to be defined with ANSI, DB2, and SQL/DS data types. These are converted internally to Oracle data types. This approach allows applications written for other database systems to be migrated to Oracle with ease.

Table definitions are obtained using the DESCRIBE command discussed in Chapter 2. Each column has an associated data type that constrains the nature of the data it can store. A NUMBER column cannot store character information.

A DATE column cannot store random characters or numbers. However, the character equivalents of both number and date information can be stored in a VARCHAR2 field.

If a function that accepts a character input parameter finds a number instead, Oracle automatically converts it into its character equivalent. If a function that accepts a number or a date parameter encounters a character value, there are specific conditions under which automatic data type conversion occurs. DATE and NUMBER data types are very strict compared to VARCHAR2 and CHAR.

Although implicit data type conversions are available, it is more reliable to explicitly convert values from one data type to another using single-row conversion functions. Converting character information to NUMBER and DATE relies on format masks, which are discussed later in this section.

on the
Óob

When numeric values are supplied as input to functions expecting character parameters, implicit data type conversion ensures that they are treated as character values. Similarly, character strings consisting of numeric digits are implicitly converted into numeric values if possible when a data type mismatch occurs. But be wary of implicit conversions. There are some cases when it does not work as expected, as in the following WHERE clause. Consider limiting data from a table T based on a character column C, which contains the string `'100'`. The condition clause `WHERE  C='100'` works as you might expect, but the condition `WHERE  C=100` returns an invalid number error.

Implicit Data Type Conversion

Values that do not share identical data types with function parameters are *implicitly converted* to the required format if possible. VARCHAR2 and CHAR data types are collectively referred to as character types. Character fields are flexible and allow the storage of almost any type of information. Therefore, DATE and NUMBER values can easily be converted to their character equivalents. These conversions are known as *number to character* and *date to character* conversions. Consider the following queries:

```
Query 1: SELECT length(1234567890) FROM dual;
Query 2: SELECT length(SYSDATE) FROM dual;
```

Both queries use the LENGTH function, which takes a character string parameter. The number 1234567890 in query 1 is implicitly converted into a character string, "1234567890", before being evaluated by the LENGTH function, which returns the number 10. Query 2 first evaluates the SYSDATE function, which is assumed to be 07-APR-38. This date is implicitly converted into the character string "07-APR-38" and the LENGTH function returns the number 9.

It is uncommon for character data to be implicitly converted into numeric data types since the only condition under which this occurs is if the character data represents a valid number. The character string "11" will be implicitly converted to a number, but "11.123.456" will not be, as the following queries demonstrate:

```
Query 3: SELECT mod('11',2) FROM dual;
Query 4: SELECT mod('11.123',2) FROM dual;
Query 5: SELECT mod('11.123.456',2) FROM dual;
Query 6: SELECT mod('$11',2) FROM dual;
```

Queries 3 and 4 implicitly convert the character strings "11" and "11.123" into the numbers 11 and 11.123, respectively, before the MOD function evaluates them and returns the results 1 and 1.123. Query 5 returns the error "ORA-1722: invalid number" when Oracle tries to perform an implicit *character to number* conversion. It fails because the string "11.123.456" is not a valid number. Query 6 also fails with the invalid number error, since the dollar symbol cannot be implicitly converted into a number.

Implicit *character to date* conversions are possible when the character string conforms to the following date patterns: [D | DD] *separator1* [MON | MONTH] *separator2* [R | RR | YYYY]. D and DD represent a single and two-digit day of the month. MON is a three-character abbreviation, while MONTH is the full name for a month. R and RR represent a single and two-digit year. YYYY represents a four-digit year. The *separator1* and *separator2* elements may be most punctuation marks, spaces, and tabs. Table 5-1 demonstrates implicit character to date conversion, listing several function calls and the results SQL Developer returns.

TABLE 5-1   Examples of Implicit Character to Date Conversion

Function Call	Format	Results
add_months('24-JAN-09',1)	DD-MON-RR	24/FEB/09
add_months('1\january/8',1)	D\MONTH/R	01/FEB/08
months_between('13*jan*8', '13/feb/2008')	DD*MON*R, DD/MON/YYYY	−1
add_months('01$jan/08',1)	DD$MON/RR	01/FEB/08
add_months('13!jana08',1)	JANA is an invalid month	ORA-1841: (full) year must be between −4713 and +9999 and not be 0
add_months('24-JAN-09 18:45',1)	DD-MON-RR HH24:MI	ORA-1830: date format picture ends before converting entire input string

Explicit Data Type Conversion

Oracle offers many functions to convert items from one data type to another, known as *explicit* data type conversion functions. These return a value guaranteed to be the type required and offer a safe and reliable method of converting data items.

NUMBER and DATE items can be converted explicitly into character items using the TO_CHAR function. A character string can be explicitly changed into a NUMBER using the TO_NUMBER function. The TO_DATE function is used to convert character strings into DATE items. Oracle's format masks enable a wide range of control over *character to number* and *character to date* conversions.

CERTIFICATION OBJECTIVE 5.02

Use the TO_CHAR, TO_NUMBER, and TO_DATE Conversion Functions

This certification objective contains a systematic description of the TO_NUMBER, TO_DATE, and TO_CHAR functions, with examples. The discussion of TO_CHAR is divided into the conversion of two types of items to characters: DATE and NUMBER. This separation is warranted by the availability of different format masks for controlling conversion to character values. These conversion functions exist alongside many others but tend to be the most widely used. This section focuses on the practicalities of using the conversion functions.

Using the Conversion Functions

Many situations demand the use of conversion functions. They may range from formatting DATE fields in a report to ensuring that numeric digits extracted from character fields are correctly converted into numbers before applying them in an arithmetic expression.

Table 5-2 illustrates the syntax of the single-row explicit data type conversion functions.

Optional national language support parameters (*nls_parameters*) are useful for specifying the language and format in which the names of date and numeric elements are returned. These parameters are usually absent, and the default values for elements such as day or month names and abbreviations are used. As Figure 5-1 shows, there is a publicly available view called NLS_SESSION_PARAMETERS that contains the NLS parameters for your current session.

The default NLS_CURRENCY value is the dollar symbol, but this can be changed at the user session level. For example, to change the currency to the three-character-long string USD, the following command may be issued:

```
ALTER SESSION SET nls_currency='USD';
```

Converting Numbers to Characters Using the TO_CHAR Function

The TO_CHAR function returns an item of data type VARCHAR2. When applied to items of type NUMBER, several formatting options are available. The syntax is as follows:

TO_CHAR(*number1*, [*format*], [*nls_parameter*]),

The *number1* parameter is mandatory and must be a value that either is or can be implicitly converted into a number. The optional *format* parameter may be used to specify numeric formatting information such as width, currency symbol, the position of a decimal point, and group (or thousands) separators, and must be enclosed

TABLE 5-2	TO_NUMBER(*char1*, [*format mask*], [*nls_parameters*]) = *num1*	TO_CHAR(*num1*, [*format mask*], [*nls_parameters*]) = *char1*
Syntax of Explicit Data Type Conversion Functions	TO_DATE(*char1*, [*format mask*], [*nls_parameters*]) = *date1*	TO_CHAR(*date1*, [*format mask*], [*nls_parameters*]) = *char1*

FIGURE 5-1

National
language support
(NLS) session
parameters

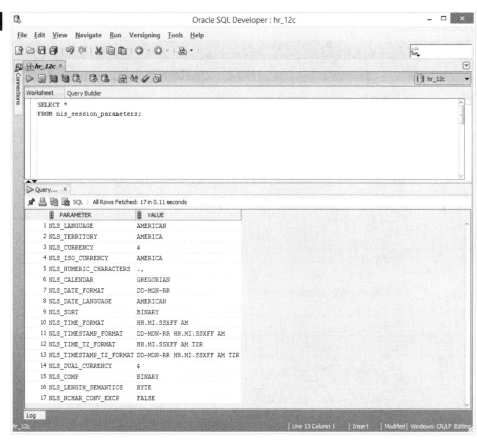

in single quotation marks. There are other formatting options for numbers being converted into characters, some of which are listed in Table 5-3.

Consider the following two queries:

```
Query 1: SELECT to_char(00001)||' is a special number' FROM dual;
Query 2: SELECT to_char(00001,'0999999')||' is a special number' FROM dual;
```

Query 1 evaluates the number 00001, removes the leading zeros, converts the number 1 into the character "1" and returns the character string "1 is a special number". Query 2 applies the numeric format mask '0999999' to the number 00001, converting it into the character string "0000001". After concatenation to the character literals, the string returned is "0000001 is a special number". The zero and six 9s in the format mask indicate to the TO_CHAR function that leading zeros must

| TABLE 5-3 | Numeric Format Masks |

Format Element	Description of Element	Format	Number	Character Result
9	Numeric width	9999	12	12
0	Displays leading zeros	09999	0012	00012
.	Position of decimal point	09999.999	030.40	00030.400
D	Decimal separator position (period is default)	09999D999	030.40	00030.400
,	Position of comma symbol	09999,999	03040	00003,040
G	Group separator position (comma is default)	09999G999	03040	00003,040
$	Dollar sign	$099999	03040	$003040
L	Local currency	L099999	03040	GBP003040 if nls_currency is set to GBP
MI	Position of minus sign for negatives	99999MI	−3040	3040−
PR	Wrap negatives in parentheses	99999PR	−3040	<3040>
EEEE	Scientific notation	99.99999EEEE	121.976	1.21976E+02
U	nls_dual_currency	U099999	03040	CAD003040 if nls_dual_currency is set to CAD
V	Multiplies by 10n times (n is the number of nines after V)	9999V99	3040	304000
S	+ or − sign is prefixed	S999999	3040	+3040

be displayed and that the display width must be set to seven characters. Therefore, the string returned by the TO_CHAR function contains seven characters.

The query in Figure 5-2 retrieves the JOB_TITLE and MAX_SALARY columns from the JOBS table for the rows with the word "PRESIDENT" in the JOB_TITLE column, regardless of the case of the characters used to store the job title. MAX_SALARY has further been formatted to have a dollar currency symbol, a comma thousands separator, and a decimal point. When a format mask is smaller than the number being converted, as illustrated in the fourth item in the SELECT list, a string of hash symbols is returned instead. When a format mask contains fewer fractional components than the number, it is first rounded to the number of decimal places in the format mask before being converted.

CHAR function
with numbers

Converting numbers into characters is a reliable way to ensure that functions
on the
Job *and general SQL syntax, which expects character input, do not return errors*
when numbers are encountered. Converting numbers into character strings is
common when numeric data must be formatted for reporting purposes. The
format masks that support currency, thousands separators, and decimal point
separators are frequently used when presenting financial data.

Converting Dates to Characters Using the TO_CHAR Function

You can take advantage of a variety of format models to convert DATE items into
almost any character representation of a date using TO_CHAR. Its syntax is as follows:

TO_CHAR(*date1*, *[format]*, *[nls_parameter]*),

Only the *date1* parameter is mandatory and must take the form of a value that can be implicitly converted to a date. The optional *format* parameter is case sensitive and must be enclosed in single quotes. The format mask specifies which date elements are extracted and whether the element should be described by a long or an abbreviated name. The names of days and months are automatically padded with spaces. These may be removed using a modifier to the format mask called the fill mode (fm) operator. By prefixing the format model with the letters "fm", Oracle is instructed to trim all spaces from the names of days and months. There are many formatting options for dates being converted into characters, some of which are listed in Table 5-4.

Consider the following three queries:

```
Query 1: SELECT to_char(sysdate)||' is today''s date' FROM dual;
Query 2: SELECT to_char(sysdate,'Month')||'is a special time' FROM dual;
Query 3: SELECT to_char(sysdate,'fmMonth')||'is a special time' FROM dual;
```

If the current system date is 03/JAN/09 and the default display format is DD/MON/RR, then Query 1 returns the character string "03/JAN/09 is today's date". There are two notable components in Query 2. First, only the month

TABLE 5-4	Format Element	Description	Result
	Y	Last digit of year	5
Date Format Masks for Days, Months, and Years	YY	Last two digits of year	75
	YYY	Last three digits of year	975
	YYYY	Four-digit year	1975
	RR	Two-digit year (see Chapter 3 for details)	75
	YEAR	Case-sensitive English spelling of year	NINETEEN SEVENTY-FIVE
	MM	Two-digit month	06
	MON	Three-letter abbreviation of month	JUN
	MONTH	Case-sensitive English spelling of month	JUNE
	D	Day of the week	2
	DD	Two-digit day of month	02
	DDD	Day of the year	153
	DY	Three-letter abbreviation of day	MON
	DAY	Case-sensitive English spelling of day	MONDAY

component of the current system date is extracted for conversion to a character type. Second, since the format mask is case sensitive and `'Month'` appears in title case, the string returned is "January is a special time". There is no need to add a space in front of the literal "is a special time" since the TO_CHAR function automatically pads the name of the month with zero or more spaces to yield a nine-character-long string. Since January is eight characters long, one space is added, but if the month was September, no spaces would be automatically added. If the format mask in query 2 was `'MONTH'`, the string returned would be "JANUARY is a special time". The *fm* modifier is applied to Query 3, and the resultant string is "Januaryis a special time". Note there is no space between January and the literal "is a special time" as a result of the *fm* modifier. In Table 5-4, assume the elements are operating on the date 02-JUN-1975 and the current year is 2009.

The date format elements pertaining to weeks, quarters, centuries, and other less commonly used format masks are listed in Table 5-5. The result column is obtained by evaluating the TO_CHAR function using the date 24-SEP-1000 BC, with the format mask from the format element column in the table.

The time component of a date time data type is extracted using the format models in Table 5-6. The result is obtained by evaluating the TO_CHAR function using the date including its time component 27-JUN-2010 21:35:13, with the format mask in the format element column in Table 5-6.

TABLE 5-5	Format Element	Description	Result
Less Commonly Used Date Format Masks	W	Week of month	4
	WW	Week of year	39
	Q	Quarter of year	3
	CC	Century	10
	S preceding CC, YYYY, or YEAR	If date is BC, a minus sign is prefixed to result	–10, –1000 or –ONE THOUSAND
	IYYY,IYY,IY,I	ISO dates of four, three, two, and one digit, respectively	1000, 000, 00, 0
	BC, AD, B.C., and A.D.	BC or AD and period-spaced B.C. or A.D.	BC
	J	Julian day—days since 31 December 4713 BC	1356075
	IW	ISO standard week (1 to 53)	39
	RM	Roman numeral month	IX

TABLE 5-6	Format Element	Description	Result
Date Format Masks for Time Components	AM, PM, A.M., and P.M.	Meridian indicators	PM
	HH, HH12, and HH24	Hour of day, 1–12 hours, and 0–23 hours	09, 09, 21
	MI	Minute (0–59)	35
	SS	Second (0–59)	13
	SSSSS	Seconds past midnight (0–86399)	77713

Several other elements that may be used in date time format models are summarized in Table 5-7. Punctuation marks are used to separate format elements. Three types of suffixes exist to format components of date time elements. Furthermore, character literals may be included in a date format model if they are enclosed in double quotation marks. The results in Table 5-7 are obtained by applying the TO_CHAR function using the date 12/SEP/08 14:31 with the format masks listed in the description and format mask column.

The JOB_HISTORY table keeps track of jobs occupied by employees in the company. The query in Figure 5-3 retrieves a descriptive sentence about the quitting date for each employee based on their END_DATE, EMPLOYEE_ID, and JOB_ID fields. A character expression is concatenated to a TO_CHAR function call with a format model of 'fmDay "the "ddth "of" Month YYYY'. The *fm* modifier is used to trim blank spaces that trail the names of the shorter days and shorter months. The two character literals enclosed in double quotation marks are the words "the" and "of". The 'th' format model is applied to the 'dd' date element to create an ordinal day such as the 17th or 31st. The 'Month' format model displays the full name of the month element of the END_DATE column in title case. Finally, the YYYY format mask retrieves the four-digit year component.

TABLE 5-7	Format Element	Description and Format Mask	Result
Miscellaneous Date Format Masks	- / . , ? # !	Punctuation marks: 'MM.YY'	09.08
	"any character literal"	Character literals: '"Week" W "of" Month'	Week 2 of September
	TH	Positional or ordinal text: 'DDth "of" Month'	12TH of September
	SP	Spelled out number: 'MmSP Month Yyyysp'	Nine September Two Thousand Eight
	THSP or SPTH	Spelled out positional or ordinal number: 'hh24SpTh'	Fourteenth

FIGURE 5-3	

TO_CHAR
function with
dates

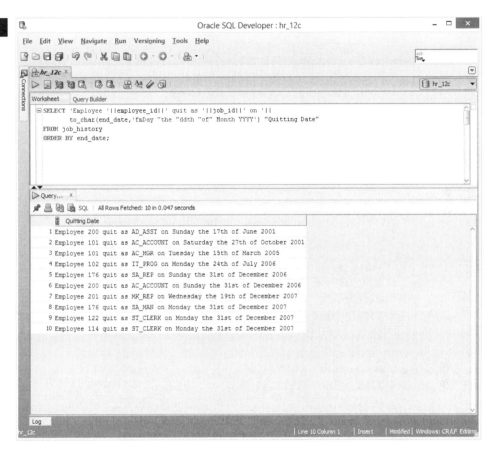

EXERCISE 5-1

Converting Dates into Characters Using the TO_CHAR Function

You are required to retrieve a list of FIRST_NAME and LAST_NAME values and an expression based on the HIRE_DATE column for employees hired on a Saturday. The expression must be aliased as START_DATE and a HIRE_DATE value of 17-FEB-1996 must return the following string:

Saturday, the 13th of January, Two Thousand One.

1. Start SQL Developer and connect to the HR schema.

2. The WHERE clause is

```
WHERE TO_CHAR(HIRE_DATE,'fmDay') = 'Saturday'
```

The *fm* modifier is necessary to remove trailing blanks since a comparison with a character literal is performed and an exact match is required.

3. The START_DATE expression is

   ```
   TO_CHAR(HIRE_DATE, 'fmDay, "the "ddth "of" Month, Yyyysp.')
   ```

   The year format mask results in it being spelled out in title case.

4. The SELECT clause is therefore

   ```
   SELECT FIRST_NAME, LAST_NAME, TO_CHAR(HIRE_DATE, 'fmDay, "the
   "ddth "of" Month, Yyyysp.') START_DATE
   ```

5. The FROM clause is

   ```
   FROM EMPLOYEES
   ```

6. Executing this statement returns employees' names and the START_DATE expression as shown in the following illustration:

Converting Characters to Dates Using the TO_DATE Function

The TO_DATE function returns an item of type DATE. Character strings converted to dates may contain all or just a subset of the date time elements comprising a DATE. When strings with only a subset of the date time elements are converted, Oracle provides default values to construct a complete date. Components of character strings are associated with different date time elements using a format model or mask. The syntax is as follows:

TO_DATE(*string1*, [*format*], [*nls_parameter*]),

Only the *string1* parameter is mandatory and if no format mask is supplied, *string1* must take the form of a value that can be implicitly converted into a date. The optional *format* parameter is almost always used and is specified in single quotation marks. The format masks are identical to those listed in Tables 5-4, 5-5, and 5-6. The TO_DATE function has an *fx* modifier which is similar to *fm* used with the TO_CHAR function. *fx* specifies an exact match for *string1* and the format mask. When the *fx* modifier is specified, character items that do not exactly match the format mask yield an error. Consider the following five queries:

```
Query 1: SELECT to_date('25-DEC-2010') FROM dual;
Query 2: SELECT to_date('25-DEC') FROM dual;
Query 3: SELECT to_date('25-DEC', 'DD-MON') FROM dual;
Query 4: SELECT to_date('25-DEC-2010 18:03:45', 'DD-MON-YYYY
HH24:MI:SS') FROM dual;
Query 5: SELECT to_date('25-DEC-10', 'fxDD-MON-YYYY') FROM dual;
```

Query 1 evaluates the string 25-DEC-2010 and has sufficient information to implicitly convert it into a DATE item with a default mask of DD-MON-YYYY. The hyphen separator could be substituted with another punctuation character. Since no time components are provided, the time for this converted date is set to midnight or 00:00:00. Query 2 cannot implicitly convert the string into a date because there is insufficient information and an "ORA-01840: input value is not long enough for date format" error is returned. By supplying a format mask DD-MON to the string 25-DEC in Query 3, Oracle can match the number 25 to DD and the abbreviated month name DEC to the MON component. Year and time components are absent, so the current year returned by the SYSDATE function is used and the time is set to midnight. If the current year is 2009, Query 3 returns the date 25/DEC/09 00:00:00. Query 4 performs a complete conversion of a string with all the date time elements present, and no default values are supplied by Oracle. Query 5 uses the *fx* modifier in its format mask. Since the year component of the string is 10 and the corresponding format mask is YYYY, the *fx* modifier results in an "ORA-01862: the numeric value does not match the length of the format item" error being returned.

FIGURE 5-4

The TO_DATE
function

```
SQL> SELECT first_name, last_name, hire_date
  2  FROM employees
  3  WHERE hire_date > to_date('01/12/2008','mm/dd/yyyy')
  4  ORDER BY hire_date;

FIRST_NAME           LAST_NAME                HIRE_DATE
-------------------  -----------------------  ---------
Douglas              Grant                    13-JAN-08
Mattea               Marvins                  24-JAN-08
Eleni                Zlotkey                  29-JAN-08
Girard               Geoni                    03-FEB-08
Hazel                Philtanker               06-FEB-08
David                Lee                      23-FEB-08
Steven               Markle                   08-MAR-08
Sundar               Ande                     24-MAR-08
Amit                 Banda                    21-APR-08
Sundita              Kumar                    21-APR-08

10 rows selected.

SQL>
```

The TO_DATE function is used in the WHERE clause in Figure 5-4 to limit the rows returned for those employees hired after 12 January 2008. The format mask matches 01 to MM, 12 to DD, and 2008 to YYYY.

Converting Characters to Numbers Using the TO_NUMBER Function

The TO_NUMBER function returns an item of type NUMBER. Character strings converted into numbers must be suitably formatted so that any nonnumeric components are translated or stripped away with an appropriate format mask. The syntax is as follows:

TO_NUMBER(*string1*, [*format*], [*nls_parameter*]),

Only the *string1* parameter is mandatory and if no format mask is supplied, it must be a value that can be implicitly converted into a number. The optional *format* parameter is specified in single quotation marks. The format masks are identical to those listed in Table 5-3. Consider the following two queries:

```
Query 1: SELECT to_number('$1,000.55') FROM dual;
Query 2: SELECT to_number('$1,000.55','$999,999.99') FROM dual;
```

Query 1 cannot perform an implicit conversion to a number because of the dollar sign, comma, and period and it returns the error "ORA-1722: invalid number." Query 2 matches the dollar symbol, comma, and period from the string to the format mask,

SCENARIO & SOLUTION

Your task is to extract the day and month portion of a date column and compare it with the corresponding components of the current system date. Can such a comparison be performed?	Yes. The TO_CHAR function used on a date item with a format mask like `'DD-MON'` causes the day and month component to be isolated. This value can be compared with the current system date using the following expression: `TO_CHAR(SYSDATE, 'DD-MON')`
A report of profit and loss is required with the results displayed as follows: if the amount is negative, it must be enclosed in angle brackets. The amount must be displayed with a leading dollar sign. Can results be retrieved in the specified format?	Yes. The numeric amount must be converted into a character string using the TO_CHAR function with a format mask that encloses it in angle brackets if it is negative and precedes it with a dollar sign. The following function call retrieves the results in the required format: `TO_CHAR(AMOUNT, '$999999PR')`
You are asked to input past employee data into the JOB_HISTORY table from a paper-based source, but the start date information is only available as the year the employee started. Can this value be converted into the first of January of the year?	Yes. Consider the conversion function call `TO_DATE('2000','YYYY')` for an employee who started in the year 2000. If this date is extracted as follows, the character string 01/01/2000 is returned: `TO_CHAR(TO_DATE('2000','YYYY'), 'MM/DD/YYYY')`

and, although the numeric width is larger than the string width, the number 1000.55 is returned.

Figure 5-5 shows how the SUBSTR function was first used to extract the last eight characters from the PHONE_NUMBER character column. The TO_NUMBER function was then used to convert these eight characters, including a decimal point, into a number that was multiplied by 10000, for employees belonging to DEPARTMENT_ID 30.

exam
ⱳatch

Read the exam questions very carefully. The TO_NUMBER function converts character items into numbers. If you convert a number using a shorter format mask, an error is returned. If you convert a number based on a longer format mask, the original number is returned. Be careful not to confuse TO_NUMBER conversions with TO_CHAR. For example, `TO_NUMBER(123.56,'999.9')` returns an error, while `TO_CHAR(123.56,'999.9')` returns 123.6.

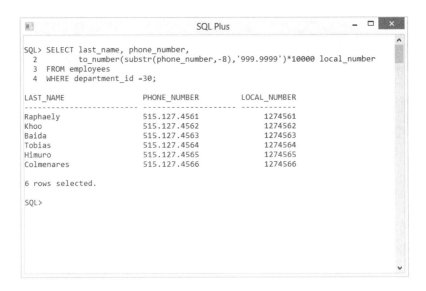

FIGURE 5-5

The TO_
NUMBER
function

```
SQL> SELECT last_name, phone_number,
  2        to_number(substr(phone_number,-8),'999.9999')*10000 local_number
  3  FROM employees
  4  WHERE department_id =30;

LAST_NAME               PHONE_NUMBER         LOCAL_NUMBER
----------------------  -------------------  ------------
Raphaely                515.127.4561              1274561
Khoo                    515.127.4562              1274562
Baida                   515.127.4563              1274563
Tobias                  515.127.4564              1274564
Himuro                  515.127.4565              1274565
Colmenares              515.127.4566              1274566

6 rows selected.

SQL>
```

CERTIFICATION OBJECTIVE 5.03

Apply Conditional Expressions in a SELECT Statement

Nested functions were introduced in Chapter 4, but a formal discussion of this concept is provided in this section. Two new categories of functions are also introduced. These include the *general functions*, which provide the language for dealing effectively with NULL values, and the *conditional functions*, which support conditional logic in expressions. This certification objective covers the following areas:

■ Nested functions
■ General functions
■ Conditional functions

Nested Functions

Nested functions use the output from one function as the input to another. Functions always return exactly one result. Therefore, you can reliably consider a function call in the same way as you would a literal value, when providing input parameters to a function. Single row functions can be nested to any level of depth. The general form of a function is as follows:

Function1(*parameter 1*, *parameter2*,...) = *result1*

Substituting function calls as parameters to other functions may lead to an expression such as the following:

F1(*param1.1*, F2(*param2.1*, *param2.2*, F3(*param3.1*)), *param1.3*)

Nested functions are first evaluated before their return values are used as parametric input to other functions. They are evaluated from the innermost to outermost levels. The preceding expression is evaluated as follows:

1. F3(*param3.1*) is evaluated and its return value provides the third parameter to function F2 and may be called: *param2.3*.

2. F2(*param2.1*, *param2.2*, *param2.3*) is evaluated and its return value provides the second parameter to function F1 and is *param1.2*.

3. F1(*param1.1*, *param1.2*, *param1.3*) is evaluated and the result is returned to the calling program.

Function F3 is said to be nested three levels deep in this example. Consider the following query:

```
SELECT length(to_char(to_date('28/10/09', 'DD/MM/RR'),'fmMonth'))FROM dual;
```

There are three functions in the SELECT list which, from inner to outer levels, are TO_DATE, TO_CHAR and LENGTH. The query is evaluated as follows:

1. The innermost function is evaluated first. TO _ DATE('28/10/09','DD/MM/RR') converts the character string 28/10/09 into the DATE value 28-OCT-2009. The RR format mask is used for the year portion. Therefore, the century component returned is the current century (the twenty-first), since the year component is between 0 and 49.

2. The second innermost function is evaluated next. TO _ CHAR('28-OCT-2009', 'fmMonth') converts the given date based on the Month format mask and returns the character string October. The *fm* modifier trims trailing blank spaces from the name of the month.

3. Finally, the LENGTH('October') function is evaluated and the query returns the number 7.

SCENARIO & SOLUTION	
Are nested functions evaluated from the outermost level to the innermost level?	No. Nested functions are resolved from the innermost nested level moving outward.
Must all functions in a nested expression return the same data type?	No. The data types of the parameters of nested functions may be different from each other. It is important to ensure that the correct data types are always supplied to functions to avoid errors.

Is there a simpler way to display the SALARY information from the EMPLOYEES table in the form $13,000 without using the following statement?
 	
`SELECT '$'|| SUBSTR(SALARY,1,`
`MOD(LENGTH(SALARY),3))||',`
`'|| SUBSTR(SALARY, MOD`
`(LENGTH(SALARY),3)+1)`
	Yes. A simple and elegant solution is to use the TO_CHAR function with the `'$99G999'` format mask:
	
	`SELECT TO_CHAR(SALARY, '$99G999') FROM`
	`EMPLOYEES;`

General Functions

General functions simplify working with columns that potentially contain null values. These functions accept input parameters of all data types. The services they offer are primarily relevant to null values.

The functions examined in the next sections include the *NVL* function, which provides an alternative value to use if a null is encountered. The *NVL2* function performs a conditional evaluation of its first parameter and returns a value if a null is encountered and an alternative if the parameter is not null. The *NULLIF* function compares two terms and returns a null result if they are equal, otherwise it returns the first term. The *COALESCE* function accepts an unlimited number of parameters and returns the first nonnull parameter, else it returns null.

The NVL Function

The NVL function evaluates whether a column or expression of any data type is null or not. If the term is null, an alternative not null value is returned; otherwise the initial term is returned.

The NVL function takes two mandatory parameters. Its syntax is:

NVL(*original, ifnull*),

where *original* represents the term being tested and *ifnull* is the result returned if the *original* term evaluates to null. The data types of the *original* and *ifnull* parameters must always be compatible. They must either be of the same type, or it must be possible to implicitly convert *ifnull* to the type of the *original* parameter. The NVL function returns a value with the same data type as the *original* parameter. Consider the following three queries:

```
Query 1: SELECT nvl(1234) FROM dual;
Query 2: SELECT nvl(null,1234) FROM dual;
Query 3: SELECT nvl(substr('abc',4),'No substring exists') FROM dual;
```

Since the NVL function takes two mandatory parameters, query 1 returns the error, "ORA-00909: invalid number of arguments." Query 2 returns 1234 after the null keyword is tested and found to be null. Query 3 involves a nested SUBSTR function that attempts to extract the fourth character from a three-character string. The inner function returns null, leaving the NVL(null,'No substring exists') function to execute, which then returns the string 'No substring exists'.

Figure 5-6 shows two almost identical queries. Both queries select rows where the LAST_NAME begins with the letter "E". The LAST_NAME, SALARY, and

FIGURE 5-6

The NVL function

COMMISSION_PCT columns are also selected. The difference between the queries is in the calculated expression aliased as MONTHLY_COMMISSION. Due to the NVL function in the first query, numeric results are returned. The second query returns some null values and one numeric item even though 1000 is added to each row.

on the
Job

It is tempting to dive in and construct a complex expression comprising many nested function calls, but this approach evolves with practice and experience. Conceptualize a solution to a query and break it down into the component function calls. The DUAL table is useful for ad hoc logical testing and debugging of separate function calls. Do not be afraid to execute queries as many times as you wish to perfect the components before assembling them into progressively larger components. Test and debug these until the final expression is formed.

The NVL2 Function

The NVL2 function provides an enhancement to NVL but serves a very similar purpose. It evaluates whether a column or expression of any data type is null or not. If the first term is not null, the second parameter is returned, else the third parameter is returned. Recall that the NVL function is different since it returns the original term if it is not null.

The NVL2 function takes three mandatory parameters. Its syntax is:

NVL2(*original, ifnotnull, ifnull*),

where *original* represents the term being tested. *Ifnotnull* is returned if *original* is not null, and *ifnull* is returned if *original* is null. The data types of the *ifnotnull* and *ifnull* parameters must be compatible, and they cannot be of type LONG. They must either be of the same type, or it must be possible to convert *ifnull* to the type of the *ifnotnull* parameter. The data type returned by the NVL2 function is the same as that of the *ifnotnull* parameter. Consider the following three queries:

```
Query 1: SELECT nvl2(1234,1,'a string') FROM dual;
Query 2: SELECT nvl2(null,1234,5678) FROM dual;
Query 3: SELECT nvl2(substr('abc',2),'Not bc','No substring') FROM dual;
```

The *ifnotnull* term in query 1 is a number and the *ifnull* parameter is `'a string'`. Since there is a data type incompatibility between them, an "ORA-01722: invalid number" error is returned. Query 2 returns the *ifnull* parameter, which is 5678. Query 3 extracts the characters "bc" using the SUBSTR function and the `NVL2('bc',Not bc','No Substring')` function is evaluated. The *ifnotnull* parameter, the string `'Not bc'`, is returned.

FIGURE 5-7

The NVL2
function

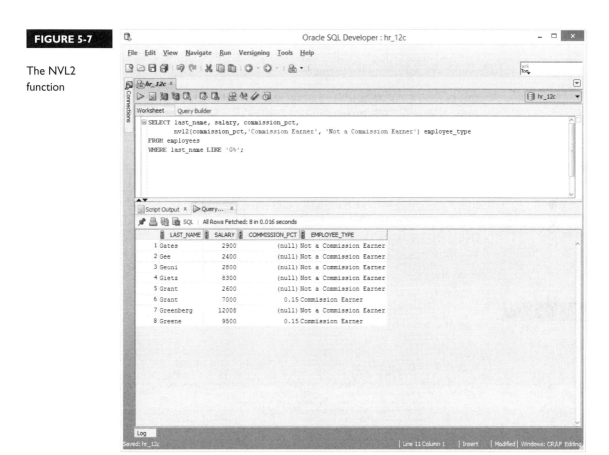

Figure 5-7 shows how the NVL2 function is used to provide descriptive text classifying employees with LAST_NAME values beginning with "F" into commission and noncommission earners based on the nullable COMMISSION_PCT column.

The NULLIF Function

The NULLIF function tests two terms for equality. If they are equal the function returns a null, else it returns the first of the two terms tested.

The NULLIF function takes two mandatory parameters of any data type. The syntax is:

NULLIF(*ifunequal*, *comparison_term*),

where the parameters *ifunequal* and *comparison_term* are compared. If they are identical, then NULL is returned. If they differ, the *ifunequal* parameter is returned. Consider the following three queries:

```
Query 1: SELECT nullif(1234,1234) FROM dual;
Query 2: SELECT nullif(1234,1233+1) FROM dual;
Query 3: SELECT nullif('24-JUL-2009','24-JUL-09') FROM dual;
```

Query 1 returns a null value since the parameters are identical. The arithmetic equation in Query 2 is implicitly evaluated, and the NULLIF function finds 1234 equivalent to 1233+1 (1234), so it returns a null value. The character literals in Query 3 are not implicitly converted to DATE items and are compared as two character strings by the NULLIF function. Since the strings are of different lengths, the *ifunequal* parameter 24-JUL-2009 is returned.

Figure 5-8 shows how NULLIF is nested as a parameter to the NVL2 function. The NULLIF function itself has the SUBSTR and UPPER character functions

FIGURE 5-8

The NULLIF function

embedded in the expression used as its *ifunequal* parameter. The EMAIL column is compared with an expression, formed by concatenating the first character of the FIRST_NAME to the uppercase equivalent of the LAST_NAME column, for employees with four-character-long first names. When these terms are equal, NULLIF returns a null, else it returns the evaluated *ifunequal* parameter. This is used as a parameter to NVL2. The NVL2 function provides descriptive text classifying rows as matching the pattern or not.

EXERCISE 5-2

Using NULLIF and NVL2 for Simple Conditional Logic

You are required to return a set of rows from the EMPLOYEES table with DEPARTMENT_ID values of 100. The set must contain FIRST_NAME and LAST_NAME values and an expression aliased as NAME_LENGTHS. This expression must return the string 'Different Length' if the length of the FIRST_NAME differs from that of the LAST_NAME, else the string 'Same Length' must be returned.

1. Start SQL Developer and connect to the HR schema.

2. The NAME_LENGTHS expression may be calculated in several ways. The solution provided uses the NULLIF function to test whether the LENGTH values returned for the FIRST_NAME and LAST_NAME columns are the same. If they are, NULL is returned, else the LENGTH of the LAST_NAME is returned. If the outer function (NVL2) gets a NULL parameter, the string 'Same Length' is returned, else the string 'Different Length' is returned.

3. The SELECT clause is therefore

```
SELECT FIRST_NAME, LAST_NAME, NVL2(NULLIF(LENGTH(LAST_NAME),
LENGTH(FIRST_NAME)), 'Different Length', 'Same Length') NAME_LENGTHS
```

4. The FROM clause is

```
FROM EMPLOYEES
```

5. The WHERE clause is

```
WHERE DEPARTMENT_ID=100
```

6. Executing this statement returns employees' names and the NAME_LENGTHS expression as shown in the following illustration:

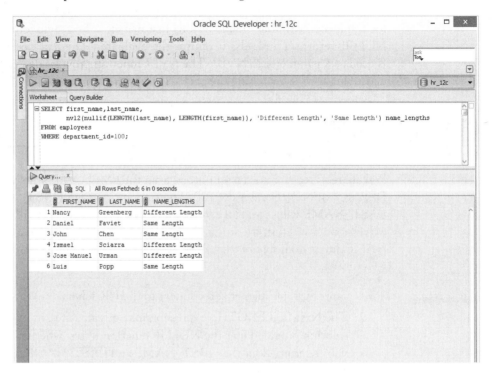

The COALESCE Function

The COALESCE function returns the first nonnull value from its parameter list. If all its parameters are null, then null is returned. The COALESCE function takes two mandatory parameters and any number of optional parameters. The syntax is:

COALESCE(*expr1*, *expr2*,…,*exprn*),

where *expr1* is returned if it is not null, else *expr2* if it is not null, and so on. COALESCE is a general form of the NVL function, as the following two equations illustrate:

COALESCE(*expr1*,*expr2*) = NVL(*expr1*,*expr2*)
COALESCE(*expr1*,*expr2*,*expr3*) = NVL(*expr1*,NVL(*expr2*,*expr3*))

The data type COALESCE returns if a not null value is found that is the same as that of the first not null parameter. To avoid an "ORA-00932: inconsistent data types" error, all not null parameters must have data types compatible with the first not null parameter. Consider the following three queries:

```
Query 1: SELECT coalesce(null, null, null, 'a string') FROM dual;
Query 2: SELECT coalesce(null, null, null) FROM dual;
Query 3: SELECT coalesce(substr('abc',4),'Not bc','No substring') FROM dual;
```

Query 1 returns the fourth parameter: a string, since this is the first not null parameter encountered. Query 2 returns null because all its parameters are null. Query 3 evaluates its first parameter, which is a nested SUBSTR function, and finds it to be null. The second parameter is not null so the string 'Not bc' is returned.

The STATE_PROVINCE, POSTAL_CODE, and CITY information was retrieved from the LOCATIONS table for the rows with COUNTRY_ID values of UK, IT, or JP. As Figure 5-9 shows, the COALESCE function returns the STATE_PROVINCE value for a row if it is not null. If it is null the POSTAL_CODE value is returned. If that is null, the CITY field is returned, else the result is null.

FIGURE 5-9	

The COALESCE function

Conditional Functions

Conditional logic, also known as *if-then-else* logic, refers to choosing a path of execution based on data values meeting certain conditions. *Conditional functions*, like DECODE and the CASE expression, return different values based on evaluating comparison conditions. These conditions are specified as parameters to the DECODE function and the CASE expression. The DECODE function is specific to Oracle, while the CASE expression is ANSI SQL compliant. Following is an example of *if-then-else* logic: if the country value is Brazil or Australia, then return Southern Hemisphere, else return Northern Hemisphere.

The DECODE Function

Although its name sounds mysterious, this function is straightforward. The DECODE function implements *if-then-else* conditional logic by testing its first two terms for equality and returns the third if they are equal and optionally returns another term if they are not.

The DECODE function takes at least three mandatory parameters, but can take many more. The syntax of the function is:

DECODE(*expr1,comp1, iftrue1, [comp2,iftrue2...[compN,iftrueN]], [iffalse]*)

These parameters are evaluated as shown in the following pseudocode example:

```
If expr1 = comp1 then return iftrue1
    else if expr1 = comp2 then return iftrue2
        . . .
        . . .
            else if expr1 = compN then return iftrueN
        else return null | iffalse;
```

Expr1 is compared to *comp1*. If they are equal, then *iftrue1* is returned. If *expr1* is not equal to *comp1*, then what happens next depends on whether the optional parameters *comp2* and *iftrue2* are present. If they are, then *expr1* is compared to *comp2*. If they are equal, then *iftrue2* is returned. If not, what happens next depends on whether further *compn,iftruen* pairs exist, and the cycle continues until no comparison terms remain. If no matches have been found and if the *iffalse* parameter is defined, then *iffalse* is returned. If the *iffalse* parameter does not exist and no matches are found, a null value is returned.

All parameters to the DECODE function may be expressions. The return data type is the same as that of the first matching comparison item. The expression *expr1* is implicitly converted to the data type of the first comparison parameter *comp1*. As the other comparison parameters *comp2…compn* are evaluated, they too are implicitly converted to the same data type as *comp1*. *Decode* considers two nulls to be equivalent, so if *expr1* is null and *comp3* is the first null comparison parameter encountered, then the corresponding result parameter *iftrue3* is returned. Consider the following three queries:

```
Query 1: SELECT decode(1234,123,'123 is a match') FROM dual;
Query 2: SELECT decode(1234,123,'123 is a match','No match') FROM dual;
Query 3: SELECT decode('search','comp1','true1', 'comp2','true2',
                  'search','true3', substr('2search',2,6),'true4',
'false')
       FROM dual;
```

Query 1 compares the number 1234 with the first comparison term 123. Since they are not equal, the first result term cannot be returned. Further, as there is no default *iffalse* parameter defined, a null is returned. Query 2 is identical to the first except that an *iffalse* parameter is defined. Therefore, since 1234 is not equal to 123, the string `'No match'` is returned. Query 3 searches through the comparison parameters for a match. The character terms `'comp1'` and `'comp2'` are not equal to search, so the results true1 and true2 are not returned. A match is found in the third comparison term `'comp3'` (parameter 6), which contains the string search. Therefore, the third result term *iftrue3* (parameter 7) containing the string `'true3'` is returned. Note that since a match has been found, no further searching takes place. So, although the fourth comparison term (parameter 8) is also a match to *expr1*, this expression is never evaluated, because a match was found in an earlier comparison term.

Distinct occurrences of the COUNTRY_ID column values in the LOCATIONS table have been classified into either Northern or Southern Hemisphere countries using a DECODE function. Figure 5-10 shows how the COUNTRY_ID column

FIGURE 5-10

The DECODE
function

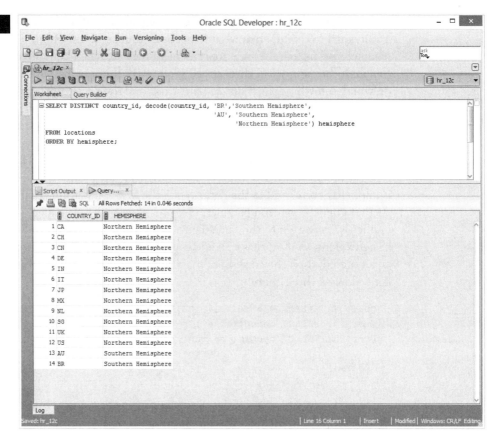

is the expression for which a match is sought. *If* the COUNTRY_ID value is
BR (Brazil) or AU (Australia), *then* the function returns the string Southern
Hemisphere, *else* Northern Hemisphere is returned.

The CASE Expression

Virtually all third and fourth generation programming languages implement a *case*
statement. Like the DECODE function, the CASE expression facilitates *if-then-else*
conditional logic. There are two variants of the CASE expression. The *simple CASE
expression* lists the conditional search item once, and equality to the search item is
tested by each comparison expression. The *searched CASE expression* lists a separate
condition for each comparison expression.

INSIDE THE EXAM

The certification objectives in this chapter are primarily measured with practical examples that require you to predict the results returned by an expression. Explicit conversion functions with their many format masks are tested. The TO_CHAR function, *fm* modifier, and the *sp*, *th*, and *spth* format models are commonly examined. Use of the TO_CHAR function to convert numbers into characters is tested, and emphasis is often placed on the format masks that determine numeric width, dollar symbol, group separator, and decimal separator formats.

Many questions consist of expressions with nested functions, and it is vital for you to know how to interpret and trace them. The innermost to outermost sequence of evaluation of nested functions is important and must be remembered.

The general functions NVL, NVL2, NULLIF, and COALESCE all pertain to

working with NULL. Since null values are prevalent in many databases, a thorough understanding of all these functions, particularly NVL and NVL2, is required.

The DECODE function and CASE expression are sometimes perceived as complex and difficult to understand. They are, however, two of the simplest and most useful functions guaranteed to be examined. Pay attention to the positional meaning of the parameters when using the DECODE function. The simple and searched CASE expression differs from the functions discussed earlier. This is due to the CASE... END block, which encloses one or more WHEN...OTHER pairs and optionally an ELSE statement. Practice with this expression and you will quickly learn its readable and standardized structure.

The CASE expression takes at least three mandatory parameters but can take many more. Its syntax depends on whether a simple or a searched CASE expression is used. The syntax for the simple CASE expression is as follows:

```
        CASE search_expr
    WHEN comparison_expr1 THEN iftrue1
    [WHEN comparison_expr2 THEN iftrue2
    …
        WHEN comparison_exprN THEN iftrueN
    ELSE iffalse]
END
```

The simple CASE expression is enclosed within a CASE…END block and consists of at least one WHEN…THEN statement. In its simplest form, with one WHEN…THEN statement, the *search_expr* is compared with the *comparison_expr1*.

If they are equal, then the result *iftrue1* is returned. If not, a null value is returned unless an ELSE component is defined, in which case, the default *iffalse* value is returned. When more than one WHEN…THEN statement exists in the CASE expression, searching for a matching comparison expression continues until a match is found.

The search, comparison, and result parameters can be column values, expressions, or literals but must all be of the same data type. Consider the following query:

```
SELECT
 CASE substr(1234,1,3)
   WHEN '134' THEN '1234 is a match'
   WHEN '1235' THEN '1235 is a match'
   WHEN concat('1','23') THEN concat('1','23')||' is a match'
   ELSE 'no match'
 END
FROM dual;
```

The search expression derived from the SUBSTR(1234,1,3) is the character string 123. The first WHEN…THEN statement compares the string 134 with 123. Since they are not equal, the result expression is not evaluated. The second WHEN…THEN statement compares the string 1235 with 123 and again, they are not equal. The third WHEN…THEN statement compares the results derived from the CONCAT('1','23') expression, which is 123, to the search expression. Since they are identical, the third results expression '123 is a match' is returned.

The LAST_NAME and HIRE_DATE columns for employees with DEPARTMENT_ID values not equal to 50, 80, 90, 100, or 110 are retrieved along with two numeric expressions and one CASE expression, as shown in Figure 5-11.

The numeric expression aliased as MONTHS returns a truncated value obtained by calculating the months of service between the 1st of January 2013 and an employee's hire date using the MONTHS_BETWEEN function.

Five categories of loyalty classification based on every two years of service are defined by truncating the quotient obtained by dividing the total months of service by 24. This forms the search expression in the CASE statement. None of the rows in the dataset match the comparison expression in the first WHEN…THEN statement, but as Figure 5-11 shows, the remaining WHEN…THEN statements catch 13 rows and 3 rows are caught by the ELSE statement. The set is then sorted by months.

FIGURE 5-11

The CASE
expression

The syntax for the searched CASE expression is as follows:

        CASE
    WHEN *condition1* THEN *iftrue1*
    [WHEN *condition2* THEN *iftrue2*
    …
        WHEN *conditionN* THEN *iftrueN*
    ELSE *iffalse*]
END

The searched CASE expression is enclosed within a CASE…END block and consists of at least one WHEN…THEN statement. In its simplest form with one

WHEN...THEN statement, *condition1* is evaluated; if it is true, then the result *iftrue1* is returned. If not, a null value is returned unless an ELSE component is defined, in which case the default *iffalse* value is returned. When more than one WHEN...THEN statement exists in the CASE expression, searching for a matching comparison expression continues until one is found. The query to retrieve the identical set of results to those obtained in Figure 5-11, using a searched CASE expression, is listed next:

```
SELECT last_name, hire_date,
trunc(months_between('01-JAN-2013',hire_date)) months,
trunc(months_between('01-JAN-2013',hire_date)/24) "Months divided by 24",
CASE
  WHEN trunc(months_between('01-JAN-2013',hire_date)/24) < 2 then 'Intern'
  WHEN trunc(months_between('01-JAN-2013',hire_date)/24) < 3 then 'Junior'
  WHEN trunc(months_between('01-JAN-2013',hire_date)/24) < 4 then 'Intermediate'
  WHEN trunc(months_between('01-JAN-2013',hire_date)/24) < 5 then 'Senior'
  ELSE 'Furniture'
END loyalty
FROM employees
where department_id NOT IN (50,80,90,100,110)
ORDER BY months;
```

EXERCISE 5-3

Using the DECODE Function

You are requested to query the LOCATIONS table for rows with the value US in the COUNTRY_ID column. An expression aliased as LOCATION_INFO is required to evaluate the STATE_PROVINCE column values and returns different information as per the following table. Sort the output based on the LOCATION_INFO expression.

If STATE_PROVINCE is	The value returned is
Washington	The string 'Headquarters'
Texas	The string 'Oil Wells'
California	The CITY column value
New Jersey	The STREET_ADDRESS column value

1. Start SQL Developer and connect to the HR schema.
2. The LOCATION_ID expression may be calculated in several different ways. This includes using a CASE expression or a DECODE function. The solution below uses DECODE.

3. The SELECT clause is

```
SELECT DECODE(STATE_PROVINCE, 'Washington', 'Headquarters',
'Texas', 'Oil Wells', 'California', CITY, 'New Jersey',
STREET_ADDRESS) LOCATION_INFO
```

Notice the mixture of character literals and columns specified as parameters to the DECODE function.

4. The FROM clause is

```
FROM EMPLOYEES
```

5. The WHERE clause is

```
WHERE COUNTRY_ID='US'
```

6. The ORDER BY clause is

```
ORDER BY LOCATION_INFO
```

7. The result of executing this statement is shown in the following illustration:

CERTIFICATION SUMMARY

This chapter builds on the single-row functions introduced previously. The concepts of implicit and explicit data type conversion are explained along with the reliability risks associated with implicit conversions.

Date to character and *number to character* conversions are described using the TO_CHAR function. A variety of format models or masks are available. The TO_NUMBER function performs *character to number* conversions, while the TO_DATE function performs *character to date* data type conversions.

Nested functions and their evaluation is one of the most valuable lessons in this chapter. Understanding this fundamental concept is crucial. The general functions NVL, NVL2, NULLIF, and COALESCE are designed to simplify working with null values and provide basic conditional logic functionality.

DECODE is an Oracle-specific function that supports *if-then-else* logic in the context of an SQL statement along with the ANSI-compliant CASE expression. The two variants are the simple CASE and searched CASE expressions. These conditional functions are straightforward and extremely useful.

The conversion, general, and conditional functions add significantly to the foundational knowledge of SQL you acquired from previous chapters and will hold you in good stead as you progress with your learning.

TWO-MINUTE DRILL

Describe Various Types of Conversion Functions Available in SQL

❏ When values do not match the defined parameters of functions, Oracle attempts to convert them into the required data types. This is known as implicit conversion.

❏ Explicit conversion occurs when a function like TO_CHAR is invoked to change the data type of a value.

❏ The TO_CHAR function performs *date to character* and *number to character* data type conversions.

❏ Character items are explicitly transformed into date values using the TO_DATE conversion function.

❏ Character items are changed into number values using the TO_NUMBER conversion function.

Use the TO_CHAR, TO_NUMBER, and TO_DATE Conversion Functions

❏ The TO_CHAR function returns an item of type VARCHAR2.

❏ Format models or masks prescribe patterns that character strings must match to facilitate accurate and consistent conversion into number or date items.

❏ When the TO_CHAR function performs *number to character* conversions, the format mask can specify currency, numeric width, position of decimal operator, thousands separator, and many other formatting codes.

❏ The format masks available when TO_CHAR is used to convert character items to date include day, week, month, quarter, year, and century.

❏ Format masks must always be specified enclosed in single quotes.

❏ When performing *date to character* conversion, the format mask specifies which date elements are extracted and whether the element should be described by a long or abbreviated name.

❏ Character terms, such as month and day names extracted from dates with the TO_CHAR function, are automatically padded with spaces that may be trimmed by prefixing the format mask with the *fm* modifier.

❏ The TO_DATE function has an *fx* modifier that specifies an exact match for the character string to be converted and the date format mask.

Apply Conditional Expressions in a SELECT Statement

❑ Nesting functions use the output from one function as the input to another.

❑ The NVL function either returns the original item unchanged or an alternative item if the initial term is null.

❑ The NVL2 function returns a new *if-null* item if the original item is null or an alternative *if-not-null* item if the original term is not null.

❑ The NULLIF function tests two terms for equality. If they are equal, the function returns null, else it returns the first of the two terms tested.

❑ The COALESCE function returns the first nonnull value from its parameter list. If all its parameters are null, then a null value is returned.

❑ The DECODE function implements *if-then-else* conditional logic by testing two terms for equality and returning the third term if they are equal or, optionally, some other term if they are not.

❑ There are two variants of the CASE expression used to facilitate *if-then-else* conditional logic: the simple CASE and searched CASE expressions.

SELF TEST

The following questions will measure your understanding of the material presented in this chapter. Read all the choices carefully because there may be more than one correct answer. Choose all the correct answers for each question.

Describe Various Types of Conversion Functions Available in SQL

I. What type of conversion is performed by the following statement? (Choose the best answer.)
```
SELECT LENGTH(3.14285) FROM DUAL;
```
A. Explicit conversion
B. Implicit conversion
C. 7
D. None of the above

2. Choose any incorrect statements regarding conversion functions. (Choose all that apply.)
A. TO_CHAR may convert date items to character items.
B. TO_DATE may convert character items to date items.
C. TO_CHAR may convert numbers to character items.
D. TO_DATE may convert date items to character items.

Use the TO_CHAR, TO_NUMBER, and TO_DATE Conversion Functions

3. What value is returned after executing the following statement? (Choose the best answer.)
```
SELECT TO_NUMBER(1234.49, 999999.9) FROM DUAL;
```
A. 1234.49
B. 001234.5
C. 1234.5
D. None of the above

4. What value is returned after executing the following statement? (Choose the best answer.)
```
SELECT TO_CHAR(1234.49, '999999.9') FROM DUAL;
```
A. 1234.49
B. 001234.5
C. 1234.5
D. None of the above

5. If SYSDATE returns 12-JUL-2009, what is returned by the following statement? (Choose the best answer.)

```
SELECT TO_CHAR(SYSDATE, 'fmMONTH, YEAR') FROM DUAL;
```

   A. JUL, 2009

   B. JULY, TWO THOUSAND NINE

   C. JUL-09

   D. None of the above

6. If SYSDATE returns 12-JUL-2009, what is returned by the following statement? (Choose the best answer.)

```
SELECT TO_CHAR(SYSDATE, 'fmDDth MONTH') FROM DUAL;
```

   A. 12TH JULY

   B. 12th July

   C. TWELFTH JULY

   D. None of the above

Apply Conditional Expressions in a SELECT Statement

7. If SYSDATE returns 12-JUL-2009, what is returned by the following statement? (Choose the best answer.)

```
SELECT TO_CHAR(TO_DATE(TO_CHAR(SYSDATE,'DD'),'DD'),'YEAR') FROM DUAL;
```

   A. 2009

   B. TWO THOUSAND NINE

   C. 12-JUL-2009

   D. None of the above

8. What value is returned after executing the following statement? (Choose the best answer.)

```
SELECT NVL2(NULLIF('CODA','SID'),'SPANIEL','TERRIER') FROM DUAL;
```

   A. SPANIEL

   B. TERRIER

   C. NULL

   D. None of the above

9. What value is returned after executing the following statement? (Choose the best answer.)

```
SELECT NVL(SUBSTR('AM I NULL',10),'YES I AM') FROM DUAL;
```

   A. NO

   B. NULL

   C. YES I AM

   D. None of the above

10. If SYSDATE returns 12-JUL-2009, what is returned by the following statement? (Choose the best answer.)
```
SELECT DECODE(TO_CHAR(SYSDATE,'MM'),'02','TAX DUE','PARTY') FROM DUAL;
```
A. TAX DUE
B. PARTY
C. 02
D. None of the above

LAB QUESTION

Using SQL Developer or SQL*Plus, connect to the OE schema and complete the following tasks.

As part of a new marketing initiative, you are asked to prepare a list of customer birthdays that occur between two days ago and seven days from any requested reference date in the current year. The list should retrieve rows from the CUSTOMERS table that include the CUST_FIRST_NAME, CUST_LAST_NAME, CUST_EMAIL, and DATE_OF_BIRTH columns in ascending order based on the day and month components of the DATE_OF_BIRTH value. An additional expression aliased as BIRTHDAY is required to return a descriptive message based on the following table. There are several approaches to solving this question. Your approach may differ from the solution described here.

SELF TEST ANSWERS

Describe Various Types of Conversion Functions Available in SQL

1. ☑ **B.** The number 3.14285 is given as a parameter to the LENGTH function. There is a data type mismatch, but Oracle implicitly converts the parameter to the character string "3.14285" allowing the function to operate correctly.

   ☒ **A, C,** and **D** are incorrect. Explicit conversion occurs when a function like TO_CHAR is executed. **C** is the correct length of the string "3.14285" but this is not asked for in the question.

2. ☑ **D.** Dates are only converted into character strings using TO_CHAR and not the TO_DATE function.

   ☒ **A, B,** and **C** are correct statements.

Use the TO_CHAR, TO_NUMBER, and TO_DATE Conversion Functions

3. ☑ **D.** An "ORA-1722: invalid number" error is returned because the statement is trying to convert a number with two digits after the decimal point using a format mask that caters for just one digit after the decimal point. If the expression was TO _ NUMBER(1234.49, '999999.99'), the number 1234.49 would be returned.

   ☒ **A, B,** and **C** are incorrect.

4. ☑ **C.** For the number 1234.49 to match the character format mask with one decimal place, the number is first rounded to 1234.5 before TO_CHAR converts it into the string "1234.5".

   ☒ **A, B,** and **D** are incorrect. **A** cannot be returned because the format mask only allows one character after the decimal point. **B** would be returned if the format mask was '009999.9'.

5. ☑ **B.** The MONTH and YEAR components of the format mask separated by a comma and a space indicate that TO_CHAR must extract the spelled out month and year values in uppercase separated by a comma and a space. The *fm* modifier removes extra blanks from the spelled out components.

   ☒ **A, C,** and **D** are incorrect. If the format mask was 'MON, YYYY' or 'MON-YY', **A** and **C**, respectively, would be returned.

6. ☑ **A.** The DD component returns the day of the month in uppercase. Since it is a number, it does not matter, unless the 'th' mask is applied, in which case that component is specified in uppercase. MONTH returns the month spelled out in uppercase.

   ☒ **B, C,** and **D** are incorrect. **B** would be returned if the format mask was 'fmddth Month', and **C** would be returned if the format mask was 'fmDDspth MONTH'.

Apply Conditional Expressions in a SELECT Statement

7. ☑ **B.** The innermost nested function is TO _ CHAR(SYSDATE,'DD'), which extracts the day component of SYSDATE and returns the character 12. The next function executed is TO _ DATE('12','DD') where the character 12 is cast as the day component. When such an incomplete date is provided, Oracle substitutes values from the SYSDATE function; since SYSDATE is 12-JUL-2009, this is the date used. The outermost function executed in TO _ CHAR('12-JUL-2009','YEAR') returns the year spelled out as TWO THOUSAND NINE.

☒ **A, C,** and **D** are incorrect.

8. ☑ **A.** The NULLIF function compares its two parameters and, since they are different, the first parameter is returned. The NVL2('CODA', 'SPANIEL','TERRIER') function call returns SPANIEL since its first parameter is not null.

☒ **B, C,** and **D** are incorrect.

9. ☑ **C.** The character literal "AM I NULL" is nine characters long. Therefore, trying to obtain a substring beginning at the tenth character returns a null. The outer function then becomes NVL(NULL,'YES I AM'), resulting in the string "YES I AM" being returned.

☒ **A, B,** and **D** are incorrect.

10. ☑ **B.** The innermost function TO _ CHAR(SYSDATE, 'MM') results in the character string "07" being returned. The outer function is DECODE('07','02','TAX DUE','PARTY'). Since "07" is not equal to "02" the else component "PARTY" is returned.

☒ **A, C,** and **D** are incorrect. **A** would only be returned if the month component extracted from SYSDATE was "02".

LAB ANSWER

Using SQL Developer or SQL*Plus, connect to the OE schema and complete the following tasks.

1. Start SQL Developer and connect to the OE schema.

2. The dataset must be restricted to rows from the CUSTOMERS table where the day component of the DATE_OF_BIRTH is between two days ago and seven days from a provided reference date in the current year. The reference date may be handled using an ampersand substitution at runtime. This solution utilizes the DDD date format mask described in Table 5-4 which provides the day of the year from a date.

3. The condition of the WHERE clause is

```
TO_CHAR(DATE_OF_BIRTH,'DDD') - TO_CHAR(&REFDATE,'DDD') BETWEEN -2 AND 7
```

4. The BIRTHDAY expression may be calculated in several ways. Based on the preceding WHERE clause, you are assured that the dataset is limited to the correct set of rows. The SELECT clause has to retrieve and manipulate the records for appropriate display. The CASE expression provides functionality for conditional logic and is well suited to this situation.

5. The case tested is based on the expression in the WHERE clause discussed above. The day of the year of the DATE_OF_BIRTH minus the day of the year of the reference date is evaluated. For example, if the difference is –2, then the string 'Day before yesterday' is returned. The different CASE conditions are tested is a similar manner. The ELSE component catches any rows not matching the CASE conditions and returns the string 'Later in the week'.

6. The SELECT clause is therefore

```
SELECT CUST_FIRST_NAME, CUST_LAST_NAME, CUST_EMAIL, DATE_OF_BIRTH,
CASE TO_CHAR(DATE_OF_BIRTH,'DDD')) -  TO_CHAR(&REFDATE,'DDD')
 WHEN -2 THEN 'Day before yesterday'
 WHEN -1 THEN 'Yesterday'
 WHEN 0  THEN 'Today'
 WHEN 1  THEN 'Tomorrow'
 WHEN 2  THEN 'Day after tomorrow'
 ELSE 'Later this week'
END BIRTHDAY
```

7. The FROM clause is

```
FROM CUSTOMERS
```

8. The ORDER BY clause is

```
ORDER BY TO_CHAR(DATE_OF_BIRTH,'MM-DD')
```

9. Executing this statement returns the set of results matching this pattern as shown in the following illustration for REFDATE=to _ date('08-JAN-2014'):

6
Reporting Aggregated Data Using the Group Functions

S ingle-row functions, explored in Chapters 4 and 5, return a single value for each row in a set of results. *Group* or *aggregate* functions operate on multiple rows. They are used to count the number of rows or to find the average of specific column values in a dataset. Many statistical operations, such as calculating standard deviation, medians, and averages, depend on executing functions against grouped data and not just single rows.

Group functions are examined in two stages. First, their purpose and syntax are discussed. Second, a detailed analysis of the AVG, SUM, MIN, MAX, and COUNT functions is conducted. The concept of grouping or segregating data based on one or more column values is explored before introducing the GROUP BY clause.

The WHERE clause restricts rows in a dataset before grouping, while the HAVING clause restricts them after grouping. This chapter concludes with a discussion of the HAVING clause.

CERTIFICATION OBJECTIVE 6.01

Describe the Group Functions

SQL *group functions* are defined and the different variants are discussed. The syntax of selected group functions is explained, their data types are discussed, and the DISTINCT keyword's effect on them is explored. This discussion is divided into two main areas:

- Definition of group functions
- Types and syntax of group functions

Definition of Group Functions

Group functions operate on aggregated data and return a single result per group. These groups usually consist of zero or more rows of data. Single-row functions are defined with the formula: $F(x, y, z, \ldots)$ = result, where $x, y, z\ldots$ are input parameters. The function F executes on one row of the data set at a time and returns a result for each row. Group functions may be defined using the following formula:

$F(g1, g2, g3, \ldots, gn)$ = *result1, result2, result3, \ldots, resultn;*

The group function executes once for each cluster of rows and returns a single result per group. These groups may be entire tables or portions of tables associated using a common value or attribute. If all the rows in tables are presented as one group to the group function, then one result is returned. One or more group functions may appear in the SELECT list as follows:

```
SELECT group_function(column or expression),…
FROM table [WHERE …] [ORDER BY…]
```

Consider the EMPLOYEES table. There are 107 rows in this table. Groups may be created based on the common values that rows share. For example, the rows that share the same DEPARTMENT_ID value may be clustered together. Thereafter, group functions are executed separately against each unique group.

As Figure 6-1 shows, there are 12 distinct DEPARTMENT_ID values in the EMPLOYEES table, including a null value. The rows are distributed into 12 groups

FIGURE 6-1

Group functions operating on 12 groups

based on common DEPARTMENT_ID values. The COUNT function executes 12 times, once for each group. Notice that the distinct groups do not contain the same number of rows.

on the **job**

*Group functions **aggregate a number of values from multiple rows into a single result. They are widely used for reporting purposes and are also known as summary or aggregate functions. Useful aggregated data such as sum totals, averages, and counts often form the basis of more sophisticated statistical calculations. It is useful to have a good understanding of the data stored in your application tables to maximize the quality of your aggregate reporting.***

Types and Syntax of Group Functions

A brief description of the most commonly used group functions is provided next. Many are examined in detail later in this chapter.

The COUNT function counts the number of rows in a group. Its syntax is as follows:

COUNT({*|[DISTINCT | ALL] *expr*}) ;

This syntax may be deconstructed into the following forms:

1. COUNT(*)
2. COUNT(DISTINCT *expr*)
3. COUNT(ALL *expr*)
4. COUNT(*expr*)

When COUNT(*) is invoked, all rows in the group, including those with nulls or duplicate values are counted. When COUNT(DISTINCT *expr*) is executed, only unique occurrences of *expr* are counted for each group. The ALL keyword is part of the default syntax, so COUNT(ALL *expr*) and COUNT(*expr*) are equivalent. These count the number of nonnull occurrences of *expr* in each group. The data type of *expr* may be NUMBER, DATE, CHAR, or VARCHAR2. If *expr* is a null, it is ignored unless it is managed using a general function like NVL, NVL2, or COALESCE.

The AVG function calculates the average value of a numeric column or expression in a group. Its syntax is as follows:

AVG([DISTINCT | ALL] *expr*) ;

This syntax may be deconstructed into the following forms:

1. AVG(DISTINCT *expr*)
2. AVG(ALL *expr*)
3. AVG(*expr*)

When AVG(DISTINCT *expr*) is invoked, the distinct values of *expr* are summed and divided by the number of unique occurrences of *expr*. AVG(ALL *expr*) and AVG(*expr*) add the nonnull values of *expr* for each row and divide the sum by the number of nonnull rows in the group. The data type of the *expr* parameter is NUMBER.

The SUM function returns the aggregated total of the nonnull numeric expression values in a group. It has the following syntax:

SUM([DISTINCT | ALL] *expr*) ;

This syntax may be deconstructed into the following forms:

1. SUM(DISTINCT *expr*)
2. SUM(ALL *expr*)
3. SUM(*expr*)

SUM(DISTINCT *expr*) provides a total by adding all the unique values returned after *expr* is evaluated for each row in the group. SUM(*expr*) and SUM(ALL *expr*) provide a total by adding *expr* for each row in the group. Null values are ignored. The data type of *expr* is NUMBER.

The MAX and MIN functions return the maximum (largest) and minimum (smallest) *expr* value in a group. Their syntax is as follows:

MAX([DISTINCT | ALL] *expr*); MIN([DISTINCT | ALL] *expr*)

This syntax may be deconstructed into the following forms:

1. MAX(DISTINCT *expr*); MIN(DISTINCT *expr*)
2. MAX(ALL *expr*); MIN(ALL *expr*)
3. MAX(*expr*); MIN(*expr*);

MAX(*expr*), MAX(ALL *expr*) and MAX(DISTINCT *expr*) examine the values for *expr* in a group of rows and return the largest value. Null values are ignored. MIN(*expr*), MIN(ALL *expr*) and MIN(DISTINCT *expr*) examine the values for *expr* in a group of rows and return the smallest value. The data type of the *expr* parameter may be NUMBER, DATE, CHAR, or VARCHAR2.

The STDDEV and VARIANCE functions are two of many statistical group functions Oracle provides. VARIANCE has the following syntax:

VARIANCE([DISTINCT | ALL] *expr*);

This syntax may be deconstructed into the following forms:

1. VARIANCE(DISTINCT *expr*)
2. VARIANCE(ALL *expr*)
3. VARIANCE(*expr*)

STDDEV has the following syntax:

STDDEV([DISTINCT | ALL] *expr*);

This syntax may be deconstructed into the following forms:

1. STDDEV(DISTINCT *expr*)
2. STDDEV(ALL *expr*)
3. STDDEV(*expr*)

Statistical variance refers to the variability of scores in a sample or set of data. VARIANCE(DISTINCT *expr*) returns the variability of unique nonnull data in a group. VARIANCE(*expr*) and VARIANCE(ALL *expr*) return the variability of nonnull data in the group.

STDDEV calculates statistical standard deviation, which is the degree of deviation from the mean value in a group. It is derived by finding the square root of the variance. STDDEV(DISTINCT *expr*) returns the standard deviation of unique nonnull data in a group. STDDEV(*expr*) and STDDEV(ALL *expr*) return the standard deviation of nonnull data in the group. The data type of the *expr* parameter is NUMBER.

There are two fundamental rules to remember when studying group functions. First, they always operate on a single group of rows at a time. The group may be one of many groups a dataset has been segmented into, or it may be an entire table. The group function executes once per group. Second, rows with nulls occurring in group columns or expressions are ignored, unless a general function like NVL, NVL2, or COALESCE is provided to handle them.

Consider the following example. If the average value for COMMISSION_PCT is retrieved from the EMPLOYEES table, only the nonnull values are considered. The expression AVG(COMMISSION_PCT) adds the 35 nonnull COMMISSION_PCT values and divides the total by 35. The average based on all 107 rows may be computed using the expression AVG(NVL(COMMISSION_PCT,0)).

CERTIFICATION OBJECTIVE 6.02

Identify the Available Group Functions

The different variants of *group functions* and their syntax were just discussed. This section provides examples demonstrating the application of these functions. The interactions of *group functions* with null values and the DISTINCT keyword are discussed, and the concept of nesting group functions is also considered. The available *group functions* are identified and explored under the following headings:

- Using the group functions
- Nesting group functions

Using the Group Functions

The practical application of *group functions* is demonstrated using AVG, SUM, MIN, MAX, and COUNT. These group functions all return numeric results. Additionally, the MIN and MAX functions may return character and date results. These five functions operate on nonnull values but, unlike the others, the COUNT(*) function call also counts rows with null values. The DISTINCT keyword is used to constrain the rows submitted to the group functions.

Analysts frequently wish to know the aggregated total or average value of a column or an expression. This is simple to achieve using most spreadsheet packages. Using the SQL group functions for reporting provides two advantages over using a spreadsheet for analysis. First, they offer a convenient platform for performing calculations using real-time live data. Second, they allow for easy analysis of every value in a dataset or of specific groups of values.

The COUNT Function

The execution of COUNT on a column or an expression returns an integer value that represents the number of rows in the group. The COUNT function has the following syntax:

COUNT({* | [DISTINCT | ALL] *expr*});

There is one parameter that can be either *, which represents all columns including null values, or a specific column or expression. It may be preceded by the DISTINCT or ALL keywords. Consider the following queries:

```
Query 1: SELECT count(*) FROM employees;
Query 2: SELECT count(commission_pct) FROM employees;
Query 3: SELECT count(DISTINCT commission_pct) FROM employees;
Query 4: SELECT count(hire_date), count(manager_id) FROM employees;
```

Query 1 counts the rows in the EMPLOYEES table and returns the integer 107. Query 2 counts the rows with nonnull COMMISSION_PCT values and returns 35. Query 3 considers the 35 nonnull rows, determines the number of unique values, and returns 7. Query 4 demonstrates two features. First, multiple group functions may be used in the same SELECT list and second, the COUNT function is used on both a DATE column and a NUMBER column. The integers 107 and 106 are returned since there are 107 nonnull HIRE_DATE values and 106 nonnull MANAGER_ID values in the group.

Three adjacent expressions using the COUNT function are shown in Figure 6-2. This query illustrates that there are 107 employee records in the EMPLOYEES table. Further, these 107 employees are allocated to 12 departments, including null departments, and work in 19 unique jobs.

FIGURE 6-2

The COUNT
function

```
                                    SQL Plus                        _  □   ×
SQL> SELECT count(*),
  2         count(DISTINCT nvl(department_id,0)),
  3         count(DISTINCT job_id)
  4  FROM employees;

 COUNT(*) COUNT(DISTINCTNVL(DEPARTMENT_ID,0)) COUNT(DISTINCTJOB_ID)
--------- ----------------------------------- ---------------------
      107                                  12                    19

SQL> ▪
```

The SUM Function

The aggregated total of a column or an expression is computed with the SUM
function. Its syntax is as follows:

SUM([DISTINCT | ALL] *expr*);

One numeric parameter, optionally preceded by the DISTINCT or ALL
keywords, is provided to the SUM function, which returns a numeric value.
Consider the following queries:

```
Query 1: SELECT sum(2) FROM employees;
Query 2: SELECT sum(salary) FROM employees;
Query 3: SELECT sum(DISTINCT salary) FROM employees;
Query 4: SELECT sum(commission_pct) FROM employees;
```

There are 107 rows in the EMPLOYEES table. Query 1 adds the number 2 across
107 rows and returns 214. Query 2 takes the SALARY column value for every row in
the group, which in this case is the entire table, and returns the total salary amount
of 691416. Query 3 returns a total of 409908 since many employees get paid the
same salary and the DISTINCT keyword only adds unique values in the column to
the total. Query 4 returns 7.8 after adding the nonnull values.

Figure 6-3 shows two queries. The first calculates the number of days between
the end of 2015 and the value in the HIRE_DATE column. The date arithmetic is
performed for every row. The number returned is added using one SUM function call.

```
SQL> SELECT sum(to_date('31-DEC-2015','DD-MON-YYYY') - hire_date) / 365.25
  2         "Years worked by End 2015"
  3  FROM employees;

Years worked by End 2015
------------------------
              1085.03491

SQL> SELECT sum(hire_date)
  2  FROM employees;
SELECT sum(hire_date)
       *
ERROR at line 1:
ORA-00932: inconsistent datatypes: expected NUMBER got DATE


SQL>
```

The result is divided by 365.25 to give the total number of years worked by all current employees. The second query shows that the SUM function returns an "ORA-00932: inconsistent datatypes" error if it is provided with a nonnumeric argument.

The AVG Function

The *average* value of a column or expression divides the sum by the number of nonnull rows in the group. The AVG function has the following syntax:

AVG([DISTINCT | ALL] *expr*);

One numeric parameter, preceded by the DISTINCT or ALL keywords, is provided to the AVG function, which returns a numeric value. Consider the following queries:

```
Query 1: SELECT avg(2) FROM employees;
Query 2: SELECT avg(salary) FROM employees;
Query 3: SELECT avg(DISTINCT salary) FROM employees;
Query 4: SELECT avg(commission_pct) FROM employees;
```

There are 107 rows in the EMPLOYEES table. Query 1 adds the number 2 across 107 rows and divides the total by the number of rows to return the number 2. Numeric literals submitted to the AVG function are returned unchanged. Query 2 adds the SALARY value for each row to obtain the total salary amount of 691400. This is divided by the 107 rows with nonnull SALARY values to return the average 6461.83178. You may expect Query 3 to return a smaller result than Query 2, but it does not. There are 58 unique salary values, which when added yield a total of 409908. Dividing 409908 by 58 returns 7067.37931 as the average of the distinct salary values. Query 4 may produce unanticipated results if not properly understood. Adding the nonnull values, including duplicates, produces a total of 7.8. There are 35 employee records with nonnull COMMISSION_PCT values. Dividing 7.8 by 35 yields an average COMMISSION_PCT of 0.222857143.

Figure 6-4 shows two queries. The first lists the LAST_NAME and JOB_ID columns with an expression that calculates the total number of years worked by programmers in the organization by the end of 2015. The second uses the AVG function to calculate the average number of years for which current programmers have been employed by the end of 2015.

The MAX and MIN Functions

The MAX and MIN functions operate on NUMBER, DATE, CHAR, and VARCHAR2 data types. They return a value of the same data type as their input arguments, which are either the largest or smallest items in the group. When applied to DATE items, MAX returns the latest date and MIN returns the earliest one. Character strings are converted to numeric representations of their constituent characters based on the NLS settings in the database. When the MIN function is

FIGURE 6-4

The AVG function

```
SQL Plus                                                          _ □ ×

SQL> SELECT last_name, job_id,
  2        (to_date('31-DEC-2015','DD-MON-YYYY') - hire_date) / 365.25
  3        "Years worked by End 2015 by IT"
  4  FROM employees
  5  WHERE job_id = 'IT_PROG';

LAST_NAME                  JOB_ID      Years worked by End 2015 by IT
------------------------   ----------  ------------------------------
Hunold                     IT_PROG                         9.99041752
Ernst                      IT_PROG                         8.61327858
Austin                     IT_PROG                         10.5160849
Pataballa                  IT_PROG                         9.90006845
Lorentz                    IT_PROG                         8.89527721

SQL> SELECT avg((to_date('31-DEC-2015','DD-MON-YYYY') - hire_date) /365.25)
  2        "Avg years IT worked by 2015"
  3  FROM employees
  4  WHERE job_id='IT_PROG';

Avg years IT worked by 2015
---------------------------
                 9.58302533

SQL>
```

applied to a group of character strings, the word that appears first alphabetically is returned, while MAX returns the word that would appear last. The MAX and MIN functions have the following syntax:

MAX([DISTINCT | ALL] *expr*); MIN([DISTINCT | ALL] *expr*)

They take one parameter preceded by the DISTINCT or ALL keywords. Consider the following queries:

```
Query 1: SELECT min(commission_pct), max(commission_pct) FROM employees;
Query 2: SELECT min(start_date),max(end_date) FROM job_history;
Query 3: SELECT min(job_id),max(job_id) FROM employees;
```

Query 1 returns the numeric values 0.1 and 0.4 for the minimum and maximum COMMISSION_PCT values in the EMPLOYEES table. Note that null values for COMMISSION_PCT are ignored. Query 2 evaluates a DATE column and indicates that the earliest START_DATE in the JOB_HISTORY table is 17-SEP-1995 and the latest END_DATE is 31-DEC-2007. Query 3 returns AC_ACCOUNT and ST_MAN as the JOB_ID values appearing first and last alphabetically in the EMPLOYEES table.

The first query shown in Figure 6-5 uses the MAX and MIN functions to obtain information about employees with JOB_ID values of SA_REP. The results indicate that

FIGURE 6-5

The MIN and MAX functions

```
SQL Plus                                              _ □ ✕

SQL> SELECT MIN(hire_date), MIN(salary), MAX(hire_date), MAX(salary)
  2  FROM employees
  3  WHERE job_id = 'SA_REP';

MIN(HIRE_ MIN(SALARY) MAX(HIRE_ MAX(SALARY)
--------- ----------- --------- -----------
30-JAN-04        6100 21-APR-08       11500

SQL> SELECT last_name, hire_date, salary
  2  FROM employees
  3  WHERE job_id  = 'SA_REP'
  4  AND salary IN (6100,11500)
  5  OR hire_date IN ('30-jan-2004','21-apr-2008');

LAST_NAME                HIRE_DATE    SALARY
------------------------ --------- ----------
King                     30-JAN-04      10000
Banda                    21-APR-08       6200
Ozer                     11-MAR-05      11500
Kumar                    21-APR-08       6100

SQL> _
```

the sales representatives working for the shortest and longest durations were hired on 21-APR-2008 and 30-JAN-2004, respectively. Furthermore, the sales representatives earning the largest and smallest salaries earn 11500 and 6100, respectively. The second query fetches the LAST_NAME values for the sales representatives to whom the minimum and maximum HIRE_DATE and SALARY values apply.

EXERCISE 6-1

Using the Group Functions

The COUNTRIES table stores a list of COUNTRY_NAME values. You are required to calculate the average length of all the country names. Any fractional components must be rounded to the nearest whole number.

1. Start SQL*Plus and connect to the HR schema.
2. The length of the country name value for each row is calculated using the LENGTH function. The average length may be determined using the AVG function. It may be rounded to the nearest whole number using the ROUND function.
3. The SELECT clause using alias AVERAGE_COUNTRY_NAME_LENGTH is

```
SELECT ROUND(AVG( LENGTH(COUNTRY_NAME)))
AVERAGE_COUNTRY_NAME_LENGTH
```

4. The FROM clause is

```
FROM COUNTRIES
```

5. Executing this statement returns a single row representing the average length of all the country names in the COUNTRIES table, as shown in the following illustration:

SCENARIO & SOLUTION	
You would like to retrieve the earliest date from a column that stores DATE information. Can a group function be utilized to retrieve this value?	Yes. The MIN function operates on numeric, date, and character data. When the MIN function is executed against a DATE column, the earliest date value is returned.
Summary statistics are required by senior management. This includes details like number of employees, total staff salary cost, lowest salary, and highest salary values. Can such a report be drawn using one query?	Yes. There is no restriction to the number of group functions listed in the SELECT clause. The requested report can be drawn using the following query: `SELECT COUNT(*) Num_Employees,` `SUM(SALARY) Tot_Salary_Cost,` `MIN(SALARY) Lowest_Salary,` `MAX(SALARY) Maximum_Salary` `FROM EMPLOYEES;`
You are asked to list the number of unique jobs performed by employees in the organization. Counting the JOB_ID records will give you all the jobs. Is it possible to count the unique jobs?	Yes. The DISTINCT keyword may be used with the aggregate functions. To count unique JOB_ID values in the EMPLOYEES table, you can issue the following query: `SELECT COUNT(DISTINCT JOB_ID)` `FROM EMPLOYEES;`

Nested Group Functions

Recall that single-row functions may be nested or embedded to any level of depth. *Group functions may only be nested two levels deep.* Three formats using group functions are shown here:

G1(*group_item*) = result
G1(G2(*group_item*)) = result
G1(G2(G3(*group_item*))) is NOT allowed.

Group functions are represented by the letter "G" followed by a number. The first simple form contains no nested functions. Examples include the SUM(*group_item*) and AVG(*group_item*) functions that return a single result per group. The second form supports two nested group functions, like SUM(AVG(*group_item*)). In this case, a GROUP BY clause is mandatory since the average value of the *group_item* per group is calculated before being aggregated by the SUM function.

The third form is disallowed by Oracle. Consider an expression that nests three group functions. If the MAX function is applied to the previous example, the expression MAX(SUM(AVG(*group_item*))) is formed. The two inner group functions return a *single value* representing the sum of a set of average values. This expression becomes MAX(*single value*). A group function cannot be applied to a single value.

FIGURE 6-6

Nested group
functions

Figure 6-6 demonstrates two queries. Both restrict the rows returned to those
with DEPARTMENT_ID values of null, 40, and 80. These are then partitioned by
their DEPARTMENT_ID values into three groups. The first query calculates the
sum of the COMMISSION_PCT values for each group and returns the values 0.15,
null, and 7.65. Query 2 contains the nested group functions, which may be evaluated
as follows: AVG(SUM(COMMISSION_PCT)) = (0.15 + 7.65) /2 = 3.9.

e x a m

w a t c h   *Single-row functions*
may be nested to any level, but group
functions may be nested to, at most,
two levels deep. The nested function
call COUNT(SUM(AVG(X))) returns
the error, "ORA-00935: group function
is nested too deeply." It is acceptable to

nest single-row functions within group
functions. Consider the following query:
*SELECT SUM(AVG(LENGTH(LAST_*
NAME))) FROM EMPLOYEES GROUP BY
DEPARTMENT_ID. It calculates the sum of
the average length of LAST_NAME values
per department.

CERTIFICATION OBJECTIVE 6.03

Group Data Using the GROUP BY Clause

The *group functions* discussed earlier use groups of rows comprising the entire table. This section explores partitioning a set of data into groups using the GROUP BY clause. Group functions may be applied to these subsets or clusters of rows. The syntax of group functions and the GROUP BY clause are discussed in the following areas:

- Creating groups of data
- The GROUP BY clause
- Grouping by multiple columns

Creating Groups of Data

A table has at least one column and zero or more rows of data. In many tables this data requires analysis to transform it into useful information. It is a common reporting requirement to calculate statistics from a set of data divided into groups using different attributes. Previous examples using group functions operated against all the rows in a table. The entire table was treated as one large group.

Groups of data within a set are created by associating rows with common properties or attributes with each other. Thereafter, group functions can execute against each of these groups. Groups of data include entire rows and not specific columns.

Consider the EMPLOYEES table. It comprises 11 columns and 107 rows. You could create groups of rows that share a common DEPARTMENT_ID value. The SUM function may then be used to create salary totals per department. Another possible set of groups may share common JOB_ID column values. The AVG group function may then be used to identify the average salary paid to employees in different jobs.

A group is defined as a subset of the entire dataset sharing one or more common attributes. These attributes are typically column values but may also be expressions. The number of groups created depends on the distinct values present in the common attribute.

As Figure 6-7 shows, there are 12 unique DEPARTMENT_ID values in the EMPLOYEES table. If rows are grouped using common DEPARTMENT_ID values, there will be 12 groups. If a group function is executed against these groups, there will be 12 values returned, as it will execute once for each group.

FIGURE 6-7

Unique
DEPARTMENT_
ID values in the
EMPLOYEES table

on the
job

Grouping data and summary functions are widely utilized for reporting purposes. It is valuable to practice the segmentation of a set of data into different groupings. Oracle provides the analytical language to deconstruct datasets into groups, divide these into further subgroups, and so on. Aggregate grouping functions can then be executed against these groups and subgroups.

The **GROUP BY** Clause

The SELECT statement is enhanced by the addition of the GROUP BY clause. This clause facilitates the creation of groups. It appears after the WHERE clause but before the ORDER BY clause, as follows:

```
SELECT column | expression | group_function(column | expression [alias]),...}
FROM table
[WHERE condition(s)]
[GROUP BY {col(s) | expr}]
[ORDER BY {col(s) | expr | numeric_pos} [ASC | DESC] [NULLS FIRST | LAST]];
```

The column or expression specified in the GROUP BY clause is also known as the *grouping attribute* and is the component that rows are grouped by. The dataset is segmented based on the grouping attribute. Consider the following query:

```
SELECT max(salary), count(*)
FROM employees
GROUP BY department_id
ORDER BY department_id;
```

The grouping attribute in this example is the DEPARTMENT_ID column. The dataset, on which the group functions in the SELECT list must operate, is divided into 12 groups, one for each department. For each group (department), the maximum salary value and the number of rows are returned. Since the results are sorted by DEPARTMENT_ID, the third row in the set of results contains the values 11000 and 6. This indicates that 6 employees have a DEPARTMENT_ID value of 30. Of these 6, the highest earner has a SALARY value of 11000. This query demonstrates that the grouping attribute does not have to be included in the SELECT list.

It is common to see the grouping attribute in the SELECT list alongside grouping functions. If an item, that is not a group function, appears in the SELECT list with other group functions and there is no GROUP BY clause, an "ORA-00937: not a single-group group function" error is raised. If a GROUP BY clause is present but that item is not a grouping attribute, then an "ORA-00979: not a GROUP BY expression" error is returned.

Any item in the SELECT list that is not a group function must be a grouping attribute of the GROUP BY clause.

If a group function is placed in a WHERE clause, an "ORA-00934: group function is not allowed here" error is returned. Imposing group-level conditions is

FIGURE 6-8

The GROUP
BY clause

```
SQL Plus                                          –  □  ×

SQL> SELECT  end_date ,count(*)
  2  FROM job_history;
SELECT  end_date ,count(*)
        *
ERROR at line 1:
ORA-00937: not a single-group group function


SQL> SELECT  end_date, start_date, count(*)
  2  FROM job_history
  3  GROUP BY end_date;
SELECT  end_date, start_date, count(*)
                  *
ERROR at line 1:
ORA-00979: not a GROUP BY expression


SQL> SELECT  to_char(end_date,'yyyy') "Year" ,
  2          count(*) "Number of Employees"
  3  FROM job_history
  4  GROUP BY to_char(end_date,'yyyy')
  5  ORDER BY count(*) DESC;

Year Number of Employees
---- -------------------
2007                   4
2006                   3
2001                   2
2005                   1

SQL> _
```

achieved using the HAVING clause discussed in the next section. Group functions may, however, be used as part of the ORDER BY clause.

The first query in Figure 6-8 raises an error since the END_DATE column is in the SELECT list with a group function and there is no GROUP BY clause. An "ORA-00979" error is returned from the second query since the START_DATE item is listed in the SELECT clause, but it is not a grouping attribute.

The third query divides the JOB_HISTORY rows into groups based on the four-digit year component from the END_DATE column. Four groups are created using this grouping attribute. These represent different years when employees ended their jobs. The COUNT shows the number of employees who quit their jobs during each of these years. The results are listed in descending order based on the "Number of Employees" expression. Note that the COUNT group function is present in the ORDER BY clause.

ⓦatch   *A dataset is divided into groups using the GROUP BY clause. The grouping attribute is the common key shared by members of each group. The grouping attribute is usually a single column but may be multiple columns or*   *an expression that cannot be based on group functions. Note that only grouping attributes and group functions are permitted in the SELECT clause when using GROUP BY.*

Grouping by Multiple Columns

A powerful extension to the GROUP BY clause uses multiple grouping attributes. Oracle permits datasets to be partitioned into groups and allows these groups to be further divided into subgroups using a different grouping attribute. Consider the following two queries:

```
Query 1: SELECT department_id, sum(commission_pct)
         FROM employees
         WHERE commission_pct IS NOT NULL
         GROUP BY department_id;
Query 2: SELECT department_id, job_id, sum(commission_pct)
         FROM employees
         WHERE commission_pct IS NOT NULL
         GROUP BY department_id, job_id;
```

Query 1 restricts the rows returned from the EMPLOYEES table to the 35 rows with nonnull COMMISSION_PCT values. These rows are then divided into two groups: 80 and NULL based on the DEPARTMENT_ID grouping attribute. The result set contains two rows, which return the sum of the COMMISSION_PCT values for each group.

Query 2 is similar to the first one except it has an additional item: JOB_ID in both the SELECT and GROUP BY clauses. This second grouping attribute decomposes the two groups based on DEPARTMENT_ID into the constituent JOB_ID components belonging to the rows in each group. The distinct JOB_ID values for rows with DEPARTMENT_ID=80 are SA_REP and SA_MAN. The distinct JOB_ID value for rows with null DEPARTMENT_ID is SA_REP. Therefore, Query 2 returns two groupings, one which consists of two subgroups, and the other with only one, as shown in Figure 6-9.

FIGURE 6-9

The GROUP
BY clause with
multiple columns

```
                                                    SQL Plus                        _  □  ×

SQL> SELECT department_id, sum(commission_pct)
  2  FROM employees
  3  WHERE commission_pct IS NOT NULL
  4  GROUP BY department_id;

DEPARTMENT_ID SUM(COMMISSION_PCT)
------------- -------------------
                              .15
           80                7.65

SQL> SELECT department_id, job_id, sum(commission_pct)
  2  FROM employees
  3  where commission_pct is not null
  4  GROUP BY department_id, job_id;

DEPARTMENT_ID JOB_ID     SUM(COMMISSION_PCT)
------------- ---------- -------------------
           80 SA_REP                    6.15
           80 SA_MAN                     1.5
              SA_REP                     .15

SQL>
```

EXERCISE 6-2

Grouping Data Based on Multiple Columns

Analysis of staff turnover is a common reporting requirement. You are required to create a report containing the number of employees who left their jobs, grouped by the year in which they left. The jobs they performed are also required. The results must be sorted in descending order based on the number of employees in each group. The report must list the year, the JOB_ID, and the number of employees who left a particular job in that year.

1. Start SQL Developer and connect to the HR schema.
2. The JOB_HISTORY table contains the END_DATE and JOB_ID columns, which constitute the source data for this report.
3. The year component is extracted using the TO_CHAR function. The number of employees who quit a particular job in each year is obtained using the COUNT(*) function.
4. The SELECT clause is

```
TO_CHAR(END_DATE,'YYYY') "Quitting Year", JOB_ID, COUNT(*)
"Number of Employees"
```

5. The FROM clause is

   ```
   FROM  JOB_HISTORY
   ```

6. There is no WHERE clause.

7. Since the report requires employees to be listed by year and JOB_ID, these two items must appear in the GROUP BY clause, which is

   ```
   GROUP BY TO_CHAR(END_DATE,'YYYY'), JOB_ID
   ```

8. The sorting is performed with

   ```
   ORDER BY COUNT(*) DESC
   ```

9. Executing this statement returns the staff turnover report requested as shown in the following illustration:

SCENARIO & SOLUTION

You wish to print name badges for the staff who work as sales representatives. Can the length of the shortest and longest LAST_NAME values be determined for these employees?	Yes. The MAX and MIN functions applied to the LAST_NAME field will determine the shortest and longest names as shown in the following query: `SELECT MIN(LENGTH(LAST_NAME)), MAX(LENGTH(LAST_NAME)) FROM EMPLOYEES WHERE JOB_ID='SA_REP';`
Is it possible to count the records in each group, first by dividing the employee records by year of employment, then by job, and finally by salary?	Yes. Grouping by multiple columns is a powerful option allowing fine-grained analysis as shown in the following query: `SELECT COUNT(*), TO_CHAR( HIRE_DATE, 'YYYY'), JOB_ID, SALARY FROM EMPLOYEES GROUP BY TO_CHAR(HIRE_DATE,'YYYY') , JOB_ID, SALARY;`
Is there a limit to the number of groups within groups that can be formed?	No. There is no limit to the number of groups and subgroups that can be formed.

CERTIFICATION OBJECTIVE 6.04

Include or Exclude Grouped Rows Using the HAVING Clause

Creating groups of data and applying aggregate functions is very useful. A refinement to these features is the ability to include or exclude results based on group-level conditions. This section introduces the HAVING clause. A clear distinction is made between the WHERE clause and the HAVING clause. The HAVING clause is explained in the following areas:

- Restricting group results
- The HAVING clause

Restricting Group Results

WHERE clause conditions restrict rows returned by a query. Rows are included based on whether they fulfill the conditions listed and are sometimes known as *row-level results*. Clustering rows using the GROUP BY clause and applying an aggregate function to these groups returns results often referred to as *group-level results*. The HAVING clause provides the language to restrict group-level results.

The following query limits the rows retrieved from the JOB_HISTORY table by specifying a WHERE condition based on the DEPARTMENT_ID column values.

```
SELECT department_id
FROM job_history
WHERE department_id IN (50,60,80,110);
```

This query returns seven rows. If the WHERE clause was absent, all 10 rows would be retrieved. Suppose you want to know how many employees were previously employed in each of these departments. There are seven rows that can be manually grouped and counted. However, if there are a large number of rows, an aggregate function like COUNT may be used, as shown in the following query:

```
SELECT department_id, count(*)
FROM job_history
WHERE department_id IN (50,60,80,110)
GROUP BY department_id;
```

This query is very similar to the previous statement. The aggregate function COUNT was added to the SELECT list, and a GROUP BY DEPARTMENT_ID clause was also added. Four rows with their aggregate row count are returned and it is clear that the original seven rows restricted by the WHERE clause were clustered into four groups based on common DEPARTMENT_ID values, as shown in the following table:

DEPARTMENT_ID	COUNT(*)
50	2
60	1
80	2
110	2

Suppose you wanted to refine this list to include only those departments with more than one employee. The HAVING clause limits or restricts the group-level rows as required.

This query must perform the following steps:

1. Consider the entire row-level dataset.

2. Limit the dataset based on any WHERE clause conditions.

3. Segment the data into one or more groups using the grouping attributes specified in the GROUP BY clause.

4. Apply any aggregate functions to create a new group-level dataset. Each row may be regarded as an aggregation of its source row-level data based on the groups created.

5. Limit or restrict the group-level data with a HAVING clause condition. Only group-level results matching these conditions are returned.

on the job   ***Choosing the appropriate context to use a WHERE or a HAVING clause depends on whether physical or group-level rows are to be restricted. Rows containing data stored in columns are sometimes called actual or physical rows. When actual (physical) rows are restricted, one or more conditions are imposed using a WHERE clause. When these rows are grouped together, one or more aggregate functions may be applied, yielding one or more group-level rows. These are not physical rows, but temporary aggregations of data. Group-level rows are restricted using conditions imposed by a HAVING clause.***

The HAVING Clause

The general form of the SELECT statement is further enhanced by the addition of the HAVING clause and becomes:

SELECT *column* | *expression* | *group_function*(*column* | *expression* [*alias*]),...}
FROM *table*
[WHERE *condition(s)*]
[GROUP BY {*col(s)* | *expr*}]
[HAVING *group_condition(s)*]
[ORDER BY {*col(s)* | *expr* | *numeric_pos*} [ASC | DESC] [NULLS FIRST | LAST]];

An important difference between the HAVING clause and the other SELECT statement clauses is that it may only be specified if a GROUP BY clause is present. This dependency is sensible since group-level rows must exist before they can be restricted. The HAVING clause can occur before the GROUP BY clause in the SELECT statement. However, it is more common to place the HAVING clause after the GROUP BY clause. All grouping is performed and group functions are executed prior to evaluating the HAVING clause.

The following query shows how the HAVING clause is used to restrict an aggregated dataset. Records from the JOB_HISTORY table are divided into four groups. The rows that meet the HAVING clause condition (contributing more than one row to the group row count) are returned:

```
SELECT department_id, count(*)
FROM job_history
WHERE department_id IN (50,60,80,110)
GROUP BY department_id
HAVING count(*) > 1
AND department_id > 50;
```

Two rows with DEPARTMENT_ID values of 80 and 110, each with a COUNT(*) value of 2 are returned. Notice the grouping attribute DEPARTMENT_ID may be present in the HAVING clause.

Figure 6-10 shows three queries. Query 1 divides the 107 records from the EMPLOYEES table into 19 groups based on common JOB_ID values. The average salary for each JOB_ID group and the aggregate row count is computed. Query 2 refines the results by conditionally excluding those aggregated rows where the average salary is less than or equal to 10000, using a HAVING clause. Query 3 demonstrates that the Boolean operators may be used to specify multiple HAVING clause conditions.

FIGURE 6-10

The HAVING
clause

```
                                      SQL Plus                        _  □  ×

SQL> SELECT job_id, avg(salary), count(*)
  2   FROM employees
  3   GROUP BY job_id;

JOB_ID     AVG(SALARY)   COUNT(*)
---------- ----------- ----------
IT_PROG           5760          5
AC_MGR           12008          1
AC_ACCOUNT        8300          1
ST_MAN            7280          5
PU_MAN           11000          1
AD_ASST           4400          1
AD_VP            17000          2
SH_CLERK          3215         20
FI_ACCOUNT        7920          5
FI_MGR           12008          1
PU_CLERK          2780          5
SA_MAN           12200          5
MK_MAN           13000          1
PR_REP           10000          1
AD_PRES          24000          1
SA_REP            8350         30
MK_REP            6000          1
ST_CLERK          2785         20
HR_REP            6500          1

19 rows selected.

SQL> SELECT job_id, avg(salary), count(*)
  2   FROM employees
  3   GROUP BY job_id
  4   HAVING avg(salary) > 10000;

JOB_ID     AVG(SALARY)   COUNT(*)
---------- ----------- ----------
AC_MGR           12008          1
PU_MAN           11000          1
AD_VP            17000          2
FI_MGR           12008          1
SA_MAN           12200          5
MK_MAN           13000          1
AD_PRES          24000          1

7 rows selected.

SQL> SELECT job_id, avg(salary), count(*)
  2   FROM employees
  3   GROUP BY job_id
  4   HAVING avg(salary) > 10000
  5   AND count(*) >1;

JOB_ID     AVG(SALARY)   COUNT(*)
---------- ----------- ----------
AD_VP            17000          2
SA_MAN           12200          5

SQL> _
```

EXERCISE 6-3

Using the HAVING Clause

The company is planning a recruitment drive and wants to identify the days of the week on which 18 or more staff members were hired. Your report must list the days and the number of employees hired on each of them.

1. Start SQL*Plus and connect to the HR schema.
2. EMPLOYEES records must be divided into groups based on the day component of the HIRE_DATE column. The number of employees per group may be obtained using the COUNT function.
3. The SELECT clause is

```
SELECT TO_CHAR(HIRE_DATE,'DAY'), COUNT(*)
```

4. No WHERE clause is required since all the physical rows of the EMPLOYEES table are considered.
5. The GROUP BY clause is

```
GROUP BY TO_CHAR(HIRE_DATE,'DAY')
```

This GROUP BY clause potentially creates seven group-level rows, one for each day of the week.

6. The COUNT function in the SELECT clause then lists the number of staff members employed on each day. The HAVING clause must be used to restrict these seven rows to only those where the count is greater than or equal to 18.
7. The HAVING clause is

```
HAVING COUNT(*) >= 18
```

8. The FROM clause is

```
FROM EMPLOYEES
```

9. Executing this statement returns the days of the week on which 18 or more employees were hired as shown in the following illustration:

```
                                    SQL Plus                        _  □   ×

SQL> SELECT to_char(hire_date,'DAY') hire_day, count(*)
  2   FROM employees
  3   GROUP BY to_char(hire_date,'DAY')
  4   HAVING count(*) >= 18;

HIRE_DAY                                          COUNT(*)
------------------------------------------------- ----------
SATURDAY                                                 19
FRIDAY                                                   19

SQL> _
```

INSIDE THE EXAM

The certification objectives in this chapter are examined using practical examples and scenarios that require you to predict the results returned from SQL queries. These queries focus on dividing datasets into groups using one or more grouping attributes.

Understand the limitations of nesting group functions. Remember that group functions or grouping attributes (or both) must exist in the SELECT clause if there is a GROUP BY clause. The HAVING clause may occur before the GROUP BY clause but usually follows it. An error is returned if the HAVING clause is used without a GROUP BY clause. Recall that the HAVING clause may contain multiple conditions, but each one must contain a group function or a grouping attribute or both.

Knowing how to interpret and trace nested group and single-row functions is vital, as many questions contain expressions with nested functions. The innermost to outermost order of evaluation of nested group and single functions is identical and must be remembered.

There are many built-in group functions available, but the exams will test your understanding of the COUNT, SUM, AVG, MAX, and MIN functions. Ensure that you have a thorough understanding of these functions and how they interact with the DISTINCT keyword and NULL values.

CERTIFICATION SUMMARY

Multiple row functions and the concept of dividing data into groups are described in this chapter. There is a multitude of group or aggregate functions available. The key functions for creating sum totals; calculating averages, minimums, or maximums; and obtaining a record count are explored in detail.

The differences between nesting group functions and single-row functions are investigated, and the limitations of the former are explained. Creating groups using common grouping attributes is concretized with the introduction of the GROUP BY clause to the SELECT statement. Row-level data is limited by conditions specified in the WHERE clause. The restriction of group-level data using the HAVING clause is also discussed.

TWO-MINUTE DRILL

Describe the Group Functions

❑ Group functions are also known as multiple row, aggregate, or summary functions. They execute once for each group of data and aggregate the data from multiple rows into a single result for each group.

❑ Groups may be entire tables or portions of a table grouped together by a common grouping attribute.

Identify the Available Group Functions

❑ The COUNT of a function returns an integer value representing the number of rows in a group.

❑ The SUM function returns an aggregated total of all the nonnull numeric expression values in a group.

❑ The AVG function divides the sum of a column or expression by the number of nonnull rows in a group.

❑ The MAX and MIN functions operate on NUMBER, DATE, CHAR, and VARCHAR2 data types. They return a value that is either the largest or smallest item in the group.

❑ Group functions may only be nested two levels deep.

Group Data Using the GROUP BY Clause

❑ The GROUP BY clause specifies the grouping attribute rows must have in common for them to be clustered together.

❑ The GROUP BY clause facilitates the creation of groups within a selected set of data and appears after the WHERE clause but before the ORDER BY clause.

❑ Any item on the SELECT list that is not a group function must be a grouping attribute.

❑ Group functions may not be placed in a WHERE clause.

❑ Datasets may be partitioned into groups and further divided into subgroups based on multiple grouping attributes.

Include or Exclude Grouped Rows Using the **HAVING** Clause

❑ Clustering rows using a common grouping attribute with the GROUP BY clause and applying an aggregate function to each of these groups returns *group-level results*.

❑ The HAVING clause provides the language to limit the group-level results returned.

❑ The HAVING clause may only be specified if there is a GROUP BY clause present.

❑ All grouping is performed and group functions are executed prior to evaluating the HAVING clause.

SELF TEST

The following questions will help you measure your understanding of the material presented in this chapter. Read all the choices carefully because there may be more than one correct answer. Choose all the correct answers for each question.

Describe the Group Functions

1. What result is returned by the following statement? (Choose the best answer.)
   ```
   SELECT COUNT(*) FROM DUAL;
   ```
   A. NULL
   B. 0
   C. 1
   D. None of the above

2. Choose one correct statement regarding group functions.
   A. Group functions may only be used when a GROUP BY clause is present.
   B. Group functions can operate on multiple rows at a time.
   C. Group functions only operate on a single row at a time.
   D. Group functions can execute multiple times within a single group.

Identify the Available Group Functions

3. What value is returned after executing the following statement? (Choose the best answer.)
   ```
   SELECT SUM(SALARY) FROM EMPLOYEES;
   ```
   Assume there are ten employee records and each contains a SALARY value of 100, except for one, which has a null value in the SALARY field.
   A. 900
   B. 1000
   C. NULL
   D. None of the above

4. Which values are returned after executing the following statement? (Choose all that apply.)
   ```
   SELECT COUNT(*), COUNT(SALARY) FROM EMPLOYEES;
   ```
   Assume there are ten employee records and each contains a SALARY value of 100, except for one, which has a null value in their SALARY field.
   A. 10 and 10
   B. 10 and NULL
   C. 10 and 9
   D. None of the above

5. What value is returned after executing the following statement? (Choose the best answer.)
```
SELECT AVG(NVL(SALARY,100)) FROM EMPLOYEES;
```
Assume there are ten employee records and each contains a SALARY value of 100, except for one employee, who has a null value in the SALARY field.

A. NULL

B. 90

C. 100

D. None of the above

Group Data Using the GROUP BY Clause

6. What value is returned after executing the following statement? (Choose the best answer.)
```
SELECT SUM((AVG(LENGTH(NVL(SALARY,0))))))
FROM EMPLOYEES
GROUP BY SALARY;
```
Assume there are ten employee records and each contains a SALARY value of 100, except for one, which has a null value in the SALARY field.

A. An error is returned

B. 3

C. 4

D. None of the above

7. How many records are returned by the following query? (Choose the best answer.)
```
SELECT SUM(SALARY), DEPARTMENT_ID FROM EMPLOYEES
GROUP BY DEPARTMENT_ID;
```
Assume there are 11 nonnull and 1 null unique DEPARTMENT_ID values. All records have a nonnull SALARY value.

A. 12

B. 11

C. NULL

D. None of the above

8. What values are returned after executing the following statement? (Choose the best answer.)
```
SELECT JOB_ID, MAX_SALARY FROM JOBS GROUP BY MAX_SALARY;
```
Assume that the JOBS table has ten records with the same JOB_ID value of DBA and the same MAX_SALARY value of 100.

A. One row of output with the values DBA, 100

B. Ten rows of output with the values DBA, 100

C. An error is returned

D. None of the above

Include or Exclude Grouped Rows Using the HAVING Clause

9. How many rows of data are returned after executing the following statement? (Choose the best answer.)

```
SELECT DEPT_ID, SUM(NVL(SALARY,100)) FROM EMP
GROUP BY DEPT_ID HAVING SUM(SALARY) > 400;
```

Assume the EMP table has ten rows and each contains a SALARY value of 100, except for one, which has a null value in the SALARY field. The first and second five rows have DEPT_ID values of 10 and 20, respectively.

A. Two rows

B. One row

C. Zero rows

D. None of the above

10. How many rows of data are returned after executing the following statement? (Choose the best answer.)

```
SELECT DEPT_ID, SUM(SALARY) FROM EMP GROUP BY DEPT_ID HAVING
SUM(NVL(SALARY,100)) > 400;
```

Assume the EMP table has ten rows and each contains a SALARY value of 100, except for one, which has a null value in the SALARY field. The first and second five rows have DEPT_ID values of 10 and 20, respectively.

A. Two rows

B. One row

C. Zero rows

D. None of the above

LAB QUESTION

Using SQL Developer or SQL*Plus, connect to the OE schema and complete the following tasks.

The PRODUCT_INFORMATION table lists items that are orderable and others that are planned, obsolete, or under development. You are required to prepare a report that groups the nonorderable products by their PRODUCT_STATUS and shows the number of products in each group and the sum of the LIST_PRICE of the products per group. Further, only the group-level rows, where the sum of the LIST_PRICE is greater than 4000, must be displayed. A product is nonorderable if the PRODUCT_STATUS value is not equal to the string "orderable". There are several approaches to solving this question. Your approach may differ from the solution proposed.

SELF TEST ANSWERS

Describe the Group Functions

1. ☑ **C.** The DUAL table has one row and one column. The COUNT(*) function returns the number of rows in a table or group.
    ☒ **A, B,** and **D** are incorrect.

2. ☑ **B.** By definition, group functions can operate on multiple rows at a time, unlike single-row functions.
    ☒ **A, C,** and **D** are incorrect statements. A group function may be used without a GROUP BY clause. In this case, the entire dataset is operated on as a group. The COUNT function is often executed against an entire table, which behaves as one group. **D** is incorrect. Once a dataset has been partitioned into different groups, any group functions execute once per group.

Identify the Available Group Functions

3. ☑ **A.** The SUM aggregate function ignores null values and adds nonnull values. Since nine rows contain the SALARY value 100, 900 is returned.
    ☒ **B, C,** and **D** are incorrect. **B** would be returned if SUM(NVL(SALARY,100)) was executed. **C** is a tempting choice since regular arithmetic with NULL values returns a NULL result. However, the aggregate functions, except for COUNT(*), ignore NULL values.

4. ☑ **C.** COUNT(*) considers all rows including those with NULL values. COUNT(SALARY) only considers the nonnull rows.
    ☒ **A, B,** and **D** are incorrect.

5. ☑ **C.** The NVL function converts the one NULL value into 100. Thereafter, the average function adds the SALARY values and obtains 1000. Dividing this by the number of records returns 100.
    ☒ **A, B,** and **D** are incorrect. **B** would be returned if AVG(NVL(SALARY,0)) was selected. It is interesting to note that if AVG(SALARY) was selected, 100 would have also been returned, since the AVG function would sum the nonnull values and divide the total by the number of rows with nonnull SALARY values. So AVG(SALARY) would be calculated as 900/9=100.

Group Data Using the GROUP BY Clause

6. ☑ **C.** The dataset is segmented based on the SALARY column. This creates two groups: one with SALARY values of 100 and the other with a null SALARY value. The average length of SALARY value 100 is 3 for the rows in the first group. The NULL salary value is first converted

into the number 0 by the NVL function, and the average length of SALARY is 1. The SUM function operates across the two groups adding the values 3 and 1, returning 4.

☒ **A, B,** and **D** are incorrect. **A** seems plausible since group functions may not be nested more than two levels deep. Although there are four functions, only two are group functions while the others are single-row functions evaluated before the group functions. **B** would be returned if the expression SUM(AVG(LENGTH(SALARY))) was selected.

7. ☑ **A.** There are 12 distinct DEPARTMENT_ID values. Since this is the grouping attribute, 12 groups are created, including 1 with a null DEPARTMENT_ID value. Therefore, 12 rows are returned.

☒ **B, C,** and **D** are incorrect.

Include or Exclude Grouped Rows Using the HAVING Clause

8. ☑ **C.** For a GROUP BY clause to be used, a group function must appear in the SELECT list.

☒ **A, B,** and **D** are incorrect. The statement is syntactically inaccurate and is disallowed by Oracle. Do not mistake the column named MAX_SALARY for the MAX(SALARY) function.

9. ☑ **B.** Two groups are created based on their common DEPT_ID values. The group with no null SALARY values consists of five rows with SALARY values of 100 in each of them. Therefore, the SUM(SALARY) function returns 500 for this group, and it satisfies the HAVING SUM(SALARY) > 400 clause. The group with the null SALARY record has four rows with SALARY values of 100 and one row with a NULL SALARY. SUM(SALARY) only returns 400 and this group does not satisfy the HAVING clause.

☒ **A, C,** and **D** are incorrect. Beware of the SUM(NVL(SALARY,100)) expression in the SELECT clause. This expression selects the format of the output. It does not restrict or limit the dataset in any way.

10. ☑ **A.** Two groups are created based on their common DEPT_ID values. The group with no null SALARY values consists of five rows with SALARY values of 100 in each of them. Therefore, the SUM(NVL(SALARY,100)) function returns 500 for this group and it satisfies the HAVING SUM(NVL(SALARY,100)) > 400 clause. The group with the null SALARY record has four rows with SALARY values of 100 and one row with a NULL SALARY. SUM(NVL(SALARY,100)) returns 500 and this group satisfies the HAVING clause. Therefore, two rows are returned.

☒ **B, C,** and **D** are incorrect. Although the SELECT clause contains SUM(SALARY), which returns 500 and 400 for the two groups, the HAVING clause contains the SUM(NVL(SALARY,100)) expression, which specifies the inclusion or exclusion criteria for a group-level row.

LAB ANSWER

Using SQL Developer or SQL*Plus, connect to the OE schema and complete the following tasks. There are several approaches to solving this question. Your approach may differ from the solution proposed here.

1. Start SQL Developer and connect to the OE schema.

2. The dataset must be restricted to rows from the PRODUCT_INFORMATION table where the PRODUCT_STATUS is not equal to the string "orderable". Since this character literal may have been input in mixed case, a case conversion function like UPPER can be used.

3. The WHERE clause is
   ```
   WHERE UPPER(PRODUCT_STATUS) <> 'ORDERABLE'
   ```

4. Since the dataset must be segmented into groups based on the PRODUCT_STATUS column, the GROUP BY statement is
   ```
   GROUP BY PRODUCT_STATUS
   ```

5. The dataset is now partitioned into different groups based on their PRODUCT_STATUS values. Therefore, the COUNT(*) function may be used to obtain the number of products in each group. The SUM(LIST_PRICE) aggregate function can be used to calculate the sum of the LIST_PRICE values for all the rows in each group.

6. The SELECT clause is therefore
   ```
   SELECT COUNT(*), SUM(LIST_PRICE), PRODUCT_STATUS
   ```

7. The HAVING clause which restricts group-level rows is therefore
   ```
   HAVING SUM(LIST_PRICE) > 4000
   ```

8. The FROM clause is
   ```
   FROM PRODUCT_INFORMATION
   ```

9. Executing this statement returns the report required as shown in the following illustration.

```
SQL Plus                                      _  □  ×

SQL> SELECT count(*) , sum(list_price), product_status
  2  FROM product_information
  3  WHERE upper(product_status) <> 'ORDERABLE'
  4  GROUP BY product_status
  5  HAVING sum(list_price)>4000;

  COUNT(*) SUM(LIST_PRICE) PRODUCT_STATUS
---------- --------------- --------------------
        11            4922 under development
        16            7389 obsolete

SQL>
```

7

Displaying Data from Multiple Tables

T he three pillars of relational theory are selection, projection, and joining. This chapter focuses on the practical implementation of *joining*. Rows from different tables are associated with each other using *joins*. Support for joining has implications for the way data is stored in database tables. Many data models such as third normal form or star schemas have emerged to exploit this feature.

Tables may be joined in several ways. The most common technique is called an *equijoin*. A row is associated with one or more rows in another table based on the *equality* of column values or expressions. Tables may also be joined using a *nonequijoin*. In this case, a row is associated with one or more rows in another table if its column values fall into a range determined by inequality operators.

A less common technique is to associate rows with other rows in the same table. This association is based on columns with logical and usually hierarchical relationships with each other. This is called a *self-join*. Rows with null or differing entries in common *join columns* are excluded when equijoins and nonequijoins, collectively known as *inner joins*, are performed. An *outer join* is available to fetch these *one-legged* or *orphaned* rows if necessary.

A *cross join* or *Cartesian product* is formed when every row from one table is joined to all rows in another. This join is often the result of missing or inadequate join conditions but is occasionally intentional.

CERTIFICATION OBJECTIVE 7.01

Write SELECT Statements to Access Data from More Than One Table Using Equijoins and Nonequijoins

This certification objective receives extensive coverage in this chapter. It is crucial to learning the concepts and language for performing joins. Different types of joins are introduced in their primitive forms outlining the broad categories that are available. An in-depth discussion of the various join clauses is then conducted. The modern ANSI-compliant and traditional Oracle syntaxes are discussed, but emphasis is placed on the modern syntax. This section concludes with a discussion of nonequijoins and additional join conditions. Joining is described by focusing on the following eight areas:

- Types of joins
- Joining tables using ANSI SQL syntax
- Qualifying ambiguous column names
- The NATURAL JOIN clause
- The JOIN USING clause
- The JOIN ON clause
- N-way joins and additional join conditions
- Nonequijoins

Types of Joins

Two basic joins are the *equijoin* and the *nonequijoin*. Equijoins are probably more frequently used. Joins may be performed between multiple tables, but much of the following discussion will use two hypothetical tables to illustrate the concepts and language of joins. The first table is called the *source* and the second is called the *target*. Rows in the source and target tables comprise one or more columns. As an example, assume that the *source* and *target* are the COUNTRIES and REGIONS tables from the HR schema, respectively.

The COUNTRIES table contains three columns named COUNTRY_ID, COUNTRY_NAME, and REGION_ID. The REGIONS table is comprised of two columns named REGION_ID and REGION_NAME. The data in these two tables is related to each other based on the common REGION_ID column. Consider the following queries:

```
Query 1: SELECT *
         FROM countries
         WHERE country_id='CA';

Query 2: SELECT region_name
         FROM regions
         WHERE region_id=2;
```

The name of the region to which a country belongs may be determined by obtaining its REGION_ID value. This value is used to join it with the row in the REGIONS table with the same REGION_ID. Query 1 retrieves the column values associated with the row from the COUNTRIES table where the COUNTRY_ID–'CA'. The REGION_ID value of this row is 2. Query 2 fetches the Americas REGION_NAME from the REGIONS table for the row with REGION_ID=2. Equijoining facilitates the retrieval of column values from multiple tables using a single query.

The source and target tables can be swapped, so the REGIONS table could be the source and the COUNTRIES table could be the target. Consider the following two queries:

```
Query 1: SELECT *
         FROM regions
         WHERE region_name='Americas';

Query 2: SELECT country_name
         FROM countries
         WHERE region_id=2;
```

Query 1 fetches one row with a REGION_ID value of 2. Joining in this reversed manner allows the following question to be asked: What countries belong to the Americas region? The answers from Query 2 are five COUNTRY_NAME values: Argentina, Brazil, Canada, Mexico, and the United States of America. These results may be obtained from a single query that joins the tables together. The language to perform equijoins, nonequijoins, outer joins, and cross joins is introduced next, along with a discussion of the traditional Oracle join syntax.

Inner Joins

The inner join is implemented using three possible *join clauses* that use the following keywords in different combinations: NATURAL JOIN, USING, and ON.

When the source and target tables share identically named columns, it is possible to perform a natural join between them without specifying a join column. In this scenario, columns with the same names in the source and target tables are automatically associated with each other. Rows with matching column values in both tables are retrieved. The REGIONS and COUNTRIES table both share the REGION_ID column. They may be naturally joined without specifying join columns, as shown in the first two queries in Figure 7-1.

The NATURAL JOIN keywords instruct Oracle to identify columns with identical names between the source and target tables. Thereafter, a join is implicitly performed between them. In the first query, the REGION_ID column is identified as the only commonly named column in both tables. REGIONS is the source table and appears after the FROM clause. The target table is therefore COUNTRIES. For each row in the REGIONS table, a match for the REGION_ID value is sought from all the rows in the COUNTRIES table. An interim result set is constructed containing rows

Natural joins and
other inner joins

```
                                    SQL Plus                    _  □  ×

SQL> SELECT region_name
  2  FROM regions
  3  NATURAL JOIN countries
  4  WHERE country_name='Canada';

REGION_NAME
------------------------
Americas

SQL>
SQL> SELECT country_name
  2  FROM countries
  3  NATURAL JOIN regions
  4  WHERE region_name='Americas';

COUNTRY_NAME
----------------------------
United States of America
Canada
Mexico
Brazil
Argentina

SQL>
SQL> SELECT region_name
  2  FROM regions
  3  JOIN countries
  4  USING (region_id)
  5  WHERE country_name='Canada';

REGION_NAME
------------------------
Americas

SQL>
SQL> SELECT country_name
  2  FROM countries
  3  JOIN regions
  4  ON (countries.region_id=regions.region_id)
  5  WHERE region_name='Americas';
```

matching the join condition. This set is then restricted by the WHERE clause. In this case, because the COUNTRY_NAME value must be "Canada", a REGION_NAME of "Americas" is returned.

The second query shows a natural join where COUNTRIES is the source table. The REGION_ID value for each row in the COUNTRIES table is identified and a search for a matching row in the REGIONS table is initiated. If matches are found, the interim results are limited by any WHERE conditions. The COUNTRY_NAME from rows with "Americas" as their REGION_NAME are returned.

Sometimes more control must be exercised regarding which columns to use for joins. When there are identical column names in the source and target tables you want to exclude as join columns, the JOIN…USING format may be used. Remember that Oracle does not impose any rules stating that columns with the same name in two discrete tables must necessarily have any relationship with each other. The third query explicitly specifies that the REGIONS table be joined to the COUNTRIES table based on common values in their REGION_ID columns. This syntax allows inner joins to be formed on specific columns instead of on all commonly named columns.

The fourth query demonstrates the JOIN…ON format of the inner join, which allows join columns to be explicitly stated. This format does not depend on the columns in the source and target tables having identical names. This form is more general and is the most widely used inner join format.

Be wary when using natural joins since database designers may assign the same name to key or unique columns. These columns may have names like ID or SEQ_NO. If a natural join is attempted between such tables, ambiguous and unexpected results may be returned.

Outer Joins

Not all tables share a perfect relationship, where every record in the source table can be matched to at least one row in the target table. It is occasionally required that rows with nonmatching join column values also be retrieved by a query. This may seem to defeat the purpose of joins but has some practical benefits.

Suppose the EMPLOYEES and DEPARTMENTS tables are joined with common DEPARTMENT_ID values. EMPLOYEES records with null DEPARTMENT_ID values are excluded along with values absent from the DEPARTMENTS table. An *outer join* fetches these rows.

Cross Joins

A *cross join* or *Cartesian product* derives its names from mathematics, where it is also referred to as a cross product between two sets or matrices. This join creates one row of output for every combination of source and target table rows.

If the source and target tables have three and four rows, respectively, a cross join between them results in ($3 \times 4 = 12$) rows being returned. Consider the row counts retrieved from the queries in Figure 7-2.

The first two row counts are performed on the COUNTRIES and REGIONS tables yielding 25 and 4 rows, respectively. Query 3 counts the number of rows returned from a cross join of these tables and yields 100. Query 4 would return 100 records if the WHERE clause was absent. Each of the four rows in the REGIONS table is joined to the one row from the COUNTRIES table. Each row returned contains every column from both tables.

FIGURE 7-2

Cross join

```
                                    SQL Plus                        -  □  ×

SQL> SELECT count(*)
  2  FROM countries;

  COUNT(*)
----------
        25

SQL>
SQL> SELECT count(*)
  2  FROM regions;

  COUNT(*)
----------
         4

SQL>
SQL> SELECT count(*)
  2  FROM regions
  3  CROSS JOIN countries;

  COUNT(*)
----------
       100

SQL>
SQL> SELECT *
  2  FROM regions
  3  CROSS JOIN countries
  4  WHERE country_id='CA';

 REGION_ID REGION_NAME              CO COUNTRY_NAME           REGION_ID
---------- --------------------     -- -------------------- ----------
         1 Europe                   CA Canada                        2
         2 Americas                 CA Canada                        2
         3 Asia                     CA Canada                        2
         4 Middle East and Africa   CA Canada                        2

SQL>
```

Oracle Join Syntax

A proprietary Oracle join syntax has evolved that is stable and understood by
millions of users. This traditional syntax is supported by Oracle and is present in
software systems across the world. You will no doubt encounter the traditional
Oracle join syntax that is now making way for the standardized ANSI-compliant
syntax discussed in this chapter.

The traditional Oracle join syntax supports inner joins, outer joins, and Cartesian
joins, as shown in the following queries:

```
Query 1: SELECT regions.region_name, countries.country_name
         FROM regions, countries
         WHERE regions.region_id=countries.region_id;
```

```
Query 2: SELECT last_name, department_name
         FROM employees, departments
         WHERE employees.department_id (+) = departments.
department_id;

Query 3: SELECT *
         FROM regions,countries;
```

Query 1 performs an inner join by specifying the join as a condition in the WHERE clause. This is the most significant difference between the traditional and ANSI SQL join syntaxes. Take note of the column aliasing using the TABLE.COLUMN_NAME notation to disambiguate the identical column names. This notation is discussed in detail later in this chapter. Query 2 specifies the join between the source and target tables as a WHERE condition. There is a plus symbol enclosed in brackets (+) to the *left* of the equal sign that indicates to Oracle that a *right outer join* must be performed. This query returns employees' LAST_NAME and their matching DEPARTMENT_NAME values. In addition, the outer join retrieves DEPARTMENT_NAME from the rows with DEPARTMENT_ID values not currently assigned to any employee records. Query 3 performs a Cartesian or cross join by excluding the join condition.

e x a m

ⓦ a t c h   *The traditional Oracle join syntax is widely used. However, the exam assesses your understanding of joins and the ANSI SQL forms of its syntax. Be prepared, though: some questions may tap your knowledge of the traditional syntax. This knowledge is useful since traditional Oracle syntax is deeply embedded across software systems worldwide.*

Joining Tables Using ANSI SQL Syntax

Prior to Oracle 9i, the traditional join syntax was the only language available to join tables. Since then, Oracle has introduced a new language that is compliant with the latest ANSI standards. It offers no performance benefits over the traditional syntax. Inner, outer, and cross joins may be written using both ANSI SQL and traditional Oracle SQL.

The general form of the SELECT statement using ANSI SQL syntax is as follows:

SELECT *table1*.*column, table2*.*column*
FROM *table1*
[NATURAL JOIN *table2*] |
[JOIN *table2* USING (*column_name*)] |
[JOIN *table2* ON (*table1*.*column_name* = *table2*.*column_name*)] |
[LEFT | RIGHT | FULL OUTER JOIN *table2*
ON (*table1*.*column_name* = *table2*.*column_name*)] |
[CROSS JOIN *table2*];

This is dissected and examples are explained in the following sections. The general form of the traditional Oracle-proprietary syntax relevant to joins is as follows:

SELECT *table1*.*column, table2*.*column*
FROM *table1, table2*
[WHERE (*table1*.*column_name* = *table2*.*column_name*)] |
[WHERE (*table1*.*column_name*(+)= *table2*.*column_name*)] |
[WHERE (*table1*.*column_name*)= *table2*.*column_name*) (+)] ;

If no joins or fewer than N-1 joins are specified in the WHERE clause conditions, where N refers to the number of tables in the query, then a Cartesian or cross join is performed. If an adequate number of join conditions is specified, then the first optional conditional clause specifies an inner join, while the second two optional clauses specify the syntax for right and left outer joins.

Qualifying Ambiguous Column Names

Columns with the same names may occur in tables involved in a join. The columns named DEPARTMENT_ID and MANAGER_ID are found in both the EMPLOYEES and DEPARTMENTS tables. The REGION_ID column is present in both the REGIONS and COUNTRIES tables. Listing such columns in a query becomes problematic when Oracle cannot resolve their origin. Columns with unique names across the tables involved in a join cause no ambiguity as Oracle can easily resolve their source table.

The problem of ambiguous column names is addressed with dot notation. A column may be prefixed by its table name and a dot or period symbol to designate its origin. This differentiates it from a column with the same name in another table. Dot notation may be used in queries involving any number of tables. Referencing some columns using dot notation does not imply that all columns must be referenced in this way.

Dot notation is enhanced with table aliases. A *table alias* provides an alternate, usually shorter name for a table. A column may be referenced as *TABLE_NAME.COLUMN_NAME* or *TABLE_ALIAS.COLUMN_NAME*. Consider the query shown in Figure 7-3.

The EMPLOYEES table is aliased with the short name EMP while the DEPARTMENTS table is not. The SELECT clause references the EMPLOYEE_ID and MANAGER_ID columns as EMP.EMPLOYEE_ID and EMP.MANAGER_ID. The MANAGER_ID column from the DEPARTMENTS table is referred to as DEPARTMENTS.MANAGER_ID. Qualifying the EMPLOYEE_ID column using dot notation is unnecessary because there is only one column with this name between the two tables. Therefore, there is no ambiguity.

The MANAGER_ID column must be qualified to avoid ambiguity because it is featured in both tables. Since the JOIN…USING format is applied, only DEPARTMENT_ID is used as the join column. If a NATURAL JOIN was employed, both the DEPARTMENT_ID and MANAGER_ID columns would be used. If the MANAGER_ID column was not qualified, an "ORA-00918:column ambiguously defined" error would be returned. If DEPARTMENT_ID was aliased, an "ORA-25154:column part of USING clause cannot have qualifier" error would be raised.

FIGURE 7-3

Dot notation

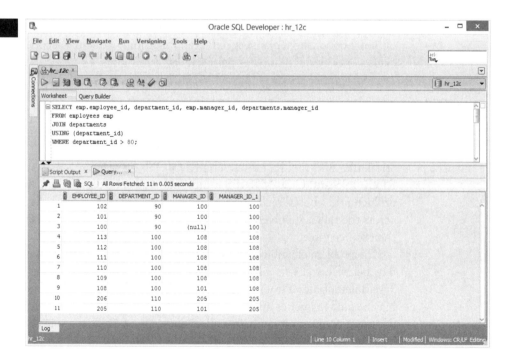

SQL Developer provides the heading MANAGER_ID to the first reference made in the SELECT clause. The string "_1" is automatically appended to the second reference, creating the heading MANAGER_ID_1.

on the
! o b

Qualifying column references with dot notation to indicate a column's table of origin has a performance benefit. Time is saved because Oracle is directed instantaneously to the appropriate table and does not have to resolve the table name.

The NATURAL JOIN Clause

The general syntax for the NATURAL JOIN clause is as follows:

SELECT *table1.column, table2.column*
FROM *table1*
NATURAL JOIN *table2;*

The natural join identifies the columns with common names in *table1* and *table2* and implicitly joins the tables using all these columns. The columns in the SELECT clause may be qualified using dot notation unless they are one of the join columns. Consider the following queries:

```
Query 1: SELECT *
         FROM locations
         NATURAL JOIN countries;

Query 2: SELECT *
         FROM locations, countries
         WHERE locations.country_id = countries.country_id;

Query 3: SELECT *
         FROM jobs
         NATURAL JOIN countries;

Query 4: SELECT *
         FROM jobs, countries;
```

The natural join identifies columns with common names between the two tables. In Query 1, COUNTRY_ID occurs in both tables and becomes the join column. Query 2 is written using traditional Oracle syntax and retrieves the same rows as Query 1. Unless you are familiar with the columns in the source and target tables, natural joins must be used with caution, as join conditions are automatically formed between all columns with shared names.

Query 3 performs a natural join between the JOBS and COUNTRIES tables. There are no columns with identical names, resulting in a Cartesian product. Query 4 is equivalent to Query 3, and a Cartesian join is performed using traditional Oracle syntax.

The natural join is simple but prone to a fundamental weakness. It suffers the risk that two columns with the same name might have no relationship and may not even have compatible data types. In Figure 7-4, the COUNTRIES, REGIONS,

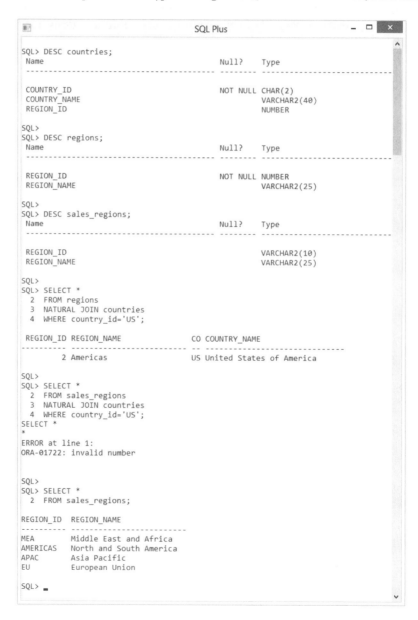

```
SQL> DESC countries;
 Name                                         Null?    Type
 --------------------------------------       --------  ------------------------

 COUNTRY_ID                                   NOT NULL CHAR(2)
 COUNTRY_NAME                                          VARCHAR2(40)
 REGION_ID                                            NUMBER

SQL>
SQL> DESC regions;
 Name                                         Null?    Type
 --------------------------------------       --------  ------------------------

 REGION_ID                                    NOT NULL NUMBER
 REGION_NAME                                          VARCHAR2(25)

SQL>
SQL> DESC sales_regions;
 Name                                         Null?    Type
 --------------------------------------       --------  ------------------------

 REGION_ID                                            VARCHAR2(10)
 REGION_NAME                                          VARCHAR2(25)

SQL>
SQL> SELECT *
  2  FROM regions
  3  NATURAL JOIN countries
  4  WHERE country_id='US';

 REGION_ID REGION_NAME                 CO COUNTRY_NAME
 ---------- ------------------------   -- -----------------------------
         2 Americas                    US United States of America

SQL>
SQL> SELECT *
  2  FROM sales_regions
  3  NATURAL JOIN countries
  4  WHERE country_id='US';
SELECT *
*
ERROR at line 1:
ORA-01722: invalid number


SQL>
SQL> SELECT *
  2  FROM sales_regions;

REGION_ID  REGION_NAME
---------- ------------------------
MEA        Middle East and Africa
AMERICAS   North and South America
APAC       Asia Pacific
EU         European Union

SQL>
```

and SALE_REGIONS tables are described. The SALES_REGIONS table was constructed to illustrate the following important point: Although it has REGION_ID in common with the COUNTRIES table, it cannot be naturally joined to it because their data types are incompatible. The data types of the COUNTRIES.REGION_ID and SALES_REGIONS.REGION_ID columns are NUMBER and VARCHAR2, respectively. The character data cannot be implicitly converted into numeric data and an "ORA-01722: invalid number" error is raised. The REGIONS.REGION_ID column is of type NUMBER and its data is related to the data in the COUNTRIES table. Therefore, the natural join between the REGIONS and COUNTRIES tables works perfectly.

EXERCISE 7-1

Using the **NATURAL JOIN**

The JOB_HISTORY table shares three identically named columns with the EMPLOYEES table: EMPLOYEE_ID, JOB_ID, and DEPARTMENT_ID. You are required to describe the tables and fetch the EMPLOYEE_ID, JOB_ID, DEPARTMENT_ID, LAST_NAME, HIRE_DATE, and END_DATE values for all rows retrieved using a natural join. Alias the EMPLOYEES table as EMP and the JOB_HISTORY table as JH and use dot notation where possible.

1. Start SQL*Plus and connect to the HR schema.
2. The tables are described using the commands DESC EMPLOYEES and DESC JOB_HISTORY, and the columns with identical names and their data types may be examined.
3. The FROM clause is
   ```
   FROM JOB_HISTORY JH
   ```
4. The JOIN clause is
   ```
   NATURAL JOIN EMPLOYEES EMP
   ```
5. The SELECT clause is
   ```
   SELECT EMPLOYEE_ID, JOB_ID, DEPARTMENT_ID, EMP.LAST_NAME,
   EMP.HIRE_DATE, JH.END_DATE
   ```

6. Executing this statement returns a single row with the same EMPLOYEE_ID, JOB_ID, and DEPARTMENT_ID values in both tables and is shown in the following illustration:

```
SQL Plus                                                    _ □ ×

SQL> DESC employees;
 Name                                    Null?    Type
 --------------------------------------- -------- --------------------------

 EMPLOYEE_ID                             NOT NULL NUMBER(6)
 FIRST_NAME                                       VARCHAR2(20)
 LAST_NAME                               NOT NULL VARCHAR2(25)
 EMAIL                                   NOT NULL VARCHAR2(25)
 PHONE_NUMBER                                     VARCHAR2(20)
 HIRE_DATE                               NOT NULL DATE
 JOB_ID                                  NOT NULL VARCHAR2(10)
 SALARY                                           NUMBER(8,2)
 COMMISSION_PCT                                   NUMBER(2,2)
 MANAGER_ID                                       NUMBER(6)
 DEPARTMENT_ID                                    NUMBER(4)

SQL>
SQL> DESC job_history;
 Name                                    Null?    Type
 --------------------------------------- -------- --------------------------

 EMPLOYEE_ID                             NOT NULL NUMBER(6)
 START_DATE                              NOT NULL DATE
 END_DATE                                NOT NULL DATE
 JOB_ID                                  NOT NULL VARCHAR2(10)
 DEPARTMENT_ID                                    NUMBER(4)

SQL>
SQL> SELECT employee_id, job_id, department_id,
  2         emp.last_name, emp.hire_date, jh.end_date
  3  FROM job_history jh
  4  NATURAL JOIN employees emp;

EMPLOYEE_ID JOB_ID     DEPARTMENT_ID LAST_NAME  HIRE_DATE END_DATE
----------- ---------- ------------- ---------- --------- ---------
        176 SA_REP                80 Taylor     24-MAR-06 31-DEC-06

SQL> _
```

The JOIN USING Clause

The format of the syntax for the JOIN USING clause is as follows:

SELECT *table1.column, table2.column*
FROM *table1*
JOIN *table2* USING (*join_column1, join_column2…*);

While the natural join contains the NATURAL keyword in its syntax, the JOIN…USING syntax does not. An error is raised if the keywords NATURAL and USING occur in the same join clause. The JOIN…USING clause allows one or more equijoin columns to be explicitly specified in brackets after the USING keyword. This avoids the shortcomings associated with the natural join. Many situations demand that tables be joined only on certain columns and this format caters for this requirement. Consider the following queries:

```
Query 1: SELECT *
         FROM locations
         JOIN countries
         USING (country_id);

Query 2: SELECT *
         FROM locations, countries
         WHERE locations.country_id = countries.country_id;
```

Query 1 specifies that the LOCATIONS and COUNTRIES tables must be joined on common COUNTRY_ID column values. All columns from these tables are retrieved for the rows with matching join column values. Query 2 shows a traditionally specified query that retrieves the same rows as Query 1. The join columns specified with the JOIN...USING syntax cannot be qualified using table names or aliases when they are referenced in the SELECT and JOIN clauses. Since this join syntax potentially excludes some columns with identical names from the join clause, these must be qualified if they are referenced to avoid ambiguity.

As Figure 7-5 shows, the JOB_HISTORY and EMPLOYEES tables were joined based on the presence of equal values in their JOB_ID and EMPLOYEE_ID columns. Rows conforming to this join condition are retrieved. These tables share

FIGURE 7-5

Natural join using the JOIN... USING clause

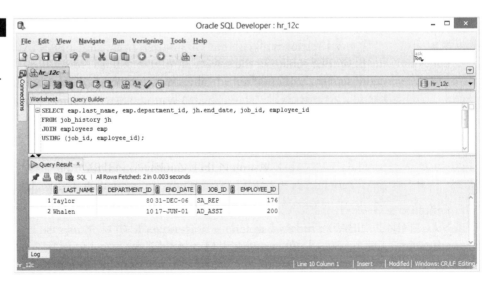

three identically named columns. In this example, only two of these are specified as join columns. Notice that although the third identically named column is DEPARTMENT_ID, it is qualified with a table alias to avoid ambiguity while the join columns specified in the SELECT clause cannot be qualified with table aliases.

The JOIN ON Clause

The format of the syntax for the JOIN ON clause is as follows:

SELECT *table1.column, table2.column*
FROM *table1*
JOIN *table2* ON (*table1.column_name* = *table2.column_name*);

The natural join and the JOIN…USING clauses depend on join columns with identical column names. The JOIN…ON clause allows the explicit specification of join columns, regardless of their column names. This is the most flexible and widely used form of the join clauses. The ON and NATURAL keywords cannot appear together in a join clause. The equijoin columns are fully qualified as *table1.column1* = *table2.column2* and are optionally specified in brackets after the ON keyword. The following queries illustrate the JOIN…ON clause:

```
Query 1: SELECT *
         FROM departments d
         JOIN employees e ON (e.employee_id=d.department_id);

Query 2: SELECT *
         FROM employees e, departments d
         WHERE e.employee_id=d.department_id;
```

Query 1 retrieves all column values from both the DEPARTMENTS and EMPLOYEES tables for the rows that meet an equijoin condition. This condition is fulfilled by EMPLOYEE_ID values matching DEPARTMENT_ID values in the DEPARTMENTS table. The traditional Oracle syntax in Query 2 returns the same results as Query 1. Notice the similarities between the traditional join condition specified in the WHERE clause and the join condition specified after the ON keyword.

The START_DATE column in the JOB_HISTORY table is joined to the HIRE_DATE column in the EMPLOYEES table in Figure 7-6. This equijoin retrieves the details of employees who worked for the organization and changed jobs.

SCENARIO & SOLUTION

You are required to retrieve information from multiple tables, group the results, and apply an aggregate function to them. Can a group function be used against data from multiple table sources?	Yes. Joining multiple tables ultimately yields a set of data comprising one or more rows and columns. Once the dataset is created, aggregate functions treat it as if the data originated from one source.
When joining two tables, there is a risk that between them they contain common column names. Does Oracle know which tables to fetch data from if such columns are present in the SELECT list?	No. Oracle does not know from which tables such columns originate, and an error is raised. Ambiguous column references can be avoided using qualifiers. Qualifiers employ dot notation to clarify a column's table of origin.
The NATURAL JOIN clause is used to join rows from two tables based on columns with common names sharing identical values. Is it possible to join two tables based on some of the shared columns and not all of them?	Yes. The clause recommended to join two tables based on one or more of the columns with identical names is JOIN…USING. A pair of brackets follows the USING clause in which the unqualified join columns are specified.

FIGURE 7-6

Inner join using the JOIN…ON clause

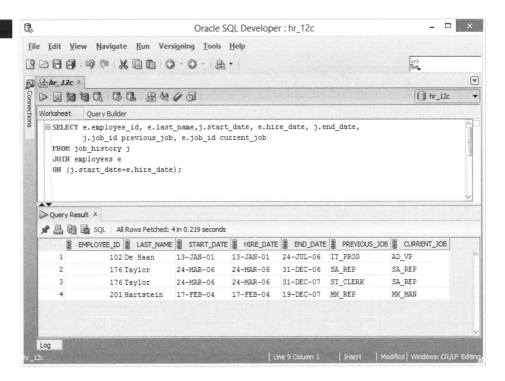

Using the **NATURAL JOIN...ON** Clause

Each record in the DEPARTMENTS table has a MANAGER_ID column matching an EMPLOYEE_ID value in the EMPLOYEES table. You are required to produce a report with one column aliased as Managers. Each row must contain a sentence of the format FIRST_NAME LAST_NAME is manager of the DEPARTMENT_NAME department. Alias the EMPLOYEES table as E and the DEPARTMENTS table as D and use dot notation where possible.

1. Start SQL Developer and connect to the HR schema.
2. The Managers column may be constructed by concatenating the required items and separating them with spaces.
3. The SELECT clause is
   ```
   SELECT E.FIRST_NAME||' '||E.LAST_NAME||' is manager of the '||
   D.DEPARTMENT_NAME||' department.' "Managers"
   ```
4. The FROM clause is
   ```
   FROM EMPLOYEES E
   ```
5. The JOIN...ON clause is
   ```
   JOIN DEPARTMENTS D
   ON (E. EMPLOYEE_ID=D.MANAGER_ID)
   ```

6. Executing this statement returns 11 rows describing the managers of each
department as shown in the following illustration:

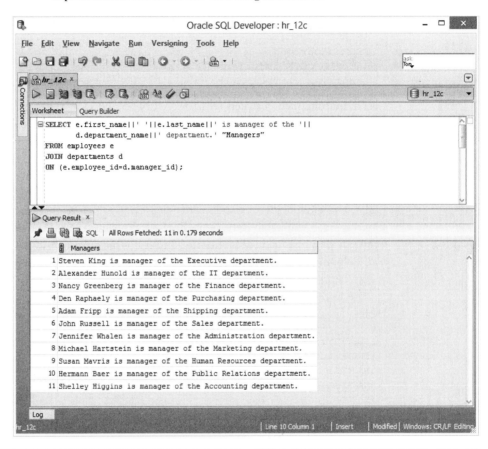

N-Way Joins and Additional Join Conditions

The joins just discussed were demonstrated using two tables. There is no restriction
on the number of tables that may be joined. Third normal form consists of a set
of tables connected through a series of primary- and foreign-key relationships.
Traversing these relationships using joins enables consistent and reliable retrieval
of data. However, there are instances when primary- and foreign-key relationships
are not defined between tables. These tables may also be joined, but the results do not

benefit from referential integrity being enforced by the database. When multiple joins exist in a statement, they are evaluated from left to right. Consider the following query using a mixture of natural joins and Oracle joins:

```
SELECT r.region_name, c.country_name, l.city, d.department_name
FROM departments d
NATURAL JOIN locations l,
countries c, regions r;
```

The natural join between DEPARTMENTS and LOCATIONS creates an interim result set consisting of 27 rows since they are implicitly joined on the LOCATION_ID column. This set is then Cartesian-joined to the COUNTRIES table since a join condition is not implicitly or explicitly specified. The 27 interim rows are joined to the 25 rows in the COUNTRIES table, yielding a new interim results set with 675 (27 × 25) rows and three columns: DEPARTMENT_NAME, CITY, and COUNTRY_NAME. This set is then joined to the REGIONS table. Once again, a Cartesian join occurs because the REGION_ID column is absent from any join condition. The final result set contains 2700 (675 × 4) rows and four columns. Using natural joins mixed with Oracle joins is error prone and not recommended since join conditions may sometimes be erroneously omitted.

The JOIN…USING and JOIN…ON syntaxes are better suited for joining multiple tables. The following query joins four tables using the natural join syntax:

```
SELECT region_id, country_id, c.country_name, l.city, d.department_name
FROM departments d
NATURAL JOIN locations l
NATURAL JOIN countries c
NATURAL JOIN regions r;
```

This query correctly yields 27 rows in the final results set since the required join columns are listed in the SELECT clause. The following query demonstrates how the JOIN…ON clause is used to fetch the same 27 rows. A join condition can reference only columns in its scope. In the following example, the join from DEPARTMENTS to LOCATIONS may not reference columns in the COUNTRIES or REGIONS tables, but the join between COUNTRIES and REGIONS may reference any column from the four tables involved in the query.

```
SELECT r.region_name, c.country_name, l.city, d.department_name
FROM departments d
JOIN locations l ON (l.location_id=d.location_id)
JOIN countries c ON (c.country_id=l.country_id)
JOIN regions r ON (r.region_id=c.region_id);
```

The JOIN…USING clause can also be used to join these four tables as follows:

```
SELECT r.region_name, c.country_name, l.city, d.department_name
FROM departments d
JOIN locations l USING (location_id)
JOIN countries c USING (country_id)
JOIN regions r USING (region_id);
```

The WHERE clause is used to specify conditions that restrict the results set of a query whether it contains joins or not. The JOIN…ON clause is also used to specify conditions that limit the results set created by the join. Consider the following two queries:

```
Query 1: SELECT d.department_name
         FROM departments d
         JOIN locations l
         ON (l.LOCATION_ID=d.LOCATION_ID)
         WHERE d.department_name LIKE 'P%';

Query 2: SELECT d.department_name
         FROM departments d
         JOIN locations l
         ON (l.LOCATION_ID=d.LOCATION_ID
         AND d.department_name like 'P%');
```

Query 1 uses a WHERE clause to restrict the 27 rows created by equijoining the DEPARTMENTS and LOCATIONS tables based on their LOCATION_ID values to the three that contain DEPARTMENT_ID values beginning with the letter "P". Query 2 implements the condition within the brackets of the ON subclause and returns the same three rows.

Five tables are joined in Figure 7-7, resulting in a list describing the top-earning employees and geographical information about their departments.

FIGURE 7-7

N-way joins and additional join conditions

Nonequijoins

Nonequijoins match column values from different tables based on an inequality expression. The value of the join column in each row in the source table is compared to the corresponding values in the target table. A match is found if the expression used in the join, based on an inequality operator, evaluates to true. When such a join is constructed, a nonequijoin is performed.

A nonequijoin is specified using the JOIN...ON syntax, but the join condition contains an inequality operator instead of an equal sign.

The format of the syntax for a nonequijoin clause is as follows:

SELECT *table1.column, table2.column*
FROM *table1*
[JOIN *table2* ON (*table1.column_name* < *table2.column_name*)] |
[JOIN *table2* ON (*table1.column_name* > *table2.column_name*)] |

[JOIN *table2* ON (*table1.column_name* <= *table2.column_name*)] |
[JOIN *table2* ON (*table1.column_name* >= *table2.column_name*)] |
[JOIN *table2* ON (*table1.column* BETWEEN *table2.col1* AND *table2.col2*)]

Consider the 16 rows returned by the query in Figure 7-8. The EMPLOYEES table is nonequijoined to the JOBS table based on the inequality join condition (`2*E.SALARY < J.MAX_SALARY`). The JOBS table stores the salary range for different jobs in the organization. The SALARY value for each employee record is doubled and compared with all MAX_SALARY values in the JOBS table. If the join condition evaluates to true, the row is returned.

on the job

Nonequijoins are not as commonly used as equijoins. The BETWEEN range operator often appears with nonequijoin conditions. It is simpler to use one BETWEEN operator in a condition than two nonequijoin conditions based on the less than or equal to (<=) and the greater than or equal to (>=) operators.

FIGURE 7-8

Nonequijoins

_Oracle SQL Developer : hr_12c_

```
SELECT e.job_id current_job,'The salary of '||last_name||' can be doubled by changing jobs to: '||
       j.job_id options, e.salary current_salary, j.max_salary potential_max_salary
FROM employees e
JOIN jobs j
ON (2*e.salary < j.max_salary)
WHERE e.salary>11000
ORDER BY last_name;
```

All Rows Fetched: 16 in 0.005 seconds

	CURRENT_JOB	OPTIONS	CURRENT_SALARY	POTENTIAL_MAX_SALARY
1	AD_VP	The salary of De Haan can be doubled by changing jobs to: AD_PRES	17000	40000
2	SA_MAN	The salary of Errazuriz can be doubled by changing jobs to: AD_PRES	12000	40000
3	SA_MAN	The salary of Errazuriz can be doubled by changing jobs to: AD_VP	12000	30000
4	FI_MGR	The salary of Greenberg can be doubled by changing jobs to: AD_VP	12008	30000
5	FI_MGR	The salary of Greenberg can be doubled by changing jobs to: AD_PRES	12008	40000
6	MK_MAN	The salary of Hartstein can be doubled by changing jobs to: AD_VP	13000	30000
7	MK_MAN	The salary of Hartstein can be doubled by changing jobs to: AD_PRES	13000	40000
8	AC_MGR	The salary of Higgins can be doubled by changing jobs to: AD_PRES	12008	40000
9	AC_MGR	The salary of Higgins can be doubled by changing jobs to: AD_VP	12008	30000
10	AD_VP	The salary of Kochhar can be doubled by changing jobs to: AD_PRES	17000	40000
11	SA_REP	The salary of Ozer can be doubled by changing jobs to: AD_VP	11500	30000
12	SA_REP	The salary of Ozer can be doubled by changing jobs to: AD_PRES	11500	40000
13	SA_MAN	The salary of Partners can be doubled by changing jobs to: AD_VP	13500	30000
14	SA_MAN	The salary of Partners can be doubled by changing jobs to: AD_PRES	13500	40000
15	SA_MAN	The salary of Russell can be doubled by changing jobs to: AD_VP	14000	30000
16	SA_MAN	The salary of Russell can be doubled by changing jobs to: AD_PRES	14000	40000

Log

CERTIFICATION OBJECTIVE 7.02

Join a Table to Itself Using a Self-Join

Storing hierarchical data in a single relational table may be accomplished by allocating at least two columns per row. One column stores an identifier of the row's parent record and the second stores the row's identifier. Associating rows with each other based on a hierarchical relationship requires Oracle to join a table to itself. This *self-join* technique is discussed in the next section.

Joining a Table to Itself Using the JOIN...ON Clause

Suppose there is a need to store a family tree in a relational table. There are several approaches one could take. One option is to use a table called FAMILY with columns named ID, NAME, MOTHER_ID, and FATHER_ID, where each row stores a person's name, unique ID number, and the ID values for their parents.

When two tables are joined, each row from the source table is subjected to the join condition with rows from the target table. If the condition evaluates to true, then the joined row, consisting of columns from both tables, is returned.

When the join columns originate from the same table, a self-join is required. Conceptually, the source table is duplicated to create the target table. The self-join works like a regular join between these tables. Note that, internally, Oracle does not duplicate the table and this description is merely provided to explain the concept of self-joining. Consider the following three queries:

```
Query 1: SELECT id, name, father_id
         FROM family;

Query 2: SELECT name
         FROM family
         WHERE id=&father_id;

Query 3: SELECT f1.name Dad, f2.name Child
         FROM family f1
         JOIN family f2
         ON(f1.id=f2.father_id);
```

To identify a person's father in the FAMILY table, you could use Query 1 to get that person's ID, NAME, and FATHER_ID value. In Query 2, the FATHER_ID value obtained from the first query can be substituted to obtain the father's NAME value. Notice that both Queries 1 and 2 source information from the FAMILY table.

Query 3 performs a self-join with the JOIN…ON clause by aliasing the FAMILY table as f1 and f2. Oracle treats these as different tables even though they point to the same physical table. The first occurrence of the FAMILY table, aliased as f1, is designated as the source table, while the second occurrence, aliased as f2, is assigned as the target table. The join condition in the ON clause is of the format *source.child_id=target.parent_id*. Figure 7-9 shows a sample of FAMILY data and demonstrates a three-way self-join to the same table.

FIGURE 7-9

Self-join

```
□                                    SQL Plus                        -  □  ×

SQL> SELECT *
  2  FROM family;

        ID NAME       MOTHER_ID  FATHER_ID
---------- ---------- ---------- ----------
         1 Harry
         2 Sabita
         3 Reg                 2          1
         4 Niresh              2          1
         5 Dee                 2          1
         6 Vee
         7 Ishwarya            6          5
         8 Yashveer            6          5
         9 Tanishka            6          5
        10 Roopesh             2          1
        11 Ameetha            15         14
        12 Coda               11         10
        13 Sid                11         10
        14 Hari
        15 Indra
        16 Fatima
        17 Kiara              16          4
        18 Amira              16          4
        19 Ramona              2          1
        20 Himal
        21 Sameer             19         20

21 rows selected.

SQL> SELECT f1.NAME mum, f3.NAME dad, f2.NAME CHILD
  2  FROM family f1
  3  JOIN family f2 ON (f2.mother_id=f1.ID)
  4  JOIN family f3 ON (f2.father_id=f3.ID);

MUM        DAD        CHILD
---------- ---------- ----------
Sabita     Harry      Ramona
Sabita     Harry      Roopesh
Sabita     Harry      Dee
Sabita     Harry      Niresh
Sabita     Harry      Reg
Fatima     Niresh     Amira
Fatima     Niresh     Kiara
Vee        Dee        Tanishka
Vee        Dee        Yashveer
Vee        Dee        Ishwarya
Ameetha    Roopesh    Sid
Ameetha    Roopesh    Coda
Indra      Hari       Ameetha
Ramona     Himal      Sameer

14 rows selected.
```

Performing a Self-Join

There is a hierarchical relationship between employees and their managers. For each row in the EMPLOYEES table, the MANAGER_ID column stores the EMPLOYEE_ID of every employee's manager. Using a self-join on the EMPLOYEES table, you are required to retrieve the employee's LAST_NAME, EMPLOYEE_ID, MANAGER_ID, manager's LAST_NAME, and employee's DEPARTMENT_ID for the rows with DEPARMENT_ID values of 10, 20, or 30. Alias the EMPLOYEES table as E and the second instance of the EMPLOYEES table as M. Sort the results based on the DEPARTMENT_ID column.

1. Start SQL Developer and connect to the HR schema.
2. The SELECT clause is

   ```
   SELECT E.LAST_NAME EMPLOYEE, E.EMPLOYEE_ID, E.MANAGER_ID,
   M.LAST_NAME MANAGER, E.DEPARTMENT_ID
   ```

3. The FROM clause with source table and alias is

   ```
   FROM EMPLOYEES E
   ```

4. The JOIN...ON clause with aliased target table is

   ```
   JOIN EMPLOYEES M ON (E.MANAGER_ID=M.EMPLOYEE_ID)
   ```

5. The WHERE clause is

   ```
   WHERE E.DEPARTMENT_ID IN (10,20,30)
   ```

6. The ORDER BY clause is

   ```
   ORDER BY E.DEPARTMENT_ID
   ```

7. Executing this statement returns nine rows describing the managers of each employee in these departments as shown in the following illustration:

CERTIFICATION OBJECTIVE 7.03

View Data That Does Not Meet a Join Condition by Using Outer Joins

Equijoins match rows between two tables based on the equality of the column data stored in each table. Nonequijoins rely on matching rows between tables based on a join condition containing an inequality expression. Target table rows with no matching join column in the source table are usually not required. When they are required, however, an *outer join* is used to fetch them. Several variations of outer joins may be used depending on whether join column data is missing from the source or target tables or both. These outer join techniques are described in the following topics:

- Inner versus outer joins
- Left outer joins
- Right outer joins
- Full outer joins

Inner Versus Outer Joins

When equijoins and nonequijoins are performed, rows from the source and target tables are matched using a join condition formulated with equality and inequality operators, respectively. These are referred to as *inner joins*. An *outer join* is performed when rows, which are not retrieved by an inner join, are returned.

Two tables sometimes share a *master-detail* or *parent-child* relationship. In the sample HR schema there are several pairs of tables with such a relationship. One pair is the DEPARTMENTS and EMPLOYEES tables. The DEPARTMENTS table stores a master list of DEPARTMENT_NAME and DEPARTMENT_ID values. Each EMPLOYEES record has a DEPARTMENT_ID column constrained to be either a value that exists in the DEPARTMENTS table or null. This leads to one of the following three scenarios. The fourth scenario could occur if the constraint between the tables was removed.

1. An employee row has a DEPARTMENT_ID value that matches a row in the DEPARTMENTS table.
2. An employee row has a null value in its DEPARTMENT_ID column.
3. There are rows in the DEPARTMENTS table with DEPARTMENT_ID values that are not stored in any employee records.
4. An employee row has a DEPARTMENT_ID value that is not featured in the DEPARTMENTS table.

The first scenario describes an inner join between the two tables. The second and third scenarios cause many problems. Joining the EMPLOYEES and DEPARTMENTS tables on the DEPARTMENT_ID column may result in rows with null DEPARTMENT_ID values being excluded. An outer join can be used to include these orphaned rows in the results set. The fourth scenario should rarely occur in a well-designed database, because foreign-key constraints would prevent the insertion of child records with no parent values. Since this row will be excluded by an inner join, it may be retrieved using an outer join.

A left outer join between the source and target tables returns the results of an inner join as well as rows from the source table excluded by that inner join. A right outer join between the source and target tables returns the results of an inner join as well as rows from the target table excluded by that inner join. If a join returns the results of an inner join as well as rows from both the source and target tables excluded by that inner join, then a full outer join has been performed.

Left Outer Joins

The format of the syntax for the LEFT OUTER JOIN clause is as follows:

SELECT *table1.column, table2.column*
FROM *table1*
LEFT OUTER JOIN *table2*
ON (*table1.column = table2.column*);

A left outer join performs an inner join of *table1* and *table2* based on the condition specified after the ON keyword. Any rows from the table on the *left* of the JOIN keyword excluded for not fulfilling the join condition are also returned. Consider the following two queries:

```
Query 1: SELECT e.employee_id, e.department_id EMP_DEPT_ID,
                d.department_id DEPT_DEPT_ID, d.department_name
         FROM departments d
         LEFT OUTER JOIN employees e
         ON (d.DEPARTMENT_ID=e.DEPARTMENT_ID)
         WHERE d.department_name like 'P%';

Query 2: SELECT e.employee_id, e.department_id EMP_DEPT_ID,
                d.department_id DEPT_DEPT_ID, d.department_name
         FROM departments d
         JOIN employees e
         ON (d.DEPARTMENT_ID=e.DEPARTMENT_ID)
         WHERE d.department_name like 'P%';
```

Queries 1 and 2 are identical except for the join clauses, which have the keywords LEFT OUTER JOIN and JOIN, respectively. Query 2 performs an inner join and seven rows are returned. These rows share identical DEPARTMENT_ID values in both tables. Query 1 returns the same seven rows and one additional row. This extra row is obtained from the table to the left of the JOIN keyword, which is the DEPARTMENTS table. It is the row containing details of the Payroll department. The inner join does not include this row since no employees are currently assigned to the department.

A left outer join is shown in Figure 7-10. The inner join produces 27 rows with matching LOCATION_ID values in both tables. There are 43 rows in total, which implies that 16 rows were retrieved from the LOCATIONS table, which is on the *left* of the JOIN keyword. None of the rows from the DEPARTMENTS table contain any of these 16 LOCATION_ID values.

FIGURE 7-10

Left outer join

```
                                    SQL Plus                        -  □  ×

SQL> SELECT city, l.location_id "l.location_id", d.location_id "d.location_id"
  2   FROM locations l
  3   LEFT OUTER JOIN departments d
  4   ON (l.location_id=d.location_id);

CITY                          l.location_id d.location_id
----------------------------- ------------- -------------
Roma                                   1000
Venice                                 1100
Tokyo                                  1200
Hiroshima                              1300
Southlake                              1400          1400
South San Francisco                    1500          1500
South Brunswick                        1600
Seattle                                1700          1700
Seattle                                1700          1700
Seattle                                1700          1700
Seattle                                1700          1700
Seattle                                1700          1700
Seattle                                1700          1700
Seattle                                1700          1700
Seattle                                1700          1700
Seattle                                1700          1700
Seattle                                1700          1700
Seattle                                1700          1700
Seattle                                1700          1700
Seattle                                1700          1700
Seattle                                1700          1700
Seattle                                1700          1700
Seattle                                1700          1700
Seattle                                1700          1700
Seattle                                1700          1700
Seattle                                1700          1700
Seattle                                1700          1700
Toronto                                1800          1800
Whitehorse                             1900
Beijing                                2000
Bombay                                 2100
Sydney                                 2200
Singapore                              2300
London                                 2400          2400
Oxford                                 2500          2500
Stretford                              2600
Munich                                 2700          2700
Sao Paulo                              2800
Geneva                                 2900
Bern                                   3000
Utrecht                                3100
Mexico City                            3200

43 rows selected.
```

Right Outer Joins

The format of the syntax for the RIGHT OUTER JOIN clause is as follows:

SELECT *table1.column, table2.column*
FROM *table1*
RIGHT OUTER JOIN *table2*
ON (*table1.column = table2.column*);

A right outer join performs an inner join of *table1* and *table2* based on the join condition specified after the ON keyword. Rows from the table to the *right* of the JOIN keyword, excluded by the join condition, are also returned. Consider the following query:

```
SELECT e.last_name, d.department_name
FROM departments d
RIGHT OUTER JOIN employees e
ON (e.department_id=d.department_id)
WHERE e.last_name LIKE 'G%';
```

The inner join produces seven rows containing details for the employees with LAST_NAME values that begin with the letter "G". The EMPLOYEES table is to the *right* of the JOIN keyword. Any employee records which do not conform to the join condition are included, provided they conform to the WHERE clause condition. In addition, the right outer join fetches one EMPLOYEE record with a LAST_NAME of Grant. This record currently has a null DEPARTMENT_ID value. The inner join excludes the record since no DEPARTMENT_ID is assigned to this employee.

A right outer join between the JOB_HISTORY and EMPLOYEES tables is shown in Figure 7-11. The EMPLOYEES table is on the right of the JOIN keyword. The DISTINCT keyword eliminates duplicate combinations of JOB_ID values from the tables. The results show the jobs that employees have historically left. The jobs that no employees have left are also returned. These have a null value in the "Jobs in JOB_HISTORY" column.

e x a m

🐾 **a t c h** *There are three types of outer join formats. Each of them performs an inner join before including rows the join condition excluded. If a left outer join is performed, then rows excluded by the inner join, to the left of the JOIN keyword, are also returned. If a right outer join is performed, then rows excluded by the inner join, to the right of the JOIN keyword, are returned as well. The full outer join performs an inner join as well as a left and right outer join.*

FIGURE 7-11

Right outer join

Full Outer Joins

The format of the syntax for the FULL OUTER JOIN clause is as follows:

SELECT *table1.column, table2.column*
FROM *table1*
FULL OUTER JOIN *table2*
ON (*table1.column = table2.column*);

A *full outer join* returns the combined results of a left and right outer join. An inner join of *table1* and *table2* is performed before rows excluded by the join condition from both tables are merged into the results set.

The traditional Oracle join syntax does not support a full outer join, which is typically performed by combining the results from a left and right outer join using the UNION set operator described in Chapter 9. Consider the full outer join shown in Figure 7-12. The WHERE clause restricting the results to rows with

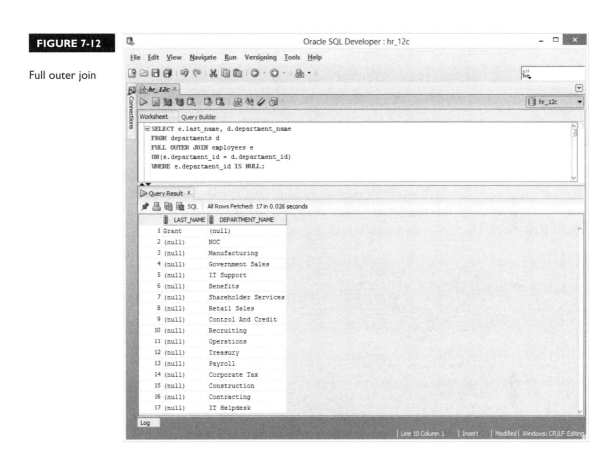

FIGURE 7-12

Full outer join

NULL DEPARTMENT_ID values shows the orphan rows in both tables. There is one record in the EMPLOYEES table that has no DEPARTMENT_ID values, and there are 16 departments to which no employees belong.

EXERCISE 7-4

Performing an Outer Join

The DEPARTMENTS table contains details of all departments in the organization. You are required to retrieve the DEPARTMENT_NAME and DEPARTMENT_ID values for those departments to which no employees are currently assigned.

1. Start SQL*Plus and connect to the HR schema.
2. The SELECT clause is

```
SELECT D.DEPARTMENT_NAME, D.DEPARTMENT_ID
```

3. The FROM clause with source table and alias is

   `FROM DEPARTMENTS D`

4. The LEFT OUTER JOIN clause with aliased target table is

   ```
   LEFT OUTER JOIN EMPLOYEES E ON
   E.DEPARTMENT_ID=D.DEPARTMENT_ID
   ```

5. The WHERE clause is

   `WHERE E.DEPARTMENT_ID IS NULL`

6. Executing this statement returns 16 rows describing the departments to which no employees are currently assigned as shown in the following illustration:

SCENARIO & SOLUTION

The data in two tables you wish to join is related but does not share any identically named columns. Is it possible to join tables using columns that do not share the same name?	Yes. The JOIN…ON clause is provided for this purpose. It provides a flexible and generic solution to joining tables based on nonidentical column names.

You wish to divide staff into four groups named after the four regions in the REGIONS table. Is it possible to obtain a list of EMPLOYEE_ID, LAST_NAME, and REGION_NAME values for each employee by joining the EMPLOYEE_ID and REGION_ID columns in a round-robin manner?	Yes. The REGION_ID value ranges from 1 to 4. Adding 1 to the remainder of EMPLOYEE_ID divided by 4 creates a value in the range 1 to 4. The round-robin assignment of employees may be done as follows:
	
	`SELECT LAST_NAME, EMPLOYEE_ID, REGION_`
	`NAME FROM EMPLOYEES JOIN REGIONS ON`
	`(MOD(EMPLOYEE_ID,4)+1= REGION_ID)`

You are required to retrieve a list of DEPARTMENT_NAME and LAST_NAME values for all departments, including those that currently have no employees assigned to them. In such cases the string `'No Employees'` should be displayed as the LAST_NAME column value. Can this be done using joins?	Yes. Depending on which side of the JOIN keyword the DEPARTMENTS table is placed, a left or right outer join may be used, since this is the table where the orphan rows originate. The following query satisfies the request:
	
	`SELECT DEPARTMENT_NAME, NVL(LAST_`
	`NAME,'No Employees') FROM EMPLOYEES`
	`RIGHT OUTER JOIN DEPARTMENTS USING`
	`(DEPARTMENT_ID)`

CERTIFICATION OBJECTIVE 7.04

Generate a Cartesian Product of Two or More Tables

A Cartesian product of two tables may be conceptualized as joining each row of the source table with every row in the target table. The number of rows in the result set created by a Cartesian product is equal to the number of rows in the source table multiplied by the number of rows in the target table. Cartesian products may be formed intentionally using the ANSI SQL cross join syntax. This technique is described in the next section.

Creating Cartesian Products Using Cross Joins

Cartesian product is a mathematical term. It refers to the set of data created by merging the rows from two or more tables together. *Cross join* is the syntax used to create a Cartesian product by joining multiple tables. Both terms are often used synonymously. The format of the syntax for the CROSS JOIN clause is as follows:

```
SELECT table1.column, table2.column
FROM table1
CROSS JOIN table2;
```

It is important to observe that no join condition is specified using the ON or USING keywords. A Cartesian product freely associates the rows from *table1* with every row in *table2*. Conditions that limit the results are permitted in the form of WHERE clause restrictions. If *table1* and *table2* contain x and y number of rows, respectively, the Cartesian product will contain x times y number of rows. The results from a cross join may be used to identify orphan rows or generate a large data set for use in application testing. Consider the following queries:

```
Query 1: SELECT *
         FROM jobs
         CROSS JOIN job_history;

Query 2: SELECT *
         FROM jobs j
         CROSS JOIN job_history jh
         WHERE j.job_id='AD_PRES';
```

Query 1 takes the 19 rows and 4 columns from the JOBS table and the 10 rows and 5 columns from the JOB_HISTORY table and generates one large set of 190 records with 9 columns. SQL*Plus presents any identically named columns as headings. SQL Developer appends an underscore and number to each shared column name and uses it as the heading. The JOB_ID column is common to both the JOBS and JOB_HISTORY tables. The headings in SQL Developer are labeled JOB_ID and JOB_ID_1, respectively. Query 2 generates the same Cartesian product as the first, but the 190 rows are constrained by the WHERE clause condition and only 10 rows are returned.

e x a m

ⓦatch

When using the cross join syntax, a Cartesian product is intentionally generated. Inadvertent Cartesian products are created when there are insufficient join conditions in a statement. Joins that specify fewer than N-1 join conditions when joining N tables or that specify invalid join conditions may inadvertently create Cartesian products. A natural join between two tables sharing no identically named columns results in a Cartesian join since two tables are joined but less than one condition is available.

Figure 7-13 shows a cross join between the REGIONS and COUNTRIES tables. There are 4 rows in REGIONS and 25 rows in COUNTRIES. Since the WHERE clause limits the REGIONS table to 2 of 4 rows, the Cartesian product produces 50 (25 × 2) records. The results are sorted alphabetically, first on the REGION_NAME and then on the COUNTRY_NAME. The first record has the pair of values, Asia and Argentina. When the REGION_NAME changes, the first record has the pair of values, Middle East and Africa and Argentina. Notice that the COUNTRY_NAME values are repeated for every REGION_NAME.

EXERCISE 7-5

Performing a Cross Join

You are required to obtain the number of rows in the EMPLOYEES and DEPARTMENTS tables as well as the number of records that would be created by a Cartesian product of these two tables. Confirm your results by explicitly counting and multiplying the number of rows present in each of these tables.

1. Start SQL*Plus and connect to the HR schema.
2. The SELECT clause to find the number of rows in the Cartesian product is
   ```
   SELECT COUNT(*)
   ```
3. The FROM clause is
   ```
   FROM EMPLOYEES
   ```
4. The Cartesian product is performed using
   ```
   CROSS JOIN DEPARTMENTS
   ```

FIGURE 7-13

The cross join

```
SQL> SELECT r.region_name, c.country_name
  2  FROM regions r
  3  CROSS JOIN countries c
  4  WHERE r.region_id in (3,4)
  5  ORDER BY region_name, country_name;

REGION_NAME               COUNTRY_NAME
------------------------  ------------------------------
Asia                      Argentina
Asia                      Australia
Asia                      Belgium
Asia                      Brazil
Asia                      Canada
Asia                      China
Asia                      Denmark
Asia                      Egypt
Asia                      France
Asia                      Germany
Asia                      India
Asia                      Israel
Asia                      Italy
Asia                      Japan
Asia                      Kuwait
Asia                      Malaysia
Asia                      Mexico
Asia                      Netherlands
Asia                      Nigeria
Asia                      Singapore
Asia                      Switzerland
Asia                      United Kingdom
Asia                      United States of America
Asia                      Zambia
Asia                      Zimbabwe
Middle East and Africa    Argentina
Middle East and Africa    Australia
Middle East and Africa    Belgium
Middle East and Africa    Brazil
Middle East and Africa    Canada
Middle East and Africa    China
Middle East and Africa    Denmark
Middle East and Africa    Egypt
Middle East and Africa    France
Middle East and Africa    Germany
Middle East and Africa    India
Middle East and Africa    Israel
Middle East and Africa    Italy
Middle East and Africa    Japan
Middle East and Africa    Kuwait
Middle East and Africa    Malaysia
Middle East and Africa    Mexico
Middle East and Africa    Netherlands
Middle East and Africa    Nigeria
Middle East and Africa    Singapore
Middle East and Africa    Switzerland
Middle East and Africa    United Kingdom
Middle East and Africa    United States of America
Middle East and Africa    Zambia
Middle East and Africa    Zimbabwe

50 rows selected.
```

FIGURE 7-13

The cross join

5. Explicit counts of the rows present in the source tables are performed using

```
SELECT COUNT(*) FROM EMPLOYEES;
SELECT COUNT(*) FROM DEPARTMENTS;
```

6. Explicit multiplication of the values resulting from the previous queries may be performed by querying the DUAL table.

7. Executing these statements reveals that there are 107 records in the EMPLOYEES table, 27 records in the DEPARTMENTS table, and 2,889 records in the Cartesian product of these two data sets as shown in the following illustration:

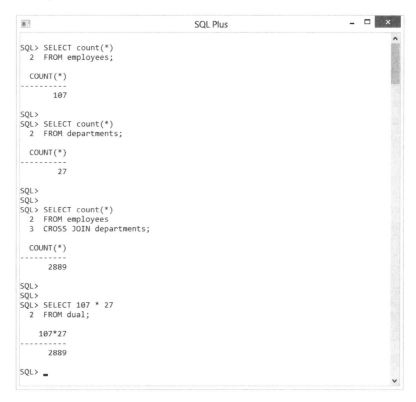

INSIDE THE EXAM

Joining is a fundamental relational principle. The certification objectives in this chapter are examined using practical scenarios in which two tables are joined. You are required to predict the number of rows returned by a join query or to assess whether it is syntactically correct or not. The inner join clauses include NATURAL JOIN, JOIN...USING, and JOIN...ON.

Remember the following simple rules. The keywords NATURAL, USING, and ON are mutually exclusive. They may not be used together in the same join clause. The NATURAL join takes no join conditions. The JOIN...USING clause requires unqualified column references in join conditions, which must appear in brackets after the USING keyword.

Self-joins are often used for searching through hierarchical data stored in separate columns in the same table. It is an uncommon join, and little emphasis is placed on testing your knowledge of self-joins in the exam. Outer joins, however, form a significant part of the exam content. Ensure that you have a solid understanding of LEFT, RIGHT, and FULL OUTER joins.

Cartesian products may be created inadvertently or intentionally using the CROSS JOIN clause. A mistake frequently made in the early stages of learning about joins is to specify fewer join conditions than are necessary when joining multiple tables. This leads to accidental Cartesian joins and is sometimes tested in the exams. Remember that when joining N tables, at least N-1 join conditions are required to avoid a Cartesian join.

CERTIFICATION SUMMARY

Data stored in separate tables may be associated with each other using various types of joins. Joins allow data to be stored in a relational manner. This prevents the need for multiple copies of the same data across multiple tables.

Equijoins and nonequijoins are referred to as inner joins. They associate rows from multiple tables that conform to join conditions and are specified using either equality or inequality operators. Rows that do not conform to these join conditions, which are ordinarily excluded by inner joins, may be retrieved with outer joins. Left, right, and full outer joins facilitate the retrieval of orphan rows.

The ANSI SQL join syntax is discussed in detail, and three forms of the inner join are explored. Each form has a purpose, and the advantages and risks associated with them are considered.

Joins associate columns from multiple tables that may share the same name. Dot notation uses a method of qualifying columns to disambiguate them. It is accompanied by table aliasing, which is not strictly essential but helps a great deal when formulating joins between tables with lengthy names.

The retrieval of hierarchical data stored in a single table using self-joins is considered. N-way joins allow more than two tables to be joined, and this generalized option is discussed. Finally, cross joins and the unique challenges associated with them are examined.

Joining is one of the fundamental pillars of relational theory and is critical to your successful exploitation of the full potential that SQL offers.

TWO-MINUTE DRILL

Write SELECT Statements to Access Data from More Than One Table Using Equijoins and Nonequijoins

❑ Equijoining occurs when one query fetches column values from multiple tables in which the rows fulfill an equality-based join condition.

❑ A natural join is performed using the NATURAL JOIN syntax when the source and target tables are implicitly equijoined using all identically named columns.

❑ The JOIN...USING syntax allows an inner join to be formed on specific columns with shared names.

❑ Dot notation refers to qualifying a column by prefixing it with its table name and a dot or period symbol. This designates the table a column originates from and differentiates it from identically named columns from other tables.

❑ The JOIN...ON clause allows the explicit specification of join columns regardless of their column names. This provides a flexible joining format.

❑ The ON, USING, and NATURAL keywords are mutually exclusive and therefore cannot appear together in a join clause.

❑ A nonequijoin is performed when the values in the join columns fulfill the join condition based on an inequality expression.

Join a Table to Itself Using a Self-Join

❑ A self-join is required when the join columns originate from the same table. Conceptually, the source table is duplicated and a target table is created. The self-join then works as a regular join between two discrete tables.

❑ Storing hierarchical data in a relational table requires a minimum of two columns per row. One column stores an identifier of the row's parent record and the second stores the row's identifier.

View Data That Does Not Meet a Join Condition Using Outer Joins

❑ When equijoins and nonequijoins are performed, rows from the source and target tables are matched. These are referred to as inner joins.

❑ An outer join is performed when rows, which are not retrieved by an inner join, are included for retrieval in addition to the rows retrieved by the inner join.

❑ A left outer join between the source and target tables returns the results of an inner join and the missing rows it excluded from the source table.

❑ A right outer join between the source and target tables returns the results of an inner join and the missing rows it excluded from the target table.

❑ A full outer join returns the combined results of a left outer join and right outer join.

Generate a Cartesian Product of Two or More Tables

❑ A Cartesian product is sometimes called a cross join. It is a mathematical term that refers to the set of data created by merging the rows from two or more tables.

❑ The count of the rows returned from a Cartesian product is equal to the number of rows in the source table multiplied by the number of rows in the target table.

❑ Joins that specify fewer than N-1 join conditions when joining N tables, or that specify invalid join conditions, inadvertently create Cartesian products.

SELF TEST

The following questions will help you measure your understanding of the material presented in this chapter. Read all the choices carefully because there may be more than one correct answer. Choose all the correct answers for each question.

Write SELECT Statements to Access Data from More Than One Table Using Equijoins and Nonequijoins

I. The EMPLOYEES and DEPARTMENTS tables have two identically named columns: DEPARTMENT_ID and MANAGER_ID. Which of these statements joins these tables based only on common DEPARTMENT_ID values? (Choose all that apply.)
    A. SELECT * FROM EMPLOYEES NATURAL JOIN DEPARTMENTS;
    B. SELECT * FROM EMPLOYEES E NATURAL JOIN DEPARTMENTS D ON E.DEPARTMENT_ID=D.DEPARTMENT_ID;
    C. SELECT * FROM EMPLOYEES NATURAL JOIN DEPARTMENTS USING (DEPARTMENT_ID);
    D. None of the above

2. The EMPLOYEES and DEPARTMENTS tables have two identically named columns: DEPARTMENT_ID and MANAGER_ID. Which statements join these tables based on both column values? (Choose all that apply.)
    A. SELECT * FROM EMPLOYEES NATURAL JOIN DEPARTMENTS;
    B. SELECT * FROM EMPLOYEES JOIN DEPARTMENTS USING (DEPARTMENT_ID,MANAGER_ID);
    C. SELECT * FROM EMPLOYEES E JOIN DEPARTMENTS D ON E.DEPARTMENT_ID=D.DEPARTMENT_ID AND E.MANAGER_ID=D.MANAGER_ID;
    D. None of the above

3. Which join is performed by the following query? (Choose the best answer.)
```
SELECT E.JOB_ID,J.JOB_ID FROM EMPLOYEES E
JOIN JOBS J ON (E.SALARY < J.MAX_SALARY);
```
   A. Equijoin
   B. Nonequijoin
   C. Cross join
   D. Outer join

4. Which of the following statements are syntactically correct? (Choose all that apply.)
   A. SELECT * FROM EMPLOYEES E JOIN DEPARTMENTS D USING (DEPARTMENT_ID);
   B. SELECT * FROM EMPLOYEES JOIN DEPARTMENTS D USING (D.DEPARTMENT_ID);
   C. SELECT D.DEPARTMENT_ID FROM EMPLOYEES JOIN DEPARTMENTS D USING (DEPARTMENT_ID);
   D. None of the above

5. Which of the following statements are syntactically correct? (Choose all that apply.)
   A. SELECT E.EMPLOYEE_ID, J.JOB_ID PREVIOUS_JOB, E.JOB_ID CURRENT_JOB FROM JOB_HISTORY J CROSS JOIN EMPLOYEES E ON (J.START_DATE=E.HIRE_DATE);
   B. SELECT E.EMPLOYEE_ID, J.JOB_ID PREVIOUS_JOB, E.JOB_ID CURRENT_JOB FROM JOB_HISTORY J JOIN EMPLOYEES E ON (J.START_DATE=E.HIRE_DATE);
   C. SELECT E.EMPLOYEE_ID, J.JOB_ID PREVIOUS_JOB, E.JOB_ID CURRENT_JOB FROM JOB_HISTORY J OUTER JOIN EMPLOYEES E ON (J.START_DATE=E.HIRE_DATE);
   D. None of the above

6. Choose one correct statement regarding the following query:
```
SELECT * FROM EMPLOYEES E
JOIN DEPARTMENTS D ON (D.DEPARTMENT_ID=E.DEPARTMENT_ID) JOIN LOCATIONS L ON
(L.LOCATION_ID =D.LOCATION_ID);
```
   A. Joining three tables is not permitted.
   B. A Cartesian product is generated.
   C. The JOIN...ON clause may be used for joins between multiple tables.
   D. None of the above

Join a Table to Itself Using a Self-Join

7. How many rows are returned after executing the following statement? (Choose the best answer.)

```
SELECT * FROM REGIONS R1 JOIN REGIONS R2 ON (R1.REGION_ID=LENGTH(R2.REGION_
NAME)/2);
```

The REGIONS table contains the following row data:

REGION_ID	REGION_NAME
1	Europe
2	Americas
3	Asia
4	Middle East and Africa

A. 2

B. 3

C. 4

D. None of the above

View Data that Does Not Meet a Join Condition Using Outer Joins

8. Choose one correct statement regarding the following query.

```
SELECT C.COUNTRY_ID
FROM LOCATIONS L RIGHT OUTER JOIN COUNTRIES C
ON (L.COUNTRY_ID=C.COUNTRY_ID) WHERE L.COUNTRY_ID is NULL;
```

A. No rows in the LOCATIONS table have the COUNTRY_ID values returned.

B. No rows in the COUNTRIES table have the COUNTRY_ID values returned.

C. The rows returned represent the COUNTRY_ID values for all the rows in the LOCATIONS table.

D. None of the above

9. Which of the following statements are syntactically correct? (Choose all that apply.)

A. SELECT JH.JOB_ID FROM JOB_HISTORY JH RIGHT OUTER JOIN JOBS J ON JH.JOB_ID=J.JOB_ID;

B. SELECT JOB_ID FROM JOB_HISTORY JH RIGHT OUTER JOIN JOBS J ON (JH.JOB_ID=J.JOB_ID);

C. SELECT JOB_HISTORY.JOB_ID FROM JOB_HISTORY OUTER JOIN JOBS ON JOB_HISTORY.JOB_ID=JOBS.JOB_ID;

D. None of the above

Generate a Cartesian Product of Two or More Tables

10. If the REGIONS table, which contains 4 rows, is cross joined to the COUNTRIES table, which contains 25 rows, how many rows appear in the final results set? (Choose the best answer.)

    A. 100 rows

    B. 4 rows

    C. 25 rows

    D. None of the above

LAB QUESTION

Using SQL Developer or SQL*Plus, connect to the OE schema and complete the following tasks.

You are required to produce a report of customers who purchased products with list prices of more than $1,000. The report must contain customer first and last names, as well as the product names and their list prices. Customer information is stored in the CUSTOMERS table, which has the CUSTOMER_ID column as its primary key. The product name and list price details are stored in the PRODUCT_INFORMATION table with the PRODUCT_ID column as its primary key. Two other related tables may assist in generating the required report: the ORDERS table, which stores the CUSTOMER_ID and ORDER_ID information, and the ORDER_ITEMS table, which stores the PRODUCT_ID values associated with each ORDER_ID.

There are several approaches to solving this question. Your approach may differ from the solution listed.

SELF TEST ANSWERS

Write SELECT Statements to Access Data from More Than One Table Using Equijoins and Nonequijoins

1. ☑ **D.** The queries in **B** and **C** incorrectly contain the NATURAL keyword. If this is removed, they will join the DEPARTMENTS and EMPLOYEES tables based on the DEPARTMENT_ID column.

   ☒ **A, B,** and **C** are incorrect. **A** performs a natural join that implicitly joins the two tables on all columns with identical names which, in this case, are DEPARTMENT_ID and MANAGER_ID.

2. ☑ **A, B,** and **C.** These clauses demonstrate different techniques to join the tables on both the DEPARTMENT_ID and MANAGER_ID columns.

   ☒ **D** is incorrect.

3. ☑ **B.** The join condition is an expression based on the *less than* inequality operator. Therefore, this join is a nonequijoin.

   ☒ **A, C,** and **D** are incorrect. **A** would be correct if the operator in the join condition expression was an equality operator. The CROSS JOIN keywords or the absence of a join condition would result in **C** being true. **D** would be true if one of the OUTER JOIN clauses was used instead of the JOIN...ON clause.

4. ☑ **A.** This statement demonstrates the correct usage of the JOIN...USING clause.

   ☒ **B, C,** and **D** are incorrect. **B** is incorrect since only nonqualified column names are allowed in the brackets after the USING keyword. **C** is incorrect because the column in brackets after the USING keyword cannot be referenced with a qualifier in the SELECT clause.

5. ☑ **B** demonstrates the correct usage of the JOIN...ON clause.

   ☒ **A, C,** and **D** are incorrect. **A** is incorrect since the CROSS JOIN clause cannot contain the ON keyword. **C** is incorrect since the OUTER JOIN keywords must be preceded by the LEFT, RIGHT, or FULL keyword.

6. ☑ **C.** The JOIN...ON clause and the other join clauses may all be used for joins between multiple tables. The JOIN...ON and JOIN...USING clauses are better suited for N-way table joins.

   ☒ **A, B,** and **D** are incorrect. **A** is false since you may join as many tables as you wish. A Cartesian product is not created since there are two join conditions and three tables.

Join a Table to Itself Using a Self-Join

7. ☑ **B.** Three rows are returned. For the row with a REGION_ID value of 2, the REGION_NAME is Asia and half the length of the REGION_NAME is also 2. Therefore, this row is returned. The same logic results in the rows with REGION_ID values of three and four and REGION_NAME values of Europe and Americas being returned.

   ☒ **A, C,** and **D** are incorrect.

View Data That Does Not Meet a Join Condition Using Outer Joins

8. ☑ **A.** The right outer join fetches the COUNTRIES rows that the inner join between the LOCATIONS and COUNTRIES tables have excluded in addition to the inner join results. The WHERE clause then restricts the results by eliminating these inner join results. This leaves the rows from the COUNTRIES table with which no records from the LOCATIONS table records are associated.

☒ **B, C,** and **D** are incorrect.

9. ☑ **A.** This statement demonstrates the correct use of the RIGHT OUTER JOIN…ON clause.

☒ **B, C,** and **D** are incorrect. The JOB_ID column in the SELECT clause in **B** is not qualified and is therefore ambiguous since the table from which this column comes is not specified. **C** uses an OUTER JOIN without the keywords LEFT, RIGHT, or FULL.

Generate a Cartesian Product of Two or More Tables

10. ☑ **A.** The cross join associates every four rows from the REGIONS table 25 times with the rows from the COUNTRIES table yielding a result set that contains 100 rows.

☒ **B, C,** and **D** are incorrect.

LAB ANSWER

Using SQL Developer or SQL*Plus, connect to the OE schema, and complete the following tasks. There are several approaches to solving this question. Your approach may differ from the following solution listed.

1. Start SQL Developer and connect to the OE schema.

2. The SELECT list consists of four columns from two tables, which will be associated with each other using several joins. The SELECT clause is

```
SELECT CUST_FIRST_NAME, CUST_LAST_NAME, PRODUCT_NAME, LIST_PRICE
```

3. The FROM clause is

```
FROM CUSTOMERS
```

4. The WHERE clause is

```
WHERE LIST_PRICE > 1000
```

5. The JOIN clauses are interesting since the PRODUCT_INFORMATION and CUSTOMERS tables not directly related. They are related through two other tables.

6. The ORDERS table must first be joined to the CUSTOMERS table based on common CUSTOMER_ID values. The first join clause following the FROM CUSTOMERS clause is

```
JOIN ORDERS USING (CUSTOMER_ID)
```

7. This set must then be joined to the ORDER_ITEMS table based on common ORDER_ID values since the ORDER_ITEMS table can ultimately link to the PRODUCT_INFORMATION table. The second join clause is

```
JOIN ORDER_ITEMS USING (ORDER_ID)
```

8. The missing link to join to the PRODUCT_INFORMATION table based on common PRODUCT_ID column values is now available. The third join clause is

```
JOIN PRODUCT_INFORMATION USING (PRODUCT_ID)
```

9. Executing this statement returns the report required as shown in the following illustration:

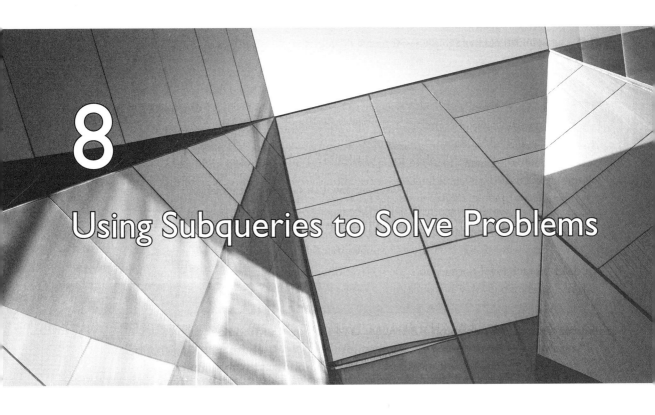

8

Using Subqueries to Solve Problems

T he previous six chapters have dealt with the SELECT statement in considerable detail, but in every case the SELECT statement has been a single, self-contained command. This chapter is the first of two that show how two or more SELECT commands can be combined into one statement. The first technique (covered in this chapter) is the use of *subqueries*. A subquery is a SELECT statement whose output is used as input to another SELECT statement (or indeed to a DML statement, as done in Chapter 10). The second technique is the use of set operators, where the results of several SELECT commands are combined into a single result set.

CERTIFICATION OBJECTIVE 8.01

Define Subqueries

A subquery is a query that is nested inside a SELECT, INSERT, UPDATE, or DELETE statement or inside another subquery. A subquery can return a set of rows or just one row to its parent query. A *scalar* subquery is a query that returns exactly one value: a single row, with a single column. Scalar subqueries can be used in most places in a SQL statement where you could use an expression or a literal value.

The places in a query where a subquery may be used are as follows:

- In the SELECT list used for column projection
- In the FROM clause
- In the WHERE clause
- In the HAVING clause

A subquery is often referred to as an *inner* query, and the statement within which it occurs is then called the *outer* query. There is nothing wrong with this terminology, except that it may imply that you can only have two levels, inner and outer. In fact, the Oracle implementation of subqueries does not impose any practical limits on the level of nesting. The depth of subquery nesting permitted is unlimited in the FROM clause and up to 255 levels in the WHERE clause.

A subquery can have any of the usual clauses for selection and projection. The following are required clauses:

- A SELECT list
- A FROM clause

The following are optional clauses:

- WHERE
- GROUP BY
- HAVING

The subquery (or subqueries) within a statement must be executed before the parent query that calls it, in order that the results of the subquery can be passed to the parent.

EXERCISE 8-1

Types of Subqueries

In this exercise, you will write code that demonstrates the places where subqueries can be used. Use either SQL*Plus or SQL Developer. All the queries should be run when connected to the HR schema.

1. Log on to your database as user HR.
2. Write a query that uses subqueries in the column projection list. The query will report on the current numbers of departments and staff:

```
SELECT sysdate Today,
  (SELECT count(*) FROM departments) Dept_count,
  (SELECT count(*) FROM employees) Emp_count
FROM dual;
```

3. Write a query to identify all the employees who are managers. This will require using a subquery in the WHERE clause to select all the employees whose EMPLOYEE_ID appears as a MANAGER_ID:

```
SELECT last_name
FROM employees
WHERE employee_id IN
  (SELECT manager_id
   FROM employees);
```

4. Write a query to identify the highest salary paid in each country. This will require using a subquery in the FROM clause:

```
SELECT max(salary),country_id
FROM (SELECT salary, country_id
```

```
            FROM employees
            NATURAL JOIN departments
            NATURAL JOIN locations)
      GROUP BY country_id;
```

See Figure 8-1.

FIGURE 8-1

Different types of
subqueries

```
SQL> SELECT sysdate Today,
  2   (SELECT count(*) FROM departments) Dept_count,
  3   (SELECT count(*) FROM employees) Emp_count
  4  FROM dual;

TODAY     DEPT_COUNT EMP_COUNT
--------- ---------- ----------
01-OCT-13         27        107

SQL> SELECT last_name
  2  FROM employees
  3  WHERE employee_id IN
  4   (SELECT manager_id
  5    FROM employees);

LAST_NAME
-------------------------
Cambrault
De Haan
Errazuriz
Fripp
Greenberg
Hartstein
Higgins
Hunold
Kaufling
King
Kochhar
Mourgos
Partners
Raphaely
Russell
Vollman
Weiss
Zlotkey

18 rows selected.

SQL> SELECT max(salary),country_id
  2  FROM (SELECT salary, country_id
  3        FROM employees
  4         NATURAL JOIN departments
  5         NATURAL JOIN locations)
  6  GROUP BY country_id;

MAX(SALARY) CO
----------- --
      17000 US
       6000 CA
      10000 UK

SQL>
```

CERTIFICATION OBJECTIVE 8.02

Describe the Types of Problems That the Subqueries Can Solve

There are many situations where you will need the result of one query as the input for another.

Use of a Subquery Result Set for Comparison Purposes

Which employees have a salary that is less than the average salary? This could be answered by two statements or by a single statement with a subquery. The following example uses two statements:

```
SELECT avg(salary)
FROM employees;

SELECT last_name
FROM employees
WHERE salary < result_of_previous_query;
```

Alternatively, this example uses one statement with a subquery:

```
SELECT last_name
FROM employees
WHERE salary <
  (SELECT avg(salary)
   FROM employees);
```

In this example, the subquery is used to substitute a value into the WHERE clause of the parent query: it is returning a single value, used for comparison with the rows retrieved by the parent query.

The subquery could return a set of rows. For example, you could use the following to find all departments that do actually have one or more employees assigned to them:

```
SELECT department_name
FROM departments
WHERE department_id IN

(SELECT DISTINCT(department_id)
  FROM employees);
```

In the preceding example, the subquery is used as an alternative to a join. The same result could have been achieved with the following as shown in Figure 8-2.

```
SELECT department_name
FROM departments
JOIN employees
ON employees.department_id = departments.department_id
GROUP BY department_name;
```

If a subquery may return more than one row, the comparison operator must be able to accept multiple values. These operators are IN, NOT IN, ANY, and ALL.

FIGURE 8-2

Subquery as
an alternative
to a join

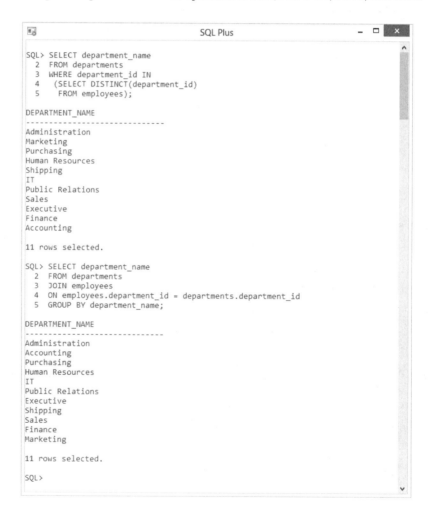

If the comparison operator is EQUAL, GREATER THAN, or LESS THAN (which each can only accept one value), the parent query will fail.

on the
i o b

Using NOT IN is fraught with problems because of the way SQL handles NULLs. As a general rule, do not use NOT IN unless you are certain that the result set will not include a NULL.

Star Transformation

An extension of the use of subqueries as an alternative to a join is to enable the *star transformation* often needed in data warehouse applications. Consider the large SALES table in the demo SH schema used for recording sales transactions. Each record captures a particular product sold to a particular customer through a particular channel. These attributes are identified by lookup codes used as foreign keys to dimension tables with rows that describe each product, customer, and channel. To identify all sales of an item called "Comic Book Heroes" to customers in the city of Oxford through Internet orders, one could run the following query:

```
SELECT count(quantity_sold)
FROM sales s, products p, customers c, channels ch
WHERE s.prod_id=p.prod_id
AND s.cust_id=c.cust_id
AND s.channel_id=ch.channel_id
AND p.prod_name='Comic Book Heroes'
AND c.cust_city='Oxford'
AND ch.channel_desc='Internet';
```

This query uses the WHERE clause to join the tables and then to filter the results. The following is an alternative query that will yield the same result as shown in Figure 8-3.

```
SELECT count(quantity_sold)
FROM sales
WHERE prod_id IN
  (SELECT prod_id
   FROM products
   WHERE prod_name='Comic Book Heroes')
AND cust_id IN
  (SELECT cust_id
   FROM customers
   WHERE cust_city='Oxford')
AND channel_id IN
  (SELECT channel_id
   FROM channels
   WHERE channel_desc='Internet');
```

FIGURE 8-3

Subqueries
used in a star
transformation

```
                                    SQL Plus                         _  ▭  ✕

SQL> SELECT count(quantity_sold)
  2  FROM sales s, products p, customers c, channels ch
  3  WHERE s.prod_id=p.prod_id
  4  AND s.cust_id=c.cust_id
  5  AND s.channel_id=ch.channel_id
  6  AND p.prod_name='Comic Book Heroes'
  7  AND c.cust_city='Oxford'
  8  AND ch.channel_desc='Internet';

COUNT(QUANTITY_SOLD)
--------------------
                   9

SQL> SELECT count(quantity_sold)
  2  FROM sales
  3  WHERE prod_id IN
  4   (SELECT prod_id
  5    FROM products
  6    WHERE prod_name='Comic Book Heroes')
  7  AND cust_id IN
  8   (SELECT cust_id
  9    FROM customers
 10    WHERE cust_city='Oxford')
 11  AND channel_id IN
 12   (SELECT channel_id
 13    FROM channels
 14    WHERE channel_desc='Internet');

COUNT(QUANTITY_SOLD)
--------------------
                   9

SQL>
```

The rewrite of the first statement to the second is the star transformation. Apart from being an inherently more elegant structure (most SQL developers with any sense of aesthetics will agree with that), there are technical reasons why the database may be able to execute it more efficiently than the original query. Also, star queries are easier to maintain; it is very simple to add more dimensions to the query or to replace the single literals ('Comic Book Heroes', 'Oxford', and 'Internet') with lists of values.

on the
⓿ o b *There is an instance initialization parameter, STAR_TRANSFORMATION_ ENABLED, which (if set to true) will permit the Oracle query optimizer to rewrite code into star queries.*

Generate a Table from Which to SELECT

Subqueries can also be used in the FROM clause where they are sometimes referred to as *inline views*. Consider the following problem based on the HR schema: Employees are assigned to a department, and departments have a location. Each location is in a country. How can you find the average salary of staff in a country, even though they work for different departments? Like this:

```
SELECT avg(salary),country_id
FROM (SELECT salary, country_id
      FROM employees
      NATURAL JOIN departments
      NATURAL JOIN locations)
GROUP BY country_id;
```

The subquery conceptually constructs a table with every employee's salary and the country in which their department is based. The parent query then addresses this table, averaging the SALARY and grouping by COUNTRY_ID.

Generate Values for Projection

The third place a subquery may be used is in the SELECT list of a query. How can you identify the highest salary and the highest commission rate and thus what the maximum commission paid would be if the highest salaried employee also had the highest commission rate? Like this, with two subqueries:

```
SELECT (SELECT max(salary) FROM employees) *
       (SELECT max(commission_pct) FROM employees) / 100
FROM dual;
```

In this usage, the SELECT list used to project columns is being populated with the results of the subqueries. A subquery used in this manner must be scalar, or the parent query will fail with an error.

Generate Rows to be Passed to a DML Statement

DML statements are covered in detail in Chapter 10. For now, consider these examples:

```
INSERT INTO sales_hist
SELECT *
FROM sales
WHERE date > sysdate-1;

UPDATE employees
SET salary = (SELECT avg(salary)
              FROM employees);

DELETE FROM departments
WHERE department_id NOT IN
(SELECT department_id
 FROM employees
 WHERE department_id is not null);
```

ⓦ**atch** *A subquery can be used to select rows for insertion but not in a VALUES clause of an INSERT statement.*

The first example uses a subquery to identify a set of rows in one table that will be inserted into another. The second example uses a subquery to calculate the average salary of all employees and passes this value (a scalar quantity) to an update statement. The third example uses a subquery to retrieve all DEPARTMENT_IDs that are in use and passes the list to a DELETE command, which will remove all departments that are not in use. Note the use of the additional WHERE clause in the subquery to ensure that no NULL values are returned by the subquery. If this clause was absent, no rows would be deleted.

Note that it is not legal to use a subquery in the VALUES clause of an insert statement; this is fine:

```
INSERT INTO dates
SELECT sysdate
FROM dual;
```

But this is not:

```
INSERT INTO dates (date_col)
VALUES
  (SELECT sysdate
   FROM dual);
```

EXERCISE 8-2

More Complex Subqueries

In this exercise, you will write more complex subqueries. Use either SQL*Plus or SQL Developer. All the queries should be run when connected to the HR schema.

1. Log on to your database as user HR.

2. Write a query that will identify all employees who work in departments located in the United Kingdom. This will require three levels of nested subqueries:

```
SELECT last_name
FROM employees
WHERE department_id IN
  (SELECT department_id
   FROM departments
   WHERE location_id IN
     (SELECT location_id
      FROM locations
```

```
  WHERE country_id =
    (SELECT country_id
     FROM countries
     WHERE country_name='United Kingdom')
  )
);
```

3. Check that the result from step 2 is correct by running the subqueries independently. First, find the COUNTRY_ID for the United Kingdom:

```
SELECT country_id
FROM countries
WHERE country_name='United Kingdom';
```

The result will be UK. Then find the corresponding locations:

```
SELECT location_id
FROM locations
WHERE country_id = 'UK';
```

The LOCATION_IDs returned will be 2400, 2500, and 2600. Then find the DEPARTMENT_IDs of departments in these locations:

```
SELECT department_id
FROM departments
WHERE location_id IN (2400,2500,2600);
```

The result will be two departments, 40 and 80. Finally, find the relevant employees:

```
SELECT last_name
FROM employees
WHERE department_id IN (40,80);
```

4. Write a query to identify all the employees who earn more than the average and who work in any of the IT departments. This will require two subqueries, not nested:

```
SELECT last_name
FROM employees
WHERE department_id IN
  (SELECT department_id
   FROM departments
   WHERE department_name LIKE 'IT%')
AND salary > (SELECT avg(salary)
              FROM employees);
```

CERTIFICATION OBJECTIVE 8.03

List the Types of Subqueries

There are three broad divisions of subquery:

- Single-row subqueries
- Multiple-row subqueries
- Correlated subqueries

Single- and Multiple-Row Subqueries

The *single-row* subquery returns one row. A special case is the scalar subquery, which returns a single row with one column. Scalar subqueries are acceptable (and often very useful) in virtually any situation where you could use a literal value, a constant, or an expression. *Multiple-row* subqueries return sets of rows. These queries are commonly used to generate result sets that will be passed to a DML or SELECT statement for further processing. Both single-row and multiple-row subqueries will be evaluated once, before the parent query is run.

Single- and multiple-row subqueries can be used in the WHERE and HAVING clauses of the parent query, but there are restrictions on the legal comparison operators. If the comparison operator corresponds with any in the following table, the subquery must be a single-row subquery:

Symbol	Meaning
=	Equal
>	Greater than
>=	Greater than or equal
<	Less than
<=	Less than or equal
<>	Not equal
!=	Not equal

If any of the operators in the preceding table are used with a subquery that returns more than one row, the query will fail. The operators in the following table can use multiple-row subqueries:

Symbol	Meaning
IN	Equal to any member in a list
NOT IN	Not equal to any member in a list
ANY	Returns rows that match any value on a list and must be used with a comparison operator
ALL	Returns rows that match all the values in a list and must be used with a comparison operator

watch *The comparison operators valid for single-row subqueries are =, >, >=, <, <=, and <>. The comparison operators* *valid for multiple-row subqueries are IN, NOT IN, ANY, and ALL.*

Correlated Subqueries

A *correlated subquery* has a more complex method of execution than single- and multiple-row subqueries and is potentially much more powerful. If a subquery references columns in the parent query, then its result will be dependent on the parent query. This makes it impossible to evaluate the subquery before evaluating the parent query. Consider this statement, which lists all employees who earn less than the average salary:

```
SELECT last_name
FROM employees
WHERE salary <
  (SELECT avg(salary)
  FROM employees);
```

The single-row subquery need only be executed once, and its result substituted into the parent query. But now consider a query that will list all employees whose salary is less than the average salary of their department. In this case, the subquery must be run for each employee to determine the average salary for her department; it is necessary to pass the employee's department code to the subquery. This can be done as follows:

```
SELECT p.last_name, p.department_id
FROM employees p
WHERE p.salary <
 (SELECT avg(s.salary)
  FROM employees s
  WHERE s.department_id=p.department_id);
```

In this example, the subquery references a column, p.department_id, from the select list of the parent query. This is the signal that, rather than evaluating the subquery once, it must be evaluated for every row in the parent query. To execute the query, Oracle will look at every row in EMPLOYEES and, as it does so, run the subquery using the DEPARTMENT_ID of the current employee row.

The flow of execution is as follows:

1. Start at the first row of the EMPLOYEES table.
2. Read the DEPARTMENT_ID and SALARY of the current row.
3. Run the subquery using the DEPARTMENT_ID from step 2.
4. Compare the result of step 3 with the SALARY from step 2, and return the row if the SALARY is less than the result.
5. Advance to the next row in the EMPLOYEES table.
6. Repeat from step 2.

A single-row or multiple-row subquery is evaluated once, before evaluating the outer query; a correlated subquery must be evaluated once for every row in the outer query. A correlated subquery can be single- or multiple-row, if the comparison operator is appropriate.

on the
ʘ o b

Correlated subqueries can be a very inefficient construct, due to the need for repeated execution of the subquery. Always try to find an alternative approach.

Investigate the Different Types of Subqueries

In this exercise, you will demonstrate problems that can occur with different types of subqueries. Use either SQL*Plus or SQL Developer. All the queries should be run when connected to the HR schema: it is assumed that the EMPLOYEES table has the standard sets of rows.

1. Log on to your database as user HR.

2. Write a query to determine who earns more than Mr. Tobias:

```
SELECT last_name
FROM employees
WHERE salary >
 (SELECT salary
  FROM employees
  WHERE last_name='Tobias')
ORDER BY last_name;
```

This will return 86 names, in alphabetical order.

3. Write a query to determine who earns more than Mr. Taylor:

```
SELECT last_name
FROM employees
WHERE salary >
 (SELECT salary
  FROM employees
  WHERE last_name='Taylor')
ORDER BY last_name;
```

This will fail with the error "ORA-01427: single-row subquery returns more than one row." The following illustration shows the last few lines of the output from step 2 followed by step 3 and the error, executed with SQL*Plus:

```
                                SQL Plus                         -  □   ×
LAST_NAME
-------------------------
Rogers
Russell
Sarchand
Sciarra
Sewall
Smith
Smith
Stiles
Sully
Taylor
Taylor
Tucker
Tuvault
Urman
Vishney
Vollman
Walsh
Weiss
Whalen
Zlotkey

86 rows selected.

SQL> SELECT last_name
  2  FROM employees
  3  WHERE salary >
  4   (SELECT salary
  5    FROM employees
  6    WHERE last_name='Taylor')
  7  ORDER by last_name;
 (SELECT salary
  *
ERROR at line 4:
ORA-01427: single-row subquery returns more than one row

SQL>
```

4. Determine why the query in step 2 succeeded but failed in step 3. The answer lies in the state of the data:

```
SELECT count(last_name)
FROM employees
WHERE last_name='Tobias';

SELECT count(last_name)
FROM employees
WHERE last_name='Taylor';
```

The use of the "greater than" operator in the queries for steps 2 and 3 requires a single-row subquery, but the subquery used may return any number of rows, depending on the search predicate used.

5. Fix the code in steps 2 and 3 so that the statements will succeed no matter what LAST_NAME is used. There are two possible solutions: one uses a different comparison operator that can handle a multiple-row subquery; the other uses a subquery that will always be single-row.
The first solution:

```
SELECT last_name
FROM employees
WHERE salary > ALL
 (SELECT salary
  FROM employees
  WHERE last_name='Taylor')
ORDER BY last_name;
```

The second solution:

```
SELECT last_name
FROM employees
WHERE salary >
 (SELECT max(salary)
  FROM employees
  WHERE last_name='Taylor')
ORDER BY last_name;
```

SCENARIO & SOLUTION

How can you best design subqueries such that they will not fail with "ORA-01427: single-row subquery returns more than one row" errors?	There are two common techniques: use an aggregation so that if you do get multiple rows they will be reduced to one, or use one of the IN, ANY, or ALL operators so that it won't matter if multiple rows are returned. But the ideal solution is to always use the primary key when identifying the row to be returned, not a nonunique key.
Sometimes there is a choice between using a subquery or using some other technique: the star transformation is a case in point. Which is better?	It depends on the circumstances. It is not uncommon for the different techniques to cause a different execution method within the database. Depending on how the instance, the database, and the data structures within it are configured, one may be much more efficient than another. Whenever such a choice arises, the statements should be subjected to a tuning analysis. Your DBA will be able to advise on this.

CERTIFICATION OBJECTIVE 8.04

Write Single-Row and Multiple-Row Subqueries

Following are examples of single- and multiple-row subqueries. They are based on the HR demonstration schema.

How would you figure out which employees have a manager who works for a department based in the United Kingdom? This is a possible solution, using multiple-row subqueries:

```
SELECT last_name
FROM employees
WHERE manager_id IN
  (SELECT employee_id
   FROM employees
   WHERE department_id IN
     (SELECT department_id
      FROM departments
      WHERE location_id IN
        (SELECT location_id
         FROM locations
         WHERE country_id='UK')));
```

In the preceding example, subqueries are nested three levels deep. Note that the subqueries use the IN operator because it is possible that the queries could return several rows.

You have been asked to find the job with the highest average salary. This can be done with a single-row subquery:

```
SELECT job_title
FROM jobs
NATURAL JOIN employees
GROUP BY job_title
HAVING avg(salary) =
  (SELECT max(avg(salary))
   FROM employees
   GROUP BY job_id);
```

The subquery returns a single value: the average salary of the department with the highest average salary. It is safe to use the equality operator for this subquery because the MAX function guarantees that only one row will be returned.

The ANY and ALL operators are supported syntax, but their function can be duplicated with other more commonly used operators combined with aggregations.

For example, these two statements, which retrieve all employees whose salary is above that of anyone in department 80, will return identical result sets:

```
SELECT last_name
FROM employees
WHERE salary > ALL
 (SELECT salary
  FROM employees
  WHERE department_id=80);

SELECT last_name
FROM employees
WHERE salary > (SELECT max(salary)
  FROM employees
  WHERE department_id=80);
```

The following table summarizes the equivalents for ANY and ALL:

Operator	Meaning
< ANY	Less than the highest
> ANY	More than the lowest
= ANY	Equivalent to IN
> ALL	More than the highest
< ALL	Less than the lowest

EXERCISE 8-4

Write a Query That Is Reliable and User Friendly

In this exercise, develop a multi-row subquery that will prompt for user input. Use either SQL*Plus or SQL Developer. All the queries should be run when connected to the HR schema; it is assumed that the tables have the standard sets of rows.

1. Log on to your database as user HR.

2. Design a query that will prompt for a department name and list the last name of every employee in that department:

```
SELECT last_name
FROM employees
WHERE department_id =
 (SELECT department_id
  FROM departments
  WHERE department_name = '&Department_name');
```

3. Run the query in step 2 three times, when prompted supplying these values:

First time, Executive

Second time, executive

Third time, Executiv

The following illustration shows the result, using SQL*Plus:

```
                                    SQL Plus                          _  □  ×

SQL> SELECT last_name
  2  FROM employees
  3  WHERE department_id =
  4   (SELECT department_id
  5    FROM departments
  6    WHERE department_name = '&Department_name');
Enter value for department_name: Executive
old   6:   WHERE department_name = '&Department_name')
new   6:   WHERE department_name = 'Executive')

LAST_NAME
-------------------------
King
Kochhar
De Haan

SQL> /
Enter value for department_name: executive
old   6:   WHERE department_name = '&Department_name')
new   6:   WHERE department_name = 'executive')

no rows selected

SQL> /
Enter value for department_name: Executiv
old   6:   WHERE department_name = '&Department_name')
new   6:   WHERE department_name = 'Executiv')

no rows selected

SQL>
```

4. Note the results from step 3. The first run succeeded because the value entered was an exact match, but the other failed. Adjust the query to make it more user friendly, so that it can handle minor variations in case or spelling:

```
SELECT last_name
FROM employees
WHERE department_id =
 (SELECT department_id
  FROM departments
  WHERE upper(department_name) LIKE upper('%&Department_name%'));
```

5. Run the query in step 4 three times, using the same values as used in step 3. This time, the query will execute successfully.

6. Run the query in step 4 again and this time enter the value Pu. The query will fail, with an "ORA-01427: single-row subquery returns more than one row" error, because the attempt to make it more user friendly means that the subquery is no longer guaranteed to be a single-row subquery. The string Pu matches two departments.

7. Adjust the query to make it resilient against the ORA-01427 error, and adjust the output to prevent any possible confusion:

```
SELECT last_name,department_name
FROM employees
JOIN departments
ON employees.department_id = departments.department_id
WHERE departments.department_id IN
 (SELECT department_id
  FROM departments
  WHERE upper(department_name) LIKE upper('%&Department_name%'));
```

The following illustration shows this final step: code that is approaching the ideal of being both bulletproof and user friendly:

INSIDE THE EXAM

Subqueries come in three general forms: single-row, multiple-row, and correlated. A special case of the single-row subquery is the scalar subquery, a subquery that returns exactly one value. This is a single-row single-column subquery. For the first SQL OCA exam, detailed knowledge is expected only of scalar subqueries and single-column multiple-row subqueries. Correlated subqueries and multiple-column subqueries are unlikely to be examined at this level, but a general knowledge of them may be tested.

When using subqueries in a WHERE clause, you must be aware of which operators will succeed with single-row subqueries and which will succeed with multiple-row subqueries.

CERTIFICATION SUMMARY

A subquery is a query embedded within another SQL statement. This statement can be another query or a DML statement. Subqueries can be nested within each other with no practical limits.

Subqueries can be used to generate values for the select list of a query to generate an inline view to be used in the FROM clause, in the WHERE clause, and in the HAVING clause. When used in the WHERE or HAVING clauses, single-row subqueries can be used with these comparison operators: =, >, >=, <, <=, <>. Multiple-row subqueries can be used with these comparison operators: IN, NOT IN, ANY, ALL.

TWO-MINUTE DRILL

Define Subqueries

❑ A subquery is a select statement embedded within another SQL statement.

❑ Subqueries can be nested within each other.

❑ With the exception of the correlated subquery, subqueries are executed before the outer query within which they are embedded.

Describe the Types of Problems That the Subqueries Can Solve

❑ Selecting rows from a table with a condition that depends on the data within the table can be implemented with a subquery.

❑ Complex joins can sometimes be replaced with subqueries.

❑ Subqueries can add values to the outer query's output that are not available in the tables the outer query addresses.

List the Types of Subqueries

❑ Multiple-row subqueries can return several rows, possibly with several columns.

❑ Single-row subqueries return one row, possibly with several columns.

❑ A scalar subquery returns a single value; it is a single-row, single-column subquery.

❑ A correlated subquery is executed once for every row in the outer query.

Write Single-Row and Multiple-Row Subqueries

❑ Single-row subqueries should be used with single-row comparison operators.

❑ Multiple-row subqueries should be used with multiple-row comparison operators.

❑ The ALL and ANY operators can be alternatives to use of aggregations.

SELF TEST

The following questions will help you measure your understanding of the material presented in this chapter. Read all the choices carefully because there may be more than one correct answer. Choose all the correct answers for each question.

Define Subqueries

1. Consider this generic description of a SELECT statement:
   ```
   SELECT select_list
   FROM table
   WHERE condition
   GROUP BY expression_1
   HAVING expression_2
   ORDER BY expression_3 ;
   ```
   Where could subqueries be used? (Choose all correct answers.)
   A. select_list
   B. table
   C. condition
   D. expression_1
   E. expression_2
   F. expression_3

2. A query can have a subquery embedded within it. Under what circumstances could there be more than one subquery? (Choose the best answer.)
   A. The outer query can include an inner query. It is not possible to have another query within the inner query.
   B. It is possible to embed a single-row subquery inside a multiple-row subquery, but not the other way around.
   C. The outer query can have multiple inner queries, but they must not be embedded within each other.
   D. Subqueries can be embedded within each other with no practical limitations on depth.

3. Consider this statement:
   ```
   SELECT employee_id, last_name
   FROM employees
   WHERE salary >
    (SELECT avg(salary)
     FROM employees);
   ```
   When will the subquery be executed? (Choose the best answer.)
   A. It will be executed before the outer query.
   B. It will be executed after the outer query.

C. It will be executed concurrently with the outer query.

D. It will be executed once for every row in the EMPLOYEES table.

4. Consider this statement:
```
SELECT o.employee_id, o.last_name
FROM employees o
WHERE o.salary >
 (SELECT avg(i.salary)
  FROM employees i
  WHERE i.department_id=o.department_id);
```
When will the subquery be executed? (Choose the best answer.)

A. It will be executed before the outer query.

B. It will be executed after the outer query.

C. It will be executed concurrently with the outer query.

D. It will be executed once for every row in the EMPLOYEES table.

Describe the Types of Problems That the Subqueries Can Solve

5. Consider the following statement:
```
SELECT last_name
FROM employees
JOIN departments
ON employees.department_id = departments.department_id
WHERE department_name='Executive';
```

and this statement:
```
SELECT last_name
FROM employees
WHERE department_id IN
 (SELECT department_id
  FROM departments
  WHERE department_name='Executive');
```

What can be said about the two statements? (Choose two correct answers.)

A. The two statements should generate the same result.

B. The two statements could generate different results.

C. The first statement will always run successfully; the second statement will error if there are two departments with DEPARTMENT_NAME='Executive'.

D. Both statements will always run successfully, even if there are two departments with DEPARTMENT_NAME='Executive'.

List the Types of Subqueries

6. What are the distinguishing characteristics of a scalar subquery? (Choose two correct answers.)
   A. A scalar subquery returns one row.
   B. A scalar subquery returns one column.
   C. A scalar subquery cannot be used in the SELECT LIST of the parent query.
   D. A scalar subquery cannot be used as a correlated subquery.

7. Which comparison operator cannot be used with multiple-row subqueries? (Choose the best answer.)
   A. ALL
   B. ANY
   C. IN
   D. NOT IN
   E. All the above can be used.

Write Single-Row and Multiple-Row Subqueries

8. Consider this statement:
```
SELECT last_name, (SELECT count(*)
                    FROM departments)
FROM employees
WHERE salary = (SELECT salary
                FROM employees);
```
What is wrong with it? (Choose the best answer.)
   A. Nothing is wrong—the statement should run without error.
   B. The statement will fail because the subquery in the SELECT list references a table that is not listed in the FROM clause.
   C. The statement will fail if the second query returns more than one row.
   D. The statement will run but is extremely inefficient because of the need to run the second subquery once for every row in EMPLOYEES.

9. Which of the following statements are equivalent? (Choose two answers.)
   A. ```
      SELECT employee_id
      FROM employees
      WHERE salary < ALL
        (SELECT salary
         FROM employees
         WHERE department_id=10);
      ```
      ```

B.
```
SELECT employee_id
FROM employees
WHERE salary <
  (SELECT min(salary)
   FROM employees
   WHERE department_id=10);
```

C.
```
SELECT employee_id
FROM employees
WHERE salary NOT >= ANY
  (SELECT salary
   FROM employees
   WHERE department_id=10);
```

D.
```
SELECT employee_id
FROM employees e
 JOIN departments d
ON e.department_id=d.department_id
WHERE e.salary <
  (SELECT min(salary)
   FROM employees)
AND d.department_id=10;
```

10. Consider this statement, which is intended to prompt for an employee's name and then find all employees who have the same job as the first employee:
```
SELECT last_name,employee_id
FROM employees
WHERE job_id =
 (SELECT job_id
  FROM employees
  WHERE last_name = '&Name');
```
What would happen if a value were given for &Name that did not match with any row in EMPLOYEES? (Choose the best answer.)

A. The statement would fail with an error.

B. The statement would return every row in the table.

C. The statement would return no rows.

D. The statement would return all rows where JOB_ID is NULL.

LAB QUESTION

Exercise 8-3 included this query that attempted to find all employees whose salary is higher than that of a nominated employee:

```
SELECT last_name
FROM employees
WHERE salary >
 (SELECT salary
  FROM employees
  WHERE last_name='Taylor')
ORDER BY last_name;
```

The query runs successfully if last_name is unique. Two variations were given that will run without error no matter what value is provided.

The first solution was as follows:

```
SELECT last_name
FROM employees
WHERE salary > ALL
 (SELECT salary
  FROM employees
  WHERE last_name='Taylor')
ORDER BY last_name;
```

The second solution was as follows:

```
SELECT last_name
FROM employees
WHERE salary >
 (SELECT max(salary)
  FROM employees
  WHERE last_name='Taylor')
ORDER BY last_name;
```

There are other queries that will run successfully; construct two other solutions, one using the ANY comparison operator, the other using the MIN aggregation function. Now that you have four solutions, do they all give the same result?

All these "solutions" are in fact just ways of avoiding error. They do not necessarily give the result the user wants, and they may not be consistent. What change needs to be made to give a consistent, unambiguous result?

SELF TEST ANSWERS

Define Subqueries

1. ☑ **A, B, C,** and **E.** Subqueries can be used at all these points.
   ☒ **D** and **F** are incorrect. A subquery cannot be used in the GROUP BY and ORDER BY clauses of a query.

2. ☑ **D.** Subquery nesting can be done to many levels.
   ☒ **A, B,** and **C** are incorrect. **A** and **C** are incorrect because subqueries can be nested. **B** is incorrect because the number of rows returned is not relevant to nesting subqueries, only to the operators being used.

3. ☑ **A.** The result set of the inner query is needed before the outer query can run.
   ☒ **B, C,** and **D** are incorrect. **B** and **C** are not possible because the result of the subquery is needed before the parent query can start. **D** is wrong because the subquery is only run once.

4. ☑ **D.** This is a correlated subquery which must be run for every row in the table.
   ☒ **A, B,** and **C** are incorrect. The result of the inner query is dependent on a value from the outer query; it must therefore be run once for every row.

Describe the Types of Problems That the Subqueries Can Solve

5. ☑ **A** and **D.** The two statements will deliver the same result, and neither will fail if the name is duplicated.
   ☒ **B** and **C** are incorrect. **B** is incorrect because the statements are functionally identical, though syntactically different. **C** is incorrect because the comparison operator used, IN, can handle a multiple-row subquery.

List the Types of Subqueries

6. ☑ **A** and **B.** A scalar subquery can be defined as a query that returns a single value.
   ☒ **C** and **D** are incorrect. **C** is incorrect because a scalar subquery is the only subquery that can be used in the SELECT LIST. **D** is incorrect because scalar subqueries can be correlated.

7. ☑ **E.** ALL, ANY, IN, and NOT IN are the multiple-row comparison operators.
   ☒ **A, B, C,** and **D** are incorrect. All of these can be used.

Write Single-Row and Multiple-Row Subqueries

8. ☑ **C.** The equality operator requires a single-row subquery, and the second subquery could return several rows.

☒ **A, B,** and **D** are incorrect. **A** is incorrect because the statement will fail in all circumstances except the unlikely case where the number of employees is zero or one. **B** is incorrect because this is not a problem; there need be no relationship between the source of data for the inner and outer queries. **D** is incorrect because the subquery will only run once; it is not a correlated subquery.

9. ☑ **A** and **B** are identical.

☒ **C** and **D** are incorrect. **C** is logically the same as **A** and **B** but syntactically is not possible; it will give an error. **D** will always return no rows, because it asks for all employees who have a salary lower than all employees. This is not an error but can never return any rows. The filter on DEPARTMENTS is not relevant.

10. ☑ **C.** If a subquery returns NULL the comparison will also return NULL, meaning that no rows will be retrieved.

☒ **A, B,** and **D** are incorrect. **A** is incorrect because this would not cause an error. **B** is incorrect because a comparison with NULL will return nothing, not everything. **D** is incorrect because a comparison with NULL can never return anything, not even other NULLs.

LAB ANSWER

The following are two possible solutions using ANY and MIN:

```
SELECT last_name
FROM employees
WHERE salary > ANY (SELECT salary
                    FROM employees
                    WHERE last_name='Taylor')
ORDER BY last_name;

SELECT last_name
FROM employees
WHERE salary > (SELECT min(salary)
                FROM employees
                WHERE last_name='Taylor')
ORDER BY last_name;
```

These are just as valid as the solutions presented earlier that used ALL and MAX, but they do not give the same result. There is no way to say that these are better or worse than the earlier solutions. The problem is that the subquery is based on a column that is not the primary key. It would not be unreasonable to say that all these solutions are wrong, and the original query is the best; it gives a result that is unambiguously correct if the LAST_NAME is unique, and if LAST_NAME is not unique, it throws an error rather than giving a questionable answer. The real answer is that the subquery should be based on EMPLOYEE_ID, not LAST_NAME.

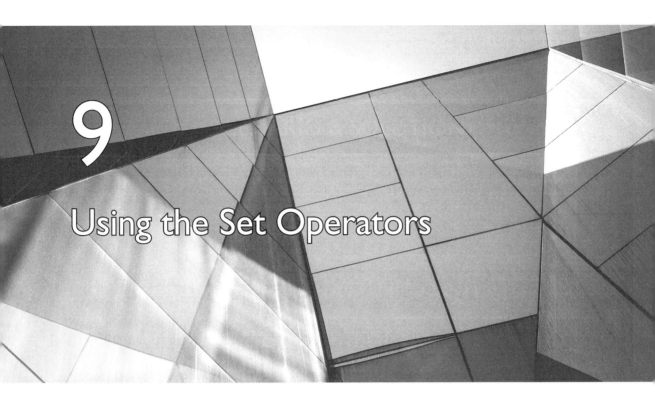

9
Using the Set Operators

A ll SELECT statements return a set of rows. The set operators take as their input the results of two or more SELECT statements and from these generate a single result set. This is known as a *compound query*. Oracle provides three set operators: UNION, INTERSECT, and MINUS. UNION can be qualified with ALL. There is a significant deviation from the ISO standard for SQL here, in that ISO SQL uses EXCEPT where Oracle uses MINUS, but the functionality is identical.

CERTIFICATION OBJECTIVE 9.01

Describe the Set Operators

The set operators used in compound queries are as follows:

- **UNION**   Returns the combined rows from two queries, sorting them and removing duplicates.
- **UNION ALL**   Returns the combined rows from two queries without sorting or removing duplicates.
- **INTERSECT**   Returns only the rows that occur in both queries' result sets, sorting them and removing duplicates.
- **MINUS**   Returns only the rows in the first result set that do not appear in the second result set, sorting them and removing duplicates.

These commands are equivalent to the standard operators used in mathematics set theory, often depicted graphically as Venn diagrams.

Sets and Venn Diagrams

Consider groupings of living creatures, classified as follows:

- **Creatures with two legs**   Humans, parrots, bats
- **Creatures that can fly**   Parrots, bats, bees
- **Creatures with fur**   Bears, bats

Each classification is known as a *set*, and each member of the set is an *element*. The *union* of the three sets is humans, parrots, bats, bees, and bears. This is all the elements in all the sets, without the duplications. The *intersection* of the sets is all elements that are common to all three sets, again removing the duplicates. In this simple example, the intersection has just one element: bats. The intersection of the two-legged set and the flying set has two elements: parrots and bats. The *minus* of the sets is the elements of one set without the elements of another, so the two-legged creatures set, minus the flying creatures set, minus the furry creatures set, results in a single element: humans.

These sets can be represented graphically as the Venn diagram shown in Figure 9-1. (Venn diagrams are named after John Venn, who formalized the theory at Cambridge University in the nineteenth century.)

The circle in the top left of the figure represents the set of two-legged creatures; the circle top right is creatures that can fly; the bottom circle is furry animals. The unions, intersections, and minuses of the sets are immediately apparent by observing the elements in the various parts of the circles that do or do not overlap. The diagram in the figure also includes the universal set, represented by the rectangle. The universal set is all elements that exist, including those that are not members of the defined sets. In this case, the universal set would be defined as all living creatures, including those that did not develop fur, two legs, or the ability to fly (such as fish).

That's enough school math; now proceed to the implementation within SQL.

FIGURE 9-1

A Venn diagram, showing three sets and the universal set

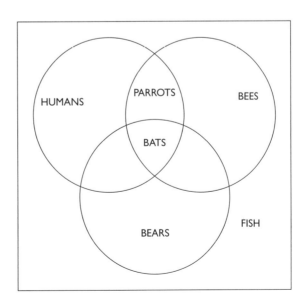

Set Operator General Principles

All set operators make compound queries by combining the result sets from two or more queries. If a SELECT statement includes more than one set operator (and therefore more than two queries), they will be applied in the order the programmer specifies: top to bottom and left to right. Although pending enhancements to ISO SQL will give INTERSECT a higher priority than the others, there is currently no priority of one operator over another. To override this possible future change in precedence, based on the order in which the operators appear, you can use parentheses: operators within brackets will be evaluated before passing the results to operators outside the brackets.

on the job *Given the pending change in operator priority, it may be good practice always to use parentheses. This will ensure that the code's function won't change when run against a later version of the database.*

Each query in a compound query will project its own list of selected columns. These lists must have the same number of elements, be nominated in the same sequence, and be of broadly similar data type. They do not have to have the same names (or column aliases), nor do they need to come from the same tables (or subqueries). If the column names (or aliases) are different, the result set of the compound query will have columns named as they were in the first query.

exam Watch *The columns in the queries that make up a compound query can have different names, but the output result set will use the names of the columns in the first query.*

While the selected column lists do not have to be exactly the same data type, they must be from the same data type group. For example, the columns selected by one query could be of data types DATE and NUMBER, and those from the second query could be TIMESTAMP and INTEGER. The result set of the compound query will have columns with the higher level of precision: in this case, they would be TIMESTAMP and NUMBER. Other than accepting data types from the same group, the set operators will not do any implicit type casting. If the second query retrieved columns of type VARCHAR2, the compound query would throw an error even if the string variables could be resolved to legitimate date and numeric values.

exam Watch *The corresponding columns in the queries that make up a compound query must be of the same data type group.*

UNION, MINUS, and INTERSECT will always combine the results sets of the input queries, then sort the results to remove duplicate rows. The sorting is based on all the columns, from left to right. If all the columns in two rows have the same value, then only the first row is returned in the compound result set. A side effect of this is that the output of a compound query will be sorted. If the sort order (which is ascending, based on the order in which the columns happen to appear in the select lists) is not the order you want, it is possible to put a single ORDER BY clause at the end of the compound query. It is not possible to use ORDER BY in any of the queries that make up the whole compound query, as this would disrupt the sorting that is necessary to remove duplicates.

e x a m

ⓦatch *A compound query will by default return rows sorted across all the columns, from left to right. The only exception is UNION ALL, where the rows will not be sorted. The only place where an ORDER BY clause is permitted is at the end of the compound query.*

UNION ALL is the exception to the sorting-no-duplicates rule: the result sets of the two input queries will be concatenated to form the result of the compound query. But you still can't use ORDER BY in the individual queries; it can only appear at the end of the compound query where it will be applied to the complete result set.

EXERCISE 9-1

Describe the Set Operators

In this exercise, you will see the effect of the set operators. Either SQL*Plus or SQL Developer can be used.

1. Connect to your database as user HR.

2. Run this query:

```
SELECT region_name
FROM regions;
```

Note the result, in particular the order of the rows. If the table is as originally created, there will be four rows returned. The order will be Europe, Americas, Asia, Middle East, and Africa.

3. Query the Regions table twice, using UNION:

```
SELECT region_name
FROM regions
UNION
SELECT region_name
FROM regions;
```

The rows returned will be as for step 1 but sorted alphabetically.

4. This time, use UNION ALL:

```
SELECT region_name
FROM regions
UNION ALL
SELECT region_name
FROM regions;
```

There will be double the number of rows, and they will not be sorted.

5. An intersection will retrieve rows common to two queries:

```
SELECT region_name
FROM regions
INTERSECT
SELECT region_name
FROM regions;
```

All four rows are common, and the result is sorted.

6. A MINUS will remove common rows:

```
SELECT region_name
FROM regions
MINUS
SELECT region_name
FROM regions;
```

The second query will remove all the rows in the first query. Result: no rows left.

CERTIFICATION OBJECTIVE 9.02

Use a Set Operator to Combine Multiple Queries into a Single Query

Compound queries are two or more queries, linked with one or more set operators. The end result is a single result set.

The examples that follow are based on two tables, OLD_DEPT and NEW_DEPT. The table OLD_DEPT is intended to represent a table created with an earlier version of Oracle, when the only data type available for representing date and time data was DATE, the only option for numeric data was NUMBER, and character data was fixed-length CHAR. The table NEW_DEPT uses the more closely defined INTEGER numeric data type (which Oracle implements as a NUMBER of up to 38 significant digits but no decimal places), the more space-efficient VARCHAR2 for character data, and the TIMESTAMP data type, which can by default store date and time values with six decimals of precision on the seconds. There are two rows in each table.

The **UNION ALL** Operator

A UNION ALL takes two result sets and concatenates them together into a single result set. The result sets come from two queries that must select the same number of columns, and the corresponding columns of the two queries (in the order in which they are specified) must be of the same data type group. The columns do not have to have the same names.

Figure 9-2 demonstrates a UNION ALL operation from two tables. The UNION ALL of the two tables converts all the values to the higher level of precision: the dates are returned as timestamps (the less precise DATEs padded with zeros), the character data is the more efficient VARCHAR2 with the length of the longer input column, and the numbers (though this is not obvious due to the nature of the data) will accept decimals. The order of the rows is the rows from the first table, in the order they are stored, followed by the rows from the second table in the order they are stored.

The **UNION** Operator

A UNION performs a UNION ALL and then sorts the result across all the columns and removes duplicates. The first query in Figure 9-3 returns all four rows because there are no duplicates. However, the rows are now in order. It may appear that

the first two rows are not in order because of the values in DATED, but they are: the DNAME in the table OLD_DEPTS is 20 bytes long (padded with spaces), whereas the DNAME in NEW_DEPT, where it is a VARCHAR2, is only as long as the name itself. The spaces give the row from OLD_DEPT a higher sort value, even though the date value is less.

ⓦ a t c h   *A UNION ALL will return rows grouped from each query in their natural order. This behavior can be modified by placing a single ORDER BY clause at the end.*

FIGURE 9-2

A UNION ALL
with data type
conversions

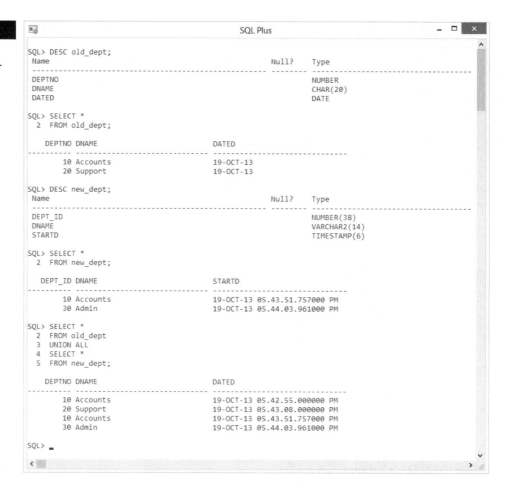

```
SQL> DESC old_dept;
 Name                                     Null?    Type
 ---------------------------------------- -------- ------------------------------
 DEPTNO                                             NUMBER
 DNAME                                              CHAR(20)
 DATED                                              DATE

SQL> SELECT *
  2  FROM old_dept;

    DEPTNO DNAME                          DATED
---------- ------------------------------ --------------------------------------
        10 Accounts                       19-OCT-13
        20 Support                        19-OCT-13

SQL> DESC new_dept;
 Name                                     Null?    Type
 ---------------------------------------- -------- ------------------------------
 DEPT_ID                                            NUMBER(38)
 DNAME                                              VARCHAR2(14)
 STARTD                                             TIMESTAMP(6)

SQL> SELECT *
  2  FROM new_dept;

   DEPT_ID DNAME                          STARTD
---------- ------------------------------ --------------------------------------
        10 Accounts                       19-OCT-13 05.43.51.757000 PM
        30 Admin                          19-OCT-13 05.44.03.961000 PM

SQL> SELECT *
  2  FROM old_dept
  3  UNION ALL
  4  SELECT *
  5  FROM new_dept;

    DEPTNO DNAME                          DATED
---------- ------------------------------ --------------------------------------
        10 Accounts                       19-OCT-13 05.42.55.000000 PM
        20 Support                        19-OCT-13 05.43.08.000000 PM
        10 Accounts                       19-OCT-13 05.43.51.757000 PM
        30 Admin                          19-OCT-13 05.44.03.961000 PM

SQL> _
```

The second query in Figure 9-3 removes any leading or trailing spaces from the DNAME columns and chops off the time elements from DATED and STARTD. Two of the rows thus become identical, so only one appears in the output.

Because of the sort, the order of the queries in a UNION compound query makes no difference to the order of the rows returned.

on the job *If you know that there can be no duplicates between two tables, then always use UNION ALL. It saves the database from doing a lot of sorting. Your DBA will not be pleased with you if you use UNION unnecessarily.*

FIGURE 9-3

UNION
compound
queries

The INTERSECT Operator

The intersection of two sets is the rows that are common to both sets, as shown in Figure 9-4.

The first query shown in Figure 9-4 returns no rows, because every row in the two tables is different. Next, applying functions to eliminate some of the differences returns the one common row. In this case, only one row is returned; had there been several common rows, they would be in order. The order in which the queries appear in the compound query has no effect on this.

The MINUS Operator

A MINUS runs both queries, sorts the results, and returns only the rows from the first result set that do not appear in the second result set.

The third query in Figure 9-4 returns all the rows in OLD_DEPT because there are no matching rows in NEW_DEPT. The last query forces some commonality, causing one of the rows to be removed. Because of the sort, the rows will be in order irrespective of the order in which the queries appear in the compound query.

FIGURE 9-4

INTERSECT and
MINUS

```
                                        SQL Plus                              _  □  ×
SQL> SELECT *
  2  FROM old_dept
  3  INTERSECT
  4  SELECT *
  5  FROM new_dept;

no rows selected

SQL> select dept_id, trim(dname), trunc(startd)
  2  FROM new_dept
  3  INTERSECT
  4  SELECT deptno, trim(dname), trunc(dated)
  5  FROM old_dept;

   DEPT_ID TRIM(DNAME)          TRUNC(STA
---------- -------------------- ---------
        10 Accounts             19-OCT-13

SQL> SELECT *
  2  FROM old_dept
  3  MINUS
  4  SELECT *
  5  FROM new_dept;

    DEPTNO DNAME                         DATED
---------- ----------------------------- -----------------------------
        10 Accounts                      19-OCT-13 05.42.55.000000 PM
        20 Support                       19-OCT-13 05.43.08.000000 PM

SQL> select dept_id, trim(dname), trunc(startd)
  2  FROM new_dept
  3  MINUS
  4  SELECT deptno, trim(dname), trunc(dated)
  5  FROM old_dept;

   DEPT_ID TRIM(DNAME)          TRUNC(STA
---------- -------------------- ---------
        30 Admin                19-OCT-13

SQL> _
```

INSIDE THE EXAM

A compound query is one query made up of several queries, but they are not subqueries. A subquery generates a result set that is used by another query; the queries in a compound query run independently, and a separate stage of execution combines the result sets.

This combining operation is accomplished by sorting the result sets and merging them together. There is an exception to this: UNION ALL does no processing after running the two queries; it simply lists the results of each.

More Complex Examples

If two queries do not return the same number of columns, it may still be possible to run them in a compound query by generating additional columns with NULL values. For example, consider a classification system for animals: all animals have a name and a weight, but the birds have a wingspan whereas the cats have a tail length. A query to list all the birds and cats might be:

```
SELECT name, tail_length, NULL
FROM cats
UNION ALL
SELECT name, NULL, wingspan
FROM birds;
```

Note the use of NULL to generate the missing values.

A compound query can consist of more than two queries, in which case operator precedence can be controlled with parentheses. Without parentheses, the set operators will be applied in the sequence in which they are specified. Consider the situation where there is a table PERMSTAFF with a listing of all permanent staff members and a table CONSULTANTS with a listing of consultant staff. There is also a table BLACKLIST of people blacklisted for one reason or another. The following query will list all the permanent and consulting staff in a certain geographical location, removing those on the blacklist:

```
SELECT name
FROM permstaff
WHERE location = 'Germany'
UNION ALL
SELECT name
FROM consultants
WHERE work_area = 'Western Europe'
MINUS
SELECT name
FROM blacklist;
```

Note the use of UNION ALL, because it is assumed that no one will be in both the PERMSTAFF and the CONSULTANTS tables; a UNION would force an unnecessary sort. The order of precedence for set operators is the order specified by the programmer, so the MINUS operation will compare the BLACKLIST with the result of the UNION ALL. The result will be all staff (permanent and consulting) who do not appear on the blacklist. If the blacklisting could be applied only to consulting staff and not to permanent staff, there would be two possibilities. First, the queries could be listed in a different order:

```
SELECT name
FROM consultants
WHERE work_area = 'Western Europe'
MINUS
SELECT name
FROM blacklist
UNION ALL
SELECT name
FROM permstaff
WHERE location = 'Germany';
```

This would return consultants who are not blacklisted and then append all permanent staff. Alternatively, parentheses could control the precedence explicitly:

```
SELECT name
FROM permstaff
WHERE location = 'Germany'
UNION ALL
  (SELECT name
  FROM consultants
  WHERE work_area = 'Western Europe'
  MINUS
  SELECT name
  FROM blacklist);
```

This query will list all permanent staff and then append all consultant staff who are not blacklisted.

These two queries will return the same rows, but the order will be different because the UNION ALL operations list the PERMSTAFF and CONSULTANTS tables in a different sequence. To ensure that the queries return identical result sets, there would need to be an ORDER BY clause at the foot of the compound queries.

on the job

The two preceding queries will return the same rows, but the second version could be considered better code because the parentheses make it more self-documenting. Furthermore, relying on implicit precedence based on the order of the queries works at the moment, but future releases of SQL may include set operator precedence.

SCENARIO & SOLUTION	
How can you present several tables with similar data as one table?	This is a common problem, often caused by bad systems analysis or perhaps by attempts to integrate systems together. Compound queries are often the answer. By using type-casting functions to force columns to the same data type and NULL to generate missing columns, you can present the data as though it were from one table.
Are there performance issues with compound queries?	Perhaps. With the exception of UNION ALL, compound queries have to sort data across the full width of the rows. This may be expensive in both memory and CPU. Also, if the two queries both address the same table, there will be two passes through the data as each query is run independently; if the same result could be achieved with one (though probably more complicated) query, this would usually be a faster solution. Compound queries are a powerful tool but should be used with caution.

EXERCISE 9-2

Using the Set Operators

In this exercise, you will run more complex compound queries.

1. Connect to your database as user HR.

2. Run this query to count the employees in three departments:

```
SELECT department_id, count(1)
FROM employees
WHERE department_id IN (20,30,40)
GROUP BY department_id;
```

3. Obtain the same result with a compound query:

```
SELECT 20,count(1)
FROM employees
WHERE department_id=20
UNION ALL
SELECT 30,count(1)
FROM employees
WHERE department_id=30
UNION ALL
SELECT 40,count(1)
FROM employees
WHERE department_id=40;
```

4. Find out if any managers manage staff in both departments 20 and 30, and exclude any managers with staff in department 40 (Figure 9-5):

```
SELECT manager_id
FROM employees
WHERE department_id=20
INTERSECT
SELECT manager_id
FROM employees
WHERE department_id=30
MINUS
SELECT manager_id
FROM employees
WHERE department_id=40;
```

5. Use a compound query to report salaries subtotaled by department, by manager, and the overall total (Figure 9-6):

```
SELECT department_id, NULL,sum(salary)
FROM employees
GROUP BY department_id
UNION
SELECT NULL, manager_id, sum(salary)
FROM employees
```

```
GROUP BY manager_id
UNION ALL
SELECT NULL, NULL,sum(salary)
FROM employees;
```

FIGURE 9-5

Using the set
operators

```
                                          SQL Plus                          _ □ ✕

SQL> SELECT department_id, count(1)
  2  FROM employees
  3  WHERE department_id IN (20,30,40)
  4  GROUP BY department_id;

DEPARTMENT_ID   COUNT(1)
------------- ----------
           20          2
           30          6
           40          1

SQL> SELECT 20,count(1)
  2  FROM employees
  3  WHERE department_id=20
  4  UNION ALL
  5  SELECT 30,count(1)
  6  FROM employees
  7  WHERE department_id=30
  8  UNION ALL
  9  SELECT 40,count(1)
 10  FROM employees
 11  WHERE department_id=40;

        20   COUNT(1)
---------- ----------
        20          2
        30          6
        40          1

SQL> SELECT manager_id
  2  FROM employees
  3  WHERE department_id=20
  4  INTERSECT
  5  SELECT manager_id
  6  FROM employees
  7  WHERE department_id=30
  8  MINUS
  9  SELECT manager_id
 10  FROM employees
 11  WHERE department_id=40;

MANAGER_ID
----------
       100
```

FIGURE 9-6

Using NULL as a pseudocolumn with the UNION ALL operator

```
SQL> SELECT department_id, NULL,sum(salary)
  2  FROM employees
  3  GROUP BY department_id
  4  UNION
  5  SELECT NULL, manager_id, sum(salary)
  6  FROM employees
  7  GROUP BY manager_id
  8  UNION ALL
  9  SELECT NULL, NULL,sum(salary)
 10  FROM employees;

DEPARTMENT_ID      NULL SUM(SALARY)
------------- ---------- -----------
           10                   4400
           20                  19000
           30                  24900
           40                   6500
           50                 156400
           60                  28800
           70                  10000
           80                 304500
           90                  58000
          100                  51608
          110                  20308
                      100      155400
                      101       44916
                      102        9000
                      103       19800
                      108       39600
                      114       13900
                      120       22100
                      121       25400
                      122       23600
                      123       25900
                      124       23000
                      145       51000
                      146       51000
                      147       46600
                      148       51900
                      149       50000
                      201        6000
                      205        8300
                                7000
                               24000
                              691416

32 rows selected.

SQL>
```

Control the Order of Rows Returned

By default, the output of a UNION ALL compound query is not sorted at all: the rows will be returned in groups in the order of which query was listed first and within the groups in the order that they happen to be stored. The output of any other set operator will be sorted in ascending order of all the columns, starting with the first column named.

It is not syntactically possible to use an ORDER BY clause in the individual queries that make up a compound query. This is because the execution of most compound queries has to sort the rows, which would conflict with the ORDER BY. It might seem theoretically possible that a UNION ALL (which does not sort the rows) could take an ORDER BY for each query, but the Oracle implementation of UNION ALL does not permit this.

There is no problem with placing an ORDER BY clause at the end of the compound query, however. This will sort the entire output of the compound query. The default sorting of rows is based on all the columns in the sequence in which they appear. A specified ORDER BY clause has no restrictions: it can be based on any columns (and functions applied to columns) in any order. For example:

```
SELECT deptno, trim(dname) name
FROM old_dept
UNION
SELECT dept_id, dname
FROM new_dept
ORDER BY name;
    DEPTNO NAME
---------- --------------------
        10 Accounts
        30 Admin
        20 Support
```

Note that the column names in the ORDER BY clause must be the name(s) (or, in this case, the alias) of the columns in the first query of the compound query.

EXERCISE 9-3

Control the Order of Rows Returned

In this exercise, you will tidy up the result of the final step in Exercise 2. This step produced a listing of salaries totaled by department and then by manager, but the results were not very well formatted.

1. Connect to your database as user HR.

2. Generate better column headings for the query (Figure 9-7):

```
SELECT department_id dept, NULL mgr, sum(salary)
FROM employees
GROUP BY department_id
UNION ALL
SELECT NULL, manager_id, sum(salary)
FROM employees
GROUP BY manager_id
UNION ALL
SELECT NULL, NULL, sum(salary)
FROM employees;
```

3. Attempt to sort the results of the queries that subtotal by using UNION instead of UNION ALL (Figure 9-8):

```
SELECT department_id dept, NULL mgr, sum(salary)
FROM employees
GROUP BY department_id
UNION
SELECT NULL, manager_id, sum(salary)
FROM employees
GROUP BY manager_id
UNION
SELECT NULL, NULL, sum(salary)
FROM employees;
```

FIGURE 9-8	
Implicit sorting using the UNION operator	

```
SQL> SELECT department_id dept, NULL mgr, sum(salary)
  2  FROM employees
  3  GROUP BY department_id
  4  UNION
  5  SELECT NULL, manager_id, sum(salary)
  6  FROM employees
  7  GROUP BY manager_id
  8  UNION
  9  SELECT NULL, NULL, sum(salary)
 10  FROM employees;

      DEPT       MGR SUM(SALARY)
---------- --------- -----------
        10                  4400
        20                 19000
        30                 24900
        40                  6500
        50                156400
        60                 28800
        70                 10000
        80                304500
        90                 58000
       100                 51608
       110                 20308
                 100      155400
                 101       44916
                 102        9000
                 103       19800
                 108       39600
                 114       13900
                 120       22100
                 121       25400
                 122       23600
                 123       25900
                 124       23000
                 145       51000
                 146       51000
                 147       46600
                 148       51900
                 149       50000
                 201        6000
                 205        8300
                            7000
                           24000
                          691416

32 rows selected.

SQL>
```

This would be fine, except that the subtotals for staff without a department or a manager are placed at the bottom of the output above the grand total, not within the sections for departments and managers. There are certainly ways to improve this output, which you should experiment with further. For example, the NVL function may be used to zero missing DEPARTMENT_ID and MANAGER_ID values, resulting in a more logically sorted output (Figure 9-9).

FIGURE 9-9

Using NVL and UNION to improve query output

```
                                         SQL Plus                              -  □  ×
SQL> SELECT 'DEP: ' || to_char(nvl(department_id, 0)) dept, 'MAN: 0' mgr, sum(salary)
  2  FROM employees
  3  GROUP BY department_id
  4  UNION
  5  SELECT 'DEP: 0', 'MAN: ' || to_char(nvl(manager_id, 0)), sum(salary)
  6  FROM employees
  7  GROUP BY manager_id
  8  UNION
  9  SELECT 'Overall ', 'Sum: ', sum(salary)
 10  FROM employees;

DEPT                  MGR                    SUM(SALARY)
--------------------  --------------------   -----------
DEP: 0                MAN: 0                        7000
DEP: 0                MAN: 0                       24000
DEP: 0                MAN: 100                    155400
DEP: 0                MAN: 101                     44916
DEP: 0                MAN: 102                      9000
DEP: 0                MAN: 103                     19800
DEP: 0                MAN: 108                     39600
DEP: 0                MAN: 114                     13900
DEP: 0                MAN: 120                     22100
DEP: 0                MAN: 121                     25400
DEP: 0                MAN: 122                     23600
DEP: 0                MAN: 123                     25900
DEP: 0                MAN: 124                     23000
DEP: 0                MAN: 145                     51000
DEP: 0                MAN: 146                     51000
DEP: 0                MAN: 147                     46600
DEP: 0                MAN: 148                     51900
DEP: 0                MAN: 149                     50000
DEP: 0                MAN: 201                      6000
DEP: 0                MAN: 205                      8300
DEP: 10               MAN: 0                        4400
DEP: 100              MAN: 0                       51608
DEP: 110              MAN: 0                       20308
DEP: 20               MAN: 0                       19000
DEP: 30               MAN: 0                       24900
DEP: 40               MAN: 0                        6500
DEP: 50               MAN: 0                      156400
DEP: 60               MAN: 0                       28800
DEP: 70               MAN: 0                       10000
DEP: 80               MAN: 0                      304500
DEP: 90               MAN: 0                       58000
Overall               Sum:                        691416

32 rows selected.

SQL>
```

CERTIFICATION SUMMARY

The set operators combine the result sets from two or more queries into one result set. A query that uses a set operator is a compound query. The set operators are UNION, UNION ALL, INTERSECT, and MINUS. They have equal precedence, and if more than one is included in a compound query they will be executed in the order in which they occur—though this can be controlled by using parentheses. All the set operators except for UNION ALL rely on sorting to merge result sets and remove duplicate rows.

The queries in a compound query must return the same number of columns. The corresponding columns in each query must be of compatible data types. The queries can use all features of the SELECT statement with the exception of ORDER BY; it is, however, permissible to place a single ORDER BY clause at the end of the compound query.

TWO-MINUTE DRILL

Describe the Set Operators

❏ UNION ALL concatenates the results of two queries.

❏ UNION sorts the results of two queries and removes duplicates.

❏ INTERSECT returns only the rows common to the result of two queries.

❏ MINUS returns the rows from the first query that do not exist in the second query.

Use a Set Operator to Combine Multiple Queries into a Single Query

❏ The queries in the compound query must return the same number of columns.

❏ The corresponding columns must be of compatible data type.

❏ The set operators have equal precedence and will be applied in the order they are specified.

Control the Order of Rows Returned

❏ It is not possible to use ORDER BY in the individual queries that make a compound query.

❏ An ORDER BY clause can be appended to the end of a compound query.

❏ The rows returned by a UNION ALL will be in the order they occur in the two source queries.

❏ The rows returned by a UNION will be sorted across all their columns, left to right.

SELF TEST

The following questions will help you measure your understanding of the material presented in this chapter. Read all the choices carefully because there may be more than one correct answer. Choose all the correct answers for each question.

Describe the Set Operators

1. Which of these set operators will not sort the rows? (Choose the best answer.)
  A. INTERSECT
  B. MINUS
  C. UNION
  D. UNION ALL

2. Which of these operators will remove duplicate rows from the final result? (Choose all that apply.)
  A. INTERSECT
  B. MINUS
  C. UNION
  D. UNION ALL

Use a Set Operator to Combine Multiple Queries into a Single Query

3. If a compound query contains both a MINUS and an INTERSECT operator, which will be applied first? (Choose the best answer.)
  A. The INTERSECT, because INTERSECT has higher precedence than MINUS.
  B. The MINUS, because MINUS has a higher precedence than INTERSECT.
  C. The precedence is determined by the order in which they are specified.
  D. It is not possible for a compound query to include both MINUS and INTERSECT.

4. There are four rows in the REGIONS table. Consider the following statements and choose how many rows will be returned for each: 0, 4, 8, or 16.
  A.
```
SELECT *
FROM regions
UNION
SELECT *
FROM regions;
```
  B.
```
SELECT *
FROM regions
UNION ALL
SELECT *
FROM regions;
```

C. ```
SELECT *
FROM regions
MINUS
SELECT *
FROM regions;
```

D. ```
SELECT *
FROM regions
INTERSECT
SELECT *
FROM regions;
```

5. Consider this compound query:

```
SELECT empno, hired
FROM emp
UNION ALL
SELECT emp_id,hired,fired
FROM ex_emp;
```

The columns EMP.EMPNO and EX_EMP.EMP_ID are integer; the column EMP.HIRED is timestamp; the columns EX_EMP.HIRED and EX_EMP.FIRED are date. Why will the statement fail? (Choose the best answer.)

A. Because the columns EMPNO and EMP_ID have different names

B. Because the columns EMP.HIRED and EX_EMP.HIRED are different data types

C. Because there are two columns in the first query and three columns in the second query

D. For all the reasons above

E. The query will succeed.

Control the Order of Rows Returned

6. Which line of this statement will cause it to fail? (Choose the best answer.)

A. `SELECT ename, hired FROM current_staff`

B. `ORDER BY ename`

C. `MINUS`

D. `SELECT ename, hired FROM current staff`

E. `WHERE deptno=10`

F. `ORDER BY ename;`

7. Study this statement:

```
SELECT ename
FROM emp
UNION ALL
SELECT ename
FROM ex_emp;
```

In what order will the rows be returned? (Choose the best answer.)

A. The rows from each table will be grouped and within each group will be sorted on ENAME.

B. The rows from each table will be grouped but not sorted.

C. The rows will not be grouped but will all be sorted on ENAME.

D. The rows will be neither grouped nor sorted.

LAB QUESTION

Working in the HR schema, design some queries that will generate reports using the set operators. The reports required are as follows:

1. Employees have their current job (identified by JOB_ID) recorded in their EMPLOYEES row. Jobs they have held previously (but not their current job) are recorded in JOB_HISTORY. Which employees have never changed jobs? The listing should include the employees' EMPLOYEE_ID and LAST_NAME.

2. Which employees were recruited into one job, then changed to a different job, but are now back in a job they held before? Again, you will need to construct a query that compares EMPLOYEES with JOB_HISTORY. The report should show the employees' names and the job titles. Job titles are stored in the table JOBS.

3. What jobs has any one employee held? This will be the JOB_ID for the employee's current job (in EMPLOYEES) and all previous jobs (in JOB_HISTORY). If the employee has held a job more than once, there is no need to list it more than once. Use a substitution variable to prompt for the EMPLOYEE_ID and display the job title(s). Employees 101 and 200 will be suitable employees for testing.

SELF TEST ANSWERS

Describe the Set Operators

1.   ☑   **D.** UNION ALL returns rows in the order that they are delivered by the two queries from which the compound query is made up.
     ☒   **A, B,** and **C** are incorrect. INTERSECT, MINUS, and UNION all use sorting as part of their execution.

2.   ☑   **A, B, C.** INTERSECT, MINUS, and UNION all remove duplicate rows.
     ☒   **D** is incorrect. UNION ALL returns all rows, duplicates included.

Use a Set Operator to Combine Multiple Queries into a Single Query

3.   ☑   **C.** All set operators have equal precedence, so the precedence is determined by the sequence in which they occur.
     ☒   **A, B,** and **D** are incorrect. A and B are incorrect because set operators have equal precedence—though this may change in future releases. D is incorrect because many set operators can be used in one compound query.

4.   ☑   A = 4; B = 8; C = 0; D = 4
     ☒   Note that 16 is not used; that would be the result of a Cartesian product query.

5.   ☑   **C.** Every query in a compound query must return the same number of columns.
     ☒   **A, B, D,** and **E** are incorrect. A is incorrect because the columns can have different names. B is incorrect because the two columns are of the same data type group, which is all that was required. It therefore follows that D and E are also incorrect.

Control the Order of Rows Returned

6.   ☑   **B.** You cannot use ORDER BY for one query of a compound query; you may only place a single ORDER BY clause at the end.
     ☒   **A, C, D, E,** and **F** are incorrect. All these lines are legal.

7.   ☑   **B.** The rows from each query will be together, but there will be no sorting.
     ☒   **A, C,** and **D** are incorrect. A is not possible with any syntax. C is incorrect because that would be the result of a UNION, not a UNION ALL. D is incorrect because UNION ALL will return the rows from each query grouped together.

LAB ANSWER

1. To identify all employees who have not changed jobs, query the EMPLOYEES table and remove all those who have a row in JOB_HISTORY:

```
SELECT employee_id, last_name
FROM employees
MINUS
SELECT employee_id,last_name
FROM job_history
JOIN employees USING (employee_id);
```

2. All employees who have changed job at least once will have a row in JOB_HISTORY; for those who are now back in a job they have held before, the JOB_ID in EMPLOYEES will be the same as the JOB_ID in one of their rows in JOB_HISTORY:

```
SELECT last_name,job_title
FROM employees
JOIN jobs USING (job_id)
INTERSECT
SELECT last_name,job_title
FROM job_history h
JOIN jobs j ON (h.job_id=j.job_id)
JOIN employees e ON (h.employee_id=e.employee_id);
```

3. This compound query will prompt for an EMPLOYEE_ID and then list the employee's current job and previous jobs:

```
SELECT job_title
FROM jobs
JOIN employees USING (job_id)
WHERE employee_id=&&Who
UNION
SELECT job_title
FROM jobs
JOIN job_history USING (job_id)
WHERE employee_id=&&Who;
```

10
Manipulating Data

T his chapter is all about the commands that change data. Syntactically, the DML commands are much simpler than the SELECT command that has been studied so far. However, there is a large amount of relational database theory that comes along with DML. As well as understanding the commands that make the changes, it is essential to understand the theory of transaction management, which is part of the relational database paradigm. The transaction management mechanisms provided by the Oracle database guarantee conformance to the relational standards for transactions: they implement what is commonly referred to as the ACID (atomicity, consistency, isolation, and durability) test.

Following detail on the DML commands, this chapter includes a full treatment of the necessary theory: transactional integrity, record locking, and read consistency.

CERTIFICATION OBJECTIVE 10.01

Describe Each Data Manipulation Language (DML) Statement

Strictly speaking, there are five DML commands:

- SELECT
- INSERT
- UPDATE
- DELETE
- MERGE

In practice, most database professionals never include SELECT as part of DML. It is considered to be a separate language in its own right, which is not unreasonable when you consider that it has taken the eight preceding chapters to describe it. The MERGE command is often dropped as well, not because it isn't clearly a data manipulation command but because it doesn't do anything that cannot be done with other commands. MERGE can be thought of as a shortcut for executing either an INSERT or an UPDATE or a DELETE, depending on some condition. A command often considered with DML is TRUNCATE. This is actually a DDL (Data Definition Language) command, but as the effect for end users is the same as a DELETE (though its implementation is totally different), it does fit with DML. So, the following commands are described in the next sections, with syntax and examples:

- INSERT
- UPDATE
- DELETE
- TRUNCATE

In addition, we will discuss, for completeness:

- MERGE

These are the commands that manipulate data.

INSERT

Oracle stores data in the form of rows in tables. Tables are *populated* with rows in several ways, but the most common method is with the INSERT statement. SQL is a set-oriented language, so one command can affect one row or a set of rows. It follows that one INSERT statement can insert one or more rows into one or many tables. The basic versions of the statement do insert just one row, but more complex variations can, with one command, insert multiple rows into multiple tables.

on the **job** **There are much faster techniques than INSERT for populating a table with large numbers of rows. These are the SQL*Loader utility, which can upload data from files produced by an external system, and Data Pump, which can transfer data in bulk from one Oracle database to another—either via disk files or through a network link.**

Tables have rules defined that control the rows that may be inserted. These rules are *constraints*. A constraint is an implementation of a business rule. The business analysts who model an organization's business processes will design a set of rules for the organization's data. Examples of such rules might be that every employee must have a unique employee number or that every employee must be assigned to a valid department. Creating constraints is described in Chapter 11—for now, remember that there is no way an INSERT command can insert a row that violates a constraint. So if you attempt to insert a row into EMPLOYEES with an EMPLOYEE_ID that already exists in another row, or with a DEPARTMENT_ID that does not match a row in the DEPARTMENTS table, the insert will fail. Constraints guarantee that the data in the database conforms to the rules that define the business procedures.

There are many possible sources for the row (or rows) inserted by an INSERT statement. A single row can be inserted by providing the values for the row's columns individually. Such a statement can be constructed by typing it into SQL*Plus or SQL Developer, or by a more sophisticated user process that presents a form that prompts for values. This is the technique used for generating the rows inserted interactively by end users. For inserts of multiple rows, the source of the rows can be a SELECT statement. The output of any and all of the SELECT statements discussed in the preceding eight chapters can be used as the input to an INSERT statement.

The end result of any SELECT statement can be thought of as a table: a two-dimensional set of rows. This "table" can be displayed to a user (perhaps in a simple tool like SQL*Plus), or it can be passed to an INSERT command for populating another table, defined within the database. Using a SELECT statement to construct rows for an INSERT statement is a very common technique. The SELECT can perform many tasks. These typically include joining tables and aggregations, so that the resulting rows inserted into the target table contain information that is much more immediately comprehensible to the end users than the raw data in the source tables.

An INSERT command can insert one row, with column values specified in the command, or a set of rows created by a SELECT statement.

UPDATE

The UPDATE command is used to change rows that already exist—rows that have been created by an INSERT command, or possibly by a tool such as Data Pump. As with any other SQL command, an UPDATE can affect one row or a set of rows. The size of the set affected by an UPDATE is determined by a WHERE clause, in exactly the same way that the set of rows retrieved by a SELECT statement is defined by a WHERE clause. The syntax is identical. All the rows updated will be in one table; it is not possible for a single UPDATE command to affect rows in multiple tables.

When updating a row or a set of rows, the UPDATE command specifies which columns of the row(s) to update. It is not necessary (or indeed common) to update every column of the row. If the column being updated already has a value, then this value is replaced with the new value specified by the UPDATE command. If the column was not previously populated—which is to say, its value was NULL—then it will be populated after the UPDATE with the new value.

A typical use of UPDATE is to retrieve one row and update one or more columns of the row. The retrieval will be done using a WHERE clause that selects a row by its primary key, the unique identifier that will ensure that only one row is retrieved. Then the columns that are updated will be any columns other than the primary key column. It is very unusual to change the value of the primary key. The lifetime of a row begins when it is inserted, then may continue through several updates, until it is deleted. Throughout this lifetime, it will not usually change its primary key.

One UPDATE statement can change rows in only one table, but it can change any number of rows in that table.

To update a set of rows, use a less restrictive WHERE clause than the primary key. To update every row in a table, do not use any WHERE clause at all. This set behavior can be disconcerting when it happens by accident. If you select the rows to be updated with any column other than the primary key, you may update several rows, not just one. If you omit the WHERE clause completely, you will update the whole table—perhaps billions of rows updated with just one statement—when you meant to change just one.

An UPDATE command must honor any constraints defined for the table, just as the original INSERT would have. For example, it will not be possible to update a column that has been marked as mandatory to a NULL value or to update a primary key column so that it will no longer be unique.

DELETE

Previously inserted rows can be removed from a table with the DELETE command. The command will remove one row or a set of rows from the table, depending on a WHERE clause. If there is no WHERE clause, every row in the table will be removed (which can be a little disconcerting if you left out the WHERE clause by mistake).

on the

Job

There are no "warning" prompts for any SQL commands. If you instruct the database to delete a million rows, it will do so. Immediately. There is none of that "Are you sure?" business that some environments offer.

A deletion is all or nothing. It is not possible to nominate columns. When rows are inserted, you can choose which columns to populate. When rows are updated, you can choose which columns to update. But a deletion applies to the whole row—the only choice is which rows in which table. This makes the DELETE command syntactically simpler than the other DML commands.

MERGE

Earlier versions of SQL did not have a MERGE command. MERGE was introduced with the SQL1999 standard, implemented by Oracle in database release 9*i*. Release 10*g* (conforming to the SQL2003 standard) provides some enhancements. Some proprietary SQL implementations had a command called UPSERT. This rather unpleasant sounding word describes the MERGE command rather well: it executes either an UPDATE or an INSERT, depending on some condition. But the term UPSERT is now definitely obsolete, because the current version of MERGE can, according to circumstances, do a DELETE as well.

There are many occasions where you want to take a set of data (the source) and integrate it into an existing table (the target). If a row in the source data already exists in the target table, you may want to update the target row, or you may want to replace it completely, or you may want to leave the target row unchanged. If a row in the source does not exist in the target, you may want to insert it. The MERGE command lets you do this. A MERGE passes through the source data, for each row attempting to locate a matching row in the target. If no match is found, a row can be inserted; if a match is found, the matching row can be updated. The release 10*g* enhancement means that the target row can even be deleted, after being matched and updated. The end result is a target table into which the data in the source has been merged.

A MERGE operation does nothing that could not be done with INSERT, UPDATE, and DELETE statements—but with one pass through the source data, it can do all three. Alternative code without a MERGE would require three passes through the data, one for each command.

on the job *MERGE may not be important for the OCP examinations, but it may be of vital importance for coding applications that perform well and use the database efficiently.*

The source data for a MERGE statement can be a table or any subquery. The condition used for finding matching rows in the target is similar to a WHERE clause. The clauses that update or insert rows are as complex as an UPDATE or an INSERT command. It follows that MERGE is the most complicated of the DML commands, which is not unreasonable, as it is (arguably) the most powerful.

TRUNCATE

The TRUNCATE command is not a DML command; it is a DDL command. The difference is enormous. When DML commands affect data, they insert, update, and delete rows as part of transactions. Transactions are defined later in this chapter in the section "Control Transactions." For now, let it be said that a transaction can be controlled, in the sense that the user has the choice of whether to make the work done in a transaction permanent or whether to reverse it. This is very useful but forces the database to do additional work behind the scenes that the user is not aware of. DDL commands are not user transactions (though within the database, they are in fact implemented as transactions—but developers cannot control them), and there is no choice about whether to make them permanent or to reverse them. Once executed, they are done. However, in comparison to DML, they are very fast.

Watch   *Transactions consisting of INSERT, UPDATE, and DELETE (or even MERGE) commands can be made permanent (with a COMMIT) or reversed* *(with a ROLLBACK). A TRUNCATE command, like any other DDL command, is immediately permanent: it can never be reversed.*

From the user's point of view, a truncation of a table is equivalent to executing a DELETE of every row: a DELETE command without a WHERE clause. But whereas a deletion may take some time (possibly hours, if there are many rows in the table) a truncation will go through instantly. It makes no difference whether the table contains one row or billions; a TRUNCATE will be virtually instantaneous. The table will still exist, but it will be empty.

on the **Job**   *DDL commands, such as TRUNCATE, will fail if there is any DML command active on the table. A transaction will block the DDL command until the DML command is terminated with a COMMIT or a ROLLBACK.*

DML Statement Failures

Commands can fail for many reasons, including the following:

- Syntax errors
- References to nonexistent objects or columns

■ Access permissions
■ Constraint violations
■ Space issues

As a SQL command can affect a set of rows, there is the complication that a command may partially succeed: the failure could occur only some way into the set. The preceding first three classes of error also apply to SELECT statements.

One purpose of reading this book is to prevent syntax errors. When they occur (and they will), they should be detected by the tool that is constructing the SQL to be sent to the database: SQL*Plus or SQL Developer if the SQL is being entered interactively, or whatever other tool is being used to generate a more sophisticated interface. There are any number of possible syntax errors, starting with simple spelling mistakes or transposition errors.

on the
job

People who type with only one finger do not make transposition errors.

Errors of this nature will not impact the database, because the database will never see them. The erroneous SQL is stopped at the source. The degree of assistance the tool provides for fixing such errors will depend on the effort the tool's developers take.

A SQL statement may be syntactically correct but refer to objects that do not exist. Typical problems are spelling mistakes, but there are more complex issues: a statement could refer to a column that existed at one time but has been dropped from the table or renamed. A statement of this nature will be sent to the database and will fail then, before the database attempts execution. This is worse for the database than a simple syntax error, but the statement is still stopped before it consumes any significant database resources.

A related error has to do with type casting. SQL is a strongly typed language: columns are defined as a certain data type, and an attempt to enter a value of a different data type will usually fail. However, you may get away with this because Oracle's implementation of SQL will, in some circumstances, do automatic type casting.

Figure 10-1 shows several attempted executions of a statement with SQL*Plus.

In Figure 10-1, a user connects as SUE (password, sue—not an example of good security) and queries the EMPLOYEES table. The statement fails because of a simple syntax error, correctly identified by SQL*Plus. Note that SQL*Plus never attempts to correct such mistakes, even when it knows exactly what you meant to type. Some third-party tools may be more helpful, offering automatic error correction.

FIGURE 10-1

Some examples
of statement
failure

```
                                    SQL Plus                          _  □  ×
SQL> CONNECT sue/sue
Connected.
SQL> SELECT count(*)
  2  FRM employees
  3  WHERE hire_date='21-APR-08';
FRM employees
    *
ERROR at line 2:
ORA-00923: FROM keyword not found where expected


SQL> SELECT count(*)
  2  FROM employees
  3  WHERE hire_date='21-APR-08';
FROM employees
    *
ERROR at line 2:
ORA-00942: table or view does not exist


SQL> SELECT count(*)
  2  FROM hr.employees
  3  WHERE hire_date='21-APR-08';

  COUNT(*)
----------
         2

SQL> SELECT count(*)
  2  FROM hr.employees
  3  WHERE hire_date='21/04/2008';
WHERE hire_date='21/04/2008'
      *
ERROR at line 3:
ORA-01843: not a valid month


SQL> SELECT * FROM nls_database_parameters WHERE parameter='NLS_DATE_FORMAT';

PARAMETER            VALUE
-------------------- --------------------
NLS_DATE_FORMAT      DD-MON-RR

SQL> ALTER SESSION SET NLS_DATE_FORMAT='DD/MM/YYYY';

Session altered.

SQL> SELECT count(*)
  2  FROM hr.employees
  3  WHERE hire_date='21/04/2008';

  COUNT(*)
----------
         2

SQL>
```

The second attempt to run the statement fails with an error stating that the object does not exist. This is because it does not exist in the current user's schema; it exists in the HR schema. Having corrected that, the third run of the statement succeeds—but only just. The value passed in the WHERE clause is a string, `'21-APR-08'`, but the column HIRE_DATE is not defined in the table as a string, it is defined as a date. To execute the statement, the database had to work out what the user really meant and cast the string as a date. In the last example, the type casting fails. This is because the string passed is formatted as a European-style date, but the database has been set up to expect an NLS_DATE_FORMAT of DD-MON-RR. Once the default date format is altered in the session the statement succeeds.

Developers should never rely on automatic type casting. It is extremely lazy programming. They should always do whatever explicit type casting is necessary, using appropriate functions as discussed in previous chapters. If automatic type casting does work, at best there is a performance hit as the database has to do extra work. This may be substantial if the type casting prevents Oracle from using indexes. In this example, if there is an index on the HIRE_DATE column, it will be an index of dates; there is no way the database can use it when you pass a string. At worst, the result will be wrong. If the date string passed in were '04/05/2007' this would succeed—but would it be the fourth of May or the fifth of April?

on the
() o b
Oracle will attempt to correct data type mismatches in SQL statements (DML and SELECT) by automatic type casting, but the results are unpredictable and no programmer should ever rely on it.

If a statement is syntactically correct and has no errors with the objects to which it refers, it can still fail because of access permissions. If the user attempting to execute the statement does not have the relevant permissions on the tables to which it refers, the database will return an error identical to that which would be returned if the object did not exist. As far as the user is concerned, it does not exist.

Errors caused by access permissions are a case where SELECT and DML statements may return different results: it is possible for a user to have permission to see the rows in a table but not to insert, update, or delete them. Such an arrangement is not uncommon; it often makes business sense. Perhaps more confusingly, permissions can be set up in such a manner that it is possible to insert rows that you are not allowed to see. And, perhaps worst of all, it is possible to delete rows that you can neither see nor update. However, such arrangements are not common.

A constraint is a business rule, implemented within the database. Typical constraints are that a table must have a primary key: a value of one column (or combination of columns) that can uniquely identify each row. An INSERT command can insert several rows into a table, and for every row the database will check whether a row already exists with the same primary key. This occurs as each row is inserted. It could be that the first few rows (or the first few million rows) go in without a problem, and then the statement encounters a row with a duplicate value. At this point it will return an error, and the statement will fail. This failure will trigger a reversal of all the insertions that had already succeeded. This is part of the SQL standard: a statement must succeed in total, or not at all. The reversal of the work is a *rollback*. The mechanisms of a rollback are described in the section of this chapter titled "Control Transactions."

If a statement fails because of space problems, the effect is similar. A part of the statement may have succeeded before the database ran out of space. The part that did succeed will be automatically rolled back. Rollback of a statement is a serious matter. It forces the database to do a lot of extra work and will usually take at least as long as the statement has taken already (sometimes much longer).

CERTIFICATION OBJECTIVE 10.02

Insert Rows into a Table

The simplest form of the INSERT statement inserts one row into one table, using values provided in line as part of the command. The syntax is as follows:

INSERT INTO *table* [(*column* [,*column*…])] VALUES (*value* [,*value*…]);

For example:

```
INSERT INTO hr.regions
VALUES (10,'Great Britain');
INSERT INTO hr.regions (region_name, region_id)
VALUES ('Australasia',11);
INSERT INTO hr.regions (region_id)
VALUES(12);
INSERT INTO hr.regions
VALUES (13,null);
```

The first of the preceding commands provides values for both the columns of the REGIONS table. If the table had a third column, the statement would fail because it relies upon *positional notation*. The statement does not say which value should be inserted into which column; it relies on the position of the values: their ordering in the command. When the database receives a statement using positional notation, it will match the order of the values to the order in which the columns of the table are defined. The statement would also fail if the column order were wrong: the database would attempt the insertion but would fail because of data type mismatches.

The second command nominates the columns to be populated and the values with which to populate them. Note that the order in which columns are mentioned now becomes irrelevant—as long as the order of the columns is the same as the order of the values.

The third example lists one column, and therefore only one value. All other columns will be left null. This statement would fail if the REGION_NAME column was not nullable. The fourth example will produce the same result, but because there is no column list, a value of some sort must be provided for each column—at the least, a NULL.

on the

Job

It is often considered good practice not to rely on positional notation and instead always to list the columns. This is more work but makes the code self-documenting (always a good idea!) and also makes the code more resilient against table structure changes. For instance, if a column is added to a table, all the INSERT statements that rely on positional notation will fail until they are rewritten to include a NULL for the new column. INSERT code that names the columns will continue to run.

Very often, an INSERT statement will include functions to do type casting or other editing work. Consider this statement:

```
INSERT INTO emp_copy (employee_id, last_name, hire_date, email, job_id)
VALUES (1000,'WATSON','03-Nov-13', 'jwatson@hr.com', 'SA_REP');
```

in contrast with this:

```
INSERT INTO emp_copy (employee_id, last_name, hire_date, email, job_id)
VALUES (1000,
        upper('Watson'),
        to_date('03-Nov-13','dd-mon-yy'),
        lower('JWatson@hr.com'),
        upper('sa_rep'));
```

The rows inserted with each statement would be identical. But the first will insert exactly the literals provided. It may well be that the application relies on employee surnames being in uppercase—without this, perhaps sort orders will be wrong and searches on surname will give unpredictable results. Also, the insertion of the date value relies on automatic type casting of a string to a date, which is always bad for performance and can result in incorrect values being entered. The second statement forces the surname into uppercase whether it was entered that way or not, and specifies exactly the format mask of the date string before explicitly converting it into a date. There is no question that the second statement is a better piece of code than the first.

The following is another example of using functions:

```
INSERT INTO emp_copy (employee_id, last_name, hire_date, email, job_id)
VALUES (1000 + 1,user,sysdate - 7,'jwatson@hr.com','SA_REP');
```

In the preceding statement, the EMPLOYEE_ID column is populated with the result of some arithmetic, the LAST_NAME column is populated with the result of the function USER (which returns the database logon name of the user), and the HIRE_DATE column is populated with the result of a function and arithmetic: the date seven days before the current system date.

Figure 10-2 shows the execution of the previous three insertions, followed by a query showing the results.

Using functions to preprocess values before inserting rows can be particularly important when running scripts with substitution variables, as they will allow the code to correct many of the unwanted variations in data input that can occur when users enter values interactively.

FIGURE 10-2

Using functions with the INSERT command

```
SQL Plus                                                    _  □  ×

SQL> CONNECT sue/sue
Connected.
SQL> DESC emp_copy
 Name                                       Null?    Type
 ---------------------------------------- -------- -------------------------
 EMPLOYEE_ID                                        NUMBER(6)
 FIRST_NAME                                         VARCHAR2(20)
 LAST_NAME                                 NOT NULL VARCHAR2(25)
 EMAIL                                     NOT NULL VARCHAR2(25)
 PHONE_NUMBER                                       VARCHAR2(20)
 HIRE_DATE                                 NOT NULL DATE
 JOB_ID                                    NOT NULL VARCHAR2(10)
 SALARY                                             NUMBER(8,2)
 COMMISSION_PCT                                     NUMBER(2,2)
 MANAGER_ID                                         NUMBER(6)
 DEPARTMENT_ID                                      NUMBER(4)

SQL> INSERT INTO emp_copy (employee_id, last_name, hire_date, email, job_id)
  2  VALUES (1000,'WATSON','03-Nov-13', 'jwatson@hr.com', 'SA_REP');

1 row created.

SQL> INSERT INTO emp_copy (employee_id, last_name, hire_date, email, job_id)
  2  VALUES (1000,
  3          upper('Watson'),
  4          to_date('03-Nov-13','dd-mon-yy'),
  5          lower('JWatson@hr.com'),
  6          upper('sa_rep'));

1 row created.

SQL> INSERT INTO emp_copy (employee_id, last_name, hire_date, email, job_id)
  2  VALUES (1000 + 1,user,sysdate - 7,'jwatson@hr.com','SA_REP');

1 row created.

SQL> SELECT employee_id, last_name, hire_date, email, job_id
  2  FROM emp_copy;

EMPLOYEE_ID LAST_NAME          HIRE_DATE EMAIL                      JOB_ID
----------- ------------------ --------- -------------------------- ----------
       1000 WATSON             03-NOV-13 jwatson@hr.com             SA_REP
       1000 WATSON             03 NOV 13 jwatson@hr.com             SA_REP
       1001 SUE                24-OCT-13 jwatson@hr.com             SA_REP

SQL>
```

To insert many rows with one INSERT command, the values for the rows must come from a query. The syntax is as follows:

INSERT INTO *table* [(*column* [, *column*…])]
subquery;

Note that this syntax does not use the VALUES keyword. If the column list is omitted, then the subquery must provide values for every column in the table. To copy every row from one table to another, if the tables have the same column structure, a command such as this is all that is needed:

```
INSERT INTO regions_copy
SELECT *
FROM hr.regions;
```

This assumes that the REGIONS_COPY table already exists (with or without any rows). The SELECT subquery reads every row from the source table, which is REGIONS, and the INSERT inserts them into the target table, which is REGIONS_COPY.

There are no restrictions on the nature of the subquery. Any query returns (eventually) a two-dimensional array of rows; if the target table (which is also a two-dimensional array) has columns to receive them, the insertion will work. A common requirement is to present data to end users in a form that will make it easy for them to extract information and impossible for them to misinterpret it. This will usually mean denormalizing relational tables, making aggregations, renaming columns, and adjusting data that can distort results if not correctly processed.

Consider a simple case within the HR schema: a need to report on the salary bill for each department. The query will need to perform a full outer join to ensure that any employees without a department are not missed, and that all departments are listed whether or not they have employees. It should also ensure that any null values will not distort any arithmetic by substituting zeros or strings for nulls. This query is perfectly straightforward for any SQL programmer, but when end users attempt to run this sort of query they are all too likely to produce inaccurate results by omitting the checks. A daily maintenance job in a data warehouse that would assemble the data in a suitable form could be a script such as this:

```
TRUNCATE TABLE department_salaries;
INSERT INTO department_salaries (department,staff,salaries)
SELECT
  coalesce(department_name,'Unassigned'),
  count(employee_id),
  sum(coalesce(salary,0))
FROM hr.employees e
FULL OUTER JOIN hr.departments d
```

```
ON e.department_id = d.department_id
GROUP BY department_name
ORDER BY department_name;
```

Figure 10-3 shows the execution of the previous INSERT statement, followed by a query showing the results.

FIGURE 10-3

Using subqueries with the INSERT command

```
SQL Plus                                                    _  □  ×

SQL> TRUNCATE TABLE department_salaries;

Table truncated.

SQL> INSERT INTO department_salaries (department,staff,salaries)
  2  SELECT
  3    coalesce(department_name,'Unassigned'),
  4    count(employee_id),
  5    sum(coalesce(salary,0))
  6  FROM hr.employees e
  7  FULL OUTER JOIN hr.departments d
  8  ON e.department_id = d.department_id
  9  GROUP BY department_name
 10  ORDER BY department_name;

28 rows created.

SQL> SELECT *
  2  FROM department_salaries;

DEPARTMENT              STAFF    SALARIES
--------------------  --------  --------
Accounting                  2     20308
Administration              1      4400
Benefits                    0         0
Construction                0         0
Contracting                 0         0
Control And Credit          0         0
Corporate Tax               0         0
Executive                   3     58000
Finance                     6     51608
Government Sales            0         0
Human Resources             1      6500
IT                          5     28800
IT Helpdesk                 0         0
IT Support                  0         0
Manufacturing               0         0
Marketing                   2     19000
NOC                         0         0
Operations                  0         0
Payroll                     0         0
Public Relations            1     10000
Purchasing                  6     24900
Recruiting                  0         0
Retail Sales                0         0
Sales                      34    304500
Shareholder Services        0         0
Shipping                   45    156400
Treasury                    0         0
Unassigned                  1      7000

28 rows selected.

SQL>
```

The TRUNCATE command will empty the table, which is then repopulated from the subquery. The end users can be let loose on this table, and it should be impossible for them to misinterpret the contents—a simple natural join with no COALESCE functions, which might be all an end user would do, might be very misleading. By doing all the complex work in the INSERT statement, users can then run much simpler queries against the denormalized and aggregated data in the summary table. Their queries will be fast, too: all the hard work has been done already.

To conclude the description of the INSERT command, it should be mentioned that it is possible to insert rows into several tables with one statement. This is not part of the SQL OCA examination, but for completeness here is an example:

```
INSERT ALL
WHEN 1=1 THEN
  INTO emp_no_name (department_id,job_id,salary,commission_pct,hire_date)
  VALUES (department_id,job_id,salary,commission_pct,hire_date)
WHEN department_id <> 80 THEN
  INTO emp_non_sales (employee_id,department_id,salary,hire_date)
  VALUES (employee_id,department_id,salary,hire_date)
WHEN department_id = 80 THEN
  INTO emp_sales (employee_id,salary,commission_pct,hire_date)
  VALUES (employee_id,salary,commission_pct,hire_date)
SELECT employee_id,department_id,job_id,salary,commission_pct,hire_date
FROM hr.employees
WHERE hire_date > sysdate - 30;
```

To read this statement, start at the bottom. The subquery retrieves all employees recruited in the last 30 days. Then go to the top. The ALL keyword means that every row selected will be considered for insertion into all the tables following, not just into the first table for which the condition applies. The first condition is 1=1, which is always true, so every source row will create a row in EMP_NO_NAME. This is a copy of the EMPLOYEES table with the personal identifiers removed, a common requirement in a data warehouse. The second condition is DEPARTMENT_ID <> 80, which will generate a row in EMP_NON_SALES for every employee who is not in the sales department; there is no need for this table to have the COMMISSION_PCT column. The third condition generates a row in EMP_SALES for all the salesmen; there is no need for the DEPARTMENT_ID column, because they will all be in department 80.

This is a simple example of a multi-table insert, but it should be apparent that with one statement, and therefore only one pass through the source data, it is possible to populate many target tables. This can take an enormous amount of strain off the database.

EXERCISE 10-1

Use the INSERT Command

In this exercise, use various techniques to insert rows into a table.

1. Connect to the HR schema, with either SQL Developer or SQL*Plus.

2. Query the REGIONS table, to check what values are already in use for the REGION_ID column:

```
SELECT *
FROM regions;
```

This exercise assumes that values above 100 are not in use. If they are, adjust the values suggested below to avoid primary key conflicts.

3. Insert a row into the REGIONS table, providing the values in line:

```
INSERT INTO regions
VALUES (101,'Great Britain');
```

4. Insert a row into the REGIONS table, providing the values as substitution variables:

```
INSERT INTO regions
VALUES (&Region_number,'&Region_name');
```

When prompted, give the values 102 for the number, Australasia for the name. Note the use of quotes around the string.

5. Insert a row into the REGIONS table, calculating the REGION_ID to be one higher than the current high value. This will need a scalar subquery:

```
INSERT INTO regions
VALUES
((SELECT max(region_id)+1
  FROM regions),
 'Oceania');
```

6. Confirm the insertion of the rows:

```
SELECT *
FROM regions;
```

7. Commit the insertions:

```
COMMIT;
```

The following illustration shows the results of the exercise, using SQL*Plus:

```
SQL> conn hr/hr
Connected.
SQL> SELECT *
  2  FROM regions;

 REGION_ID REGION_NAME
---------- -------------------------
         1 Europe
         2 Americas
         3 Asia
         4 Middle East and Africa

SQL> INSERT INTO regions
  2  VALUES (101,'Great Britain');

1 row created.

SQL> INSERT INTO regions
  2  VALUES (&Region_number,'&Region_name');
Enter value for region_number: 102
Enter value for region_name: Australasia
old    2: VALUES (&Region_number,'&Region_name')
new    2: VALUES (102,'Australasia')

1 row created.

SQL> INSERT INTO regions
  2  VALUES
  3  ((SELECT max(region_id)+1
  4    FROM regions),
  5  'Oceania');

1 row created.

SQL> SELECT *
  2  FROM regions;

 REGION_ID REGION_NAME
---------- -------------------------
         1 Europe
         2 Americas
         3 Asia
         4 Middle East and Africa
       101 Great Britain
       102 Australasia
       103 Oceania

7 rows selected.

SQL> COMMIT;

Commit complete.

SQL>
```

Update Rows in a Table

The UPDATE command changes column values in one or more existing rows in a single table. The basic syntax is the following:

UPDATE *table* SET *column=value* [,*column=value*…] [WHERE *condition*];

The more complex form of the command uses subqueries for one or more of the column values and for the WHERE condition. Figure 10-4 shows updates of varying complexity, executed from SQL*Plus.

The first example is the simplest. One column of one row is set to a literal value. Because the row is chosen with a WHERE clause that uses the equality predicate on the table's primary key, there is an absolute guarantee that at most only one row will be affected. No row will be changed if the WHERE clause fails to find any rows at all.

FIGURE 10-4

Examples of using the UPDATE statement

```
SQL Plus                                              _ □ ×

SQL> UPDATE employees
  2   SET salary=10000
  3   WHERE employee_id=206;

1 row updated.

SQL> UPDATE employees
  2   SET salary=salary*1.1
  3   WHERE last_name='Cambrault';

2 rows updated.

SQL> UPDATE employees
  2   SET salary=salary*1.1
  3   WHERE department_id IN
  4   (SELECT department_id
  5    FROM departments
  6    WHERE department_name LIKE '%&Which_department%');
Enter value for which_department: IT
old    6:  WHERE department_name LIKE '%&Which_department%')
new    6:  WHERE department_name LIKE '%IT%')

5 rows updated.

SQL> UPDATE employees
  2   SET department_id=80,
  3        commission_pct=
  4   (SELECT min(commission_pct)
  5    FROM employees
  6    WHERE department_id=80)
  7   WHERE employee_id=206;

1 row updated.

SQL> _
```

The second example shows use of arithmetic and an existing column to set the new value, and the row selection is not done on the primary key column. If the selection is not done on the primary key, or if a nonequality predicate (such as BETWEEN) is used, then the number of rows updated may be more than one. If the WHERE clause is omitted entirely, the update will be applied to every row in the table.

The third example in Figure 10-4 introduces the use of a subquery to define the set of rows to be updated. A minor additional complication is the use of a replacement variable to prompt the user for a value to use in the WHERE clause of the subquery. In this example, the subquery (lines 4, 5, and 6) will select every employee who is in a department whose name includes the string 'IT' and increment their current salary by 10 percent (unlikely to happen in practice).

It is also possible to use subqueries to determine the value to which a column will be set, as in the fourth example. In this case, one employee (identified by primary key, in line 7) is transferred to department 80 (the sales department), and then the subquery in lines 4, 5, and 6 set his commission rate to whatever the lowest commission rate in the department happens to be.

The syntax of an update that uses subqueries is as follows:

UPDATE *table*

SET *column=[subquery] [,column=subquery…]*

WHERE *column* = (*subquery*)
[AND *column=subquery…*] ;

There is a rigid restriction on the subqueries using update columns in the SET clause: the subquery must return a *scalar* value. A scalar value is a single value of whatever data type is needed: the query must return one row, with one column. If the query returns several values, the UPDATE will fail. Consider these two examples:

```
UPDATE employees
SET salary=
  (SELECT salary
   FROM employees
   WHERE employee_id=206);
UPDATE employees
SET salary=
  (SELECT salary
   FROM employees
   WHERE last_name='Abel');
```

The first example, using an equality predicate on the primary key, will always succeed. Even if the subquery does not retrieve a row (as would be the case if there were no employee with EMPLOYEE_ID equal to 206), the query will still return a scalar value: a null. In that case, all the rows in EMPLOYEES would have their SALARY set to NULL—which might not be desired but is not an error as far as SQL is concerned. The second example uses an equality predicate on the LAST_NAME, which is not guaranteed to be unique. The statement will succeed if there is only one employee with that name, but if there were more than one it would fail with the error "ORA-01427: single-row subquery returns more than one row." For code that will work reliably, no matter what the state of the data, it is vital to ensure that the subqueries used for setting column values are scalar.

on the

Job

A common fix for making sure that queries are scalar is to use MAX or MIN. This version of the statement will always succeed:

```
UPDATE employees
SET salary=
  (SELECT max(salary)
   FROM employees
   WHERE last_name='Abel');
```

However, just because it will work doesn't necessarily mean that it does what is wanted.

The subqueries in the WHERE clause must also be scalar, if it is using the equality predicate (as in the preceding examples) or the greater/less than predicates. If it is using the IN predicate, then the query can return multiple rows, as in this example which uses IN:

```
UPDATE employees
SET salary=10000
WHERE department_id IN
  (SELECT department_id
   FROM departments
   WHERE department_name LIKE '%IT%');
```

This will apply the update to all employees in a department whose name includes the string 'IT'. There are several of these. But even though the query can return several rows, it must still return only one column.

Use the UPDATE Command

In this exercise, use various techniques to update rows in a table. It is assumed that the HR.REGIONS table is as seen in the illustration at the end of Exercise 10-1. If not, adjust the values as necessary.

1. Connect to the HR schema using SQL Developer or SQL*Plus.

2. Update a single row, identified by primary key:

```
UPDATE regions
SET region_name='Scandinavia'
WHERE region_id=101;
```

This statement should return the message "1 row updated."

3. Update a set of rows, using a nonequality predicate:

```
UPDATE regions
SET region_name='Iberia'
WHERE region_id > 100;
```

This statement should return the message "3 rows updated."

4. Update a set of rows, using subqueries to select the rows and to provide values:

```
UPDATE regions
SET region_id=
 (region_id +
  (SELECT max(region_id)
   FROM regions))
WHERE region_id IN
 (SELECT region_id
  FROM regions
  WHERE region_id > 100);
```

This statement should return the message "3 rows updated."

5. Confirm the state of the rows:

```
SELECT *
FROM regions;
```

6. Commit the changes made:

```
COMMIT;
```

The following illustration shows the exercise, as done from SQL*Plus:

```
SQL> UPDATE regions
  2  SET region_name='Scandinavia'
  3  WHERE region_id=101;

1 row updated.

SQL> UPDATE regions
  2  SET region_name='Iberia'
  3  WHERE region_id > 100;

3 rows updated.

SQL> UPDATE regions
  2  SET region_id=
  3  (region_id +
  4    (SELECT max(region_id)
  5      FROM regions))
  6  WHERE region_id IN
  7    (SELECT region_id
  8      FROM regions
  9      WHERE region_id > 100);

3 rows updated.

SQL> SELECT *
  2  FROM regions;

 REGION_ID REGION_NAME
---------- -------------------------
         1 Europe
         2 Americas
         3 Asia
         4 Middle East and Africa
       204 Iberia
       205 Iberia
       206 Iberia

7 rows selected.

SQL> COMMIT;

Commit complete.

SQL> _
```

CERTIFICATION OBJECTIVE 10.04

Delete Rows from a Table

To remove rows from a table, there are two options: the DELETE command and the TRUNCATE command. DELETE is less drastic, in that a deletion can be rolled back whereas a truncation cannot be. DELETE is also more controllable, in that it is possible to choose which rows to delete, whereas a truncation always affects the whole table. DELETE is, however, a lot slower and can place a lot of strain on the database. TRUNCATE is virtually instantaneous and effortless.

Removing Rows with DELETE

The DELETE commands removes rows from a single table. The syntax is as follows:

DELETE FROM *table*
[WHERE *condition*];

This is the simplest of the DML commands, particularly if the condition is omitted. In that case, every row in the table will be removed with no prompt. The only complication is in the condition. This can be a simple match of a column to a literal:

```
DELETE FROM employees
WHERE employee_id=206;
DELETE FROM employees
WHERE last_name LIKE 'S%';
DELETE FROM employees
WHERE department_id=&Which_department;
DELETE FROM employees
WHERE department_id IS NULL;
```

The first statement identifies a row by primary key. One row only will be removed—or no row at all, if the value given does not find a match. The second statement uses a nonequality predicate that could result in the deletion of many rows: every employee whose surname begins with an uppercase "S". The third statement uses an equality predicate but not on the primary key. It prompts for a department number with a substitution variable, and all employees in that department will go. The final statement removes all employees who are not currently assigned to a department.

The condition can also be a subquery:

```
DELETE FROM employees
WHERE department_id IN
 (SELECT department_id
  FROM departments
  WHERE location_id IN
   (SELECT location_id
    FROM locations
    WHERE country_id IN
     (SELECT country_id
      FROM countries
      WHERE region_id IN
       (SELECT region_id
        FROM regions
        WHERE region_name='Europe')))));
```

This example uses a subquery for row selection that navigates the HR geographical tree (with more subqueries) to delete every employee who works for any department that is based in Europe. The same rule for the number of values returned by the subquery applies as for an UPDATE command: if the row selection is based on an equality predicate (as in the preceding example) the subquery must be scalar, but if it uses IN the subquery can return several rows.

If the DELETE command finds no rows to delete, this is not an error. The command will return the message "0 rows deleted" rather than an error message because the statement did complete successfully—it just didn't find anything to do.

EXERCISE 10-3

Use the DELETE Command

In this exercise, use various techniques to delete rows in a table. It is assumed that the HR.REGIONS table is as seen in the illustration at the end of Exercise 10-2. If not, adjust the values as necessary.

1. Connect to the HR schema using SQL Developer or SQL*Plus.

2. Remove one row, using the equality predicate on the primary key:

```
DELETE FROM regions
WHERE region_id=204;
```

This should return the message "1 row deleted."

3. Attempt to remove every row in the table by omitting a WHERE clause:

```
DELETE FROM regions;
```

This will fail due to a constraint violation.

4. Remove rows with the row selection based on a subquery:

```
DELETE FROM regions
WHERE region_id IN
 (SELECT region_id
  FROM regions
  WHERE region_name='Iberia');
```

This will return the message "2 rows deleted."

5. Confirm that the REGIONS table now contains just the original four rows:

```
SELECT *
FROM regions;
```

6. Commit the deletions:

```
COMMIT;
```

The following illustration shows the exercise as done from SQL*Plus:

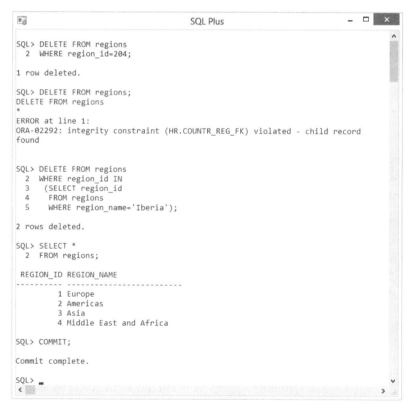

Removing Rows with TRUNCATE

TRUNCATE is a DDL (Data Definition Language) command. It operates within the data dictionary and affects the structure of the table, not the contents of the table. However, the change it makes to the structure has the side effect of destroying all the rows in the table.

One part of the definition of a table as stored in the data dictionary is the table's physical location. When first created, a table is allocated a single area of space, of fixed size, in the database's data files. This is known as an *extent* and will be empty. Then, as rows are inserted, the extent fills up. Once it is full, more extents will be allocated to the table automatically. A table therefore consists of one or more extents, which hold the rows. As well as tracking the extent allocation, the data dictionary also tracks how much of the space allocated to the table has been used. This is done with the *high water mark*. The high water mark is the last position in the last extent that has been used; all space below the high water mark has been used for rows at one time or another, and none of the space above the high water mark has been used yet.

Note that it is possible for there to be plenty of space below the high water mark that is not being used at the moment; this is because of rows having been removed with a DELETE command. Inserting rows into a table pushes the high water mark up. Deleting them leaves the high water mark where it is; the space they occupied remains assigned to the table but is freed up for inserting more rows.

Truncating a table resets the high water mark. Within the data dictionary, the recorded position of the high water mark is moved to the beginning of the table's first extent. As Oracle assumes that there can be no rows above the high water mark, this has the effect of removing every row from the table. The table is emptied and remains empty until subsequent insertions begin to push the high water mark back up again. In this manner, one DDL command, which does little more than make an update in the data dictionary, can annihilate billions of rows in a table.

on the job *A truncation is fast: virtually instantaneous, irrespective of whether the table has many millions of rows or none. A deletion may take seconds, minutes, hours—and it places much more strain on the database than a truncation. But a truncation is all or nothing.*

The syntax to truncate a table couldn't be simpler:

TRUNCATE TABLE *table*;

Figure 10-5 shows access to the TRUNCATE command through the SQL Developer navigation tree, but of course it can also be executed from SQL*Plus.

MERGE

The MERGE command is often ignored, because it does nothing that cannot be done with INSERT, UPDATE, and DELETE. It is, however, very powerful, in that with one pass through the data it can carry out all three operations. This can improve performance dramatically. Use of MERGE is not in the OCA syllabus, but for completeness here is a simple example:

```
MERGE INTO employees e
USING new_employees n
ON (e.employee_id = n.employee_id)
WHEN MATCHED THEN
UPDATE SET e.salary=n.salary
WHEN NOT MATCHED THEN
   INSERT (employee_id, last_name, salary, email, job_id)
   VALUES (n.employee_id, n.last_name, n.salary, n.email, n.job_id);
```

FIGURE 10-5

The TRUNCATE command in SQL Developer

The preceding statement uses the contents of a table NEW_EMPLOYEES to update or insert rows in EMPLOYEES. The situation could be that EMPLOYEES is a table of all staff, and NEW_EMPLOYEES is a table with rows for new staff and for salary changes for existing staff. The command will pass through NEW_EMPLOYEES, and for each row, attempt to find a row in EMPLOYEES with the same EMPLOYEE_ID. If there is a row found, its SALARY column will be updated with the value of the row in NEW_EMPLOYEES. If there is not such a row, one will be inserted. Variations on the syntax allow the use of a subquery to select the source rows, and it is even possible to delete matching rows.

CERTIFICATION OBJECTIVE 10.05

Control Transactions

The concepts behind a *transaction* are a part of the relational database paradigm. A transaction consists of one or more DML statements, followed by either a ROLLBACK or a COMMIT command. It is possible to use the SAVEPOINT command to give a degree of control within the transaction. Before going into the syntax, it is necessary to review the concept of a transaction. Related topics are read consistency; this is automatically implemented by the Oracle server, but to a certain extent programmers can manage it by the way they use the SELECT statement.

Database Transactions

This is not the place to go into detail on the relational database transactional paradigm—there are any number of academic texts on this, and there is not space to cover this topic in a practical guide. Following is a quick review of some of the principles of a relational database to which all databases (not just Oracle's) must conform. Other database vendors comply with the same standards with their own mechanisms, but with varying levels of effectiveness. In brief, any relational database must be able to pass the ACID test: it must guarantee atomicity, consistency, isolation, and durability.

A is for Atomicity

The principle of *atomicity* states that all parts of a transaction must complete or none of them. (The reasoning behind the term is that an atom cannot be split—now well known to be a false assumption). For example, if your business analysts have said that every time you change an employee's salary you must also change the employee's grade, then the atomic transaction will consist of two updates. The database must guarantee that both go through or neither. If only one of the updates were to succeed, you would have an employee on a salary that was incompatible with his grade: a data corruption, in business terms. If anything (anything at all!) goes wrong before the transaction is complete, the database itself must guarantee that any parts that did go through are reversed; this must happen automatically. But although an atomic transaction sounds small (like an atom), it can be enormous. To take another example, it is logically impossible for an accounting suite nominal ledger to be half in August and half in September: the end-of-month rollover is therefore (in business terms) one atomic transaction, which may affect millions of rows in thousands of tables and take hours to complete (or to roll back, if anything goes wrong). The rollback of an incomplete transaction may be manual (as when you issue the ROLLBACK command), but it must be automatic and unstoppable in the case of an error.

C is for Consistency

The principle of *consistency* states that the results of a query must be consistent with the state of the database at the time the query started. Imagine a simple query that averages the value of a column of a table. If the table is large, it will take many minutes to pass through the table. If other users are updating the column while the query is in progress, should the query include the new or the old values? Should it include rows that were inserted or deleted after the query started? The principle of consistency requires that the database ensure that changed values are not seen by the query; it will give you an average of the column as it was when the query started, no matter how long the query takes or what other activity is occurring on the tables concerned. Oracle guarantees that if a query succeeds, the result will be consistent. However, if the database administrator has not configured the database appropriately, the query may not succeed: there is a famous Oracle error, "ORA-1555 snapshot too old," that is raised. This used to be an extremely difficult problem to fix with earlier releases of the database, but with recent versions the database administrator should always be able to prevent this.

I is for Isolation

The principle of *isolation* states that an incomplete (that is, uncommitted) transaction must be invisible to the rest of the world. While the transaction is in progress, only the one session that is executing the transaction is allowed to see the changes; all other sessions must see the unchanged data, not the new values. The logic behind this is, first, that the full transaction might not go through (remember the principle of atomicity and automatic or manual rollback?) and that therefore no other users should be allowed to see changes that might be reversed. And second, during the progress of a transaction the data is (in business terms) incoherent: there is a short time when the employee has had his salary changed but not his grade. Transaction isolation requires that the database must conceal transactions in progress from other users: they will see the preupdate version of the data until the transaction completes, when they will see all the changes as a consistent set. Oracle guarantees transaction isolation: there is no way any session (other than that making the changes) can see uncommitted data. A read of uncommitted data is known as a *dirty read*, which Oracle does not permit (though some other databases do).

D is for Durable

The principle of *durability* states that once a transaction completes, it must be impossible for the database to lose it. During the time that the transaction is in progress, the principle of isolation requires that no one (other than the session concerned) can see the changes it has made so far. But the instant the transaction completes, it must be broadcast to the world, and the database must guarantee that the change is never lost; a relational database is not allowed to lose data. Oracle fulfills this requirement by writing out all change vectors that are applied to data to log files as the changes are done. By applying this log of changes to backups taken earlier, it is possible to repeat any work done in the event of the database being damaged. Of course, data can be lost through user error such as inappropriate DML, or dropping or truncating tables. But as far as Oracle and the DBA are concerned, such events are transactions like any other: according to the principle of durability, they are absolutely nonreversible.

The Start and End of a Transaction

A session begins a transaction the moment it issues any INSERT, UPDATE, or DELETE statement (but not a TRUNCATE—that is a DDL command, not DML). The transaction continues through any number of further DML commands until the session issues either a COMMIT or a ROLLBACK statement. Only then will the changes be made permanent and become visible to other sessions (if it is committed, rather than rolled back). It is impossible to nest transactions. The SQL standard does not allow a user to start one transaction and then start another before terminating the first. This can be done with PL/SQL (Oracle's proprietary third-generation language), but not with industry-standard SQL.

The explicit transaction control statements are COMMIT, ROLLBACK, and SAVEPOINT. There are also circumstances other than a user-issued COMMIT or ROLLBACK that will implicitly terminate a transaction:

- Issuing a DDL or DCL statement
- Exiting from the user tool (SQL*Plus or SQL Developer or anything else)
- If the client session dies
- If the system crashes

If a user issues a DDL (CREATE, ALTER, or DROP) or DCL (GRANT or REVOKE) command, the transaction in progress (if any) will be committed: it will be made permanent and become visible to all other users. This is because the DDL and DCL commands are themselves transactions. If it were possible to see the source code for these commands, it would be obvious. They adjust the data structures by performing DML commands against the tables that make up the data dictionary, and these commands are terminated with a COMMIT. If they were not, the changes made couldn't be guaranteed to be permanent. As it is not possible in SQL to nest transactions, if the user already has a transaction running, the statements the user has run will be committed along with the statements that make up the DDL or DCL command.

If a user starts a transaction by issuing a DML command and then exits from the tool he is using without explicitly issuing either a COMMIT or a ROLLBACK, the transaction will terminate—but whether it terminates with a COMMIT or a ROLLBACK is entirely dependent on how the tool is written. Many tools will have different behavior, depending on how the tool is exited. (For instance, in the Microsoft Windows environment, it is common to be able to terminate a program either by selecting the File | Exit options from a menu on the top left of the window, or by clicking an "X" in the top-right corner. The programmers who wrote the tool may well have coded different logic into these functions.) In either case, it will be a controlled exit, so the programmers should issue either a COMMIT or a ROLLBACK, but the choice is up to them.

If a client's session fails for some reason, the database will always roll back the transaction. Such failure could be for a number of reasons: the user process can die or be killed at the operating system level, the network connection to the database server may go down, or the machine where the client tool is running can crash. In any of these cases, there is no orderly issue of a COMMIT or ROLLBACK statement, and it is up to the database to detect what has happened. The behavior is that the session is killed, and an active transaction is rolled back. The behavior is the same if the failure is on the server side. If the database server crashes for any reason, when it next starts up all transactions from any sessions that were in progress will be rolled back.

The Transaction Control Statements

A transaction begins implicitly with the first DML statement. There is no command to explicitly start a transaction. The transaction continues through all subsequent DML statements issued by the session. These statements can be against any number of tables: a transaction is not restricted to one table. It terminates (barring any of the events listed in the previous section) when the session issues a COMMIT or ROLLBACK command. The SAVEPOINT command can be used to set markers that will stage the action of a ROLLBACK, but the same transaction remains in progress irrespective of the use of SAVEPOINT.

COMMIT

Syntactically, COMMIT is the simplest SQL command. The syntax is as follows:

COMMIT;

This will end the current transaction, which has the dual effect of making the changes both permanent and visible to other sessions. Until a transaction is committed, it cannot be seen by any other sessions, even if they are logged on to the database with the same username as that of the session executing the transactions. Until a transaction is committed, it is invisible to other sessions and can be reversed. But once it is committed, it is absolutely nonreversible. The principle of durability applies.

The state of the data before the COMMIT is that the changes have been made, but all sessions other than the one that made the changes are redirected to copies of the data in its prechanged form. So if a session has inserted rows, other sessions that SELECT from that table will not see them. If the transaction has deleted rows, other sessions selecting from the table will still see them. If the transaction has made updates, it will be the unupdated versions of the rows that are presented to other sessions. This is in accordance with the principle of isolation: no session can be in any way dependent on the state of an uncommitted transaction.

After the COMMIT, all sessions will immediately see the new data in any queries they issue: they will see the new rows, they will not see the deleted rows, they will see the new versions of the updated rows. This is in accordance with the principle of durability.

ROLLBACK

While a transaction is in progress, Oracle keeps an image of the data as it was before the transaction. This image is presented to other sessions that query the data while the transaction is in progress. It is also used to roll back the transaction automatically if anything goes wrong, or deliberately if the session requests it. The syntax to request a rollback is as follows:

ROLLBACK [TO SAVEPOINT *savepoint*] ;

The optional use of savepoints is detailed in the section following.

The state of the data before the rollback is that the data has been changed, but the information needed to reverse the changes is available. This information is presented to all other sessions, in order to implement the principle of isolation. The rollback will discard all the changes by restoring the prechange image of the data; any rows the transaction inserted will be deleted, rows the transaction deleted will be inserted back into the table, and any rows that were updated will be returned to their original state. Other sessions will not be aware that anything has happened at all; they never saw the changes. The session that did the transaction will now see the data as it was before the transaction started.

on the
job

A COMMIT is instantaneous, because it doesn't really have to do anything. The work has already been done. A ROLLBACK can be very slow: it will usually take as long (if not longer) to reverse a transaction than it took to make the changes in the first place. Rollbacks are not good for database performance.

EXERCISE 10-4

Use the **COMMIT and ROLLBACK** Commands

In this exercise, demonstrate the use of transaction control statements and transaction isolation. It is assumed that the HR.REGIONS table is as seen in the illustration at the end of Exercise 10-3. If not, adjust the values as necessary. Connect to the HR schema with two sessions concurrently. These can be two SQL*Plus sessions or two

SQL Developer sessions or one of each. The following table lists steps to follow in each session.

Step	In your first session	In your second session
1	`SELECT *` `FROM regions;`	`SELECT *` `FROM regions;`
Both sessions see the same data.		
2	`INSERT INTO regions` `VALUES (100,'UK');`	`INSERT INTO regions` `VALUES (101,'GB');`
3	`SELECT *` `FROM regions;`	`SELECT *` `FROM regions;`
Both sessions see different results: the original data, plus their own change.		
4	`COMMIT;`	
5	`SELECT *` `FROM regions;`	`SELECT *` `FROM regions;`
One transaction has been published to the world; the other is still visible to only one session.		
6	`ROLLBACK;`	`ROLLBACK;`
7	`SELECT *` `FROM regions;`	`SELECT *` `FROM regions;`
The committed transaction was not reversed because it has already been committed, but the uncommitted one is now completely gone, having been terminated by rolling back the change.		
8	`DELETE FROM regions` `WHERE region_id=100;`	`INSERT INTO regions` `VALUES (101,'GB');`
8		`COMMIT;`
9		`DELETE FROM REGIONS` `WHERE region_id=101;`
10	`SELECT *` `FROM regions;`	`SELECT *` `FROM regions;`
Each deleted row is still visible in the session that did not delete it, until you do the following:		
10	`COMMIT;`	`COMMIT;`
11	`SELECT *` `FROM regions;`	`SELECT *` `FROM regions;`
With all transactions terminated, both sessions see a consistent view of the table.		

SAVEPOINT

The use of savepoints is to allow a programmer to set a marker in a transaction that can be used to control the effect of the ROLLBACK command. Rather than rolling back the whole transaction and terminating it, it becomes possible to reverse all changes made after a particular point but leave changes made before that point intact. The transaction itself remains in progress: still uncommitted, still rollbackable, and still invisible to other sessions.

The syntax is as follows:

SAVEPOINT *savepoint*;

This creates a named point in the transaction that can be used in a subsequent ROLLBACK command. The following table illustrates the number of rows in a table at various stages in a transaction. The table is a very simple table called TAB1, with one column.

Command	Rows Visible to the User	Rows Visible to Others
TRUNCATE TABLE tab1;	0	0
INSERT INTO TAB1 VALUES ('one');	1	0
SAVEPOINT first;	1	0
INSERT INTO tab1 VALUES ('two');	2	0
SAVEPOINT second;	2	0
INSERT INTO tab1 VALUES ('three');	3	0
ROLLBACK TO SAVEPOINT second;	2	0
ROLLBACK TO SAVEPOINT first;	1	0
COMMIT;	1	1
DELETE FROM tab1;	0	1
ROLLBACK;	1	1

The example in the table shows two transactions: the first terminated with a COMMIT, the second with a ROLLBACK. It can be seen that the use of savepoints is visible only within the transaction: other sessions see nothing that is not committed.

on the !
①o b

The SAVEPOINT command is not (yet) part of the official SQL standard, so it may be considered good practice to avoid it in production systems. It can be very useful in development, though, when you are testing the effect of DML statements and walking through a complex transaction step by step.

The AUTOCOMMIT in SQL*Plus and SQL Developer

The standard behavior of SQL*Plus and SQL Developer is to follow the SQL standard: a transaction begins implicitly with a DML statement and ends explicitly with a COMMIT or a ROLLBACK. It is possible to change this behavior in both tools so that every DML statement commits immediately, in its own transaction. If this is done, there is no need for any COMMIT statements, and the ROLLBACK statement can never have any effect: all DML statements become permanent and visible to others as soon as they execute.

In SQL*Plus, enable the autocommit mode with the command:

SET AUTOCOMMIT ON

To return to normal:

SET AUTOCOMMIT OFF

In SQL Developer, from the Tools menu, select Preferences. Then expand Database and Advanced: you will see the Autocommit check box.

on the !
①o b

*It may be hard to justify enabling the autocommit mode of the SQL*Plus and SQL Developer tools. Perhaps the only reason is for compatibility with some third-party products that do not follow the SQL standard. SQL scripts written for such products may not have any COMMIT statements.*

SELECT FOR UPDATE

One last transaction control statement is SELECT FOR UPDATE. Oracle, by default, provides the highest possible level of concurrency: readers do not block writers, and writers do not block readers. Or in plain language, there is no problem with one session querying data that another session is updating, or one session updating data that another session is querying. However, there are times when you may wish to change this behavior and prevent changes to data that is being queried.

It is not unusual for an application to retrieve a set of rows with a SELECT command, present them to a user for perusal, and prompt him for any changes. Because Oracle is a multiuser database, it is not impossible that another session has also retrieved the same rows. If both sessions attempt to make changes, there can be some rather odd effects. The following table depicts such a situation.

First User	Second User
SELECT * FROM regions;	SELECT * FROM regions;
	DELETE FROM regions WHERE region_id=5;
	COMMIT;
UPDATE regions SET region_name='GB' WHERE region_id=5;	

This is what the first user will see, from a SQL*Plus prompt:

```
SELECT *
FROM regions;
REGION_ID REGION_NAME
--------- ------------------------
        5 UK
        1 Europe
        2 Americas
        3 Asia
        4 Middle East and Africa

UPDATE regions
SET region_name='GB'
WHERE region_id=5;
0 rows updated.
```

This is a bit disconcerting. One way around this problem is to lock the rows in which one is interested:

```
SELECT *
FROM regions FOR UPDATE;
```

The FOR UPDATE clause will place a lock on all the rows retrieved. No changes can be made to them by any session other than that which issued the command, and therefore the subsequent updates will succeed: it is not possible for the rows to have been changed. This means that one session will have a consistent view of the data

INSIDE THE EXAM

Understanding Transaction Isolation

All DML statements are private to the session that makes them, until the transaction commits. The transaction is started implicitly with the first DML statement executed. Until it is committed, it can be reversed with a ROLLBACK. No other session will ever see changes that have not been committed, but the instant they are committed they will be visible to all other sessions.

Transaction structure is vital for good programming. A transaction is a logical unit of work: the changes made by the transaction, whether it is one statement affecting one row in one table, or many

statements affecting any number of rows in many tables, should be self contained. It should not be in any way dependent on statements executed outside the transaction, and it should not be divisible into smaller, self-contained transactions. A transaction should be the right size; it should contain all the statements that cannot be separated in terms of business logic and no statements that can be.

The decisions on transaction structure may be complex, but with some thought and investigation, they can be made for any situation. Business and systems analysts can and should advise on transaction structure.

SCENARIO & SOLUTION

Transactions, like constraints, are business rules: a technique whereby the database can enforce rules developed by business analysts. If the "logical unit of work" is huge, such as an accounting suite period rollover, should this actually be implemented as one transaction?	Not necessarily. Such a transaction might take hours, occupying a vast amount of database resources. In such cases, you must discuss with your business analysts and DBA whether it is possible to break up the one business transaction into a number of database transactions. Of course, if something goes wrong partway through, you will have an accounting suite that is partly in one period and partly in another. The application will need to be able to sort out the mess.
Being able to do DML operations, look at the result, then roll back and try them again can be very useful. But is it really a good idea?	No, not really. If the application is designed so that end users can do this, the DBA will not be happy. He will see many transactions being rolled back, which stresses the database. It is much better for the application to do all such work on the client side and only submit the work to the database when it is ready and can be committed immediately.

(it won't change), but the price to be paid is that other sessions will hang if they try to update any of the locked rows (they can, of course, query them).

The locks placed by a FOR UPDATE clause will be held until the session issuing the command issues a COMMIT or ROLLBACK. This must be done to release the locks, even if no DML commands have been executed.

CERTIFICATION SUMMARY

There are four DML commands that affect data: INSERT, UPDATE, DELETE, and (the optional command) MERGE. TRUNCATE is a DDL command that is functionally equivalent to a DELETE command without a WHERE clause, but it is far faster. All DML commands can be rolled back, either automatically in the case of error, or manually with the ROLLBACK command—unless they have been committed with a COMMIT. Once committed, the changes can never be reversed. TRUNCATE, like all DDL commands, has a built-in COMMIT that is unstoppable.

TWO-MINUTE DRILL

Describe Each Data Manipulation Language (DML) Statement

❑ INSERT enters rows into a table.

❑ UPDATE adjusts the values in existing rows.

❑ DELETE removes rows.

❑ MERGE can combine the functions of INSERT, UPDATE, and DELETE.

❑ Even though TRUNCATE is not DML, it does remove all rows in a table.

Insert Rows into a Table

❑ INSERT can add one row or a set of rows.

❑ It is possible for an INSERT to enter rows into multiple tables.

❑ Subqueries can be used to generate the rows to be inserted.

❑ Subqueries and functions can be used to generate column values.

❑ An INSERT is not permanent until it is committed.

Update Rows in a Table

❑ UPDATE can affect one row or a set of rows in one table.

❑ Subqueries can be used to select the rows to be updated.

❑ Subqueries and functions can be used to generate column values.

❑ An UPDATE is not permanent until it is committed.

Delete Rows from a Table

❑ DELETE can remove one row or a set of rows from one table.

❑ A subquery can be used to select the rows to be deleted.

❑ A DELETE is not permanent until it is committed.

❑ TRUNCATE removes every row from a table.

❑ A TRUNCATE is immediately permanent: it cannot be rolled back.

Control Transactions

❑ A transaction is a logical unit of work possibly made up of several DML statements.

❑ Transactions are invisible to other sessions until committed.

❑ Until committed, transactions can be rolled back.

❑ Once committed, a transaction cannot be reversed.

❑ A SAVEPOINT lets a session roll back part of a transaction.

SELF TEST

The following questions will help you measure your understanding of the material presented in this chapter. Read all the choices carefully because there might be more than one correct answer. Choose all the correct answers for each question.

Describe Each Data Manipulation Language (DML) Statement

1. Which of the following commands can be rolled back?
   A. COMMIT
   B. DELETE
   C. INSERT
   D. MERGE
   E. TRUNCATE
   F. UPDATE

2. How can you change the primary key value of a row? (Choose the best answer.)
   A. You cannot change the primary key value.
   B. Change it with a simple UPDATE statement.
   C. The row must be removed with a DELETE and reentered with an INSERT.
   D. This is only possible if the row is first locked with a SELECT FOR UPDATE.

3. If an UPDATE or DELETE command has a WHERE clause that gives it a scope of several rows, what will happen if there is an error part way through execution? The command is one of several in a multistatement transaction. (Choose the best answer.)
   A. The command will skip the row that caused the error and continue.
   B. The command will stop at the error, and the rows that have been updated or deleted will remain updated or deleted.
   C. Whatever work the command had done before hitting the error will be rolled back, but work done already by the transaction will remain.
   D. The whole transaction will be rolled back.

Insert Rows into a Table

4. If a table T1 has four numeric columns, C1, C2, C3, and C4, which of these statements will succeed? (Choose the best answer.)
   A. INSERT INTO T1 VALUES (1,2,3,null);
   B. INSERT INTO T1 values ('1','2','3','4');
   C. INSERT INTO T1
      SELECT *
      FROM T1;
   D. All the statements (A, B, and C) will succeed.
   E. None of the statements (A, B, or C) will succeed.

5. Study the result of this SELECT statement:

```
SELECT *
FROM t1;
        C1          C2          C3          C4
---------- ---------- ---------- ----------
         1           2           3           4
         5           6           7           8
```

If you issue this statement:

```
INSERT INTO t1 (c1,c2)
VALUES
  (SELECT c1,c2
   FROM t1);
```

why will it fail? (Choose the best answer.)

   A. Because values are not provided for all the table's columns: there should be NULLs for C3 and C4.
   B. Because the subquery returns multiple rows: it requires a WHERE clause to restrict the number of rows returned to one.
   C. Because the subquery is not scalar: it should use MAX or MIN to generate scalar values.
   D. Because the VALUES keyword is not used with a subquery.
   E. It will succeed, inserting two rows with NULLs for C3 and C4.

6. Consider this statement:

```
INSERT INTO regions (region_id,region_name)
VALUES
((SELECT max(region_id)+1
  FROM regions),
 'Great Britain');
```

What will the result be? (Choose the best answer.)

    A. The statement will not succeed if the value generated for REGION_ID is not unique, because REGION_ID is the primary key of the REGIONS table.

    B. The statement has a syntax error because you cannot use the VALUES keyword with a subquery.

    C. The statement will execute without error.

    D. The statement will fail if the REGIONS table has a third column.

Update Rows in a Table

7. You want to insert a row and then update it. What sequence of steps should you follow? (Choose the best answer.)

    A. INSERT, UPDATE, COMMIT

    B. INSERT, COMMIT, UPDATE, COMMIT

    C. INSERT, SELECT FOR UPDATE, UPDATE, COMMIT

    D. INSERT, COMMIT, SELECT FOR UPDATE, UPDATE, COMMIT

8. If you issue this command:

```
UPDATE employees
SET salary=salary * 1.1;
```

what will be the result? (Choose the best answer.)

    A. The statement will fail because there is no WHERE clause to restrict the rows affected.

    B. The first row in the table will be updated.

    C. There will be an error if any row has its SALARY column NULL.

    D. Every row will have SALARY incremented by 10 percent, unless SALARY was NULL.

Delete Rows from a Table

9. How can you delete the values from one column of every row in a table? (Choose the best answer.)
   A. Use the DELETE COLUMN command.
   B. Use the TRUNCATE COLUMN command.
   C. Use the UPDATE command.
   D. Use the DROP COLUMN command.

10. Which of these commands will remove every row in a table while keeping its structure intact? (Choose one or more correct answers.)
    A. A DELETE command with no WHERE clause
    B. A DROP TABLE command
    C. A TRUNCATE command
    D. An UPDATE command, setting every column to NULL and with no WHERE clause

Control Transactions

11. User JOHN updates some rows and asks user ROOPESH to log in and check the changes before he commits them. Which of the following statements is true? (Choose the best answer.)
    A. ROOPESH can see the changes but cannot alter them because JOHN will have locked the rows.
    B. ROOPESH will not be able to see the changes.
    C. JOHN must commit the changes so that ROOPESH can see them and, if necessary, roll them back.
    D. JOHN must commit the changes so that ROOPESH can see them, but only JOHN can roll them back.

12. User JOHN updates some rows but does not commit the changes. User ROOPESH queries the rows that JOHN updated. Which of the following statements is true? (Choose the best answer.)
    A. ROOPESH will not be able to see the rows because they will be locked.
    B. ROOPESH will be able to see the new values, but only if he logs in as JOHN.
    C. ROOPESH will see the old versions of the rows.
    D. ROOPESH will see the state of the data as it was when JOHN last created a SAVEPOINT.

13. Which of these commands will terminate a transaction? (Choose three correct answers.)
    A. COMMIT
    B. DELETE
    C. ROLLBACK
    D. ROLLBACK TO SAVEPOINT
    E. SAVEPOINT
    F. TRUNCATE

LAB QUESTION

Carry out this exercise in the OE schema.

I. Insert a customer into CUSTOMERS, using a function to generate a unique customer number:

```
INSERT INTO customers
(customer_id,cust_first_name,cust_last_name)
VALUES (
  (SELECT max(customer_id)+1
   FROM customers),
   'John','Watson');
```

2. Give him a credit limit equal to the average credit limit:

```
UPDATE customers
SET credit_limit=
  (SELECT avg(credit_limit)
   FROM customers)
   WHERE cust_last_name='Watson';
```

3. Create another customer using the customer just created, but make sure the CUSTOMER_ID is unique:

```
INSERT INTO customers
(customer_id,cust_first_name,cust_last_name,credit_limit)
SELECT customer_id+1,cust_first_name,cust_last_name,credit_limit
FROM customers
WHERE cust_last_name='Watson';
```

4. Change the name of the second entered customer:

```
UPDATE customers
SET cust_last_name='Ramklass',cust_first_name='Roopesh'
WHERE customer_id=
  (SELECT max(customer_id)
   FROM customers);
```

5. Commit this transaction:

```
COMMIT;
```

6. Determine the CUSTOMER_IDs of the two new customers and lock the rows:

```
SELECT customer_id,cust_last_name
FROM customers
WHERE cust_last_name IN ('Watson','Ramklass') FOR UPDATE;
```

From another session connected to the OE schema, attempt to update one of the locked rows:

```
UPDATE customers
SET credit_limit=0
WHERE cust_last_name='Ramklass';
```

7. This command will hang. In the first session, release the locks by issuing a commit:

```
COMMIT;
```

8. The second session will now complete its update. In the second session, delete the two rows:

```
DELETE FROM customers
WHERE cust_last_name IN ('Watson','Ramklass');
```

9. In the first session, attempt to truncate the CUSTOMERS table:

```
TRUNCATE TABLE customers;
```

10. This will fail because there is a transaction in progress against the table, which will block all DDL commands. In the second session, commit the transaction:

```
COMMIT;
```

11. The CUSTOMERS table will now be back in the state it was in at the start of the exercise. Confirm this by checking the value of the highest CUSTOMER_ID:

```
SELECT max(customer_id)
FROM customers;
```

SELF TEST ANSWERS

Describe Each Data Manipulation Language (DML) Statement

1. ☑ **B, C, D,** and **F.** These are the DML commands: they can all be rolled back.
    ☒ **A** and **E** are incorrect. COMMIT terminates a transaction, which can then never be rolled back. TRUNCATE is a DDL command and includes a built-in COMMIT.

2. ☑ **B.** Assuming no constraint violations, the primary key can be updated like any other column.
    ☒ **A, C,** and **D** are incorrect. **A** is incorrect because there is no restriction on updating primary keys (other than constraints). **C** is incorrect because there is no need to do it in such a complex manner. **D** is incorrect because the UPDATE will apply its own lock: you do not have to lock the row first.

3. ☑ **C.** This is the expected behavior: the statement is rolled back, and the rest of the transaction remains uncommitted.
    ☒ **A, B,** and **D** are incorrect. **A** is incorrect because, while this behavior is in fact configurable, it is not enabled by default. **B** is incorrect because, while this is in fact possible in the event of space errors, it is not enabled by default. **D** is incorrect because only the one statement will be rolled back, not the whole transaction.

Insert Rows into a Table

4. ☑ **D. A, B,** and **C** will all succeed, even though **B** will force the database to do some automatic type casting.
    ☒ **A, B, C,** and **E** are incorrect. **A, B,** and **C** are each valid, but **D** groups them into the appropriate single valid response. **E** is incorrect because **A, B,** and **C** will all succeed.

5. ☑ **D.** The syntax is wrong: use either the VALUES keyword or a subquery, but not both. Remove the VALUES keyword, and it will run. C3 and C4 would be populated with NULLs.
    ☒ **A, B, C,** and **E** are incorrect. **A** is incorrect because there is no need to provide values for columns not listed. **B** and **C** are incorrect because an INSERT can insert a set of rows, so there is no need to restrict the number with a WHERE clause or by using MAX or MIN to return only one row. **E** is incorrect because the statement is not syntactically correct.

6. ☑ **C.** The statement is syntactically correct, and the use of "MAX(REGION_ID) + 1" guarantees generating a unique number for the primary key column.
    ☒ **A, B,** and **D** are incorrect. **A** is incorrect because the function will generate a unique value for the primary key. **B** is incorrect because there is no problem using a scalar subquery to generate a value for a VALUES list. What cannot be done is to use the VALUES keyword and then a single nonscalar subquery to provide all the values. **D** is incorrect because if there is a third column, it will be populated with a NULL value.

Update Rows in a Table

7. ☑ **A.** This is the simplest (and therefore the best) way.
☒ **B, C,** and **D** are incorrect. All these will work, but they are all needlessly complicated: no programmer should use unnecessary statements.

8. ☑ **D.** Any arithmetic operation on a NULL returns a NULL, but all other rows will be updated.
☒ **A, B,** and **C** are incorrect. **A** and **B** are incorrect because the lack of a WHERE clause means that every row will be processed. **C** is incorrect because trying to do arithmetic against a NULL is not an error (though it isn't very useful, either).

Delete Rows from a Table

9. ☑ **C.** An UPDATE, without a WHERE clause, is the only way.
☒ **A, B,** and **D** are incorrect. **A** is incorrect because there is no such syntax: a DELETE affects the whole row. **B** is incorrect because there is no such syntax: a TRUNCATE affects the whole table. **D** is incorrect because, while this command does exist (it is part of the ALTER TABLE command), it will remove the column completely, not just clear the values out of it.

10. ☑ **A** and **C.** The TRUNCATE will be faster, but the DELETE will get there too.
☒ **B** and **D** are incorrect. **B** is incorrect because this will remove the table as well as the rows within it. **D** is incorrect because the rows will still be there—even though they are populated with NULLs.

Control Transactions

11. ☑ **B.** The principle of isolation means that only JOHN can see his uncommitted transaction.
☒ **A, C,** and **D** are incorrect. **A** is incorrect because transaction isolation means that no other session will be able to see the changes. **C** and **D** are incorrect because a committed transaction can never be rolled back.

12. ☑ **C.** Transaction isolation means that no other session will be able to see the changes until they are committed.
☒ **A, B,** and **D** are incorrect. **A** is incorrect because locking is not relevant; writers do not block readers. **B** is incorrect because isolation restricts visibility of in-progress transactions to the session making the changes; the schema the users are connecting to does not matter. **D** is incorrect because savepoints are only markers in a transaction; they do not affect publishing changes to other sessions.

13. ☑ **A, C,** and **F.** COMMIT and ROLLBACK are the commands to terminate a transaction explicitly; TRUNCATE will do it implicitly.

☒ **B, D,** and **E** are incorrect. **B** is incorrect because DELETE is a DML command that can be executed within a transaction. **D** and **E** are incorrect because creating savepoints and rolling back to them leaves the transaction in progress.

LAB ANSWER

Figure 10-6 shows the first five steps of the exercise.

Figure 10-7 shows the final seven steps of the exercise, as seen from the point of view of the first session.

FIGURE 10-6

Steps 1 through 5 of the lab exercise

```
                                    SQL Plus                              _ □ ✕

SQL> CONNECT oe/oe
Connected.
SQL> INSERT INTO customers(customer_id, cust_first_name,cust_last_name)
  2  VALUES(
  3  (SELECT max(customer_id) + 1
  4    FROM customers),
  5  'John','Watson');

1 row created.

SQL> UPDATE customers
  2  SET credit_limit=
  3  (SELECT avg(credit_limit)
  4    FROM customers)
  5  WHERE cust_last_name='Watson';

1 row updated.

SQL> INSERT INTO customers(customer_id, cust_first_name,cust_last_name,credit_limit)
  2  SELECT customer_id+1,cust_first_name,cust_last_name,credit_limit
  3  FROM customers
  4  WHERE cust_last_name='Watson';

1 row created.

SQL> UPDATE customers
  2  SET cust_last_name='Ramklass',
  3     cust_first_name='Roopesh'
  4  WHERE customer_id=
  5  (SELECT max(customer_id)
  6    FROM customers);

1 row updated.

SQL> COMMIT;

Commit complete.

SQL>
```

The final steps of
the lab exercise,
including the
TRUNCATE
error

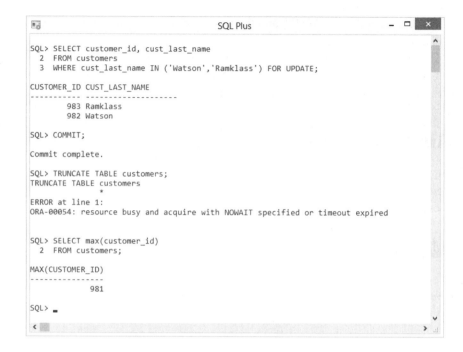

```
SQL> SELECT customer_id, cust_last_name
  2  FROM customers
  3  WHERE cust_last_name IN ('Watson','Ramklass') FOR UPDATE;

CUSTOMER_ID CUST_LAST_NAME
----------- --------------------
        983 Ramklass
        982 Watson

SQL> COMMIT;

Commit complete.

SQL> TRUNCATE TABLE customers;
TRUNCATE TABLE customers
               *
ERROR at line 1:
ORA-00054: resource busy and acquire with NOWAIT specified or timeout expired


SQL> SELECT max(customer_id)
  2  FROM customers;

MAX(CUSTOMER_ID)
---------------
            981

SQL>
```

11
Using DDL Statements to Create and Manage Tables

CERTIFICATION OBJECTIVES

here are several types of data objects in a database that can be accessed using SQL. The most commonly used type of object is the table. Tables come in various forms, but SQL is independent of their forms. A table may also be associated with other objects such as indexes or LOBs (a large object—a structure designed for storing big items of information, such as video recordings) that are addressed implicitly. The SQL statement will address only the table with which the other objects are associated. This chapter details table creation.

When creating a table, there are certain rules that must be followed regarding the table's structure: its columns may only be of certain data types. There are also rules that can be defined for the individual rows; these are known as *constraints*. The structural rules and the constraint rules together restrict the data that can be inserted into the table.

CERTIFICATION OBJECTIVE 11.01

Categorize the Main Database Objects

There are various types of objects that can exist within a database, many more with the current release than with earlier versions. All objects have names, and all objects are owned by someone. The "someone" is a database user, such as HR. The objects the user owns are their *schema*. An object's name must conform to certain rules.

Object Types

This query lists the object types that happen to exist in this particular database, with a count of how many there are:

```
SELECT object_type, count(object_type)
FROM dba_objects
GROUP BY object_type
ORDER BY object_type;

OBJECT_TYPE            COUNT(OBJECT_TYPE)
------------------     ------------------
CLUSTER                               10
CONSUMER GROUP                        12
CONTEXT                                6
```

```
DIMENSION                             5
DIRECTORY                             9
EDITION                               1
EVALUATION CONTEXT                   13
FUNCTION                            286
INDEX                              3023
INDEX PARTITION                     342
INDEXTYPE                            12
JAVA CLASS                        22018
JAVA DATA                           322
JAVA RESOURCE                       820
JOB                                  11
JOB CLASS                            11
LIBRARY                             177
LOB                                 769
LOB PARTITION                         7
MATERIALIZED VIEW                     3
OPERATOR                             60
PACKAGE                            1240
PACKAGE BODY                       1178
PROCEDURE                           118
PROGRAM                              17
QUEUE                                37
RESOURCE PLAN                         7
RULE                                  1
RULE SET                             21
SCHEDULE                              2
SEQUENCE                            204
SYNONYM                           26493
TABLE                              2464
TABLE PARTITION                     199
TRIGGER                             413
TYPE                               2630
TYPE BODY                           231
UNDEFINED                             6
VIEW                               4669
WINDOW                                9
WINDOW GROUP                          4
XML SCHEMA                           93
42 rows selected.
```

This query addresses the view DBA_OBJECTS, which has one row for every object in the database. The numbers are low, because the database is a very small one used only for teaching. A database used for a business application might have hundreds of thousands of objects. You may not be able to see the view DBA_OBJECTS, depending on what permissions your account has. Alternate views are USER_OBJECTS, which will show all the objects owned by you, and ALL_OBJECTS, which will show all the objects to which you have been granted access (including your own). All users have access to these.

The objects of greatest interest to a SQL programmer are those that contain, or give access to, data. These are

- Tables
- Views
- Synonyms
- Indexes
- Sequences

This chapter covers tables; the others are out of scope of the SQL exam. Briefly, a view is a stored SELECT statement that can be addressed as though it were a table. It is nothing more than a named SELECT statement, but rather than running the statement itself, the user issues a SELECT statement against the view instead. In effect, the user is selecting from the result of another selection. A synonym is an alias for a table (or a view). Users can execute SQL statements against the synonym, and the database will map them into statements against the object to which the synonym points. Indexes are a means of improving access times to rows in tables. If a query requires only one row, then rather than scanning the entire table to find the row, an index can give a pointer to the row's exact location. Of course, the index itself must be searched, but this is often faster than scanning the table. A sequence is a construct that generates unique numbers. There are many cases where unique numbers are needed. Sequences issue numbers in order, on demand: it is absolutely impossible for the same number to be issued twice.

The remaining object types are less commonly relevant to a SQL programmer. Their use falls more within the realm of PL/SQL programmers and database administrators.

Users and Schemas

Many people use the terms "user" and "schema" interchangeably. In the Oracle environment, you can get away with this (though not necessarily with other database management systems). A *user* is a person who can connect to the database. The user will have a username and a password. A *schema* is a container for the objects owned by a user. When a user is created, their schema is created too. A schema is the objects owned by a user; initially, it will be empty.

Some schemas will always be empty: the user will never create any objects, because they do not need to and (if the user is set up correctly) will not have the necessary privileges anyway. Users such as this will have been granted permissions, either through direct privileges or through roles, to use code and access data in other schemas, owned by other users. Other users may be the reverse of this: they will own many objects but will never actually log on to the database. They need not even have been granted the CREATE SESSION privilege, so the account is effectively disabled (or indeed it can be locked)—these schemas are used as repositories for code and data accessed by others.

Schema objects are objects with an owner. The unique identifier for an object of a particular type is not its name—it is its name prefixed with the name of the schema to which it belongs. Thus, the table HR.REGIONS is a table called REGIONS, which is owned by user HR. There could be another table SYSTEM.REGIONS that would be a completely different table (perhaps different in both structure and contents) owned by user SYSTEM and residing in its schema.

A number of users (and their associated schemas) are created automatically at database creation time. Principal among these are SYS and SYSTEM. User SYS owns the data dictionary: a set of tables (in the SYS schema) that define the database and its contents. SYS also owns several hundred PL/SQL packages: code that is provided for the use of database administrators and developers. Objects in the SYS schema should never be modified with DML commands. If you were to execute DML against the data dictionary tables, you would run the risk of corrupting the data dictionary, with disastrous results. You update the data dictionary by running DDL commands (such as CREATE TABLE), which provide a layer of abstraction between you and the data dictionary itself. The SYSTEM schema stores various additional objects used for administration and monitoring.

Depending on the options selected during database creation, there may be more users created. These users store code and data required by various database options. For example, the user MDSYS stores the objects used by Spatial, an option that extends the capabilities of the Oracle database to manage geographical information.

Naming Schema Objects

A schema object is an object that is owned by a user. All schema object names must conform to certain rules:

- The name may be from 1 to 30 characters long (with the exception of database link names that may be up to 128 characters long).
- Reserved words (such as SELECT) cannot be used as object names.

- All names must begin with a letter from A through Z.
- The characters in a name can only be letters, numbers, an underscore (_), the dollar sign ($), or the hash symbol (#).
- Lowercase letters will be converted to uppercase.

By enclosing the name within double quotes, all these rules (with the exception of the length) can be broken, but to get to the object, subsequently, it must always be specified with double quotes, as in the examples in Figure 11-1. Note that the same restrictions also apply to column names.

Although tools such as SQL*Plus and SQL Developer will automatically convert lowercase letters to uppercase unless the name is enclosed within double quotes,

FIGURE 11-1

Using double quotes to use nonstandard names

```
                            SQL Plus            —  □  ×

SQL> CREATE TABLE "with space" ("-Hyphen" date);

Table created.

SQL> INSERT INTO "with space"
  2  VALUES (sysdate);

1 row created.

SQL> SELECT *
  2  FROM with space;
FROM with space
     *
ERROR at line 2:
ORA-00903: invalid table name


SQL> SELECT -Hyphen
  2  FROM "with space";
SELECT -Hyphen
       *
ERROR at line 1:
ORA-00904: "HYPHEN": invalid identifier


SQL> SELECT "-Hyphen"
  2  FROM "with space";

-Hyphen
---------
08-DEC-13

SQL>
```

remember that object names are always case sensitive. In this example, the two tables are completely different:

```
CREATE TABLE lower (c1 date);
Table created.

CREATE TABLE "lower" (col1 varchar2(2));
Table created.

SELECT table_name
FROM user_tables
WHERE lower(table_name) = 'lower';

TABLE_NAME
----------------------------
lower
LOWER
```

on the job *While it is possible to use lowercase names and nonstandard characters (even spaces), it is considered bad practice because of the confusion it can cause.*

Object Namespaces

It is often said that the unique identifier for an object is the object name, prefixed with the schema name. While this is generally true, for a full understanding of naming, it is necessary to introduce the concept of a *namespace*. A namespace defines a group of object types, within which all names must be uniquely identified by schema and name. Objects in different namespaces can share the same name.

These object types all share the same namespace:

- Tables
- Views
- Sequences
- Private synonyms

Thus, it is impossible to create a view with the same name as a table—at least, it is impossible if they are in the same schema. And once created, SQL statements can address a view or a synonym as though it were a table. The fact that tables, views, and private synonyms share the same namespace means that you can set up several layers of abstraction between what the users see and the actual tables, which can be invaluable for both for security and for simplifying application development. Indexes and constraints each have their own namespace. Thus, it is possible for an index to have the same name as a table, even within the same schema.

Determine What Objects Are Accessible to Your Session

In this exercise, query various data dictionary views as user HR to determine what objects are in the HR schema and what objects in other schemas HR has access to.

1. Connect to the database with SQL*Plus or SQL Developer as user HR.

2. Determine how many objects of each type are in the HR schema:

```
SELECT object_type, count(*)
FROM user_objects
GROUP BY object_type;
```

The USER_OBJECTS view lists all objects owned by the schema to which the current session is connected, in this case HR.

3. Determine how many objects in total HR has permissions on:

```
SELECT object_type, count(*)
FROM all_objects
GROUP BY object_type;
```

The ALL_OBJECTS view lists all objects to which the user has some sort of access.

4. Determine who owns the objects HR can see:

```
SELECT DISTINCT owner
FROM all_objects;
```

CERTIFICATION OBJECTIVE 11.02

Review the Table Structure

According to the relational database paradigm, a table is a two-dimensional structure storing rows. A row is one or more columns. Every row in the table has the same columns, as defined by the structure of the table. The Oracle database does permit variations on this two-dimensional model. Some columns can be defined as nested tables, which themselves have several columns. Other columns may be of an unbounded data type such as a binary large object, theoretically terabytes big. It is also possible to define columns as objects. The object will have an internal structure (possibly based on columns) that is not visible as part of the table.

The systems analysis phase of the system development lifecycle will have modeled the data structures needed to store the system's information into third normal form, as described in Chapter 1. The result is a set of two-dimensional tables, each with a primary key and linked to each other with foreign keys. The system design phase may have compromised this structure, perhaps by denormalizing the tables or by taking advantage of Oracle-specific capabilities such as nested tables. But the end result, as far as the SQL developer is concerned, is a set of tables.

Each table exists as a definition in the data dictionary. On creation, the table will have been assigned a limited amount of space (known as an *extent*) within the database. This may be small, perhaps only a few kilobytes or megabytes. As rows are inserted into the table, this extent will fill. When it is full, the database will (automatically) assign another extent to the table. As rows are deleted, space within the assigned extents becomes available for reuse. Even if every row is deleted, the extents remain allocated to the table. They will only be freed up and returned to the database for use elsewhere if the table is dropped or truncated (as described in Chapter 10).

EXERCISE 11-2

Investigate Table Structures

In this exercise, query various data dictionary views as user HR to determine the structure of a table.

1. Connect to the database with SQL*Plus or SQL Developer as user HR.
2. Determine the names and types of tables that exist in the HR schema:

```
SELECT table_name, cluster_name, iot_type
FROM user_tables;
```

Clustered tables and index organized tables (IOTs) are advanced table structures. In the HR schema, all tables are standard heap tables except for COUNTRIES, which is an IOT.

3. Use the DESCRIBE command to display the structure of a table:

```
DESCRIBE regions;
```

4. Retrieve similar information by querying a data dictionary view:

```
SELECT column_name, data_type, nullable
FROM user_tab_columns
WHERE table_name='REGIONS';
```

CERTIFICATION OBJECTIVE 11.03

List the Data Types That Are Available for Columns

When creating tables, each column must be assigned a data type, which determines the nature of the values that can be inserted into the column. These data types are also used to specify the nature of the arguments for PL/SQL procedures and functions. When selecting a data type, you must consider the data that you need to store and the operations you will want to perform upon it. Space is also a consideration: some data types are fixed length, taking up the same number of bytes no matter what data is actually in it; others are variable. If a column is not populated, then Oracle will not give it any space at all. If you later update the row to populate the column, then the row will get bigger, no matter whether the data type is fixed length or variable. In 12c database, a new system parameter, MAX_STRING_SIZE, allows string data types to be much larger than in previous versions when it is changed from its default value of STANDARD to EXTENDED.

The following are the data types for alphanumeric data:

- **VARCHAR2**   Variable-length character data, from 1 byte to 4000 bytes if MAX_STRING_SIZE=STANDARD or 32767 bytes if MAX_STRING_SIZE=EXTENDED. The data is stored in the database character set.
- **NVARCHAR2**   Like VARCHAR2, but the data is stored in the alternative national language character set, one of the permitted Unicode character sets.
- **CHAR**   Fixed-length character data, from 1 byte to 2000 bytes, in the database character set. If the data is not the length of the column, then it will be padded with spaces.

on the *For ISO/ANSI compliance, you can specify a VARCHAR data type, but any*
job *columns of this type will be automatically converted to VARCHAR2.*

The following is the data type for binary data:

■ **RAW**   Variable-length binary data, from 1 byte to 4000 bytes if MAX_STRING_SIZE=STANDARD or 32767 bytes if MAX_STRING_ SIZE=EXTENDED. Unlike the CHAR and VARCHAR2 data types, RAW data is not converted by Oracle Net from the database's character set to the user process's character set on SELECT or the other way on INSERT.

The following are the data types for numeric data, all variable length:

■ **NUMBER**   Numeric data, for which you can specify precision and scale. The precision can range from to 1 to 38, the scale can range from −84 to 127.

■ **FLOAT**   This is an ANSI data type, floating-point number with precision of 126 binary (or 38 decimal). Oracle also provides BINARY_FLOAT and BINARY_DOUBLE as alternatives.

■ **INTEGER**   Equivalent to NUMBER, with scale zero.

The following are the data types for date and time data, all fixed length:

■ **DATE**   This is either length zero, if the column is empty, or 7 bytes. All DATE data includes century, year, month, day, hour, minute, and second. The valid range is from January 1, 4712 BC to December 31, 9999 AD.

■ **TIMESTAMP**   This is length zero if the column is empty, or up to 11 bytes, depending on the precision specified. Similar to DATE, but with precision of up to 9 decimal places for the seconds, 6 places by default.

■ **TIMESTAMP WITH TIMEZONE**   Like TIMESTAMP, but the data is stored with a record kept of the time zone to which it refers. The length may be up to 13 bytes, depending on precision. This data type lets Oracle determine the difference between two times by normalizing them to UTC, even if the times are for different time zones.

■ **TIMESTAMP WITH LOCAL TIMEZONE**   Like TIMESTAMP, but the data is normalized to the database time zone on saving. When retrieved, it is normalized to the time zone of the user process selecting it.

■ **INTERVAL YEAR TO MONTH**   Used for recording a period in years and months between two DATEs or TIMESTAMPs.

■ **INTERVAL DAY TO SECOND**   Used for recording a period in days and seconds between two DATEs or TIMESTAMPs.

The following are the large object data types:

- **CLOB** Character data stored in the database character set, size effectively unlimited: (4GB –1) multiplied by the database block size.
- **NCLOB** Like CLOB, but the data is stored in the alternative national language character set, one of the permitted Unicode character sets.
- **BLOB** Like CLOB, but binary data that will not undergo character set conversion by Oracle Net.
- **BFILE** A locator pointing to a file stored on the operating system of the database server. The size of the files is limited to 4GB.
- **LONG** Character data in the database character set, up to 2GB. All the functionality of LONG (and more) is provided by CLOB; LONGs should not be used in a modern database, and if your database has any columns of this type they should be converted to CLOB. There can only be one LONG column in a table.
- **LONG RAW** Like LONG, but binary data that will not be converted by Oracle Net. Any LONG RAW columns should be converted to BLOBs.

The following is the ROWID data type:

- **ROWID** A value coded in base 64 that is the pointer to the location of a row in a table. Encrypted within it is the exact physical address. ROWID is an Oracle proprietary data type, not visible unless specifically selected.

e x a m

ⓦatch   *All examinees will be expected to know about these data types: VARCHAR2, CHAR, NUMBER, DATE, TIMESTAMP, INTERVAL, RAW, LONG,*   *LONG RAW, CLOB, BLOB, BFILE, and ROWID. Detailed knowledge will also be needed for VARCHAR2, NUMBER, and DATE.*

The VARCHAR2 data type must be qualified with a number indicating the maximum length of the column. If a value is inserted into the column that is less than this, it is not a problem: the value will only take up as much space as it needs. If the value is longer than this maximum, the INSERT will fail with an error. If the value is updated to a longer or shorter value, the length of the column (and therefore the row itself) will change accordingly. If it is not entered at all or is updated to NULL, then it will take up no space at all.

The NUMBER data type may optionally be qualified with a precision and a scale. The precision sets the maximum number of significant decimal digits, where the most significant digit is the left-most nonzero digit, and the least significant digit is the right-most known digit in the number. The scale is the number of digits from the decimal point to the least significant digit. A positive scale is the number of significant digits to the right of the decimal point to (and including) the least significant digit. A negative scale is the number of significant digits to the left of the decimal point to (but not including) the least significant digit.

The DATE data type always includes century, year, month, day, hour, minute, and second—even if all these elements are not specified at insert time. Year, month, and day must be specified; if the hours, minutes, and seconds are omitted they will default to midnight. Using the TRUNC function on a date also has the effect of setting the hours, minutes, and seconds to midnight.

Oracle provides a range of type casting functions for converting between data types and in some circumstances will do automatic type casting. Figure 11-2 illustrates using both the manual and the automatic type casting techniques.

In the preceding example, the first INSERT uses type casting functions to convert the character data entered to the data types specified for the table columns. The second INSERT attempts to insert character strings into all three columns, but the insert still succeeds because Oracle can convert data types automatically if

FIGURE 11-2

Use of type casting functions and automatic type casting

```
SQL> CREATE TABLE typecast (d_col DATE, n_col NUMBER, v_col VARCHAR2(20));

Table created.

SQL> ALTER SESSION
  2  SET nls_date_format='dd-mm-yy';

Session altered.

SQL> INSERT INTO typecast
  2  VALUES (to_date('23-11-13'), to_number(1000), 'done correctly');

1 row created.

SQL> INSERT INTO typecast
  2  VALUES ('23-11-13', '1000', 'automatic casting');

1 row created.

SQL> SELECT *
  2  FROM typecast;

D_COL        N_COL V_COL
-------- --------- --------------------
23-11-13      1000 done correctly
23-11-13      1000 automatic casting

SQL>
```

necessary—but only if the format of the data is suitable. Note that if the value for the date has been entered in any format other than DD-MM-YY, such as '23-Nov-13', it would have failed.

on the

Ọ o b

Do not rely on automatic type casting. It can impact performance and may not always work. The Oracle environment is strongly typed, and programmers should respect this.

EXERCISE 11-3

Investigate the Data Types in the HR schema

In this exercise, find out what data types are used in the tables in the HR schema, using two techniques.

1. Connect to the database as user HR with SQL*Plus or SQL Developer.

2. Use the DESCRIBE command to show the data types in some tables:

   ```
   DESCRIBE employees;
   DESCRIBE departments;
   ```

3. Use a query against a data dictionary view to show what columns make up the EMPLOYEES table, as the DESCRIBE command would:

   ```
   SELECT column_name, data_type, nullable, data_length, data_precision,
   data_scale
   FROM user_tab_columns
   WHERE table_name='EMPLOYEES';
   ```

   The view USER_TAB_COLUMNS shows the detail of every column in every table in the current user's schema.

CERTIFICATION OBJECTIVE 11.04

Create a Simple Table

Tables can be stored in the database in several ways. The simplest is the *heap* table. A heap is variable length rows in random order. There may be some correlation between the order in which rows are entered and the order in which they are stored, but this is a matter of luck. More advanced table structures, such as the following, may impose ordering and grouping on the rows or force a random distribution:

- **Index organized tables**   Store rows in the order of an index key.
- **Index clusters**   Can denormalize tables in parent-child relationships so that related rows from different tables are stored together.
- **Hash clusters**   Force a random distribution of rows, which will break down any ordering based on the entry sequence.
- **Partitioned tables**   Store rows in separate physical structures, the partitions, allocating rows according to the value of a column.

Using the more advanced table structures has no effect whatsoever on SQL. Every SQL statement executed against tables defined with these options will return exactly the same results as though the tables were standard heap tables, so use of these features will not affect code. But while their use is transparent to programmers, they do give enormous benefits in performance.

Creating Tables with Column Specifications

To create a standard heap table, use this syntax:

CREATE TABLE [schema.]table [ORGANIZATION HEAP]
(column datatype [DEFAULT expression]
[,column datatype [DEFAULT expression]...]);

As a minimum, specify the table name (it will be created in your own schema, if you don't specify someone else's) and at least one column with a data type. There are very few developers who ever specify ORGANIZATION HEAP, as this is the default and is industry standard SQL. The DEFAULT keyword in a column definition lets you provide an expression that will generate a value for the column when a row is inserted if a value is not provided by the INSERT statement.
Consider this statement:

```
CREATE TABLE SCOTT.EMP
(EMPNO NUMBER(4),
ENAME VARCHAR2(10),
HIREDATE DATE DEFAULT TRUNC(SYSDATE),
SAL NUMBER(7,2),
COMM NUMBER(7,2) DEFAULT 0.03);
```

This will create a table called EMP in the SCOTT schema. Either user SCOTT himself has to issue the statement (in which case nominating the schema would not actually be necessary), or another user could issue it if he has been granted permission to create tables in another user's schema. Taking the columns one by one:

- EMPNO can be 4 digits long, with no decimal places. If any decimals are included in an INSERT statement, they will be rounded (up or down) to the nearest integer.
- ENAME can store any characters at all, up to 10 of them.
- HIREDATE will accept any date, optionally with the time, but if a value is not provided, today's date will be entered as at midnight.
- SAL, intended for the employee's salary, will accept numeric values with up to 7 digits. If any digits over 7 are to the right of the decimal point, they will be rounded off.
- COMM (for commission percentage) has a default value of 0.03, which will be entered if the INSERT statement does not include a value for this column.

Following creation of the table, these statements insert a row and select the result:

```
INSERT INTO scott.emp (empno, ename, sal)
VALUES (1000, 'John', 1000.789);
1 row created.

SELECT *
FROM scott.emp;

     EMPNO ENAME       HIREDATE         SAL       COMM
---------- ---------- --------- ---------- ----------
      1000 John       19-NOV-13    1000.79        .03
```

Note that values for the columns not mentioned in the INSERT statement have been generated by the DEFAULT clauses. Had those clauses not been defined in the table definition, the columns would have been NULL. Also note the rounding of the value provided for SAL.

on the **Ob**   *The DEFAULT clause can be useful, but it is of limited functionality. You cannot use a subquery to generate the default value: you can only specify literal values or functions.*

Creating Tables from Subqueries

Rather than creating a table from nothing and then inserting rows into it (as in the previous section), tables can be created from other tables by using a subquery. This technique lets you create the table definition and populate the table with rows with just one statement. Any query at all can be used as the source of both the table structure and the rows. The syntax is as follows:

CREATE TABLE [*schema.*]*table* AS *subquery*;

All queries return a two-dimensional set of rows; this result is stored as the new table. A simple example of creating a table with a subquery is:

```
CREATE TABLE employees_copy AS
SELECT *
FROM employees;
```

This statement will create a table EMPLOYEES_COPY, which is an exact copy of the EMPLOYEES table, identical in both definition and the rows it contains. Any not null and check constraints on the columns will also be applied to the new table, but any primary-key, unique, or foreign-key constraints will not be. (Constraints are discussed in the section titled "Explain How Constraints Are Created at the Time of Table Creation.") This is because these three types of constraints require indexes that might not be available or desired.

The following is a more complex example:

```
CREATE TABLE emp_dept AS
SELECT last_name ename, department_name dname, round(sysdate - hire_date)
service
FROM employees
NATURAL JOIN departments
ORDER BY dname, ename;
```

The rows in the new table will be the result of joining the two source tables, with two of the selected columns having their names changed. The new SERVICE column will be populated with the result of the arithmetic that computes the number of days since the employee was hired. The rows will be inserted in the order specified. This ordering will not be maintained by subsequent DML, but assuming the standard HR schema data, the new table will look like this:

```
SELECT *
FROM emp_dept
WHERE rownum < 10;

ENAME            DNAME             SERVICE
---------------  ---------------   ----------
Gietz            Accounting             4203
De Haan          Executive              4713
Kochhar          Executive              3001
Chen             Finance                2994
```

```
Faviet          Finance              4133
Popp            Finance              2194
Sciarra         Finance              2992
Urman           Finance              2834
Austin          IT                   3089
9 rows selected.
```

The subquery can of course include a WHERE clause to restrict the rows inserted into the new table. To create a table with no rows, use a WHERE clause that will exclude all rows:

```
CREATE TABLE no_emps AS
SELECT *
FROM employees
WHERE 1=2;
```

The WHERE clause 1=2 can never return TRUE, so the table structure will be created ready for use, but no rows will be inserted at creation time.

Altering Table Definitions After Creation

There are many alterations that can be made to a table after creation. Those that affect the physical storage fall into the domain of the database administrator, but many changes are purely logical and will be carried out by the SQL developers. The following are examples (for the most part self-explanatory):

- Adding columns:

    ```
    ALTER TABLE emp
    ADD (job_id number);
    ```

- Modifying columns:

    ```
    ALTER TABLE emp
    MODIFY (comm number(4,2) DEFAULT 0.05);
    ```

- Dropping columns:

    ```
    ALTER TABLE emp
    DROP COLUMN comm;
    ```

- Marking columns as unused:

    ```
    ALTER TABLE emp
    SET UNUSED COLUMN job_id;
    ```

▓ Renaming columns:

```
ALTER TABLE emp
RENAME COLUMN hiredate TO recruited;
```

▓ Marking the table as read-only:

```
ALTER TABLE emp
READ ONLY;
```

All of these changes are DDL commands with the built-in COMMIT. They are therefore nonreversible and will fail if there is an active transaction against the table. They are also virtually instantaneous with the exception of dropping a column. Dropping a column can be a time-consuming exercise because as each column is dropped, every row must be restructured to remove the column's data. The SET UNUSED command, which makes columns nonexistent as far as SQL is concerned, is often a better alternative, followed when convenient by

```
ALTER TABLE tablename
DROP UNUSED COLUMNS;
```

which will drop all the unused columns in one pass through the table.

Marking a table as read-only will cause errors for any attempted DML commands. But the table can still be dropped. This can be disconcerting but is perfectly logical when you think it through. A DROP command doesn't actually affect the table: it affects the tables in the data dictionary that define the table, and these are not read-only.

Dropping and Truncating Tables

The TRUNCATE TABLE command was described in Chapter 10: it has the effect of removing every row from a table, while leaving the table definition intact. DROP TABLE is more drastic in that the table definition is removed as well. The syntax is as follows:

DROP TABLE [*schema.*]*tablename*;

If *schema* is not specified, then the table called *tablename* in your currently logged on schema will be dropped.

As with a TRUNCATE, SQL will not produce a warning before the table is dropped, and furthermore, as with any DDL command, it includes a COMMIT. But there are some restrictions: if any session (even your own) has a transaction in progress that includes a row in the table, then the DROP will fail, and it is also impossible to drop a table that is referred to in a foreign key constraint defined for a another table. This table (or the constraint) must be dropped first.

on the **Oracle 12c includes a recycle bin option, which is enabled by default. This**
Ⓘob **allows any dropped table to be restored unless it was dropped with the**
PURGE option or if the recycle bin option has been disabled.

EXERCISE 11-4

Create Tables

In this exercise, use SQL Developer to create a heap table, insert some rows with a subquery, and modify the table. Do some more modifications with SQL*Plus, then drop the table.

1. Connect to the database as user HR with SQL Developer.

2. Right-click the Tables branch of the navigation tree, and click New Table.

3. Name the new table emps, and use the Add Column button to set it up as in the following illustration:

4. Click the DDL tab to see if the statement has been constructed. It should look like this:

```
CREATE TABLE EMPS
(
EMPNO NUMBER
,ENAME VARCHAR2(25)
```

```
,SALARY NUMBER
,DEPTNO NUMBER(4, 0)
);
```

Return to the Table tab (as in the preceding illustration) and click OK to create the table.

5. Run this statement:

```
INSERT INTO emps
SELECT employee_id, last_name, salary, department_id
FROM employees;
```

and commit the insert:

```
COMMIT;
```

6. Right-click the EMPS table in the SQL Developer navigator, click Column and Add.

7. Define a new column HIRED, type DATE, as in the following illustration below; and click Apply to create the column.

8. Connect to the database as HR with SQL*Plus.

9. Define a default for HIRED column in the EMPS table:

```
ALTER TABLE emps
MODIFY (hired DEFAULT sysdate);
```

10. Insert a row without specifying a value for HIRED and check that the new row does have a HIRED date but that the other rows do not:

```
INSERT INTO emps (empno, ename)
VALUES (99, 'Newman');

SELECT hired, count(1)
FROM emps
GROUP BY hired;
```

11. Tidy up by dropping the new table:

```
DROP TABLE emps;
```

CERTIFICATION OBJECTIVE 11.05

Explain How Constraints Are Created at the Time of Table Creation

Table constraints are a means by which the database can enforce business rules, and guarantee that the data conforms to the entity-relationship model determined by the systems analysis that defines the application data structures. For example, the business analysts of your organization may have decided that every customer and every invoice must be uniquely identifiable by number, that no invoices can be issued to a customer before that customer has been created, and that every invoice must have a valid date and a value greater than zero. These would be implemented by creating primary-key constraints on the CUSTOMER_NUMBER column of the CUSTOMERS table and the INVOICE_NUMBER column of the INVOICES table, a foreign-key constraint on the INVOICES table referencing the CUSTOMERS table, a not-null constraint on the DATE column of the INVOICES table (the DATE data type will itself ensure that that any dates are valid automatically—it will not accept invalid dates), and a check constraint on the AMOUNT column on the INVOICES table.

When any DML is executed against a table with constraints defined, if the DML violates a constraint, then the whole statement will be rolled back automatically. Remember that a DML statement that affects many rows might partially succeed before it hits a constraint problem with a particular row. If the statement is part of a multistatement transaction, then the statements that have already succeeded will remain intact but uncommitted.

The Types of Constraints

The constraint types supported by the Oracle database are as follows:

- UNIQUE
- NOT NULL
- PRIMARY KEY
- FOREIGN KEY
- CHECK

Constraints have names. It is good practice to specify the names with a standard naming convention, but if they are not explicitly named, Oracle will generate names.

Unique Constraints

A unique constraint nominates a column (or combination of columns) for which the value must be different for every row in the table. If based on a single column, this is known as the *key* column. If the constraint is composed of more than one column (known as a *composite key* unique constraint), the columns do not have to be the same data type or be adjacent in the table definition.

An oddity of unique constraints is that it is possible to enter a NULL value into the key column(s); it is indeed possible to have any number of rows with NULL values in their key column(s). So selecting rows on a key column will guarantee that only one row is returned—unless you search for NULL, in which case all the rows where the key columns are NULL will be returned.

Unique constraints are enforced by an index. When a unique constraint is defined, Oracle will look for an index on the key column(s), and if one does not exist it will be created. Then whenever a row is inserted, Oracle will search the index to see if the values of the key columns are already present: if they are, it will reject the insert. The structure of these indexes (known as B*Tree indexes) does not include NULL values, which is why many rows with NULL are permitted: they simply do not exist in the index. While the first purpose of the index is to enforce the constraint, it has a secondary effect: improving performance if the key columns are used in the WHERE clauses of SQL statements. However, selecting `WHERE key_column IS NULL` cannot use the index because it doesn't include the NULLs and will therefore always result in a scan of the entire table.

Not Null Constraints

The not null constraint forces values to be entered into the key column. Not null constraints are defined per column: if the business requirement is that a group of columns should all have values, you cannot define one not null constraint for the whole group, but instead must define a not null constraint for each column.

Any attempt to insert a row without specifying values for the not null constrained columns results in an error. It is possible to bypass the need to specify a value by including a DEFAULT clause on the column when creating the table, as discussed in the previous section on creating tables.

Primary Key Constraints

The primary key is the means of locating a single row in a table. The relational database paradigm includes a requirement that every table should have a primary key, a column (or combination of columns) that can be used to distinguish every row. The Oracle database deviates from the paradigm (as do some other RDBMS implementations) by permitting tables without primary keys.

on the Job *Tables without primary keys are possible but not a good idea. Even if the business rules do not require the ability to identify every row, primary keys are often needed for maintenance work.*

The implementation of a primary key constraint is, in effect, the union of a unique constraint and a not null constraint. The key columns must have unique values, and they may not be null. As with unique constraints, an index must exist on the constrained column(s). If one does not exist already, an index will be created when the constraint is defined. A table can have only one primary key. Try to create a second, and you will get an error. A table can, however, have any number of unique constraints and not null columns, so if there are several columns that

e x a m

Watch *A primary key constraint is a unique constraint combined with a not null constraint.*

the business analysts have decided must be unique and populated, one of these can be designated the primary key and the others made unique and not null. An example could be a table of employees, where e-mail address, Social Security number, and employee number should all be required and unique.

Foreign Key Constraints

A foreign key constraint is defined on the child table in a parent-child relationship. The constraint nominates a column (or columns) in the child table that corresponds to the primary key column(s) in the parent table. The columns do not have to have the same names, but they must be of the same data type. Foreign key constraints define the relational structure of the database: the many-to-one relationships that connect the table, in their third normal form.

If the parent table has unique constraints as well as (or instead of) a primary key constraint, these columns can be used as the basis of foreign key constraints, even if they are nullable.

Just as a unique constraint permits null values in the constrained column, so does a foreign key constraint. You can insert rows into the child table with null foreign key columns—even if there is not a row in the parent table with a null value. This creates *orphan* rows and can cause dreadful confusion. As a general rule, all the columns in a unique constraint and all the columns in a foreign key constraint are best defined with not null constraints as well; this will often be a business requirement.

Attempting to insert a row in the child table for which there is no matching row in the parent table will give an error. Similarly, deleting a row in the parent table will give an error if there are already rows referring to it in the child table. There are two techniques for changing this behavior. First, the constraint may be created as ON DELETE CASCADE. This means that if a row in the parent table is deleted, Oracle will search the child table for all the matching rows and delete them too. This will happen automatically. A less drastic technique is to create the constraint as ON DELETE SET NULL. In this case, if a row in the parent table is deleted, Oracle will search the child table for all the matching rows and set the foreign key columns to null. This means that the child rows will be orphaned but will still exist. If the columns in the child table also have a not null constraint, then the deletion from the parent table will fail.

It is not possible to drop the parent table in a foreign key relationship, even if there are no rows in the child table. This still applies if the ON DELETE SET NULL or ON DELETE CASCADE clauses were used.

A variation on the foreign key constraint is the *self-referencing* foreign key constraint. This defines a condition where the parent and child rows exist in the same table. An example would be a table of employees, which includes a column for the employee's manager. The manager is himself an employee and must exist in the table. So if the primary key is the EMPLOYEE_NUMBER column, and the manager is identified by a column MANAGER_NUMBER, then the foreign key constraint will state that the value of the MANAGER_NUMBER column must refer back to a valid EMPLOYEE_NUMBER. If an employee is his own manager, then the row would refer to itself.

Check Constraints

A check constraint can be used to enforce simple rules, such as that the value entered in a column must be within a range of values. The rule must be an expression which will evaluate to TRUE or FALSE. The rules can refer to absolute values entered as literals or to other columns in the same row and may make use of some functions. As many check constraints as you want can be applied to one column, but it is not possible to use a subquery to evaluate whether a value is permissible or to use functions such as SYSDATE.

on the
() o b

The not null constraint is in fact implemented as a preconfigured check constraint.

Defining Constraints

Constraints can be defined when creating a table or added to the table later. When defining constraints at table creation time, the constraint can be defined in line with the column to which it refers or at the end of the table definition. There is more flexibility to using the latter technique. For example, it is impossible to define a foreign key constraint that refers to two columns, or a check constraint that refers to any column other than that being constrained if the constraint is defined in line, but both of these are possible if the constraint is defined at the end of the table.

For the constraints that require an index (the unique and primary key constraints), the index will be created with the table if the constraint is defined at table creation time.

SCENARIO & SOLUTION

You are designing table structures for a human resources application. The business analysts have said that when an employee leaves the company, his employee record should be moved to an archive table. Can constraints help?	Probably not. Constraints are intended to enforce simple business rules: this may be too complicated. It may well be necessary to use a DML trigger on the live table, which will automatically insert a row into the archive table whenever an employee is deleted from the live table. Triggers can do much more complicated processing than a constraint.
Active transactions block some DDL statements against tables. If you want to add a constraint or rename a column in a busy table and find the statement always fails with "ORA-00054: resource busy and acquire with NOWAIT specified or timeout expired," what can you do?	Perhaps you shouldn't be doing this sort of thing when the database is in use, but should wait until the next period of scheduled downtime. However, if you really need to make the change in a hurry, ask the database administrator to quiesce the database: this is a process that will freeze all user sessions. If you are very quick, you can make the change then unquiesce the database before end users complain.

Consider these two table creation statements (to which line numbers have been added):

```
1    CREATE TABLE dept(
2    deptno NUMBER(2,0) CONSTRAINT dept_deptno_pk PRIMARY KEY
3    CONSTRAINT dept_deptno_ck CHECK (deptno BETWEEN 10 AND 90),
4    dname VARCHAR2(20) CONSTRAINT dept_dname_nn NOT NULL);

5    CREATE TABLE emp(
6    empno NUMBER(4,0) CONSTRAINT emp_empno_pk PRIMARY KEY,
7    ename VARCHAR2(20) CONSTRAINT emp_ename_nn NOT NULL,
8    mgr NUMBER(4,0) CONSTRAINT emp_mgr_fk REFERENCES emp (empno),
9    dob DATE,
10   hiredate DATE,
11   deptno NUMBER(2,0) CONSTRAINT emp_deptno_fk REFERENCES
dept(deptno)
12   ON DELETE SET NULL,
13   email VARCHAR2(30) CONSTRAINT emp_email_uk UNIQUE,
14   CONSTRAINT emp_hiredate_ck CHECK(hiredate>= dob + 365*16),
15   CONSTRAINT emp_email_ck
16   CHECK ((instr(email,'@') > 0) AND (instr(email,'.') > 0)));
```

Taking these statements line by line:

1. The first table created is DEPT, intended to have one row for each department.

2. DEPTNO is numeric, 2 digits, no decimals. This is the table's primary key. The constraint is named DEPT_DEPTNO_PK.

3. A second constraint applied to DEPTNO is a check limiting it to numbers in the range 10 to 90. The constraint is named DEPT_DEPTNO_CK.

4. The DNAME column is variable length characters, with a constraint DEPT_DNAME_NN making it not nullable.

5. The second table created is EMP, intended to have one row for every employee.

6. EMPNO is numeric, up to 4 digits with no decimals. Constraint EMP_EMPNO_PK marks this as the table's primary key.

7. ENAME is variable length characters, with a constraint EMP_ENAME_NN making it not nullable.

8. MGR is the employee's manager, who must himself be an employee. The column is defined in the same way as the table's primary key column of EMPNO. The constraint EMP_MGR_FK defines this column as a self-referencing foreign key, so any value entered must refer to an already extant row in EMP (though it is not constrained to be not null, so can be left blank).

9. DOB, the employee's birthdate, is a date and not constrained.

10. HIREDATE is the date the employee was hired and is not constrained. At least, not yet.

11. DEPTNO is the department with which the employee is associated. The column is defined in the same way as the DEPT table's primary key column of DEPTNO, and the constraint EMP_DEPTNO_FK enforces a foreign key relationship: it is not possible to assign an employee to a department that does not exist, though this is nullable.

12. The EMP_DEPTO_FK constraint is further defined as ON DELETE SET NULL, so if the parent row in DEPT is deleted, all matching child rows in EMPNO will have DEPTNO set to NULL.

13. EMAIL is variable length character data, and must be unique if entered (though it can be left empty).

14. This defines an additional table-level constraint EMP_HIREDATE_CK. The constraint checks for use of child labor by rejecting any rows where the date of hiring is not at least 16 years later than the birthdate. This constraint could not be defined in line with HIREDATE, because the syntax does not allow references to other columns at that point.

15. An additional constraint EMP_EMAIL_CK is added to the EMAIL column, which makes two checks on the e-mail address. The INSTR functions search for the at symbol (@) and dot (.) characters (which will always be present in a valid e-mail address); if it can't find both of them, the check condition will return FALSE and the row will be rejected.

The preceding examples show several possibilities for defining constraints at table creation time. The following are further possibilities not covered:

- Controlling the index creation for the unique and primary key constraints
- Defining whether the constraint should be checked at insert time (which it is by default) or later on when the transaction is committed
- Stating whether the constraint is in fact being enforced at all (which is the default) or is disabled

It is possible to create tables with no constraints and then to add them later with an ALTER TABLE command. The end result will be the same, but this technique does make the code less self-documenting, as the complete table definition will then be spread over several statements rather than being in one.

INSIDE THE EXAM

Using DDL Statements to Create and Manage Tables

The CREATE TABLE statement can be very complex indeed. The SQL Reference volume of the Oracle Database 12c documentation set devotes 86 pages to it, with another 104 pages for ALTER TABLE (by contrast,

DROP TABLE takes only four pages). For examination purposes, only knowledge of the simplest table structure—the heap table—is required, with knowledge of the most basic data types. Understanding, defining, and using constraints is needed but not the methods for controlling when (or if) they are enforced.

EXERCISE 11-5

Work with Constraints

Use SQL*Plus or SQL Developer to create tables, add constraints, and demonstrate their use.

1. Connect to the database as user HR.

2. Create a table EMP as a copy of some columns from EMPLOYEES:

```
CREATE TABLE emp AS
SELECT employee_id empno, last_name ename, department_id deptno
FROM employees;
```

3. Create a table DEPT as a copy of some columns from DEPARTMENTS:

```
CREATE TABLE dept AS
SELECT department_id deptno, department_name dname
FROM departments;
```

4. Use DESCRIBE to describe the structure of the new tables. Note that the not null constraint on ENAME and DNAME has been carried over from the source tables.

5. Add a primary key constraint to EMP and to DEPT and a foreign key constraint linking the tables:

```
ALTER TABLE emp
ADD CONSTRAINT emp_pk PRIMARY KEY (empno);

ALTER TABLE dept
ADD CONSTRAINT dept_pk PRIMARY KEY (deptno);

ALTER TABLE emp
ADD CONSTRAINT dept_fk FOREIGN KEY (deptno) REFERENCES dept ON
DELETE SET NULL;
```

The preceding last constraint does not specify which column of DEPT to reference; this will default to the primary key column.

6. Demonstrate the effectiveness of the constraints by trying to insert data that will violate them:

```
INSERT INTO dept
VALUES (10,'New Department');
```

```
INSERT INTO emp
VALUES (9999,'New emp',99);

TRUNCATE TABLE dept;
```

7. Tidy up by dropping the tables. Note that this must be done in the correct order:

```
DROP TABLE emp;
DROP TABLE dept;
```

CERTIFICATION SUMMARY

Tables are two-dimensional structures consisting of rows of columns of defined data types. The Oracle database does permit user-defined data types, but for the most part you will be using the built-in data types.

Tables can be created from scratch: defining every column and then inserting rows. Alternatively, tables can be created using the output of a query. This latter technique can define the table and insert rows in one command, but there are limitations: it will be necessary to add primary key and unique constraints later, whereas they can be defined at table creation time using the former technique.

To assist with enforcing business rules, constraints can be defined for columns. These will maintain data integrity by making it absolutely impossible to insert data that breaks the rules.

TWO-MINUTE DRILL

Categorize the Main Database Objects

- ❏ Some objects contain data, principally tables and indexes.
- ❏ Programmatic objects such as stored procedures and functions are executable code.
- ❏ Views and synonyms are objects that give access to other objects.

Review the Table Structure

- ❏ Tables are two-dimensional structures, storing rows defined with columns.
- ❏ Tables exist within a schema. The schema name with the table name make a unique identifier.

List the Data Types That Are Available for Columns

- ❏ The most common data types are VARCHAR2, NUMBER, and DATE.
- ❏ There are many other data types.

Create a Simple Table

- ❏ Tables can be created from nothing or with a subquery.
- ❏ After creation, column definitions can be added, dropped, or modified.
- ❏ The table definition can include default values for columns.

Explain How Constraints Are Created at the Time of Table Creation

- ❏ Constraints can be defined at table creation time or added later.
- ❏ A constraint can be defined in line with its column or at the table level after the columns.
- ❏ Table-level constraints can be more complex than those defined in line.
- ❏ A table may only have one primary key but can have many unique keys.
- ❏ A primary key is functionally equivalent to unique plus not null.
- ❏ A unique constraint does not stop insertion of many null values.
- ❏ Foreign key constraints define the relationships between tables.

SELF TEST

The following questions will help you measure your understanding of the material presented in this chapter. Read all the choices carefully because there might be more than one correct answer. Choose all the correct answers for each question.

Categorize the Main Database Objects

1. If a table is created without specifying a schema, in which schema will it be? (Choose the best answer.)
   A. It will be an *orphaned* table, without a schema.
   B. The creation will fail.
   C. It will be in the SYS schema.
   D. It will be in the schema of the user creating it.
   E. It will be in the PUBLIC schema.

2. Several object types share the same namespace, and therefore cannot have the same name in the same schema. Which of the following object types is not in the same namespace as the others? (Choose the best answer.)
   A. Index
   B. PL/SQL stored procedure
   C. Synonym
   D. Table
   E. View

3. Which of these statements will fail because the table name is not legal? (Choose two answers.)
   A. `create table "SELECT" (col1 date);`
   B. `create table "lowercase" (col1 date);`
   C. `create table number1 (col1 date);`
   D. `create table 1number (col1 date);`
   E. `create table update (col1 date);`

Review the Table Structure

4. What are distinguishing characteristics of heap tables? (Choose two answers.)
   A. A heap can store variable length rows.
   B. More than one table can store rows in a single heap.
   C. Rows in a heap are in random order.
   D. Heap tables cannot be indexed.
   E. Tables in a heap do not have a primary key.

List the Data Types That Are Available for Columns

5. Which of the following data types are variable length? (Choose all correct answers.)
   A. BLOB
   B. CHAR
   C. LONG
   D. NUMBER
   E. RAW
   F. VARCHAR2

6. Study these statements:
   ```
   CREATE TABLE tab1 (c1 NUMBER(1), c2 DATE);
   ALTER SESSION SET nls_date_format='dd-mm-yy';
   INSERT INTO tab1 VALUES (1.1,'31-01-07');
   ```
   Will the insert succeed? (Choose the best answer)
   A. The insert will fail because the 1.1 is too long.
   B. The insert will fail because the '31-01-07' is a string, not a date.
   C. The insert will fail for both reasons A and B.
   D. The insert will succeed.

7. Which of the following is not supported by Oracle as an internal data type? (Choose the best answer.)
   A. CHAR
   B. FLOAT
   C. INTEGER
   D. STRING

Create a Simple Table

8. Consider this statement:
   ```
   CREATE TABLE t1 AS SELECT * FROM regions WHERE 1=2;
   ```
   What will be the result? (Choose the best answer.)
   A. There will be an error because of the impossible condition.
   B. No table will be created because the condition returns FALSE.
   C. The table T1 will be created but no rows inserted because the condition returns FALSE.
   D. The table T1 will be created and every row in REGIONS inserted because the condition returns a NULL as a row filter.

9. When a table is created with a statement such as the following:

```
CREATE TABLE newtab AS SELECT * FROM tab;
```

will there be any constraints on the new table? (Choose the best answer.)

A. The new table will have no constraints, because constraints are not copied when creating tables with a subquery.

B. All the constraints on TAB will be copied to NEWTAB.

C. Primary key and unique constraints will be copied but not check and not null constraints.

D. Check and not null constraints will be copied but not unique or primary key.

E. All constraints will be copied, except foreign key constraints.

Explain How Constraints Are Created at the Time of Table Creation

10. Which types of constraint require an index? (Choose all that apply.)

A. CHECK

B. NOT NULL

C. PRIMARY KEY

D. UNIQUE

11. A transaction consists of two statements. The first succeeds, but the second (which updates several rows) fails partway through because of a constraint violation. What will happen? (Choose the best answer.)

A. The whole transaction will be rolled back.

B. The second statement will be rolled back completely, and the first will be committed.

C. The second statement will be rolled back completely, and the first will remain uncommitted.

D. Only the one update that caused the violation will be rolled back; everything else will be committed.

E. Only the one update that caused the violation will be rolled back; everything else will remain uncommitted.

LAB QUESTION

Consider this simple analysis of a telephone billing system:

A subscriber is identified by a customer number and also has a name and possibly one or more telephones.

A telephone is identified by its number, which must be a 7-digit integer beginning with 2 or 3, and also has a make, an activation date, and a flag for whether it is active. Inactive telephones are not assigned to a subscriber; active telephones are.

For every call, it is necessary to record the time it started and the time it finished.

Create tables with constraints and defaults that can be used to implement this system.

SELF TEST ANSWERS

Categorize the Main Database Objects

1. ☑ **D.** The schema will default to the current user.
    ☒ **A, B, C,** and **E** are incorrect. **A** is incorrect because all tables must be in a schema. **B** is incorrect because the creation will succeed. **C** is incorrect because the SYS schema is not a default schema. **E** is incorrect because while there is a notional user PUBLIC, he does not have a schema at all.

2. ☑ **A.** Indexes have their own namespace.
    ☒ **B, C, D,** and **E** are incorrect. Stored procedures, synonyms, tables, and views exist in the same namespace.

3. ☑ **D** and **E. D** violates the rule that a table name must begin with a letter, and **E** violates the rule that a table name cannot be a reserved word. Both rules can be bypassed by using double quotes.
    ☒ **A, B,** and **C** are incorrect. These are incorrect because all will succeed (though **A** and **B** are not exactly sensible).

Review the Table Structure

4. ☑ **A** and **C.** A heap is a table of variable length rows in random order.
    ☒ **B, D,** and **E** are incorrect. **B** is incorrect because a heap table can only be one table. **D** and **E** are incorrect because a heap table can (and usually will) have indexes and a primary key.

List the Data Types That Are Available for Columns

5. ☑ **A, C, D, E,** and **F.** All these are variable length data types.
    ☒ **B** is incorrect. CHAR columns are fixed length.

6. ☑ **D.** The number will be rounded to 1 digit, and the string will be cast as a date.
    ☒ **A, B,** and **C** are incorrect. Automatic rounding and type casting will correct the "errors," though ideally they would not occur.

7. ☑ **D.** STRING is not an internal data type.
    ☒ **A, B,** and **C** are incorrect. CHAR, FLOAT, and INTEGER are all internal data types, though not as widely used as some others.

Create a Simple Table

8. ☑ **C.** The condition applies only to the rows selected for insert, not to the table creation.
☒ **A, B,** and **D** are incorrect. **A** is incorrect because the statement is syntactically correct. **B** is incorrect because the condition does not apply to the DDL, only to the DML. **D** is incorrect because the condition will exclude all rows from selection.

9. ☑ **D.** Check and not null constraints are not dependent on any structures other than the table to which they apply and so can safely be copied to a new table.
☒ **A, B, C,** and **E** are incorrect. **A** is incorrect because not null and check constraint will be applied to the new table. **B, C,** and **E** are incorrect because these constraints need other objects (indexes or a parent table) and so are not copied.

Explain How Constraints Are Created at the Time of Table Creation

10. ☑ **C and D.** Unique and primary key constraints are enforced with indexes.
☒ **A and B** are incorrect. Check and not null constraints do not rely on indexes.

11. ☑ **C.** A constraint violation will force a rollback of the current statement but nothing else.
☒ **A, B, D,** and **E** are incorrect. **A** is incorrect because all statements that have succeeded remain intact. **B** and **D** are incorrect because there is no commit of anything until it is specifically requested. **E** is incorrect because the whole statement will be rolled back, not just the failed row.

LAB ANSWER

A possible solution:

■ The SUBSCRIBERS table:

```
CREATE TABLE subscribers
(id NUMBER(4,0) CONSTRAINT sub_id_pk PRIMARY KEY,
name VARCHAR2(20) CONSTRAINT sub_name_nn NOT NULL);
```

■ The TELEPHONES table:

```
CREATE TABLE telephones
(telno NUMBER(7,0) CONSTRAINT tel_telno_pk PRIMARY KEY
CONSTRAINT tel_telno_ck CHECK (telno BETWEEN 2000000 AND 3999999),
activated DATE DEFAULT sysdate,
active VARCHAR2(1) CONSTRAINT tel_active_nn NOT NULL
CONSTRAINT tel_active_ck CHECK(active='Y' OR active='N'),
subscriber NUMBER(4,0) CONSTRAINT tel_sub_fk REFERENCES subscribers,
CONSTRAINT tel_active_yn CHECK((active='Y' AND subscriber IS NOT NULL)
  OR (active='N' AND subscriber IS NULL))
);
```

This table has a constraint on the ACTIVE column that will permit only Y or N, depending on whether there is a value in the SUBSCRIBER column. This constraint is too complex to define in line with the column, because it references other columns. SUBSCRIBER, if not null, must match a row in SUBSCRIBERS.

- The CALLS table:

```
CREATE TABLE calls
(telno NUMBER (7,0) CONSTRAINT calls_telno_fk REFERENCES telephones,
starttime DATE CONSTRAINT calls_start_nn NOT NULL,
endtime DATE CONSTRAINT calls_end_nn NOT NULL,
CONSTRAINT calls_pk PRIMARY KEY(telno, starttime),
CONSTRAINT calls_endtime_ck CHECK (endtime >= starttime));
```

Two constraints are defined at the table level, not the column level. The primary key cannot be defined in line with a column because it is based on two columns: one telephone can make many calls, but not two that begin at the same time (at least, not with current technology). The final constraint compares the start and end times of the call and so cannot be defined in line.

A

About the CD-ROM

The CD-ROM included with this book comes complete with Total Tester customizable practice exam software with more than 150 practice exam questions and the electronic book in PDF format.

System Requirements

The software requires Windows XP or higher and 30MB of hard disk space for full installation. To run, the screen resolution must be set to 1024 × 768 or higher. The electronic copy of the book requires Adobe Acrobat Reader, which is available for installation on the CD-ROM.

Total Tester Premium Practice Exam Software

Total Tester provides you with a simulation of the Oracle OCA-1Z0-061 exam. You can create practice exams from selected domains or chapters. You can further customize the number of questions and time allowed.

The exams can be taken in either Practice mode or Exam Simulation mode. Practice mode provides an assistance window with hints, references to the book, an explanation of the answer, and the option to check your answer as you take the test. Both Practice mode and Exam Simulation mode provide an overall grade and a grade broken down by domain.

To take a test, launch the program and select OCA-1Z0-061 from the Installed Question Packs list. You can then select either a Practice Exam or an Exam Simulation, or create a Custom Exam.

Installing and Running Total Tester Premium Practice Exam Software

From the main screen you may install the Total Tester by clicking the Total Tester Practice Exams button. This will begin the installation process and place an icon on your desktop and in your Start menu. To run Total Tester, navigate to Start | (All) Programs | Total Seminars, or double-click the icon on your desktop.

To uninstall the Total Tester software, go to Start | Settings | Control Panel | Add/Remove Programs (XP) or Programs And Features (Vista/7/8), and then select the Total Tester program. Select Remove, and Windows will completely uninstall the software.

Electronic Book

The entire contents of the book are provided in PDF format on the CD. This file is viewable on your computer and many portable devices. Adobe's Acrobat Reader is required to view the file on your PC and has been included on the CD. You may also use Adobe Digital Editions to access your electronic book.

For more information on Adobe Reader and to check for the most recent version of the software, visit Adobe's web site at www.adobe.com and search for the free Adobe Reader or look for Adobe Reader on the product page. Adobe Digital Editions can also be downloaded from the Adobe web site.

To view the electronic book on a portable device, copy the PDF file to your computer from the CD, and then copy the file to your portable device using a USB or other connection. Adobe offers a mobile version of Adobe Reader, the Adobe Reader mobile app, which currently supports iOS and Android. For customers using Adobe Digital Editions and the iPad, you may have to download and install a separate reader program on your device. The Adobe web site has a list of recommended applications, and McGraw-Hill Education recommends the Bluefire Reader.

Technical Support

Technical Support information is provided in the following sections by feature.

Total Seminars Technical Support

For questions regarding the Total Tester software or operation of the CD-ROM, visit www.totalsem.com or e-mail support@totalsem.com.

McGraw-Hill Content Support

For questions regarding the electronic book, e-mail techsolutions@mhedu.com or visit http://mhp.softwareassist.com.

For questions regarding book content, e-mail customer.service@mheducation.com. For customers outside the United States, e-mail international_cs@mheducation.com.

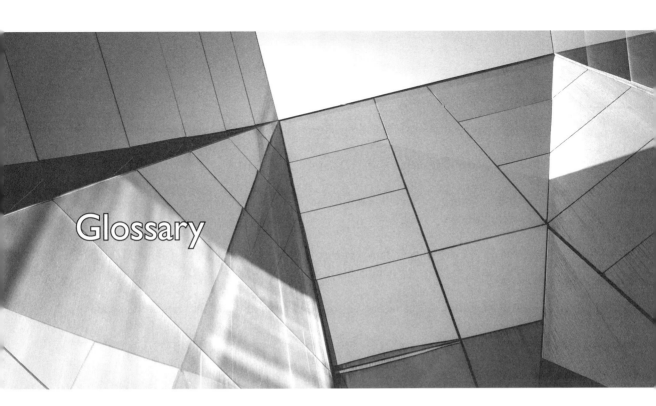

Glossary

ACID Atomicity, consistency, isolation, and durability. Four characteristics that a relational database must be able to maintain for transactions.

AL16UTF16 A Unicode fixed-width, 2-byte character set, commonly specified for the NLS character set used for NVARCHAR2, NCHAR, and NCLOB data types.

alias (1) In Oracle SQL, an alternative name for a table, view, or set of data used in a query. (2) In Oracle Net, a pointer to a connect string. An alias must be resolved into the address of a listener and the name of a service or instance.

ANSI American National Standards Institute. A U.S. body that defines a number of standards relevant to computing.

API Application Programming Interface. A defined method for manipulating data, typically implemented as a set of PL/SQL procedures in a package.

ASCII American Standard Code for Information Interchange. A standard (with many variations) for coding letters and other characters as bytes.

attribute One element of a tuple (aka a column).

AVG A function that divides the sum of a column or expression by the number of nonnull rows in a group.

BFILE A large object data type that is stored as an operating system file. The value in the table column is a pointer to the file.

bind variable A value passed from a user process to a SQL statement at statement execution time.

BLOB Binary Large Object. A LOB data type for binary data, such as photographs and video clips.

block The units of storage into which data files are formatted. The size can be 2KB, 4KB, 8KB, 16KB, 32KB, or 64KB. Some platforms will not permit all these sizes.

Cartesian product Sometimes called a cross join. A mathematical term that refers to the set of data created by merging the rows from two or more tables.

CET Central European Time. A time zone used in much of Europe (though not Great Britain) that is one hour ahead of UTC with daylight saving time in effect during the summer months.

character set The encoding system for representing data within bytes. Different character sets can store different characters and may not be suitable for all languages. Unicode character sets can store any character.

check constraint A simple rule enforced by the database that restricts the values that can be entered into a column.

client-server architecture A processing paradigm where the application is divided into client software that interacts with the user and server software that interacts with the data.

CLOB   Character Large Object. A LOB data type for character data, such as text documents, stored in the database character set.

cluster   A hardware environment where more than one computer shares access to storage. A RAC database consists of several instances on several computers opening one database on the shared storage.

cluster segment   A segment that can contain one or more tables, denormalized into a single structure.

COALESCE   A function that returns the first nonnull value from its parameter list. If all its parameters are null, then a null value is returned.

column   An element of a row: tables are two-dimensional structures, divided horizontally into rows and vertically into columns.

commit   To make permanent a change to data.

connect identifier   An Oracle Net alias.

connect string   The database connection details needed to establish a session: the address of the listener and the service or instance name.

consistent backup   A backup made while the database is closed.

constraint   A mechanism for enforcing rules on data: that a column value must be unique or may only contain certain values. A primary key constraint specifies that the column must be both unique and not null.

control file   The file containing pointers to the rest of the database, critical sequence information, and the RMAN repository.

CPU   Central Processing Unit. The chip that provides the processing capability of a computer, such as an Intel Xeon or an Oracle SPARC T6.

data blocks   The units into which data files are formatted.

data dictionary   The tables owned by SYS in the SYSTEM tablespace that define the database and the objects within it.

data dictionary views   Views on the data dictionary tables that let the DBA investigate the state of the database.

data file   The disk-based structure for storing data.

data guard   A facility whereby a copy of the production database is created and updated (possibly in real time) with all changes applied to the production database.

data pump   A facility for transferring large amounts of data at high speed into, out of, or between databases.

database buffer cache   An area of memory in the SGA used for working on blocks copied from data files.

database link   A connection from one database to another, based on a username and password and a connect string.

DBA   Database Administrator. The person responsible for creating and managing Oracle databases—this could be you.

DBA role   A preseeded role provided for backward compatibility that includes all the privileges needed to manage a database, except those needed to start up or shut down.

DBCA   The Database Configuration Assistant. A GUI tool for creating, modifying, and dropping instances and databases.

DBMS   Database Management System. Often used interchangeably with RDBMS.

DDL   Data Definition Language. The subset of SQL commands that change object definitions within the data dictionary: CREATE, ALTER, DROP, and TRUNCATE.

deadlock   A situation where two sessions block each other, such that neither can do anything. Deadlocks are detected and resolved automatically by the database.

DECODE   A function that implements if-then-else conditional logic by testing two terms for equality and returning the third term if they are equal or, optionally, returning some other term if they are not.

DHCP   Dynamic Host Configuration Protocol. The standard for configuring the network characteristics of a computer, such as its IP address, in a changing environment where computers may be moved from one location to another.

directory object   An Oracle directory: an object within the database that points to an operating system directory.

DML   Data Manipulation Language. The subset of SQL commands that change data within the database: INSERT, UPDATE, DELETE, and MERGE.

DNS   Domain Name Service. The TCP mechanism for resolving network names into IP addresses.

domain   The set of values an attribute is allowed to take. Terminology: tables have rows; rows have columns with values. Or: relations have tuples; tuples have attributes with values taken from their domain.

DSS   Decision Support System. A database, such as a data warehouse, optimized for running queries as opposed to OLTP work.

easy connect   A method of establishing a session against a database by specifying the address on the listener and the service name without using an Oracle Net alias.

EBCDIC   Extended Binary Coded Decimal Interchange Code. A standard developed by IBM for coding letters and other characters in bytes.

environment variable   A variable set in the operating system shell that can be used by application software and by shell scripts.

equijoin   A join condition using an equality operator.

fact table   The central table in a star schema, with columns for values relevant to the row and columns used as foreign keys to the dimension tables.

FGA   Fine Grained Auditing. A facility for tracking user access to data based on the rows that are seen or manipulated.

full backup   A backup containing all blocks of the files backed up, not only those blocks changed since the last backup.

GMT   Greenwich Mean Time. Now referred to as UTC, this is the time zone of the meridian through Greenwich Observatory in London.

grid computing   An architecture where the delivery of a service to end users is not tied to certain server resources but can be provided from anywhere in a pool of resources.

GROUP BY   A clause that specifies the grouping attribute rows must have in common for them to be clustered together.

GUI   Graphical User Interface. A layer of an application that lets users work with the application through a graphical terminal, such as a PC with a mouse.

HTTP   Hypertext Transfer Protocol. The protocol that enables the World Wide Web (both invented at the European Organization for Nuclear Research in 1989), this is a layered protocol that runs over TCP/IP.

HWM   High water mark. This is the last block of a segment that has ever been used—blocks above this are part of the segment but are not yet formatted for use.

inconsistent backup   A backup made while the database was open.

incremental backup   A backup containing only blocks that have been changed since the last backup was made.

INITCAP   A function that accepts a string of characters and returns each word in title case.

inner join When equijoins and nonequijoins are performed, rows from the source and target tables are matched. These are referred to as inner joins.

instance recovery The automatic repair of damage caused by a disorderly shutdown of the database.

INSTR A function that returns the positional location of the nth occurrence of a specified string of characters in a source string.

I/O Input/output. The activity of reading from or writing to disks—often the slowest point of a data processing operation.

IOT Index organized table. A table type where the rows are stored in the leaf blocks of an index segment.

IP Internet Protocol. Together with the Transmission Control Protocol, TCP/IP: the de facto standard communication protocol used for client/server communication over a network.

IPC Interprocess Communications Protocol. The platform-specific protocol, provided by your OS vendor, used for processes running on the same machine to communicate with each other.

ISO International Organization for Standardization. A group that defines many standards, including SQL.

JEE Java Enterprise Edition. The standard for developing Java applications.

JOIN...ON A clause that allows the explicit specification of join columns regardless of their column names. This provides a flexible joining format.

JOIN...USING A syntax that allows a natural join to be formed on specific columns with shared names.

joining Involves linking two or more tables based on common attributes. Joining allows data to be stored in third normal form in discrete tables, instead of in one large table.

JVM   Java Virtual Machine. The run-time environment needed for running code written in Java. Oracle provides a JVM within the database, and there will be one provided by your operating system.

LAST_DAY   A function used to obtain the last day in a month given any valid date item.

LDAP   Lightweight Directory Access Protocol. The TCP implementation of the X25 directory standard, used by the Oracle Internet Directory for name resolution, security, and authentication. LDAP is also used by other software vendors, including Microsoft and IBM.

LENGTH   A function that computes the number of characters in a string including spaces and special characters.

LGWR   Log writer. The background process responsible for flushing change vectors from the log buffer in memory to the online redo logfiles on disk.

listener   The server-side process that listens for database connection requests from user processes and launches server processes to establish sessions.

LOB   Large object. A data structure that is too large to store within a table. LOBs (Oracle supports several types) are defined as columns of a table but are physically stored in a separate segment.

log switch   The action of closing one online logfile group and opening another; triggered by the LGWR process filling the first group.

MOD   Modulus operation, a function that returns the remainder of a division operation.

MONTHS_BETWEEN   A function that computes the number of months between two given date parameters and is based on a 31-day month.

mounted database   A situation where the instance has opened the database control file but not the online redo logfiles or the data files.

MTBF   Mean time between failure. A measure of the average length of running time for a database between unplanned shutdowns.

MTTR   Mean time to recover. The average time it takes to make the database available for normal use after a failure.

multiplexing   To maintain multiple copies of files.

namespace   A logical grouping of objects within which no two objects may have the same name.

natural join   A join performed using the NATURAL JOIN syntax when the source and target tables are implicitly equijoined using all identically named columns.

NCLOB   National Character Large Object. A LOB data type for character data, such as text documents, stored in the alternative national database character set.

NLS   National Language Support. The capability of the Oracle database to support many linguistic, geographical, and cultural environments—now usually referred to as globalization.

node   A computer attached to a network.

nonequijoin   Performed when the values in the join columns fulfill the join condition based on an inequality expression.

null   The absence of a value, indicating that the value is not known, missing, or inapplicable.

NULLIF   A function that tests two terms for equality. If they are equal, the function returns null; else it returns the first of the two terms tested.

NVL   A function that returns either the original item unchanged or an alternative item if the initial term is null.

NVL2   A function that returns a new if-null item if the original item is null or an alternative if-not-null item if the original term is not null.

OCA Oracle Certified Associate.

OCI Oracle Call Interface. An API, published as a set of C libraries, that programmers can use to write user processes that will use an Oracle database.

OCM Oracle Certified Master. An advanced qualification you may ultimately wish to pursue.

OCP Oracle Certified Professional. The qualification you are working toward.

ODBC Open Database Connectivity. A standard developed by Microsoft for communicating with relational databases. Oracle provides an ODBC driver that will allow clients running Microsoft products to connect to an Oracle database.

offline backup A backup made while the database is closed.

OLAP Online Analytical Processing. Select intensive work involving running queries against a (usually) large database. Oracle provides OLAP capabilities as an option, in addition to the standard query facilities.

OLTP Online Transaction Processing. A pattern of activity within a database typified by a large number of small, short, transactions.

online backup A backup made while the database is open.

online redo log The files to which change vectors are streamed by the LGWR.

ORACLE_BASE The root directory into which Oracle products are installed.

ORACLE_HOME The root directory of any one Oracle product, typically for a given release. This value is located beneath ORACLE_BASE.

Oracle Net Oracle's proprietary communications protocol, layered on top of an industry standard protocol.

OS Operating system. Typically, in the Oracle environment, this will be a version of Unix (perhaps Linux) or Microsoft Windows.

outer join A join performed when rows, which are not retrieved by an inner join, are included for retrieval.

parse An action that converts SQL statements into a form suitable for execution.

PGA Program Global Area. The variable-sized block of memory used to maintain the state of a database session. PGAs are private to the session and controlled by the session's server process.

PL/SQL Procedural Language/Structured Query Language. Oracle's proprietary programming language, which combines procedural constructs, such as flow control, and user interface capabilities with SQL.

PMON Process monitor. The background process responsible for monitoring the state of user sessions against an instance.

primary key The column (or combination of columns) whose value(s) can be used to uniquely identify each row in a table.

projection The restriction of columns selected from a table. Using projection, you retrieve only the columns of interest and not every possible column.

RAC Real Application Clusters. Oracle's clustering technology, which allows several instances in different machines to open the same database for scalability, performance, and fault tolerance.

RAID Redundant Array of Inexpensive Disks. Techniques for enhancing performance and/or fault tolerance by using a volume manager to present a number of physical disks to the operating system as a single logical disk.

RAM Random Access Memory. The chips that make up the real memory in your computer hardware, as opposed to the virtual memory presented to software by the operating system.

raw device An unformatted disk or disk partition.

RDBMS Relational Database Management System. Often used interchangeably with DBMS.

referential integrity   A rule defined on a table specifying that the values in a column (or columns) must map onto those of a row in another table.

relation   A two-dimensional structure consisting of tuples with attributes (aka a table).

REPLACE   A function that substitutes each occurrence of a search item in the source string with a replacement term and returns the modified source string.

RMAN   Recovery Manager. Oracle's backup and recovery tool.

rowid   The unique identifier of every row in the database, used as a pointer to the physical location of the row.

schema   The objects owned by a database user.

SCN   System Change Number. The continually incrementing number used to track the sequence and exact time of all events within a database.

segment   A database object, within a schema, that stores data.

selection   The extraction of rows from a table. Selection includes the further restriction of the extracted rows based on various criteria or conditions. This allows you to retrieve only the rows that are of interest and not every row in the table.

self-join   A join required when the join columns originate from the same table. Conceptually, the source table is duplicated and a target table is created. The self-join then works as a regular join between two discrete tables.

sequence   A database object, within a schema, that can generate consecutive numbers.

service name   A logical name registered by an instance with a listener, which can be specified by a user process when it issues a connect request.

session   A user process and a server process, connected to the instance.

SGA   System Global Area. The block of shared memory that contains the memory structures that make up an Oracle instance.

SID   (1) System Identifier. The name of an instance, which must be unique on the computer the instance is running on. (2) Session Identifier. The number used to uniquely identify a session logged on to an Oracle instance.

SMON   System Monitor. The background process responsible for opening a database and monitoring the instance.

spfile   Server parameter file. The file containing the parameters used to build an instance in memory.

SQL   Structured Query Language. An international standard language for extracting data from and manipulating data in relational databases.

SSL   Secure Sockets Layer. A standard for securing data transmission, using encryption, checksumming, and digital certificates.

SUBSTR   A function that extracts and returns a segment from a given source string.

SUM   A function that returns an aggregated total of all the nonnull numeric expression values in a group.

synonym   An alternative name for a database object.

sysdba   The privilege that lets a user connect with operating system or password file authentication and create, start up, and shut down a database.

sysoper   The privilege that lets a user connect with operating system or password file authentication and start up and shut down (but not create) a database.

system   A preseeded schema used for database administration purposes.

table   A logical two-dimensional data storage structure, consisting of rows and columns.

tablespace   The logical structure that abstracts logical data storage in tables from physical data storage in data files.

TCP   Transmission Control Protocol. Together with the Internet Protocol, TCP/IP: the de facto standard communication protocol used for client/server communication over a network.

TCPS   TCP with SSL. The secure sockets version of TCP.

tempfile   The physical storage that makes up a temporary tablespace, used for storing temporary segments.

TNS   Transparent Network Substrate. The heart of Oracle Net, a proprietary layered protocol running on top of whatever underlying network transport protocol you choose to use—probably TCP/IP.

TO_CHAR   A function that performs date-to-character and number-to-character data type conversions.

TO_DATE   A function that explicitly transforms character items into date values.

TO_NUMBER   A function that changes character items into number values.

transaction   A logical unit of work that will complete in total or not at all.

tuple   A one-dimensional structure consisting of attributes (aka a row).

UGA   User Global Area. That part of the PGA that is stored in the SGA for sessions running through shared servers.

UI   User interface. The layer of an application that communicates with end users—nowadays, frequently graphical: a GUI.

URL   Uniform Resource Locator. A standard for specifying the location of an object on the Internet consisting of a protocol, a host name and domain, an IP port number, a path and filename, and a series of parameters.

UTC Coordinated Universal Time. Previously known as Greenwich Mean Time (GMT), UTC is the global standard time zone; all others relate to it as offsets, ahead or behind.

X Window System The standard GUI environment used on most computers, except those that run Microsoft Windows.

XML Extensible Markup Language. A standard for data interchange using documents, where the format of the data is defined by tags within the document.

INDEX

A

A.D. in date format masks, 243
A.M. in date format masks, 244
access permissions, 432
ACID test, 451–453
AD in date format masks, 243
Add Column option, 494
ADD_MONTHS function
    description, 179
    working with, 215–216
addition
    dates, 211
    evaluation order, 76
Advanced Connection Type setting, 41
aggregated data. *See* group functions
algebra, relational, 62
aliases
    columns, 79–81
    purpose, 66
    tables, 324
ALL keyword
    AVG, 286
    COUNT, 280, 284
    INSERT, 438
    MAX and MIN, 288
    subqueries, 370, 377, 382–383
    SUM, 285
ALL_OBJECTS view, 478
ALTER TABLE command, 492–493
altering table definitions, 492–493
alternative quote operator, 84–87
AM in date format masks, 244
ambiguous column names, 323–325

American National Standards Institute (ANSI)
    joins, 322–323
    SQL standards, 27
ampersand (&) substitution
    define and verify, 157–162
    variables. *See* substitution variables
AND operator
    overview, 134–136
    precedence, 140
    ranges, 124
anomalies, insert update and deletion, 15
ANSI (American National Standards Institute)
    joins, 322–323
    SQL standards, 27
ANY operators, 370, 377, 382–383
application tiers in web applications, 6
arithmetic and arithmetic operators
    dates, 211–212
    with NULL, 90
    overview, 76–78
    precedence, 139
    row updates, 442
AS keyword, 81–82
ascending sorts, 144–146
asterisks (*)
    columns, 65
    COUNT, 280
    evaluation order, 76
    precedence, 140
atomicity in ACID test, 451–452
attention to detail, 71
attributes
    entities, 12–13
    grouping, 294

O

Reach More than 700,000 Oracle Customers with Oracle Publishing Group

Connect with the Audience that Matters Most to Your Business

Oracle Magazine
The Largest IT Publication in the World
Circulation: 550,000
Audience: IT Managers, DBAs, Programmers, and Developers

Profit
Business Insight for Enterprise-Class Business Leaders to Help Them Build a Better Business Using Oracle Technology
Circulation: 100,000
Audience: Top Executives and Line of Business Managers

Java Magazine
The Essential Source on Java Technology, the Java Programming Language, and Java-Based Applications
Circulation: 125,000 and Growing Steady
Audience: Corporate and Independent Java Developers, Programmers, and Architects

For more information or to sign up for a FREE subscription:
Scan the QR code to visit Oracle Publishing online.

LICENSE AGREEMENT